THE SECRET OF CULTURE

CONSULTING EDITOR

Anthony F. C. Wallace, *University of Pennsylvania*

LAURA THOMPSON

THE SECRET
OF CULTURE

NINE COMMUNITY STUDIES

RANDOM HOUSE NEW YORK

Properly speaking, the only real
human "specialization" is culture . . .

C. LORING BRACE (1964:6)

102837

What is meant by "culture"? How do human beings create culture, experience it, manifest it, change it, pass it on from generation to generation? What is the relation of a community's culture to its natural environment, its social structure, its history, its well-being? Does the comparative study of cultures afford clues toward understanding and coping with the acute social problems of our time? For example, does it throw light on the processes of community development? The population explosion? Migration? Racial integration? The nature of poverty? Mental illness? The conservation of natural resources? What can the comparative study of cultures teach us regarding a "healthy" community versus an "unhealthy" one?

As an undergraduate in the 1920s I failed to find satisfying answers to these questions in the sociology, economics, or social work of the time. Eventually I discovered anthropology, with its on-the-spot, face-to-face methods of investigating the peoples of the world—*all* of them, not merely those we may consider attractive, familiar, or admirable. So I chose this discipline as my life's work. Now, after a forty-year search, I am beginning to find in anthropology answers to these crucial social problems of our time—answers that make sense to me.

When asked to deliver a course of lectures on educational television for North Carolina State University, I therefore decided to attempt an inquiry into the nature of culture. I thought that it would be interesting to take an armchair audience on an imaginary field expedition and to revisit some of the communities that I had studied at first hand. I had in mind an anthropologically guided tour, illustrated with maps and museum specimens. Observations might be compared. The findings might serve as the basis for drawing tentative conclusions about the behaviors of people living in groups and their relevance to the world.

From about thirty-five communities investigated on the spot, I selected nine case studies belonging to several culture areas of the world for the lessons about culture that might be learned from them. The result was *Peoples I Have Known,* a program of thirteen illustrated half-hour broadcasts presented over WUNC, Raleigh, channel 4, between February and May, 1960. These broadcasts have served as the nucleus for the present book. The original script has been revised and elaborated. Several new chapters have been added, and selected references have been inserted.

The book differs in several ways from cross-cultural analyses based mainly on secondhand reports. The aim of each case study has been not merely to present a *simple description* of the behavior of the group under consideration but also to strive for an *understanding description* of behavior in situational context. As Alfred N. Whitehead pointed out, only an understanding description of an event provides the background necessary for predicting future change. In this instance the effort is keyed toward limited prediction of probable changes in group behavior under certain conditions.

To project a dynamic, processual image of the changing group behavior as a complex historical "event," the approach had to be empirical, situational in depth, and holistic. Field notes and records collected on the spot, while I was working either alone or as part of a team, have been supplemented with information obtained from the available literature or by correspondence with appropriate authorities.

In each case the focus has been on changing group behavior in geographic, ecological, and historical perspective. An attempt has been made step by step to build up an understanding of variations in human group behavior in the complex setting of the community as part of a larger inclusive ecosystem (a natural community viewed as a bioenvironmental whole). Most of the selected communities have a history of settlement and cultural development for at least a thousand years in a near-isolated homeland. (Unless otherwise indicated, events are described as of the date when the fieldwork was done.)

An attempt has been made to present the relevant data that anthropologists, archaeologists, linguists, ecologists, geneticists, and others have collected so that the reader may compare them and reach his own conclusions. Thus the reader may move from certain happenings and events to a comparison of them and finally to generalizations and hypotheses about them. He may make up his own mind on the basis of the available facts.

It should be emphasized that the aim of this endeavor is not to make an exhaustive inquiry in the orthodox historical tradition. Obviously the available data regarding some of the communities under investigation are so extensive that a whole lifetime and more would be needed for complete review and critical analysis. Rather, this book has been undertaken as a pioneer attempt to view diverse firsthand field materials—living histories, one might say—supplemented by available reports and background data, according to universal, multidimensional perspective. It aims to seek out and project, on a planetary scale according to the pulsations of cosmic time, persistence and change in the cultures of certain indigenous populations as revealed by group behavior and behavioral productions. For once the culture-change process has been isolated under favorable conditions and defined correctly, it may be identified in every human group, even the most complexly organized urban communities, and used as a basic research tool for understanding and, to a degree, controlling group behavior.

Accordingly, we shall not concentrate on nations, national characters, races, or cultures as usually conceived. Rather, we shall take as our intelligible fields of study the behavior of contemporary ethnic communities apprehended not only from the outside but also from the inside as continuous developments from prehistoric times to the present. For a heuristic approach toward history today does not lie in studiously adding fact to fact in an endless chain. Rather, it lies in using the available evidence from many points of view in order to penetrate below the outer surface of events and discover their hidden meanings.

Of course, only a small fraction of the available data on each community could be presented in this form. Space limitations and the need to compare comparable phenomena necessitated a rigorous selection of materials relevant to the book's primary purpose, to inquire empirically into the structure and dynamics of culture in the hope of uncovering its secret. If the book succeeds in shedding some light on this intricate problem, it will have fulfilled its purpose.

L. T.

Brooklyn, New York

ACKNOWLEDGMENTS

A great many people have contributed to the research on which this book is based. Although my primary debts will be acknowledged in footnotes to each chapter and in the text, I take this opportunity to express my appreciation especially to the host of friends and informants in each of the nine communities used as case studies who have aided me in the field and to the many colleagues on whose work I have drawn. I thank also Anthony F. C. Wallace, D. P. Sinha, Martin Silverman, Edwin H. Bryan, Jr., Alexander S. Preminger and Sam Duker for reading the manuscript in various stages of completion and for their helpful suggestions. I am very grateful to Virginia Andrews for her tireless secretarial assistance.

CONTENTS

PART 4

PART 1

1 /

INTRODUCTION

> One day I looked around my study and thought, "In these books, field notes, specimens, tapes, and films is hidden the secret of culture. We have but to find the key to unlock it."

Culture: The Missing Ingredient

We live in an era when significant scientific gains are being made toward improving human welfare. Ecologists and other scientists are helping man to increase his control over his environment. Psychologists and psychiatrists are discovering the meaning of behavior even at the unconscious level. Social scientists are beginning to fathom the dynamics of society from a universal viewpoint. And biologists are uncovering the hidden mechanisms of genetics and human variability.

In our search for improved welfare on a global scale, however, there remains a focal area about which our information is confused and fragmentary, even misleading: the realm of culture. Crucial data relating to the cultural factor are often missing from decision-making considerations in antipoverty and economic development projects, city and regional planning, population control and nutrition, political and military strategy. Absence of cultural sophistication also handicaps communication between nations, diplomatic negotiations, and the drafting of international treaties. Until decision makers gain a deeper understanding of cultural differences we shall probably continue trying to solve human problems by such unavailing and costly methods as fighting alien customs and ideologies with bullets and bombs.

Why are cultural phenomena so often neglected and so grossly misunderstood? In view of the basic role of culture in human behavior, what can be done to remedy the situation?

A widespread notion precluding cultural sophistication is that "after all, human nature is the same all over the world" and that

3

all we need do to understand other peoples is to project our own feelings and ideas onto them. The basic flaw in this approach stems from the fact that, to an overwhelming extent, human nature is culturally molded nature. Studies by anthropologists, biologists, geneticists, linguists, archaeologists, and psychologists all conclude that most human problems are cultural problems. Our knowledge of the role of culture in human development is expanding rapidly, and if we are to assess man's character and aspirations or predict his behavior, an understanding of the culture of his social groups is crucial. Besides enhancing our understanding of human behavior, a thorough grasp of the nature of culture enables us to exercise a measure of control over our destiny. Without such grasp we remain inept and helpless. Despite the extraordinary technical achievements of modern man, our schemes for human betterment turn out to be impractical and unrealistic.

Culture: A Difficult Concept

The concept of culture is not a simple one. The term stems from the Latin *cultivare*, to till or cultivate. Webster's primary definition is "the art or practice of cultivating; manner or method of cultivating; tillage." It is not surprising, therefore, that "culture" is frequently interpreted to mean refinement or civilization. This meaning recalls the German term *Kultur*, the ideal of a classical education based on study of Greek, Latin, and the humanities. In the eighteenth century the notion of culture as *Kultur* became basic to education in Europe, especially in the Anglo-Saxon countries, and a "civilized" man was judged by his knowledge of history, languages, literature, and the arts. As science and technology developed, this notion played a part in the establishment of a rigid separation between the sciences and the humanities.

On the other hand, many people think of culture as a thing of "shreds and patches," an aggregation of discrete items that are associated by historical chance and that do not make sense as a whole. For example, a person may profess a religious code of ethics on the Sabbath and a totally different, pragmatic code for the remainder of the week. According to the "shreds and patches" notion, he may deplore the moral discrepancy but will not perceive it as symptomatic of a cultural malaise. He will not link psychological stress with cultural ambivalence.

Another approach treats a culture as though it were a mechanical system. If a part, that is, a culture "trait," breaks down or wears out, we need merely replace it with a new one. For example, government officials often attempt to alter the culture of their constituents by this sort of cultural repair. Disinfectants are substituted for magical incantations; taxes for chiefly tribute; and stooges for troublesome native leaders banished to a distant province.

On the other hand, if the entire indigenous culture is condemned, attempts may be made simply to substitute another model, usually some version of Western technological civilization. The history of the American administration of the Pueblo Indians of Arizona and New Mexico between about 1850 and 1930 well illustrates an attempt to implement this conception of culture (see Dozier 1964: 90–91).

Although the fallacies of past approaches to culture are becoming apparent, often in highly dramatic ways, deeply ingrained habits of feeling and thought linger on and confuse us. How may we transform them into concepts consistent with the findings of modern scientific research?

Many scholars have worked on this problem—Alfred North Whitehead, John Dewey, F. S. C. Northrop, Ernst Cassirer, Nicolai Hartmann, C. S. Peirce, Lancelot Law Whyte, and Pierre Teilhard de Chardin, to mention a few. Each has made his contribution, and, little by little, a new image of man has begun to emerge. Hermann Wein (1952) has suggested that the work of certain American philosophers and anthropologists—Charles Morris, Clyde Kluckhohn, and John Collier, among others—is helping to build this new image. We might add the names of geneticist Theodocius Dobzhansky, biologists George Gaylord Simpson and Sir Julian Huxley, ecologists Marston Bates and Alfred E. Emerson, social psychiatrist Alexander H. Leighton, semanticist Alfred Korzybski, linguists Edward Sapir and Benjamin Lee Whorf, economic historian Karl Polanyi, and theoretical anthropologists Dorothy Lee and David Bidney.

Under such scrutiny the concept of culture is undergoing radical revision. Anthropologists are struggling to move out of a primarily descriptive, natural-history phase of scientific endeavor to a more mature phase of deductively formulated theory. Traditional definitions of a culture as a sum total of elements, traits, and patterns have long been outmoded. The view of culture as a mechanical-type system is also obsolete. But anthropologists are having difficulty developing a working concept of culture adequate to the complex, multidimensional requirements of modern biocultural research, which involves several disciplines focused on the behavior of human communities.

In a critical review of concepts and definitions of culture, A. L. Kroeber and Clyde Kluckhohn (1952: 181) came to the conclusion that we do not yet have an adequate theory of culture. If we are to ameliorate world problems, however, we must systematically implement a scientifically viable, universally applicable concept of culture.

Culture as Coping

As we know, Homo sapiens is a relatively unspecialized species. Man's complex symbolizing brain differentiates him from the rest of the animal world (see Count 1958; Kubie 1953). Culture, then, is the brainchild of man. Viewed holistically a culture is the supreme creation of a human community—the product of its deep-seated urge to fulfill and perpetuate itself.

My thesis is that, whatever else a culture may be, it is primarily a group problem-solving device instituted by a human community to cope with its basic practical problems. This is the secret of culture. From today's perspective it is the essential pragmatic fact about the cultures of mankind.

This thesis, of course, is not new. Similar notions have been expressed by many students of culture, including W. G. Sumner and A. G. Keller, Clellan S. Ford, A. L. Kroeber and Clyde Kluckhohn, Kimball Young, John J. Honigmann, and others. But the problem-solving function of culture is by no means fully accepted by all students of culture; nor have the implications of culture's problem-solving role been spelled out.

The Anthropologist

Perhaps the precise meaning of culture as coping can be grasped only through firsthand experience. Perhaps we must study and compare the development of different cultural wholes to realize their significance and indeed that of our own culture. But a culture is difficult to study for many reasons. One obstacle, for example, is that the concept of culture is an abstraction. We cannot actually observe culture. We can only observe its manifestations: people's behavior in many different kinds of situations and their behavioral productions, such as houses, tools, weapons, boats, poems, and paintings. From an analysis of such observations we can often make valid generalizations about the culture as a whole.

A second difficulty is that we tend to project the familiar onto what we observe. In regard to behavior, we notice what we need to notice, what we admire, what we approve. We tend to close our eyes to the distasteful, the "peculiar" and "primitive." We are, in a way, prisoners of our own culture and its values. Without special training we tend to observe the behavior of others only through our own culturally tinted lenses.

So the training that goes into the making of an anthropologist is long and arduous. He must cultivate an open mind, self-discipline, and scientific restraint from making generalizations until sufficient evidence is available, and then only as working hypotheses. An anthropologist works toward entertaining simultaneously a great many kinds of facts without superimposing a formal structure upon them until their inner relationships, such as group perception patterns, ideology, and "logic," emerge as an organized whole.

Suspension of judgment is perhaps the most difficult skill that an anthropologist must acquire. Western anthropologists in particular need to resist a tendency to superimpose well-known models prematurely upon their data. If we are to gain an accurate description of a native culture, we must inhibit this habit and allow native perception patterns, cognitive categories, and value orientations to emerge from the field data, an approach that may require new forms of logic and the creation of original models appropriate to unique structural arrangements.

A fieldworker has to cope with many unfamiliar situations. He may have to learn a new language. He may have to adjust to life in the tropics, as in sunny Fiji, or in the subarctic, as in the fjord-indented coast of northern Iceland. He has also to accustom himself to different food and eating customs, various work rhythms, patterns of waking and sleeping, sanitary conditions, and ideas of privacy. A fieldworker may be transported to his place of work by outrigger sailing canoe in Lau or on horseback in rural Iceland. And he may observe local ceremonies seated cross-legged and cramped in a sun-baked village in Lau or standing in an icy Lutheran chapel in Iceland.

When he goes to live in a community with an unfamiliar setting and culture, every anthropologist experiences a nervous tension known as culture shock to some degree. The stresses of the new environment may relate to climate, diseases, poisonous plants, dangerous fish, and wild animals; strange patterns of color, light, motion, and sound; natural catastrophes such as earthquakes, volcanic eruptions, or tidal waves. But mainly the stresses are connected with the need to adjust quickly to unfamiliar behavioral habits and other culturally structured phenomena while functioning effectively in his professional role.

An anthropologist must not only cope with unfamiliar situations but must do so with grace and tact twenty-four hours a day for many months, even years. As part of his professional discipline he must overcome culture shock and learn to handle and understand the new way of life. He must never forget that a single *faux pas* may mean the failure of a carefully cultivated rapport, an end to his investigation, or in extreme cases the termination of his career and even his life. It may also jeopardize the work of his colleagues.

To become ill or die in the field is considered a serious flaw in field technique. I'll never forget the case of a woman anthropologist who was murdered on an Indian reservation in the Southwest when I was a graduate student. It was her first field trip and she was collecting information for her doctor's dissertation. The story was that she had become involved with an Indian youth and had behaved foolishly. I heard no one express sympathy for the girl. The case was used as an example of what not to do in the field.

How I envied the geologist and the botanist who were visiting Lau when I was doing fieldwork there! Having finished their day's work, they could act as they pleased and wear what they liked because they remained in a native village only long enough to complete a chore requiring from one to twenty days, whereas I had to key my behavior and dress to a residence of many months. During this time the tolerance and approval of the natives, based on their own standards of conduct for foreigners, were my only passport. For example, despite the warm muggy weather, shorts, lavalavas, and bikinis were out, and even modern bathing suits were considered immodest. In remote islands, where communication with the outside world is minimal, one's welfare and even one's life may depend on the goodwill of the people.

It is extremely difficult to win the friendship of a Melanesian, a fact that was brought home to me forcefully during fieldwork in Tokalau village on Kambara island, Fiji. I had moved with the villagers to a temporary camp near their fishing grounds. One night a young girl was speared in the thigh by a swordfish. She was bleeding profusely and was expected to die. Upon the urgent request of the family, I treated her as best I could with the help of a Boy Scout manual. Fortunately, the wound healed. Failure would have meant a severe setback in the fieldwork. Soon, however, I noticed a change in the relations of the girl's family toward me. Semitchi, her father, began to ask many small favors: tobacco, some kava, trade goods, even my sunglasses. I asked a native the meaning of this behavior. Was I expected to pay the father for successfully treating his child, perhaps saving her life? "Oh," he replied, "that is natural. Semitchi assumes that you would not have bothered to treat his daughter if you had not thought that it would somehow work to your advantage."

A field anthropologist's position is often very delicate. Not only must he work closely with the natives, but he must get along well with their administrators and officials, often living in a distant capital town. Without local government help and protection, he should not expect to reach his destination in the field, let alone remain there for the duration of his tour of duty or be permitted to return at a later date for followup checks. Besides, since his destination is often a little-known, rarely visited part of the world, he is in a favorable position to operate as an intelligence agent for his government. Hence he may be doubly suspect by officials of the host country.

Searching for Favorable Laboratories

Anthropologists have found that the first step toward becoming culturally sophisticated is to shift attention from cultural similarities to cultural differences and that certain communities represent natural experiments of human populations in culture building. Such communities, it should be emphasized, are not found in modern urban areas with complex plural cultures but in habitats far removed from the strains of modern urban and industrial civilization.

In a small, near-isolated community the investigator is an eyewitness to a biocultural experiment within a group deeply rooted in its natural setting. The population can be studied clinically as a complex, ongoing event—behavioral, biopsychological, and cultural—in geographical and historical perspective. In contrast to the usual contrived scientific laboratory, all relevant factors have been built by nature into the natural laboratory. Geographic isolation affords the researcher greater control over these factors, and historical depth ensures that biocultural processes operating in every human community have had time to manifest themselves in mature forms. Remote areas also prove ideal for research into the role of cultural factors in the evolution of microraces.

Most large nations, and many small ones, have groups of aborigines or indigenous peoples among whom persist behavior patterns, languages, attitudes, and values that differ markedly from those of the dominant group. Later comers often conquer the aborigines and relegate them to an inferior status. For example, in Fiji the Land People of Lau were conquered by the Ndaunisai invaders and demoted to form the lower class in a local social hierarchy. When India was conquered by invaders of the subcontinent, the hill tribes were demoted to outcasts. Australia and Japan have low-class aboriginal populations. Europe has its indigenous rural groups, called "peasants," whose cultures stem from Neolithic and Mesolithic roots. In this exploration we shall consider two European indigenous peoples: certain Lower Saxons of West Germany and the Icelanders, who have recently reforged their sovereign nation.

The American Indians number more than half a million and constitute the largest native group in the United States. In this study we shall consider four Indian tribes: the Hopi, the Navaho, the Dakota Sioux, and the Papago. The natives of American Samoa and the Pacific Trust Territory, as well as those of Hawaii and Guam, which we shall also investigate, are aboriginal peoples who form local units in the United States.

Investigating Human Behavior

After he has selected a favorable natural laboratory as the locus of investigation, how does a field anthropologist go about the job of studying a culture?

The goal is to investigate the behavior of the community members viewed as a biological group or population in geographic and historical perspective and to study their cultural productions, such as tools, house types, arts and crafts, literature, and language. This type of investigation is called *ethnography*. From a systematic analysis on both of his observations the behavior of the group in temporal and spatial perspective and of the records he has collected, an anthropologist abstracts the community's covert attitudes, beliefs, and values. Finally, by comparing these empirical findings with other comparable data, he makes generalizations about the group's culture as a whole. This type of comparison and generalization is called *ethnology*.

An anthropologist's job, first of all, is to record the daily round of activities in the community throughout the year and to search for their meaning. When an anthropologist visits a Lauan village, for example, he does not observe Lauan culture directly. Rather, he sees a group of colorful South Sea islanders in a brilliant tropical setting behaving in certain unfamiliar ways. For example, he may observe Lauans of diverse ages waiting on the beach for the return of a fishing expedition. Or he may note a crew of muscular young men sailing an outrigger canoe or a group of people in gala attire—colorful barkcloth kilts and garlands—preparing for a kava ceremony. If he records the behavior of the members over a period of time—several months to a year or more—he notes that their actions fall into describable patterns that tend to be repeated over and over again.

An anthropologist in the field must also obtain many different kinds of records, such as clan and family genealogies, lists of kinship terms, and censuses; sketch maps of land use and village plans; specimens of useful plants with their native names and the purposes for which they are employed; tapes of native music; texts of chants, poems, and songs; films of dances; and designs for barkcloth, mats, baskets, pottery, and woodwork. Indeed, a fieldworker frequently makes a collection of such cultural resources to be deposited for analysis and classification in a home, museum or library.

To accomplish his ends a cultural anthropologist not only observes and records native behavior down to the tiniest detail but also participates in the daily life of the community. This method of study is called participant observation (see, for example, F. Kluckholm 1940; Powdermaker 1966: 285–296). Often he becomes a member of a native family or clan, an affiliation that gives him a place and role in the native social structure (which usually is based on kinship ties). And, of course, a fieldworker begins immediately to learn the native language or languages. Interviewing community members first through an interpreter and later in the native tongue is a subtle and delicate field technique.

Many anthropologists consider learning the native language the most difficult part of a field investigation. The linguistic chore may become more arduous if over the years the anthropologist must acquire several unrelated native languages such as Fijian, an eastern Malayo-Polynesian speech; Papago, a Utaztecan language; and Icelandic, an archaic Indo-European tongue. Many

American Indian languages are so difficult that few fieldworkers master them unless they spend many years studying a single tribe.

One of the obvious advantages of learning a language on the spot as you go is that its nuances may be grasped as a functional part of the culture and as a reflection of its structure. One's growing knowledge of the language illuminates the culture, and vice versa. Of course, learning to speak a people's language is also an excellent way to get acquainted. It is also a sure means of pleasing, because it indicates a genuine interest in them and their affairs. A beginner's mistakes may also serve to break the ice and to channel hostility into laughter.

Linguistic misunderstandings can be amusing. While I was living among the Lower Saxons I accompanied my Saxon family on a visit to a neighboring farm. To put me at ease and help in my linguistic struggles, the company conversed in High German instead of Plattdeutsch, their usual idiom. They were questioning me about my field trip to Fiji. As I was telling how the natives train the brilliant jungle parakeets to talk, our hostess exclaimed, "*Na, ya,* to think of all those parrots in the *Südsee* speaking German!"

An anthropologist goes into the field with relatively little gear —notebooks, maps and cameras, typewriter and record player, tape recorder and calipers, and a few reference books and dictionaries. But traveling light can sometimes be embarrassing. I remember an incident that occurred on my first field trip. While awaiting transportation to the isolated and rarely visited Lau islands, I decided to see the mountainous interior of Viti Levu, Fiji's main island. Because there were no roads to this remote area at the time, the government-sponsored journey involved a launch ride up the Rewa River and a cross-country hike to a native village that boasted a government rest house. Packing all my gear except a camera in an ingeniously designed knapsack, I set out. When the launch reached the jumping-off place I discovered to my dismay that, besides a guide, twenty Fijian bearers were waiting. How amused they were and, yes, a little condescending, when the foreign *marama* (lady) disembarked with but two small pieces of luggage! I had not yet discovered that in Fiji one's prestige is directly related to the quantity of one's visible worldly goods.

Conclusion

I have tried to describe some of the practical problems, hardships, and hazards of anthropological fieldwork. I hope that I have also conveyed some sense of its fascination, challenge, and rewards. An anthropologist differs from other students of man and culture because he seeks to learn about people by describing and comparing all types of human groups, their biological heritages as well as their distinctive ways of living and communicating—not merely those groups near at hand, familiar, or admired. To accomplish this he seeks out human populations with distinctive cultures, behaviors, and gene pools wherever they may be found, even in the most remote corners of the earth.

These natural settings form the anthropologist's "laboratory." On-the-spot observations, sketch maps of settlement patterns, recordings of music and oral literature are among the basic documents and empirical evidence from which an anthropologist generalizes about man's symbolizing, culture-creating propensities in relation to his way of solving his situational problems. On the basis of such observations and documents, as well as those of biologists, geneticists, archaeologists, and linguists, anthropologists strive to develop working hypotheses about the nature and dynamics of culture and the role of culture in human evolution.

2 /

EARLY MAN IN THE PACIFIC

The handle of my steering paddle thrills to action,
My paddle named Kautu-ki-te-rangi.
It guides to the horizon but dimly discerned.
To the horizon that lifts before us,
To the horizon that ever recedes,
To the horizon that ever draws near,
To the horizon that causes doubt,
To the horizon that instils dread,
The horizon with unknown power,
The horizon not hitherto pierced.
The lowering skies above,
The raging seas below,
Oppose the untraced path
Our ship must go.

Polynesian deep-sea chant (Buck 1938: 40)*

One of the major concerns that has preoccupied anthropologists
is the relation between culture and environment, and our first
series of explorations will be concerned especially with the nature-culture problem.

The influence of geography on humanity has, of course, received the attention of many writers from antiquity to modern
times. In the late nineteenth century, environmental determinism
was stressed by geographers and anthropogeographers, especially Friedrich Ratzel. Although taking a less extreme stand
than some of his contemporaries, Ratzel (1899) gave considerable weight to the influence of geography on humanity. His
position has been called "tempered environmentalism." Extreme
environmentalists maintain that environmental influences play a

15

dominant role in building cultures. Ellsworth Huntington (1945) explained human behavior as largely determined by geographic factors, especially climate. A school of environmental determinists has developed and has had far-reaching effects on the ideologies and behavior of peoples and on international conflicts.

By means of empirical findings from their field investigations, anthropologists are in a favorable position to test the theories of the environmental determinists. Alexander A. Goldenweiser (1937: 443–454) was, I believe, the first anthropologist to assemble systematically the available field data and to refute the theory of environmental determinism.

Recently the problem of the interrelationship between man and nature has been undergoing a revival of interest on the part of scientists from many disciplines. These include biogeography (for example, Butzer 1964; Fosberg 1963a); ecology (for example, Bates 1960); archaeology (for example, Clark 1962: Ch. 1); comparative anatomy, genetics and physical anthropology (for example, Dobzhansky 1962); history (for example, L. White 1967); and cultural ecology (for example, Thomas 1956).

Opposed to the extreme environmentalists are the cultural ecologists, whose orientation and basic concepts have been borrowed from modern biological ecology. Cultural ecologists treat a human community as a population of the human species that is integrally part of a larger multispecies unit designated by ecologists as a population system. According to Alfred E. Emerson (1965: 50), "Population systems are highly evolved integrated biological entities, ranking in importance with such analogous units as the gene, the cell, and the multicellular individual organism." A population system transacts adaptively with the environment through circular (feedback) and spiral processes by which energy and materials constantly flow into, through, and out of the system and back into the environment.

C. S. Pittendrigh (1958: 391–394) defines adaptation as the "total organization of a living system." He emphasizes that the adaptive process is keyed not to completion of the life cycle of a single organism, according to the species biogram or way of self-actualization, but to that of future generations of the species. He refers to this process as "teleonomy," defined as movement with direction toward improved organization in terms of probable future function. "Teleonomy" is frequently confused with "teleology," defined as movement toward a predetermined goal.

The teleonomic process is thus responsible for the fact that a population system that is undisturbed for a period of time tends to move toward a mature, self-perpetuating steady state or climax in which all available ecological niches are filled and the relationship of the component species toward one another and toward the natural environment is characterized by homeostasis, a process defined as "the self-regulation of optimal conditions for maintenance and continuation" (Emerson 1965: 54).

According to this culture-ecological school of thought, human culture is perceived as an adaptive device, unique to the biogram (mode of life) of the human species. To understand the complex interrelationships between a human community as part of a larger ecosystem and its natural environment we would thus need to consider the human population in relation to its changing culture in geographical, climatic, ecological, and historical perspective. In our concern with the nature-culture problem we shall keep the requirements of this relatively broad view of the problem in mind.

A Favorable Laboratory

When, after years of preparation, the time came to embark on my first field expedition, I chose the Lau islands of eastern Fiji.[1] The area seemed to afford an unusually favorable natural laboratory for my purpose—to study a small isolated community where processes of cultural change under pressure from other native groups as well as Westerners might be examined in the context of a scarcity type of environment. Having written a dissertation on native trade areas of Melanesia, I wanted to investigate a Melanesian trade area at first hand.

The vast Pacific area of Oceania encompasses one-third of the earth's surface and is inhabited by an estimated 17.5 million people, less than 5 million of which are native peoples, the remainder being settlers from other parts of the world. Many communities in this culture area, particularly on small tropical islands, are little protected by man-made devices from direct contact with natural forces and are directly exposed to solar radiation and other possible cosmic influences, to atmospheric pressures including winds and cyclones, to temperature changes, to precipitation, and to ocean tides and currents. Isolated peoples living in many Pacific habitats are more directly dependent on local geology and natural resources than are peoples in many other environments. The population of relatively isolated, sea-girt islands thus affords an opportunity to investigate a human group as an integral part of a total ecosystem in natural setting (Spate 1963: 253).

It is generally agreed that early man evolved in central and southern Africa, and during the greater part of his 2-million-year history Homo sapiens has inhabited tropical regions and lived in small, near-isolated groups. Many human communities in the Pacific are located within or just outside the tropics and therefore can be studied under conditions similar in many respects to those that prevailed throughout most of man's evolutionary history. Continental biotics are more stable and less liable to disturbance from external forces than those of insular origin, and oceanic islands are particularly vulnerable to disturbance from alien species. Therefore, the Pacific area is especially suitable for a study of the effects of changing conditions on human communities and for research in the dynamics of culture change, a vital area of concern for modern man.

To set the stage we shall consider certain facts about the geography of the Pacific and then try to reconstruct the history of man's settlement there. It should be borne in mind, however, that exploration of the area is proceeding rapidly among archaeologists, geologists, botanists, zoologists, entomologists, marine biologists, oceanographers, and other scientists using mainly natural-history methods of research. Geneticists and anthropologists are also hard at work, and new facts are constantly being reported.

Climate

In exploring the natural forces that create man's environment, we may well start with the effects of solar radiation on that part of the spinning earth nearest the sun—the heat equator. Because the earth tilts as it rotates around the sun, the heat equator fluctuates. It moves north of the true equator during most of the northern summer and south of it during the southern summer. In general, the heat equator forms a zone of low pressure that attracts atmospheric movements to it from high-pressure centers to the northeast and the southeast. In the eastern Pacific this process brings cooling winds called trade winds.

In the Northern Hemisphere the trades blow from the northeast during the summer and in the Southern Hemisphere, from the southeast during the summer. In localities where they blow regularly, the trade winds, by lowering both temperature and humidity, influence human comfort and activity. Because barriers such as hills and mountain ranges obstruct winds and influence precipitation, villages located on the windward side of an island are appreciably cooler and often healthier than those to the leeward, where semiarid conditions may be found. The trades therefore figure as a major factor in the selection of habitation sites.

During the winter season, which varies of course with the hemisphere, the trade winds tend to die down and monsoon winds may take over. The monsoons blow irregularly from a general direction opposite that of the trades. They bring tropical thunderstorms and at times hurricanes. Although of great destructive force, hurricanes bring needed rain to dry areas.

In the immediate vicinity of the equator is a windless area known as the doldrums, and beyond the 30-degree or 40-degree parallels of latitude in both hemispheres blow the prevailing westerlies. Here the weather is highly changeable and cyclones are common, a situation of crucial concern to navigators, especially islanders in frail outrigger canoes.

In studying the climate of the Pacific as it affects human migration and settlement, we must consider the great riverlike ocean currents that directly affect navigation, especially in small native vessels. The movements of ocean currents are related to the eastward rotation of the earth, the north-south extension of the continents, the prevailing winds, and the tendency of cold water to flow toward warmer zones, where it forces warm water to rise. These currents are called the north equatorial and the south equatorial currents, and they flank the warm, eastward-flowing equatorial countercurrent.

The warm north equatorial current becomes the warm Japan current as it sweeps northward along the Asiatic coast. The cold, eastward-moving Kamchatka and subarctic currents, bifurcated by the North American landmass, flow northward into the cold Alaska current and southward into the cold California current. South of the southern continents the cold west wind drift moves eastward around the world. Supplemented by upwelling colder water from the depths, part of it is diverted by the South American continent into the cold Peruvian, or Humboldt, current, which moves northward almost to the equator.

The Pacific Ocean controls, to a considerable extent, the temperatures of small islands rising out of the deep sea in the eastern Pacific, which have an equable maritime climate. Mean air temperatures correspond closely to those of the ocean surface, the annual range being around 10 degrees F. Many tropical Pacific islands have year-around temperatures between 70 and 80 degrees F. throughout the day, which directly affects the choice of house types, clothing, and activities. People who live in the tropics become very sensitive to minute changes in temperature. At 70 degrees it is not unusual for Lauans to shiver with cold in the early morning or when fishing in the lagoon.

Rainfall, on the other hand, is highly variable by day, season, and year. Maximum precipitation occurs on the windward slopes of high mountains on volcanic islands. Because of the seasonal shifting of the intertropical front, most islands north of the equator receive maximum rainfall in summer and early fall, July to October, and those to the south have their rainy season during their summer months, between November and April.

Geography and Geology

The Pacific Ocean is the earth's largest single feature.[2] This vast sea, averaging 14,000 feet in depth, covers more than 68 million square miles. Such great expanses have significantly affected the migration and colonization of organic species, microorganisms, plants, animals, and men in this region.

Another feature of the Pacific that bore upon human settlement is the so-called continental shelf. This submarine platform extends along the ocean floor eastward from the Asiatic continent far out into the Pacific. The andesite line extends northward and westward beyond the eastern margins of New Zealand and Fiji and along the north coasts of the Solomons, Bismarck, and the islands north of the New Guinea coast. It continues eastward, past Palau and Yap, the Marianas, Japan, and the Kamchatka peninsula in eastern Siberia. On islands west of the line are schist, gneiss, granite, slate, and other metamorphic rocks, such as andesite, and gold and other minerals. Islands east of the line lack these continental resources.

Apparently parts of the east Asiatic continent have sunk since the Cenozoic era, and sea levels have fluctuated. It is believed that Australia and the islands east of Wallace's line (which runs east of Bali and Borneo through the Makassar Strait) were separated from Asia during the Miocene epoch, about 20 million years ago. On islands west of Wallace's line are found animals characteristic of southeast Asia today or fossils from the past, such as the tiger, orangutan, gibbon, tapir, deer, wild dog, Sumatran rhinoceros, and squirrel. On the islands east of Wallace's line animals that distinguish Asiatic from Australian fauna are absent. Instead, there are primitive Australian animals like the duckbill, spiny anteater, kangaroo, wombat, wallaby, and koala and such distinctive plants as the eucalyptus. Only about 50 percent of the 9,000 species of flowering plants in Australia are endemic. Weber's line, east of Celebes and Timor and west of New Guinea, separates Australian and Indonesian flora and fauna from those of Oceania. The presence or absence of continental resources is reflected directly in the native cultures of the Pacific area.

Pacific Basin

By noting the occurrence of metamorphic and plutonic rocks, Harry A. Ladd (1934: 49–53, fig. 6) locates the structural boundary and the probable limits of the former "Melanesian continent." Thus the area included Tasmania, New Zealand,

Chatham, Kermadec, Tonga, all of Melanesia, the Western Carolines as far as Truk, and the Marianas. Ladd suggests that the destruction of this continent, probably by faulting, constituted one of the major events of earth history.

East of the continental shelf the Pacific Basin tends to drop abruptly. The greatest ocean deep, the Mariana Trench, between Guam and Yap, is 35,636 feet in depth; and the Tonga-Kermadec Trench, east of Tonga and the Kermadecs, reaches 34,898 feet. Oceanic island groups rise from the ocean floor and tend to be separated by great distances, whereas most groups on the shelf are less widely spaced. Apparently it is no accident that the early Papuo-Melanesians did not manufacture or use large seagoing double canoes, for they settled on islands on the shelf, where there is little need for long-distance travel. Deep-sea canoes are characteristic of the Polynesians, who much later found and settled the far-flung islands to the east.

Geologically, most of this vast Pacific area is still in the process of formation. The Pacific Basin is rimmed with more than 300 volcanoes, such as those of New Zealand, Tonga, the Marianas, and Japan. A new volcano, Taal, near Manila in the Philippines, recently erupted; a new island, Krakatoa, appeared in the Sunda Strait; and volcanic craters long inactive, such as Kilauea-iki on Hawaii, may suddenly burst forth. The ever-present threat of volcanic inundation is reflected in many aspects of the native culture of Ka'u (see Chapter 5).

Oceanic Islands

Geologists define oceanic islands as those that rise from submarine platforms built by outpourings of lava from rifts in the ocean floor. They may be "high" islands, like those of the Society group, the Marquesas, and Hawaii. The Hawaiian islands, for example, rise 18,000 feet from the ocean floor, and their highest peaks tower almost 14,000 feet higher.

"Low" islands rise not more than a few hundred feet above the sea. Some low islands, called atolls, such as the Tuamotus, the Gilberts, and the Marshalls, have been built on submarine volcanic platforms and cones by colonies of tiny lime-secreting organisms like the coral polyp. Such organisms only grow near the surface (not below 150 feet) in clear waters with a saline content at least 80 percent of that of sea water. The temperature of the water is usually 73 degrees F. or higher. Other low islands, such as Fulanga in Lau, or parts of islands like the northern plateau of Guam have been formed of solidified coral limestone deposits that have been raised several hundred feet above sea level, probably by faulting.

The volcanic islands of the Pacific usually have richer natural resources, including more fertile garden land, than islands formed of coral or limestone. For example, taro, a nutritious tuber that is the basic food for many Pacific islanders, generally will not grow on limestone islands. Because of their reef-protected lagoons, however, atolls and raised limestone islands frequently have safer and more propitious offshore fishing conditions than volcanic islands.

Changes During the Ice Age

During the Pleistocene epoch, dated approximately from 2 million to 10,000 years ago, the ice sheet at its maximum depth is estimated to have been 3,000 to 4,000 feet thick. Sea levels fluctuated from 394 to 590 feet higher to 492 feet lower than they are today. Shorelines were reduced or extended, and land bridges emerged in several parts of the world, including shelves between the islands of Indonesia, between Australia and New Guinea, and in the Bering Strait area (Butzer 1964: figs. 70, 71). During the fourth (Würm) recession of the icecap (12,000–8,000 B.C.), the stage was set for the migration of large prehistoric mammals from one continent to another and even between the hemispheres. Paleolithic human hunters followed such prey as bison, mastodon, mammoth, and reindeer.

During cold maximum periods rainfall was heavy immediately south of the great glaciers. Beyond this rainy belt were savannahs. Consequently, areas of the world that are desiccated today (such as the Lower Sonoran desert in the American Southwest, parts of the great Australian desert, and the Sahara) were grasslands well stocked with game. There were far more inland seas

and lakes than there are today. Between the great pulses of the
ice sheet, the climate of Europe was temperate to subtropical. In
Africa the rains diminished, lakes shrank, and deserts developed.

Thus, in the Late Pleistocene, quantities of ocean water had
been impounded in the great glaciers that still covered much of
the Northern Hemisphere as well as the mountain peaks in the
south and Antarctica. By the Late Würm period sea levels
may have been 150 to 300 feet lower than they are now. Suma-
tra, Java, and Borneo were attached to Malaya by the Sunda
Shelf, and the Sahul Shelf connected New Guinea to Australia
(Butzer 1964: fig. 71, 396–398). However, small boats or rafts
were probably required for man to cross from the Sunda area
to Australia and New Guinea.

First Settlements in the Pacific

Hominids of the genus Pithecanthropus from the Middle
Pleistocene have been found west of Wallace's line. But anthropologists believe that the first groups of Homo sapiens moved
as hunters and gatherers into the New Guinea region during
the Late Pleistocene or early post-Pleistocene era. Although the
oldest fossil remains of Homo sapiens so far discovered in the
area are dated about the middle of the seventh millennium
B.C. (Clark 1962: 244), other finds indicate the presence of
man here by 10900 B.C. and probably earlier (Bulmer 1964).

Some anthropologists postulate that the early penetration of
modern human groups into the Pacific was accomplished by
two subspecies of Homo sapiens. They class one subspecies with
the Australoid stock, represented today in the area, for example,
by the fast-disappearing aborigines of Australia. The other subspecies is classed with the Negrito stock, represented today by
pygmy communities in the forested, mountainous interior of
western New Guinea and large islands of Melanesia, as well
as in the Philippines, Malaya, and the Andaman Islands.

Judging from present-day distributions, both Australoids and
Negritos formerly may have occupied a far greater area than
they do today. Dravidians of southern India and Ceylon may
be Asiatic relatives of the Pacific Australoids. The Australoids

seem to have sought out arid, savannahlike habitats, while Negritos settled in equatorial rain forests. They are thought to have taken refuge from later invaders in the marginal areas they now occupy.

Pacific Negritos have recently been reclassified by biological anthropologists as a separate geographic race, the "Pacific Negrito" (Garn 1961: 130; Newman 1963), consisting of a series of microraces found from the Philippines to Queensland and characterized by small stature, dark skin, and frizzy hair. Although their genetic constitution is little known, Pacific Negritos are believed by this school of thought to have "no necessary connection" with African pygmies. The small stature of the African pygmies is thought to result from isolation and natural selection during the early expansion of populations.

Australian Aborigines[3]

During the next ten millenniums the Australoids of Australia, somewhat mixed with Negritos, apparently developed a number of local cultures under relatively undisturbed conditions. This population evolved into several local races that together form what some biological anthropologists, according to serological factors, call the Australian geographic race (Garn 1961: 120), which is related to the extinct Tasmanians. Serological factors, called blood groups, are inherited gene frequencies that have been found, mainly during the last half-century, to aid in the scientific study of genetics. Systems of alleomorphs, like the A-B-O, M-N, Rhesus, Duffy, and Diego afford a dependable means of analyzing, comparing, and classifying human populations by blood types into local races such as geographic and microraces. They also help in reconstructing the origin of recently mixed populations.

According to research in blood typing, the Australian aborigines, now numbering some 50,000 fullbloods, show a very high incidence of N in the M-N system, and a very low (probably recent) frequency of blood group B. All are classed as Duffy positive.[4] They have long narrow skulls, broadest at the base; moderately heavy brow ridges with a low or retreating forehead; bright eyes; nose depressed at the root and wide at the nostrils; prognathous jaws; large, strong teeth; dark brown skin; black wavy hair; erect posture; and an average height of five feet five inches. While sleeping in the nude, the aborigines are able to withstand very low night temperatures.

When Europeans settled Australia in 1788, the aborigines numbered about 300,000 and were divided into about 500 tribes, each numbering 500 or 600 members. Each tribe spoke its own language. According to A. P. Elkin (1964: 13), all these languages belonged to a single linguistic stock characterized by

> Precision, brevity of expression, an emphasis on concreteness and an endeavour to express in one word or in as few as possible, a complete picture of the situation or desire; this is done by the inflexions of the word or words used . . . there is a wide-spread similarity in word order; in poverty of conjunctions; in absence of relative pronouns; in richness of the forms of the verb; in the use of the dual; in the use of phrase-order for expressing comparison and similarity; in distinguishing by suffixes between the nominative subject as a name and as an active agent; in the wealth of inflexions for the noun and pronoun; and in the significance of some of the case affixes.

Based on a locally self-sufficient collecting and hunting economy, the Australian aborigines developed some of the most interesting cultures known to man. In their semiarid environment such self-sufficiency required considerable knowledge of local natural resources and great skill with chipped-stone tools and weapons. Neither farming nor metal implements were known in Australia until introduced by Europeans.

The aborigines regulate interclan marriage through an elaborate system of kinship groups based on clan affiliations. Their eight-class system, based on the principle of unilinear descent through either the male or female line, is the most complicated kinship network ever devised. Through intertribal gatherings for ceremonial purposes, during the last sixty years this system has spread from the Kimberley mountains in the northwest to Arnhem Land in the north, from Fitzroy Crossing to the south, and to central Australia (Elkin 1964: 32–33).

The natives of Australia not only regulate interpersonal relations by means of kinship but tie together, by means of kinship bonds, the living members of a clan with ancestors and unborn members. They identify with species of animals and plants and with other natural phenomena important to their way of life. Such extension of the kinship system onto the world of nature is called totemism.

The world is perceived by the aborigines as a circular and cyclical whole in which the domain of the living contrasts to the domain of the dead, the spirits, and the unborn souls. At death the soul is believed to return to the spirit home of the tribe where it existed before birth. Some tribes locate their spirit home beneath the earth, others in the sky, beyond the sea, or on an island. The spirit home is conceived as the province of the sacred, the supernatural, myth, and dream, which to the natives represents the real world. Conversely, the domain of the living appears transitory and dreamlike. Their universe is an ordered world in which man is believed to be but one power unit among many in nature. If mutual welfare is to be achieved, they believe all power units must work together, according to the rhythms of nature, to create and conserve life. As a power unit man must fulfill his role actively by means of certain prescribed deeds, especially dances, songs, and ceremonies.

Among Murngin aborigines of Arnhem Land on the north coast of Australia, according to W. Lloyd Warner (1937: 445–449), every man is believed to have two souls: a true soul and a trickster. Before his birth his true soul emerges from the depths of the water hole or well belonging to his father's clan and enters his mother's womb. This soul lodges throughout life in the man's heart and links him to his clan's subterranean reservoir of magical power through the souls of his clan's ancestors and his clan's sacred totems. After death the true soul descends through the clan's water hole into the sacred world. Later it may be born again of another clan wife. The trickster soul is a shadowy entity that may leave a living man's body at any time and play pranks on other persons. After death the trickster soul vanishes into the bush, where it joins other spirits for good or ill.

Australian cultures manifest an elegance of structure and an economy of parts that may elude us if we measure value and success in terms of the numerical accretion of "traits" or the elaboration and proliferation of forms. Recently a hitherto unknown tribe called the Bindibu was discovered near a well in a canyon of the Great Sandy Desert north of Lake Mackay. The tribe numbers about forty members. They wear no clothing and appear "friendly, fearless, poised and happy" (Hillaby 1965, from Donald F. Thomson). The entire tool kit of this group consists of a digging stick, a throwing stick, a long wooden spear, and "an all-purpose tool of about two feet long and four inches wide resembling a model of a shallow canoe that is used as a spear thrower, shield, chopper, knife and food container." The Bindibu also use their bodies as tools. They trim their stone implements with their large incisor teeth. Clenched jaws function as a combined vise and knife during tool-making operations; and feet double as clamps and anvils. The seminomadic aborigines apparently take pride in requiring as few artifacts as possible and using one tool in many ways.

Economy of movement is characteristic among the natives of both sexes. Their body movements are graceful both in the ballet-like ceremonial dances and in everyday activities. They also use their bodies as musical instruments: their voices for singing; their hands and thighs for clapping; their breath, tongue, lips, and diaphragm for playing the *didjeridu*, a musical instrument of the eastern Kimberleys and part of the Northern Territory, remarkable for the precision and sustained quality of its tone and for the variety of rhythms that a skilled player can produce with it. Economy may also be detected in the aborigines' songs and chants, which express with accuracy and completeness an episode or story in few words, perhaps only four or five.

Preferred Relationship Pattern

Designed to conserve and perpetuate the natural resources needed for their subsistence pattern, the aborigines' customs express this economy principle and the idea of transmigration of souls in relation to the strength and perpetuation of their clans. Even their kinship system, which appears so complicated in comparison with simple Euro-American bilateral family types, is an efficient device for arranging marriage ties and reciprocal exchanges between clans within the native preferred relationship pattern.

An understanding of the aborigine's culture, and especially his image of the world and preferred relationship pattern, not only enhances our understanding of aboriginal behavior but gives a clue to the behavior and world images of many other native peoples of Oceania and southeast Asia. For example, a similarly structured world image seems implicit in the traditional religion of the Lauans (Chapter 3), the Polynesians to some extent (Handy 1940b), and certain aboriginal tribes of India such as the Hill Saora (Elwin 1955: Ch. 2). This holistic, cyclical model of the universe seems to have evolved in unbroken sequence from Stone Age man's conception of unity with his natural surroundings and with himself as part of his group. Such continuity and affinity with nature are implicit in Hinduism, Buddhism, and other religions of Asia. The concept differs radically, however, from the traditional world views implicit in Judaism, Christianity, Islam, and other revealed religions stemming from the Near East.

Peoples of Oceania

Australoids and Negritos interbred in varying degrees as they gradually entrenched themselves in most of the islands of the Melanesian continental shelf. Settlements in New Guinea and the continental islands to the east in time acquired Neolithic skills from southeast Asia: stone grinding and polishing and pottery making (Chang, Solheim, and Grace 1964: 382–384). The complex of plants and animals associated with the Neolithic period in Oceania includes certain nonseed root plants such as taro, yams, and sugar cane, as well as breadfruit, fowl, pigs, and dogs. They are believed to have been domesticated in southeast Asia, which has been proposed as the region of earliest agriculture by Carl O. Sauer (1952: 24ff.).

At the time of their discovery by Europeans, the native peoples of the immense region of Oceania were fishermen and farmers. They used no metals but had cutting tools of stone, shell, and bone. Except for Papuan speakers in the interiors of large islands, these peoples speak languages belonging to the Austronesian (Malayo-Polynesian) linguistic stock.

Melanesians

Within Oceania, the culture area of Melanesia includes New Guinea just north of Australia, the Bismarcks, the Solomons, the New Hebrides, New Caledonia, and Fiji. The entire culture area lies south of the equator and is peopled mainly by the Melanesian-Papuan geographic race (Garn 1961: 119–120).

The Papuo-Melanesians are a long-headed, muscular, dark-skinned people of short to medium height with Negroid facial features and bushy black hair. Cut off until World War II from the rest of the world for ten millenniums, they constitute a genetic isolate with certain describable characteristics. Recent research in blood group typing, disease susceptibility, and other physical-anthropology techniques reveals that they differ from the Australian aborigines by a greater incidence of type B blood. They also differ morphologically and serologically from the Polynesians to the east, and they exhibit a number of unique gene-determined diseases such as kuru, a hereditary neurological disorder that seems to be restricted to the eastern highlands of New Guinea. The prevalence of kuru has necessitated the quarantine of an entire tribe. Another neuromuscular heredo-familial disease that is apparently population limited has been reported from the New Guinea Trust Territory.

Lau, our first case study, belongs to the Melanesian culture area.

Micronesians

The Micronesian culture area of Oceania is located east of the Philippines and north of Melanesia. The entire ocean area of 3 million square miles and land area of 1200 square miles lies in the Northern Hemisphere. It includes the Carolines, Palaus (sometimes considered part of the Western Carolines), Marshalls, Gilberts, and Marianas, of which Guam is the southernmost island.

In several respects the Marianas and the Palaus should be classified with the Philippine-Indonesian culture area to the west rather than with Micronesia. The natives of these islands speak languages affiliated with the western branch of the Austronesian stock, along with those of the Philippines, Taiwan, Malaysia, and Madagascar (Chang, Solheim, and Grace 1964: 365–367), whereas the languages of the remainder of Micronesia are affiliated with the eastern branch of Austronesian, along with those of the New Hebrides-Banks, Loyalty, New Caledonia, Rotuma, and Fiji. The natives of the Marianas and the Palaus formerly made pottery, a skill unknown on the islands to the east. The distribution of the A-B-O blood-group system among the Chamorros of the Marianas is similar to that among the Palauans but differs from other Micronesian groups tested (Myrianthopoulos and Pieper 1959: 106). Of special interest is the fact that the Marianas and Palaus, like the Philippines, are formed partly of continental rocks. The remaining islands of this culture area are of volcanic formation or of coral limestone. Continental-type natural resources were built into their native cultures by the Chamorros and Palauans. Continental rock was used in making stone money, which was traded to neighboring islands.

There is archaeological evidence of the spread, by island hopping, of mixed Australoid-Negrito explorers eastward along the continental shelf during the Late Pleistocene and early post-Pleistocene period; and a strong Oceanic Negroid strain, less conspicuous in the islands to the east, is well documented in the present population of the Palaus (Barnett 1949: ii). Information concerning the prehistory of these islands, however, is limited. Some of the extinct aborigines of the Marianas may also have been Negroid in type (see Chapter 4).

Although in appearance most Micronesians somewhat resemble Polynesians, their blood-group affiliations are different and they are classed as a separate geographic race. Among the Micronesians phenotype frequency of blood type A exceeds 50 percent. Blood type N exceeds M in the N-M system except in the Kapingamarangi Polynesian outlyer. Micronesians are largely Duffy positive and entirely Diego negative. According to Garn (1961: 119), "The Micronesians occupy a unique serological niche. With Ro practically absent there can be no recent contact with Africa. With a moderate frequency of B, the Micronesians are set off from Polynesia and Australia while the absence of Diego positive individuals sets them off from Asia as well." Absence of the Diego positive factor also distinguishes Micronesians from American Indians.

The natives of Guam will be the subject of our second case study.

Polynesians

The culture area of Polynesia, within Oceania, extends in a great triangle north and south of the equator. Its apex is formed by tropical Hawaii, and its base includes temperate New Zealand on the southwest and remote, rockbound Easter Island on the southeast.

Possibly 4,000 years ago the Polynesians, a seafaring people with a Neolithic culture, began to move out in large double sailing canoes from southern China, southeast Asia, and Indonesia. They tried to gain a foothold on islands on the continental shelf, but, because most of the desirable land was already occupied and fiercely defended, many of the groups moved farther eastward. They settled in a few remote islands such as the central New Hebrides, which, if we can trust linguistic evidence (Chang, Solheim, and Grace 1964: 366), apparently served as a jumping-off place. With navigational skill and daring the Polynesians pushed beyond the shallow seas of Melanesia into the deep Pacific. They gradually populated most of the habitable islands in Polynesia and probably also reached the coasts of the Americas. Linguistic and cultural evidence on such Polynesian outliers as Tikopia, Ontong, Java, Rennell, Bellona, and Kapingamarangi indicates that they also moved northward and westward into Melanesia and Micronesia. The Maori anthropologist Sir Peter Buck (1938) gave a vivid picture of some of the problems solved by these native navigators as they successfully crossed and recrossed vast expanses of open sea.

The beauty of the Polynesian women was much admired by

early European navigators and whalers. Although one may gather the impression that all Polynesians are tall, handsome, well formed, and brown-skinned, with dark eyes and black wavy hair, there is considerable variation in physical type among the island groups. This polymorphism has long been explained as resulting from inbreeding among Caucasoid, Mongoloid, and Negroid stocks. Recent serological research, however, reveals that Polynesians have a high N to M ratio, a characteristic of Pacific peoples; a low incidence of blood group B; and a high frequency of the Duffy factor (Garn 1961: 118–119; Shapiro 1940). The high N frequencies set the Polynesians off from and rule out any recent major contact with the Americas, and the low incidence of B does the same with Asia. From the genetics viewpoint, therefore, the hybrid theory appears oversimplified. Living in one of the most remote regions of the planet and one of the last to be settled by man, Polynesians were isolated from the rest of the world for perhaps two millenniums. An inbreeding population until recently, they are classed as a separate geographic race.

The several Polynesian groups show variant forms and elaborations of a basic Polynesian culture complex. They also speak closely related languages—one might almost say dialects—of a single Polynesian language. Polynesian, together with Fijian and Rotuman, is believed by George W. Grace (Chang, Solheim, and Grace 1964: 367–368) to have differentiated from the languages of the Efate-Epi area of the New Hebrides more than 3,000 years ago.

Hawaii, our third case study, belongs to the Polynesian culture area.

Conclusion

In this chapter I have tried to convey something of the natural environment of the Australia-Pacific island region and to outline some of the problems it poses to human groups seeking a livelihood there. Certain current assumptions regarding the peopling of the Pacific have been noted, based on the available evidence—archaeological findings, historical documents, blood groupings, somatological types, native languages and cultures. Some facts concerning the culture areas of Oceania have been cited and have set the stage for an investigation of three native communities: Lau, Guam, and Hawaii.

Notes

* From *Vikings of the Sunrise* by Peter H. Buck. Copyright, 1938, by J. P. Lippincott Company, reprinted by arrangement with the publishers.
1. I am indebted to Edwin H. Bryan, Jr., and Harry S. Ladd for supplying information regarding some problems dealt with in this chapter.
2. Otis W. Freeman, ed., *Geography of the Pacific* (1951), and Douglas L. Oliver, *The Pacific Islands* (1961), are helpful sources regarding the geography and geology of the Pacific basin.
3. A. P. Elkin's classic *The Australian Aborigines* (1964) is recommended for background reading.
4. See Garn 1961: 121; Elkin 1964: 4, 339; Howells 1937.

3 /

LAUANS OF FIJI

Na vatu manawa, na vau i rama,
Yau talatala, vakaselotaki mana wangga,
Tambu wangga ko ira na kai Mathuata
Laki kele sara i matamatana.

Like a stone that floats, like the fruit of light,
Heavy with goods to be given, the canoes are welcomed,
Canoes of the people of Mathuata
Anchoring at the mouth of the passage.

> Ancient Fijian club dance recorded by Thompson
> (1940a: 60) and interpreted by Manu Tupou
> Taunaolo

Remote from the usual haunts of tourists and adventurers, Lau
is one of the South Sea's most beautiful spots.[1] Located about
200 miles from Suva, the capital of Fiji, and 170 miles from
Tonga, this sea-girt world consists of a hundred small islands
strung like an emerald necklace on the eastern margin of the
Fijian archipelago.

In this inquiry we shall focus on a group of about fifteen
small islands forming a native trade area in southern Lau. Only
six of the islands are inhabited—Kambara, Namuka, Komo,
Mothe, Fulanga, and Ongea. The uninhabited islands are Wangava, Marambo, Tavunasithi, Karoni, Yangasa, Navutu-i-loma,
Navutu-i-ra, Tuvutha, and Ongea Ndriki. At the time of my
visit the estimated population of the six islands was 1,500.
Twenty years later (1956) it had increased to 2,407 (Colony of
Fiji 1958: 85, 87, 89). The inhabitants were native Fijians except for one Chinese trader on Kambara, one on Namuka, and

35

one on Mothe. There were no East Indians or Europeans in the southern islands.

Physical Type and Language

Now numbering about 200,000, the Fijians form a local race characterized by moderately long heads, Negroid facial features, dark skin, and frizzy black hair. Serological analysis reveals the following approximate blood group frequencies: "O—43.8 percent; A—43.1 percent; B—9.4 percent; AB—3.8 percent; Rh factor—66.1 percent (Howells 1933: 325).

The Lauans of eastern Fiji have interbred with Tongans and, less frequently, with Samoans (Gifford 1951a: 123). Norman E. Gabel (1958: 25) wrote:

> The eastern Fijians stand in considerable contrast to the interior tribes and are the most Polynesian in appearance. They have lighter skins, greater stature, and heavier musculature. Their heads are broader as are their faces and jaws, their noses are larger, narrower, and higher bridged, and their chins are more pronounced.

Hair tends to be more wavy than frizzy, and they have less facial and body hair than the Fijians proper.

Lauans speak a dialect of the Mbauan language of Viti Levu, the largest island of Fiji, enriched with Tongan words, and some Lauans also speak Tongan. The Fijian languages belong to the eastern branch of the Austronesian stock, and some are so diverse as to be mutually unintelligible.

Geography and Natural Resources

The Lau islands were formed mainly by volcanic activity and coral limestone deposits beginning some 30 million years ago in the Lower Miocene (Ladd and Hoffmeister 1945: 25). Today they rise from 100 to 1,100 feet above sea level from an ocean floor more than 600 feet deep. In southern Lau natural resources valued by the natives are distributed sparsely and sporadically. Their occurrence is related to geological structure, reef and lagoon formation, climate, natural and man-made erosion, availability of garden land and fresh water, and small local variations in the ecosystems that characterize the several island types.

For example, only Mothe and Komo are so-called high islands composed almost wholly of weathered volcanic (andesite) rock. They rise to central ridges at 590 feet and 226 feet, respectively. These islands contain the best garden lands in the group. Only on them do the favored cultivated yam and the best paper mulberry, used in the production of superior-quality barkcloth, grow well. Indeed, all garden and tree crops important to the Lauan nutrition pattern grow well on Mothe and Komo, including the sweet potato, manioc, banana, Tahitian chestnut, breadfruit, mango, and papaya. The people have food to spare, and both islands are well endowed with barrier reefs enclosing calm turquoise lagoons with good fishing grounds. Mothe even has two freshwater creeks and a limestone satellite. Because of Komo's location and small size (two miles by half a mile), it is economically and socially less significant than Mothe, which is the canoe port of entry from Tonga.

Except for Kambara, the remaining islands in the trade area are formed almost entirely of coral limestone rock that has been elevated, apparently by faulting along the ocean floor, up to 250 feet. Although predominantly composed of raised limestone, Kambara has a 470-foot volcanic outcrop that affords good but limited garden land. Indeed, Kambara, Fulanga, and Ongea are known as the famine islands of Fiji because for a month at the end of the rainy season there is not enough nourishing food to feed their populations.

With the exception of Namuka, the heavily wooded limestone islands all lack good garden land. Even manioc, considered the least desirable staple of Lau, grows rather poorly on porous limestone soil, but reasonably good crops of breadfruit, Tahitian chestnut, papaya, and mango are produced. Coconuts, used for drinking, in the making of coconut cream, and for pig and chicken fodder, also thrive here. Pandanus, used to make mats, and a poor quality of paper mulberry grow in abundance.

The most valued resource of the limestone islands is hardwood. In all of Fiji and Tonga superior hardwoods grow only on the forested limestone plateaus of southern Lau, especially on Kambara, Wangava, Fulanga, and Ongea. The wood is used for canoes (formerly for the large double war canoe) and in the manufacture of hand-carved kava and food bowls. Wooden craft articles from these islands find their way, through a system of chiefly tribute and ceremonial exchange, to all parts of Fiji.

Besides the sporadic distribution of resources basic to the native economy, there are other imbalances in natural resources that are significant from an ecocultural viewpoint. For example, a species of shellfish highly prized by Lauans lives only in a lake on uninhabited Wangava. Lobsters, another prized delicacy, are found only off the Marambo shore. Another scarce item in southern Lau is potter's clay, which, according to native informants, was formerly quarried at Matanimoko near Lomatchi village, Kambara.

Archaeology and History

According to archaeological evidence (Gifford 1951a, 1951b: 235), the large islands of Fiji have been occupied since 2000 ±500 years B.C. Papuo-Melanesians settled in Fiji on the eastern margin of the continental shelf and developed Stone Age cultures that included fishing and eventually gardening. The aborigines spread to the eastern islands and, according to archaeological evidence (Thompson 1940b: 220–221) and the statements of informants, they occupied hamlets (*i tokatoka*) in the bush near their garden lands.

Aborigines

Today a large majority of southern Lauans (twenty-seven of the thirty-seven existing clans in the islands studied) belong to the Land People (*kai vanua*), who believe themselves descended from the aborigines. The Land People believe that they have always lived in their present habitat and that deceased members go to a local abode of the dead. On each island they trace their origin to a different local phenomenon. The Land People of Kambara trace their origin to a *ngingia* tree; those of Mothe to a Tahitian chestnut tree; those of Namuka, now extinct, to a white dog. In times of crisis such as drought, hurricane, tidal wave, or epidemic, the head of the priest (*mbete*) clan, a Land People's group, propitiates the totem of the island with offerings of food, fragrant garlands, and kava.

The Land People still own most of the land and constitute the best farmers in southern Lau. The title of the chief's herald (*mata-ni-vanua*), who assists in the first-fruits ceremony and mediates between the people and their chiefs and administrators, is hereditary in a Land People's clan on each island, as is that of the chief of the ceremonial ground (*tui rara*), who has responsibility for dividing into shares every village feast and offering of first fruits, according to the number and rank of each clan. One Land clan on each island also retains the important hereditary office of crop master (*vaka vanua*). By placing a tabu on the gathering of important crops before they mature, the crop master controls the conserving, harvesting, and ceremonial offering of first fruits. The basic ceremony in southern Lau, on which all other rites are to some degree variations, is the first-fruits rite, by which tribute is presented to a chief on the ceremonial ground. First fruits were formerly presented to the priest at the god house, a thatched hut that sheltered the god's image.

On most islands a Land clan also retains the master-fisherman hereditary office (*ndau ni ika*). The master fisherman controls and conserves the island's fishing grounds and plays a major role in ceremonial offerings of fish. This role requires specialized knowledge of weather, seasonal changes, tides and currents, and lunar and solar influences. It relates to the habits of local species of fish, turtles, and crustaceans, poisonous varieties and other hazards, configuration of the lagoon and reef, and proprietary offshore rights. Without a literary tradition such specialized information can be amassed only by years of apprenticeship, observation, and experience and by a notable feat of memory. Besides the sheer accumulation of this knowledge, it must be considered in the context of the native culture: its technology, social structure, economy, resources rights, ceremonies, attitudes, and values, as well as its human idiosyncracies. The master fisherman is only one of the specialized roles in Lauan society that involves precise and often secret knowledge for its successful implementation. The crop master of each island must have comparable skills and knowledge of the land and its potential for food and goods.

Despite their control of the use of those resources related to food and production from land, shores, reefs, and lagoons and to the redistribution of resources in the form of chiefly tribute, the Land People constitute the lower class in Lau. Their idiom, the southern Lauan dialect of the Mbauan language, is unembellished with the polite phrases of chiefly discourse. It is greeted with a superior smile in Lakemba, home of the high chief of Lau.

Ndaunisai Invasion

Some fifteen generations ago, according to tradition, the culture hero Ndaunisai and his two-canoe war party of sailors and fishermen came from Viti Levu to southern Lau in search of hardwoods. Fortified village sites and fortresses (Thompson 1940b: 216–221) substantiate the statements of informants that the invaders conquered the islands, entrenched themselves, and established a chiefdom (*mata-ni-tu*) centered in Kambara, but except during periods of raiding the people still occupied hamlet sites in the bush near the garden land. On the larger islands such as Kambara, the hamlets aligned themselves into two rival factions, one associated with the east side of the island, the other with the west. On Mothe the factions divided north and south. Competition between the two sides and between islands occasionally broke out in cannibalistic raiding. Eventually Kambara lost its paramount position in Lau by becoming, along with its allies and dependencies, a tribute-paying subsidiary to the chiefdom of Lakemba. How this happened is unclear (Hocart 1929:25).

By marrying women of the Land People and acquiring land, Ndaunisai and his sons and grandsons founded five ranking clans on Kambara, Wangava (now uninhabited), Lakemba, and Mothe. Members of these clans are established as the upper class (*yavusa turanga*) in Lau, who specialize in sailing and fishing, and one noble clan on Kambara, Lakemba, and Mothe respectively holds the hereditary title of island chief. The members of each noble clan believe themselves related to three totems that are thought to incarnate deified ancestors: a species of tree, a species of fish, and a species of bird. To obtain mana (diffused, nonpersonalized superhuman power) they also propitiate Ndengei, the snake god of Viti Levu, who is Ndaunisai's putative forefather; and Ndaunisai, who is considered to have brought *rarama* (light, civilization) to the *mbutombuto* (darkness) of the aborigines.

Carpenters and Sea People

Before Ndaunisai a professional carpenter is reputed to have come to southern Lau from Viti Levu. His descendants form two clans of professional carpenters known as *matai sau*, one on Namuka and one on Fulanga. After Ndaunisai a professional carpenter came from Samoa to Kambara and his descendants form one clan known as *matai lemaki*. Professional carpenters subsist mainly on food presented to them in exchange for their services.

The Sea People (*kai wai*), fishermen and potters reputed to have migrated to southern Lau from Ngau, an island in the Lomai Viti group, Fiji, have founded one clan on Fulanga and one on Ongea.

Tongans

Beginning three centuries ago Tongans began to visit the jungle-clad southern Lau islands to build large double canoes from hardwoods, which were absent in their homeland, but they founded no clans in southern Lau. Early in the nineteenth century Tongan traders obtained sandalwood from Mbua on Vanua Levu, Fiji, and red parakeet feathers from Taveuni for exchange with Samoa. Chinese and European traders also began to visit Fiji, chiefly to collect sandalwood and *bêche-de-mer*, and introduced firearms and military tactics. As a result, competitive struggling among the leading chiefdoms intensified and the scale of native warfare and cannibalism increased. Eventually the chiefdom of Mbau in Viti Levu reduced most of the other chiefdoms to tributary status.

This centralization of power in Fiji was used by the Tongans to further their own interests. The Tongans were themselves used, by Wesleyan Methodist missionaries who had gained a foothold in Tonga, as a wedge to establish a mission on Lakemba, seat of the high chief of Lau, in 1835. At first their only converts in Fiji were Tongans. By 1850 the paramount chief at Lakemba decided that because the Christians had so many goods their God must have more powerful mana than the Lauan deities. He therefore allowed himself to be baptized. With the high chief went the entire chiefdom of Lau, including the southern islands. Native religious ceremonies, god houses, hereditary priesthood, totemism, cannibalism, human sacrifice, warfare, polygamy, infanticide, and the tattooing of women were outlawed. The native deities were reduced to the status of devils in a revised supernatural hierarchy dominated by the Christian God.

Recent History

Tongan conquest of the entire Fijian archipelago was averted in 1874 when Fiji, by request of the high chief of Mbau, became a British Crown colony and native warfare and raiding were abolished. The next year one-third of the population of Lau perished in a measles epidemic. Although the colonial governors tried to implement a policy of indirect rule whereby the native chieftainship system would be upheld, their administration actually split the authority formerly held exclusively by the chiefs and thereby lowered their status.

During the last quarter of the nineteenth century copra became an important export of Fiji and coconut acreage increased in value. The southern Lauans neglected their gardening, fishing, and crafts to develop coconut plantations. They traded copra for knives, cloth, and canned food. The ensuing prosperity lasted until the Great Depression, when trade virtually ceased. By the mid-1930s the Lauans had reestablished their traditional economy and most of their economic independence.

After the government outlawed raiding, related hamlets united and moved to more convenient coast sites near anchorages or canoe landings to form a village (koro) under a government-sponsored village chief, but rivalry persisted between the two factions of an island. In the southern group there are from one to four villages on each inhabited island. A village site, usually a sandy flat along the shore, is divided into strips extending from shore to cliffs around a ceremonial ground. Each clan occupies a strip, with the highest-ranking clan facing the ceremonial ground. Several villages form a minor chiefdom (*mata-ni-tu*) that stands in tributary relationship to the paramount chief of the chiefdom of Lakemba.

Land Use and Social Structure

The patrilineal clan (*matanggali*) headed by a clan chief is the main land-owning and land-use unit in southern Lau. Membership in the clan of one's father is established at birth and maintained throughout life regardless of sex, marriage, or other affiliations, except in the case of children born out of wedlock, who usually follow the mother's clan.

Volcanic islands like Mothe are divided into as many pie-shaped sections as there are clans on the island. The boundaries of each section are natural ridges that separate fertile valleys. The ridges run from interior uplands (usually eroded volcanic cones) down to the shore. Each section, therefore, includes three types of resources: upland bush, fertile valley lands, and shore. Proprietary rights to each section are vested in a clan, whose name it bears. The clan's chief is responsible for allocating garden land from his clan's fertile valley section to each of the subclans within it.

On the limestone islands there are no valleys, ridges, or freshwater streams. Garden land is found only in shallow patches on porous wooded plateaus. The central lagoon at Fulanga is divided into three sections, each of which is accessible to the inhabitants of the village adjacent to it. The bush is divided in similar fashion. The meager garden-land patches and the islands in the central lagoon are claimed by clans inhabiting villages adjacent to the section or island. Such lands are parceled out by the clan's headman to constituent subclans.

Clans or villages may also hold proprietary rights over uninhabited islands. The entire island of Wangava, for example, is claimed by Naivotavota clan of Nggalinggali village, Kambara. Marambo is claimed by Undu village, Kambara; Tavunasithi by Naivotavota clan of Tokalau, Kambara; Yangasa by Fulanga; and Ongea Ndriki by Naithulaianga village, Ongea.

Subclan, Food-Group, and Nutrition Pattern

A clan is divided into subclans or food groups, which usually consist of two or more related families who occupy adjacent sleeping houses and cooperate in producing, collecting, and preparing their daily food.

Lauans eat one main meal a day. Served just after sundown, this meal is a semiceremonial occasion consisting of two parts: steamed "true food" and boiled relish. For a major feast a sweet pudding is also served. Because there is no refrigeration or electricity in Lau, nor modern methods of food preservation, virtually all ingredients for a meal must be collected the day they are to be consumed. The men and circumcised boys of each subclan or other food group within a clan are responsible for gathering, preparing, and cooking the group's "true food," consisting of a carbohydrate, which may be sweet potato, yam, manioc, or Tahitian chestnut, depending on the season of the year. Under the leader of the group, usually the oldest active male, the men gather this part from the lands accessible to their clan. They also prepare any fish they have caught. After cleaning the fish, and extracting poisonous ingredients in the case of manioc, they wrap each individual food portion in a banana or ti leaf, then steam the packages in a large earth oven.

The women, girls, and uncircumcised boys of each food group are responsible for the relish, which forms a protein, fat, and mineral complement to true food. They work under the leadership of the oldest active woman. Every morning the girls of the group gather protein-rich edible leaves from the jungle or garden land of their clan and fish or shellfish from lagoons available to them. These ingredients are combined with coconut cream and vitamin-rich bird's-eye pepper and boiled in pots over an open fire. Evaporated sea salt may be added.

When the two parts of the meal are ready, the true food is

brought to the kitchen hut. First the true food and then the relish are carefully divided into shares by the male head of the group according to the number and rank of each individual in each household to be fed. The head of a large fish, as the locus of its mana, goes to the highest-ranking or oldest male. Usually the meal is consumed in or near the kitchen hut.

Note that the meal roughly meets the requirements of modern nutritionists for a balanced daily diet, if the vitamin D–supplying function of intense solar radiation on lightly clad or exposed bodies is considered. Thus without benefit of modern science or education, the Lauans have found a way to organize themselves, pattern their daily behavior, and distribute their meager resources systematically to serve a nutritious daily meal to every member of the community. Even in an emergency such as drought, hurricane, or tidal wave, everyone eats in Lau if anyone eats, although the size of the portions may be reduced and less desirable wild foods may be substituted for cultivated ones.

Intervillage Exchange

The villages of southern Lau use a system of intervillage competitive ceremonial exchange called *solevu* to even up discrepancies in natural resources. The people of a village with good garden lands, like those on Mothe, Komo and Namuka, exchange food for craft goods made by people of a village on an island that is poor in garden land, such as Fulanga or Ongea. The village that presents the most goods, in terms of the native value system, gains prestige and wins the contest. This potlatch type of redistribution system thus operates on the principle that "they who give the most receive the most."

A form of nonceremonial, solicited exchange of goods with deferred payment, called *kerekere* (begging), may occur between relatives of unequal rank at a *solevu*, which is a pleasurable social occasion with much feasting, kava drinking, and gossip. Young people from the two competing villages have a chance to meet, play games together, exchange dances, and arrange trysts at night in the bush.

Vasu and Preferred Mates

A man is related to his mother's clan through the *vasu* privilege, which gives him the right to appropriate, without permission, property belonging to members of his mother's clan, especially to his *vungo*. In Lau the term *veivungoni* refers to all relatives in the class of one's mother's brother and his wife, father's sister and her husband, father-in-law and mother-in-law, son-in-law and daughter-in-law, and the child of one's sibling of the opposite sex. Strict reciprocal avoidance is observed between *veivungoni* but, according to the *vasu* custom, a man is allowed to take without asking the property of his *vungo*.

The rights of a high chief as *vasu* permit him to demand tribute from all his mother's people. As *vasu* a man may demand in marriage his mother's brother's daughter or his father's sister's daughter. These preferred mates are called *watchi* (wife or female cross-cousin, male-speaking; husband or male cross-cousin, female-speaking). In this context, all a man's unmarried or widowed female cross-cousins are potentially available to him, if not overtly in the role of wife, then covertly as mistress.

Conversely, mating with females within one's own clan, especially one's father's brother's daughter or mother's sister's daughter, called *weka* (sister or female parallel cousin, male-speaking), is rated as incest in Lau. Such behavior would be as severely censored as union with a sister. Parallel cousins and siblings of opposite sex, called *veiwekani*, strictly avoid each other after the age of seven years, when a child is believed to "come into his mind."

Kinship Terminology

The Lauan kinship-terminology system is formally classed as Dakota in type (Murdock 1949: 236–238), misnamed after that of the Dakota Sioux, who practice a different system (see Chapter 16). The Dakota type of kinship structure includes all patrilineal societies with cousin terminology like that of Lau. It is usually associated with patrilineal extension of incest tabus and special terms for aunts and nieces. It is also widely characterized by patrilineal clans and by a family organization either of the patrilocal extended type as in Lau or of the independent non-sororal polygynous type (whereby a man may marry more than one wife but the wives are usually not sisters).

Birth Spacing

The Lauans practice birth spacing. For two years or more, until the child is weaned, the father sleeps in the men's house of his clan rather than with his wife in the family dwelling house. According to statistics obtained from clan genealogies, this custom tends to be rather strictly observed. A breach is severely censored throughout the island. The tabu functions to protect the health of both mother and child. At the same time it spaces births in the family and may have helped in the past to control population growth.

Native informants say that several methods of abortion are used in Lau, chiefly by unmarried girls. The withdrawal practice is also known. Formerly the Lauans practiced infanticide and cannibalism under certain circumstances. On Fulanga I was told that old persons who could no longer work were formerly abandoned on certain islets in the central lagoon.

Anxieties, Myths, and Dreams

As might be expected, the precarious economic situation of the famine islanders and the stringent devices that they have devised to cope with it take their toll in anxiety manifest in overt behavior, myths, and dreams. For example, the windwomen are perceived as twin evil spirits that disturb a man's sleep by appearing to him in the form of two beautiful young women who offer him food, symbolizing sexual intercourse. If he accepts food, the natives say, he will become ill or die. Tutumatua, conceived as an ugly old man with elephantiasis of the leg (a phallic symbol), is believed to have the power to appear as a handsome young man and to trouble young women whom he desires. Outside the entrance to the thatched house in which I lived in Tokalau grew a giant taro plant. This served as a pro-phylactic against Tutumatua, who, on seeing the swollen tuba, would be shamed and refrain from entering, according to the owner.

The Fiji islands are famous for the practice of witchcraft called *ndrau ni kau* (leaf of a tree), which despite its prohibition by the colonial government is used extensively as a protective device. How much the Lauans value their hardwoods I discovered in the following manner. Soon after establishing headquarters in Tokalau, I decided to visit the other three villages on Kambara. At Nggalinggali, Tokalau's chief rival, all the men of the village had been summoned by the village chief to gather at dusk in the house that had been vacated for my temporary use. Through my interpreter (I was just beginning to speak the Lauan language) I tried to explain the purpose of my presence on the island. After they left, following a lively discussion lasting several hours, I discerned in the moonlight that a couple of men huddled over another man, who seemed to be scratching the ground. Inspecting the spot later with a flashlight, I saw that a circle had been drawn around a small cross ingeniously fashioned from a piece of dried pandanus leaf. Suspecting witchcraft, I found that the pandanus frond forming the cross matched the mat on which I had been sitting. At the village meeting the next evening I held up the leaf cross for all to see and asked in Lauan, "What's this?" There was a dead silence. Finally the head of the lemaki carpenter clan spoke: "It's a bad trick," he said. Subsequently I learned that the people of Nggalinggali feared I was involved in a plan to build a sawmill for exporting hardwood from Kambara and had indeed attempted to rid themselves of my presence by witchcraft. On my departure from the village I was ceremonially presented with a 200-pound sea turtle, a chiefly gift of atonement and one that, after a canoe journey to the other side of the island, provided a highly esteemed feast for the people of Tokalau.

Preferred Relationship Pattern

Human relations in southern Lau, whether with other people, putative devils, spirits, ancestor ghosts, or totems, involve an exchange of values usually expressed in material goods indispensable to maintain group life. Lauans also believe that such goods can be exchanged for mana. If the transaction involves a high chief or administrator, a sacred whale's tooth is presented, the most precious object in Fiji. Transactions may be classed as either reciprocal, involving an exchange of identical values, or correlative, involving equivalent but not identical values. The return payment is usually deferred. Gift thus both solicits and elicits countergift (either as a social obligation or by magical compulsion). Such exchanges are given social significance by being raised to the level of social ceremonies, enacted in an atmosphere of sweet-smelling plants and fragrant coconut oil and frequently accompanied by chanting, dancing, and kava drinking. There is an undertone of rivalry between the two parties to a transaction and perhaps even between a human group and its totem or ancestor god. The winning side is always the one that gives "a great deal" (*levu*), according to the Lauan perception of the event.

Conclusion

The findings reveal that southern Lauan culture expresses an amalgam stemming from at least two separate cultural heritages: that of the Land People and that of the Ndaunisai invaders plus some Tongan traits. In an isolated tropical habitat, where garden land and other natural resources are scarce and sporadically distributed and where hunger, drought, and hurricanes are a constant threat, the Lauans developed their traditions into a homeostatic relationship with the local ecosystem. Through resources conservation, patrilineage, clan and chiefly obligations, a judicious division of labor, land use, craft specialization, and other man-made devices, they organized themselves and fashioned their culture into an effective problem-solving tool. They are therefore able to live virtually self-sufficiently in an environment that otherwise would be inviable to nonindustrialized village-dwelling fishermen-agriculturists.

The production and distribution system of the Lauans is thus not accidental or sporadic but has been built into the fabric of the culture. The system was formerly reinforced by ceremonial and religious practices and beliefs, many of which persist despite the nominal conversion of the natives to Christianity. It is still embedded in social institutions, sanctions, and tabus. Should an individual default on his contribution or responsibility he would lose prestige, an eventuality difficult for a Lauan to endure.

The Lauans' relation to their famine islands is a lesson in how a community that would fall unequivocally in the "poverty" class by current American standards can fashion and use its culture to survive and fulfill itself with gusto despite meager resources and strong directive pressures from the outside world.

Recent population growth indicates, however, that the old system of demographic control is breaking down. Many practices that formerly operated as checks on population growth have been banned: intergroup warfare, cannibalism, the death penalty for certain tabu violations, infanticide, and euthanasia. Recent changes, such as the introduction of Western medical practices for child and maternal care, have also contributed to population increases on the southern islands. The colonial government failed to uphold the native system of resources conservation and was thus unwittingly one of many influences that disturbed the traditional balance between population size and food supply.

Notes

1. This chapter is based on fieldwork in the islands of Kambara, Wangava, Namuka, Mothe, Fulanga, Ongea, Lakemba, and Viti Levu in 1933–1934 as well as library and museum work in Suva, Hawaii, New York, and Berlin. The description of the social structure of southern Lau is based both on observed behavior and on an analysis of genealogies of the thirty-seven clans in the area, each extending back six to thirteen generations. The genealogies, which include the pedigrees of all the living inhabitants of the inhabited islands visited, were recorded in the field in the native language and stored in the Human Relations Area File, New Haven. Generalizations regarding rules of descent, marriage, resources use, and so on have been made as a result of counting all the individual cases from the area as far back as the memory of the living extends and relating the oral record to sketch maps of each village, of

garden land and lagoon areas, as well as of archaeological sites. The information was recorded prior to the investigation of land titles in southern Lau by the Fijian Land Commission and the publication of the "official version" of Fijian social structure. For an analysis of the major differences between the social structure of southern Lau and that of Fiji proper as described by G. K. Roth (1953), A. Capell, and R. H. Lester (1941–1942, 1945–1946), Rusiate R. Nayacakalou (1955, 1957), and W. R. Geddes (1959), see Thompson 1947b. The present study is the result of three analyses of the field data: a primary processing immediately after the fieldwork (Thompson 1940, 1940b); a second analysis twelve years later (Thompson 1947b; 1949); and a third analysis for this volume. I thank the former director and trustees of the B. P. Bishop Museum for a fellowship that made possible the field expedition and Edwin H. Bryan, Jr., Clellan S. Ford, and Manu Tupou Taunaolo for reading the manuscript in an earlier draft and for helpful comments.

4 /

PEOPLE OF GUAM

An numa' piniti hau tautau,
Nanga mana' pinitimu;
Masea apmaman na tiempo,
Un apase sa dibimu.

When you cause a person pain,
Wait for pain to come to you;
Though it be a very long time,
You will pay it as it is a debt.

> A Chamorran children's song sung to the *tsamorita*
> refrain recorded and translated by Gertrude Horn-
> bostel[1]

When I was a beginning student of anthropology, my first professional job was to describe and classify the archaeological
artifacts from the Mariana Islands collected by Hans G. Hornbostel during the 1920s and stored in the Bishop Museum in
Honolulu. I handled more than 10,000 specimens of stone, shell,
clay, and bone from this remote island group. This experience
stimulated my interest in the culture of the Marianas and led
me to spend six months in Guam shortly before the outbreak
of World War II. As consultant to the naval governor in educational anthropology I worked in the capital city of Agaña and in
Merizo village, on the southwest coast of the island. And, on a
trip to the Philippines, China, and Japan sponsored by my

superiors, I gathered valuable comparative data for the Guam research.[2]

Geography and Geology

The Mariana Islands form an isolated archipelago on the northwestern boundary of Micronesia. They are the exposed tips of submerged volcanos, several of them active, rising nearly six miles above the ocean floor in one of the deepest parts of the Pacific. The chain includes Guam, Saipan, Tinian, Rota, and several islets. The Marianas are located about 1,500 miles east of Manila and 1,300 miles south of Japan. Situated 300 miles and more to the south are the Caroline atolls of Ulithi, Woleai, and Lamotrek. Yap is 450 miles to the southwest. The Palau group, located 700 miles southwest of Guam, is only 600 miles east of the Philippines and about the same distance north of New Guinea. The Bonins, Iwo Jima, the Marianas, Yap, and Palau form an arc from Japan and the Asiatic mainland to the Philippines and the Malay archipelago to the west and southwest.

Guam covers 209 square miles and is the largest and southernmost island in the Marianas. Although Guam is basically an eroded volcanic cone (elevation 1,334 feet), the northern half of Guam forms a coral limestone plateau. The plateau (elevation 600 feet) is heavily wooded except where it has been cleared for military installations and economic development. This region is so wild that a Japanese soldier hid in it from World War II until his capture in 1960. Other Japanese fugitives, ignorant of the war's end, may still be there.

Ecologically, Guam is a favored tropical island, with resources from both volcanic and coral limestone soils. Located some 13 degrees north of the equator, the island has a warm and humid climate with temperatures averaging about 87 degrees F. The dry season, cooled by northeast trades, extends from January to June, and the rainy season, punctuated by the irregular southwest monsoon, lasts from July to December. Most of the rainfall (85–100 inches annually), falls from July to September. Droughts, earthquakes, and typhoons are not uncommon and often take a heavy toll in property and lives.

Prehistory

Knowledge of Marianas prehistory is increasing rapidly.[3] Recent archaeological investigations by Alexander Spoehr (1957: 168) on Saipan and Tinian islands north of Guam revealed the presence of a pottery sequence. The earliest level has been dated 1527 B.C. ± 200. Impressed lime-accented decorations on sherds found at this level resemble those found on wood, stone, and clay objects in New Guinea, the Bismarck archipelago, and the Solomon Islands and thus strongly suggest early Melanesian cultural influences in the Marianas. A more common form of early Marianas pottery is Marianas Red, which has been found with human burials in sand-lined pits along with pecked and polished adzes of stone and shell.

Aborigines

Historical, ethnographic, and archaelogical evidence indicates that the aborigines of the Marianas arrived more than 3,500 years ago. They were fishermen and farmers and produced Marianas Red pottery and either made the lime-impressed pottery or traded for it with Melanesia. They buried their dead extended in pits, the floors of which were covered with beach sand. For about two and a half millenniums the aborigines built a unique culture in relative isolation. Closely attached to the land, they are comparable to the Land People of Lau (Chapter 3) and the first settlers in Hawaii (Chapter 5).

Invasion by the *Latte* Builders

Around the ninth century A.D. (845 ± 145 according to C-14 dating), the Marianas were invaded by a taller, more robust Polynesian type of people who were sailors, deep-sea fishermen, and warriors. The invaders brought superior fishing equipment, new methods of warfare, and new weapons, including spears tipped with human bone. Conquering the aborigines, they apparently established themselves as a noble class (*matua*) and reduced the natives to an endogamous caste with its own low-status subculture.

The newcomers probably built the *latte* (stone-pillared ruins) found in profusion throughout the islands (for Guam, see Hornbostel n.d.: map; Reed 1952: map 1; Reinman n.d.: map). Interest in Marianas archaeology centered for years on these spectacular sites. For example, a *latte* site on Tinian island described in 1742 by Sir George Anson (1748), had twelve stone pillars capped with inverted coral heads. Since Anson's visit earthquakes and typhoons have caused caps to fall from their pillars, or they have been removed by the natives. An aura of mystery surrounds them. Between the pillars and in surrounding areas have been found human burials, sometimes without skulls. Several types of interments are associated with the *latte* builders, including burial of cremated remains, extended burial beneath house platforms, and subsequent disposal of skeletal remains. The skeletal material is accompanied by stone, bone, shell, and clay artifacts such as adzes, scrapers, slingstones, pounders, and potsherds of the Marianas Plain, Marianas Fine-Line Incised, Marianas Cord-Marked, and Marianas Trailed pottery types.

Following the early sources, I assumed at first that the *latte* marked the graves of important people. On measuring the ground plan and the number, alignment, and height of wooden piles of the modern thatched houses in Merizo, however, I discovered that they corresponded exactly to the coral and stone pillars of neighboring *latte*. Because the inverted coral heads would prevent rats from entering a structure built above them (rats are known to have been stowaways in the early Polynesian canoes), I concluded that they were the stone foundations of dwelling houses or, if located near the shore, canoe houses built for the nobility. This simple piece of archaeological detective work cleared away the mystery of the stone "monuments." The Taga site was evidently the homestead of a Tinian paramount chief named Taga.

Population and Food Supply

At the time of their discovery by Fernando Magellan in 1521 the Marianas had a relatively isolated population. During the Spanish period the natives were described as highly class conscious with three distinct castes (see Thompson 1945: 13–14). The noble caste (*matua*) was by custom endogamous, and its members belonged to high-ranking clans that controlled not only the land and other resources but also certain wealth-getting prerogatives such as the manufacture of shell money and large sailing canoes, which gave them a monopoly on seagoing traffic. The nobles were deep-sea fishermen, professional canoe builders, sailors, traders, and war leaders. The middle class (*atchaot*) assisted the nobles in these activities. The members of the two upper classes, according to reports (Freycinet 1829 [2]: 364–365, 378), were tall, robust, and brown-skinned, with long, wavy black hair like that of the Polynesians. They were well formed, strong, and muscular. Members of a low caste (*mangatchang*) were not allowed to marry out of their caste. They were darker and smaller in stature than the rest of the population and were restricted by certain tabus. For example, they were required to crouch before the nobles and to remain seated while talking to them. They were not allowed to participate in the professions reserved for nobles, and their fishing was restricted to hunting river eels with wooden-tipped spears.

In 1668, at the time of the first Christian mission to the Marianas, the population in Guam alone was estimated at around 50,000 (Garcia 1937: 20–21). According to archaeological evidence, the Chamorros, as the Marianas natives are called, lived in villages along the shores and in the well-watered interior valleys. Soil erosion near archaeological sites suggests that garden land was cultivated intensively. Taro, yams, and breadfruit were the main carbohydrate foods. Rice was grown in the fertile lowlands at the mouths of streams and was prized for feasts. On the limestone plateau the federico palm grew abundantly. After being depoisoned and ground in a stone mortar with a stone pestle, the nut of the federico was quite nutritious. Seafood, fish, and freshwater eels constituted an important source of protein. Sinkers and lures ingeniously designed to cope with deep-sea fishing problems posed by the Marianas Trench are found in archaeological sites. Some types, reported nowhere else in the world, are still in use. Hornbostel (Thompson 1932: 47–48) observed that at a certain time daily a fisherman in a small canoe off Rota lowered with a line a half coconut shell filled with coconut meat chewed fine and attached to a limestone sinker. The meat, spread by jiggling the line, attracted *atsumen,* a deep-sea fish. From an initial depth of fifty or more feet the lure, drawing increasingly large numbers of fish for regular feeding, was raised slightly each day until large catches could be netted near the surface over a period of several months.

The widespread habit of chewing betelnut with a pepper leaf and lime contributed certain nutriments to the native diet.[4]

Land Use and Political Organization

An island was divided into one or more land-use districts, each consisting of garden land, bush, and fishing grounds. Whether pie-shaped divisions characterized districts in the Marianas is not clear. It seems that each district was inhabited by a matrilineal kinship group, probably a clan. The first-born male (*maga-lahe*) of the ranking line in the clan was traditionally the paramount chief of the district. He shared the office with his sister (*maga-haga*). The chief's prestige was based both on rank by inheritance and on wealth. He monopolized certain wealth-getting prerogatives mentioned above. A paramount chief was accorded elaborate funeral ceremonies.

Succession passed to a younger brother. A paramount chief's younger brothers, cousins, and nephews headed subsidiary clan groups and ranked as subsidiary chiefs (*maga*) of the district. The chief and his retinue lived in well-built *latte* built in rows parallel to the shore as at Taga, Tinian. The chief used elaborate canoe houses located on the shore. Other members of the community inhabited small thatched huts.

The people of each district supported their chief and accorded him great respect. The evidence suggests that there was strong interdistrict competition for prestige, expressed in ceremonial exchanges between districts similar to the intervillage and interisland exchanges in Lau. In the prehistoric Marianas such exchanges frequently developed into warfare between the supporters of rival paramount chiefs. The main weapons were wooden spears hardened by fire and tipped with bone, and slings, which the Chamorros used with great precision. But they depended primarily on agility and clever strategy.

Culture Changes Under Spain

In 1668 the Spaniards began their conquest of the archipelago, ostensibly to introduce the Roman Catholic religion. Even with the help of gunpowder and organized units of trained soldiers, it took the Spaniards thirty years to subdue the fierce Chamorros.

By 1710 slaughter, disease, and migration to the Carolines had reduced the population of the Marianas to about 3,500. The survivors, except for a few renegades who hid out in Rota, were forced to leave their traditional homes and to settle in village sites on the coast of Guam. Each village became a religious and civic center headed by a Spanish Jesuit. Ancestor and spirit worship, the skull cult (skulls of ancestors, believed of magical efficacy in bringing rain, were kept in houses), native ceremonies, interdistrict warfare, cremation, bachelor houses, premarital consorting of the sexes, infanticide, and abortion were suppressed.

The Spaniards also brought new customs, plants, and animals, including maize from Mexico and water buffalo from the Philippines. Most families maintained not only a dwelling in a rural village or town but also a family farm some distance away. After four o'clock mass every morning, men and boys walked to work on their family garden lands, returning the long road home at dusk. The family was thus able to keep in touch with its traditional land base despite enforced change in its residence pattern. But in rural areas especially, anxiety from failure to carry out traditional rites continued to disturb the people. For example, after the Spanish conquest a belief emerged among the natives that their former chiefs had not perished but continued to inhabit their districts as headless men of supernatural strength called *taotaomona*. The *taotaomona* were believed to guard their districts jealously. If a stranger entered a district he was not allowed to pick fruit, cut wood, catch fish, dig yams, hunt fruit bats, camp out for the night, or defile the ground unless he first asked permission from its *taotaomona*. Violation was believed to bring about illness or death. Until recently the *taotaomona* belief persisted in the rural districts of the Marianas. It was found among old people on the island of Rota by Hornbostel (n.d.) in the 1920s.

In Guam some people in the rural districts were afraid to pass a large banyan tree after nightfall, or even a spot where such a tree had once stood, because ancestors called *bihu* were thought to inhabit it. The bark of the banyan was used by herb doctors to cure illness, especially those believed to be caused by supernatural agents.

Under the Laws of the Indies the Spaniards attempted to implement a system of indirect rule. Controlled by a Spanish governor and military commander with headquarters in Agaña, four municipalities were established on Guam. Local chiefs loyal to Spain were appointed to head each municipality. They were assisted by subordinate chiefs who administered lesser settlements within a municipality. In each municipality native officials served as local judges. This system was later extended to include Rota and other islands of the northern Marianas.

Changes Under the United States

In 1899–1900, after a bloodless coup during the Spanish-American War, Guam became a United States possession and a strategic naval base. The remainder of the Mariana Islands were purchased from Spain by Germany and fell into Japanese hands after World War I. Under the U.S. Navy Department a government staffed by naval officers was established in Guam. The Spanish municipality system was retained, and the number of municipalities was increased from four to fifteen.

A hospital was built in the capital city of Agaña with field stations under navy corpsmen located in every municipality. English-speaking elementary schools staffed by native teachers were established in every village, and a high school was located in Agaña. Although attempts were made to stimulate industry and commercial fishing, the people of Guam continued to cultivate their family lands and to fish and to hunt according to traditional methods.

Guam was the first American soil to be overcome by enemy forces in World War II. Under Japanese attack and occupation Guamanians were beaten, raped and killed for refusing to betray an American signal corpsman whom they protected. The islanders showed exceptional bravery and loyalty to the United States. They rendered invaluable assistance when the island was recaptured by the American navy.

Finally, in 1950, after 230 years under Spanish rule, 49 years under the American navy, and 3 years of Japanese occupation, Guam's status was changed from a possession to an unincorporated territory of the United States. The island was granted an organic act and its people became American citizens. The new civilian territory, administered by the Department of Interior, is organized on the basis of the old local municipality units. Even their prewar boundaries have been retained (Solenberger 1964: 56). Their changed political status has wrought great changes in the lives of the islanders. Economic development is proceeding rapidly, and for the first time under American rule the people of Guam are guaranteed due process of law.

A subgroup of the Micronesian geographic race at the time of their discovery by Magellan, the Guamanians who survived decimation by war and disease mixed with Spaniards, Filipinos, Mexicans, Carolinians, Americans, and others. Today they are a multihybrid population numbering about 67,000.

Cultural Persistence

Although the Guamanians have lost most of their visible native characteristics, some directly observable cultural traits apparently have persisted with little or no change since prehistoric times. Many have been given new functions. Conspicuous among the cultural productions that have survived is the thatched pile house. In the rural villages this dwelling type has persisted from ancient times, even to such details as the number, spacing, height, and alignment of the piles. Moreover, the double lean-to used as a shed in rural Guam seems to be a replica of an ancient prototype. The persistence of these two early house forms in modern Guam corroborates evidence found in other parts of the world as to the marked stability of house forms.

The ground plan of a prehistoric *latte* village site at Agingan, Saipan, sketched by Hornbostel in the 1920s, shows twelve stone-pile house sites in two parallel rows along the seashore (see Thompson 1932: fig. 11a). The ground plan of Merizo, a typical rural village in modern Guam, reveals two rows of wooden pile houses, one on each side of a highway that runs parallel to the shoreline. Furthermore, the largest and most imposing *latte* structure at the Taga site on Tinian is located at the center of the village, indicating that the residence of the paramount chief was centrally located. In today's Merizo the church and residence of the missionary, a high-prestige figure since the Spanish conquest of the island, occupy the central location in the village. Since the ground plans of prehistoric and modern villages show identical proportions and orientations, the comparison suggests that an affinity not only for certain house types but also for a characteristic village plan and social organization is part of the persisting Chamorran cultural heritage.

Stone mortars unchanged from prehistoric times were used daily for husking rice, grinding federico nuts, and crushing herbs in the prewar villages. Obtained by the natives directly from archaeological sites, mortars have long been associated with the preparation of Chamorran food and medicines. The basic subsistence diet in rural Guam persisted from pre-Spanish times until the war with only one major addition, maize from Mexico. Except for the importation of the metal-bladed thrusting hoe, the water buffalo, and the plow (which in Guam could be used only in volcanic soils), the whole indigenous wet-rice culture and gardening complex survived practically intact. It may be noted that rice in Guam has long been not merely a favorite food but a feastday food, indispensable to all important festivals. Rice cultivation was discontinued after the war, and this highly desired food must now be imported.

Although most deep-sea fishing and deep-sea sailing techniques have long been lost, many traditional offshore fishing methods survive, together with the paraphernalia associated with them. Guamanians also use a type of inshore canoe that is probably ancient (Thompson 1947a: plate 25).

Several types of plaited articles reproducing traditional models, including mats and baskets, are still made, and exceptional skill in plaiting, noted in early records, has been retained to some extent. Persisting as late as the 1930s were three apparently indigenous types of musical instruments: the bamboo flute, the bamboo reed, and the musical bow. Also conspicuous was the *tsamorita*, a native folk refrain. Improvisation of rhymed couplets to variations on the *tsamorita* pattern still affords creative expression and a culturally sanctioned outlet for aggression. They are sung by fishermen to bring luck, by lovers as a charm, and by travelers to ward off evil influences.

Stone throwing, another habit dating from prehistoric times, figures prominently in Chamorran folktales. The sling was one of the main weapons of the ancient Chamorros, and their dexterity in its manipulation is well documented (Garcia 1937: 38). The modern natives use stones in deer hunting and as a means of expressing hostility.

Associated with the stone-throwing habit seems to be that of starting fires. The ancient Chamorros threw burning spears on the thatched houses of their enemies. Modern natives ambush their game by burning the bush. Incidents involving thwarted individuals who started fires for revenge or to cover an illicit love affair have been recorded. For example, while I was living in Merizo a young man was accused of starting two bush fires. While the villagers, warned by the blast from a conch shell, were putting out first one fire and then the other, the young man went to his girl in the village. On another occasion a Merizo youth, after being scolded by his father for drinking too much *tuba* (the fermented sap of the coconut spathe), was reported to have knocked his father unconscious with a club and then set fire to the sword grass near a neighboring farmhouse.

Discoloration due to betel chewing has been found on the teeth of skulls unearthed at archaeological sites. Betel chewing gives the individual the satisfaction of a narcotic and also has ceremonial significance. A gift of betelnut plays a prominent role in life-crisis rites of birth, naming, betrothal, marriage, and death. It also figures in communal functions such as thatching parties, as well as at such nonnative festivals as Catholic saints' days, Christmas, and Easter.

Social Structure

Robert R. Solenberger (1964: 53–60) has called attention to the continuity of local political institutions in the Marianas. As noted, the district or island chiefdom was ruled by a paramount chief who was the elder of the first-ranking clan. The district land-use pattern associated with the chiefdoms was continued by the Spaniards, with a military governor substituted for the paramount chief and local chiefs installed as officials in the four municipalities. The American regime upheld the Spanish system and increased the number of municipalities. "Thus we see in contemporary Guam," states Solenberger (1964: 56), "the survival of the oldest political institution in the Marianas, the *municipio*, complete with its original features of a paramount chief over the entire area, assisted by one or more subordinate village or hamlet chiefs." Furthermore, the ancient hamlet organization of the Marianas is reflected in the rural community, the village, and the prewar barrios (sections within a town) of Agaña. In rural villages the economic organization and work calendar followed the old pattern. Until the system of patrilineal descent was enforced by American authorities, reckoning by matrilineal descent survived—children bore the surnames of their mothers. Even now some older natives bear their mothers' names. The father is head of the family. But the real power is still the mother, who, besides having the main responsibility and care of the children and the housework, takes charge of the family ceremonies, guards its physical well-being, and usually distributes the pooled earnings of its members.

A strongly entrenched trait seems to be cooperation among relatives. Formerly clan solidarity was manifest in mutual economic, social, and ceremonial obligations in the subsistence patterns and life crises of its members. The modern extended family is also a tightly knit unit, engaging in many cooperative economic, religious, and social activities. Native officials may show partiality toward their relatives, a common administrative problem in areas where loyalty to the kinship group is strong.

Individuals within the kin group are united by mutual obligations and privileges. These center in the nuclear family forming a household group and extend to families related by marriage or by godparenthood, especially those living in close proximity. Obligations are fulfilled largely through the ceremonial exchange of goods and services between groups and individuals. The persistence of ancient prototypes is most clear in death, birth, betrothal, and marriage ceremonies and in such cooperative activities as house building, gardening, and fishing. The traditional division of labor by sex has also survived.

The indigenous class structure has persisted to the present in modified form. The two castes established by the early inhabitants set the pattern for the two classes, "high people" and "low people," in native society, a social distinction of far-reaching significance in island life. Similarity in structural type among the indigenous social organization, the Roman Catholic hierarchy, and the prewar American military government organization is marked.

In sum, it appears that to understand the modern natives and problems of Guam, the observer should take into account in historical and geographic perspective, not only visible productions and habits but the structure of human relations by which such artifacts and habits are woven into the fabric of daily life. For it is the deep-rooted institutional systems and preferred patterns of relationship, not the visible habits and objects themselves, that regulate behavior and that have fundamental meaning for those who attempt to understand a native culture.

Attitudes and Values

In Guam, as in Lau and Hawaii, there is evidence of a traditional belief in an invisible generalized superhuman power, as the primary creative force in the universe. This power, referred to as mana, could be manifest in human beings and transmitted especially through the first-born, male or female, of a family line. The mana concept became the foundation for the ranking system, ancestor worship, and a concept of a sacred chieftainship similar to that found in Hawaii and among the upper class in Lau. In the Marianas mana was conceived as also abiding in animals, plants, and objects. If a weapon proved particularly potent in warfare, it was considered imbued with mana. As the most sacred part of a person, the head was believed the repository of mana. Such a belief underlies the skull cult, whereby the skulls of power-dispensing deceased ancestors were stored in dwelling houses and cherished in the Marianas.

Another persisting attitude is respect for authority, which is instilled into the Guamanian child from birth throughout the formative years. Respect for parents and ancestors is reinforced by respect for supernatural powers, clergy, and government officials. In prewar Guam the authority system developed into a hierarchy upheld by sanctions. Fear of the *taotaomona,* the *bihu* in the banyan tree, the Catholic clergy, and the patrolman is acquired at an early age. Ridicule by members of one's own community is especially feared. The sanction pattern has persisted from prehistoric times and is now associated with many new objects and practices. Also related to the authority constellation is the class consciousness, pride, and intense loyalty to family, community, and country characteristic of the Guamanians.

Cooperation within the kinship group and certain village activities, such as house thatching and fishing, mirror traditional prototypes. So do competitive attitudes in games and sports, dancing and singing, ceremonial exchange and barter, and intervillage and interdistrict activities. Cock fighting, with its gambling procedures and magical lore, was introduced from the Philippines in historic times and fits well into the indigenous recreation pattern. The ancient competitive singing found an echo in the Roman Catholic novena and other Christian services and has persisted in the *tsamorita* refrain. Competitive dancing finds a modern counterpart in the fandango, which gives an opportunity for expressing rivalry between families and villages.

Interdistrict competition, which formerly found an outlet in warfare, now is expressed in economic, political, and social spheres. Similar cultural substitutions took place in Lau.

Persistent among Chamorran attitudes is close attachment of males to the mother and jealousy toward the father. This was noted by Padre Diego Luis de Sanvitores among the ancients and by me among the modern males. Modern Guamanians admire the same personal traits that the Chamorros admired at the time of their discovery. Love of laughter, buffoonery, mimicry, ingenuity, manual dexterity, and cleverness are firmly entrenched Guamanian character values (see Thompson 1945: 9–10).

Deep-rooted attitudes—prejudices, fears, loves, attachments, kinds of pride and jealousy, supernatural beliefs—are easily overlooked because they are often unconscious. Group attitudes are of utmost significance because they are not isolated phenomena but combine to give consistency or logic to a culture. These hidden patterns explain how a society "ticks" and reveal what structures the behavior of its members. Thus, they give clues as to how both the culture of a community and the character of an individual member may be understood and, to a degree, foreseen. On this basis, for example, I was able when officially asked to do so to predict correctly and in detail how the Guamanians would act under Japanese rule, information relevant when plans were formulated to recapture the island.

Language and Character Traits

Although most Guamanians speak English and some speak Spanish, virtually all speak their native Chamorro language. Chamorro persists not as an aggregate of words but as an organized system of symbolic verbal expression. Although words and modes of expression have been added from Spanish, English, and other languages, the basic Chamorran grammar survives intact.

According to early voyagers and missionaries, the people of the Mariana Islands were ingenious, quick to learn, adaptable, tricky, gay, and boisterous. They were playful and fond of mimicry, buffoonery, and competitions of all sorts. They were kind and tractable if treated with consideration but violent and vengeful when thwarted.

From historical documents and archaeological evidence about the culture itself, the picture of native Chamorro personality is substantiated by internal evidence; for example, in myths, songs, and tales, and in an ingenious technology and elaborate social structure.

All these traits are characteristic of the modern natives to some extent. Obviously, the aspects of Chamorro personality that have persisted are not isolated traits but form a pattern expressing their group personality. It appears probable that this personality structure is directly related not to the visible cultural traits that have survived from prehistoric times but rather to the preferred relationship patterns that underlie them. Reference is made especially to the sociocultural organization and to the hidden symbols, attitudes, beliefs, and values at the core of the culture.

Conclusion

Like Lau, Guam is a favorable natural laboratory for studying colonization by a new organic species, Homo sapiens, of an isolated island community of known geological formation and limited natural resources. Here, on the basis of island geology and biotics, the shaping of a many-stranded indigenous culture by an isolated population may be reconstructed over at least three millenniums. We may also review the rediscovery of the group by Europeans, the subsequent decimation of its population by war, disease and migration, and the suppression of much of its culture. The Marianas record also affords an opportunity to study the results of a native effort to solve changing living problems by rebuilding a new biocultural balance upon a prehistoric base.

The record suggests that the culture the Chamorros developed in relation to their tropical environment and to neighboring human groups was of a balanced, viable type. It fostered the growth and well-being of a relatively large population within the limitations of island resources. Under ordinary circumstances, when thrown off balance, it was reestablished in somewhat changed form. Even under extreme pressures, its basic structures tended to persist or to reemerge.

From the historical point of view the Guam analysis suggests the persistence of indigenous culture and character patterns through four centuries of outside influences, including a long period of alien domination. These forces brought about a change in the native physical type. They destroyed the traditional religion. But they did not succeed in suppressing the native language. And they did not completely sever the relationship between native social groups and their lands.

The significance of the survival of the Chamorro language and land-use divisions as whole systems in context rather than as isolated traits of the native culture now becomes apparent. And we begin to understand how it has been possible for other culturally preferred relationship patterns of the prehistoric Chamorros, including even the group personality structure, to survive in association with the indigenous language.

The analysis also reveals the inaccuracy of the popular belief that race, culture, and personality or temperament are causally related. In other words, it disproves the theory that certain racial types are linked inevitably with certain patterns of culture or of character, for in Guam aspects of the group culture and character have persisted long after the racial type with which they were originally associated has died out.

The Guam record also suggests that native personality is closely related to structural regularities of the culture, including the grammar of the language. Chamorro culture-personality links seem to be ancient and remarkably tenacious. The Guamanians are not simply another brown-skinned people to be lumped together and stereotyped. They are a unique human community with their own deep-rooted ancient culture and character. Finally, the record reveals the significance of looking beyond directly observable artifacts and behavior to discover patterns of feeling, thought, and symbolic expression that underlie them. Only through the study of the culture of a community in geographic and historical perspective, especially the organized invisible aspects, including linguistic phenomena, may we begin to understand culture as a problem-solving instrument.

Notes

1. Thompson 1932: 70. This Chamorran children's song expresses a native version of the concept of immanent punishment. The Spanish word *tiempo* is used to signify the European concept of time.
2. The field data on which this chapter is based were collected in Guam in 1938–1939 under a Rosenwald Fellowship supplemented by a grant-in-aid from the Social Science Research Council. The project was sponsored by the University of Hawaii's Department of Anthropology, chaired by Felix Keesing, and by the United States Naval Government of Guam. I take this opportunity to thank the donors and the sponsors of the project for their help and encouragement. The chapter is based mainly on Thompson 1945, 1947a.
3. Hornbostel n.d.; Osborne 1947, Reed 1952; Reinman n.d.; Spoehr 1957; Thompson 1932, 1945. Excavations are underway near Inarajan, Guam, according to reports.
4. On the other hand, *tuba* (the fermented sap of the coconut spathe) has contributed to the undernutrition and malnutrition frequently found among Guamanian farmers with rather easy access to food. The habit of *tuba* drinking was introduced into the Marianas from the Philippines in historic times and may thus be regarded as a phenomenon associated with stress and culture change. In 1938–1939 most farmers tapped one or two trees at a time (the maximum allowed tax-free). The sap, which ferments in a few hours, was collected daily. Consumption of fermented sap is estimated to have averaged one or two quarts per farmer per day. The effect was to numb the senses slightly and dull the appetite.

5 /

NATIVE HAWAIIANS

O ke au i kahuli wela ka honua
O ke au i kahuli lole ka lani
O ke au i kukaʻiaka ka la
E hoʻomalamalama i ka malama
O ke au o Makaliʻi ka po
O ka walewale hoʻokumu honua ia
O ke kumu o ka lipo, i lipo ai
O ke kumu o ka Po, i po ai
O ka lipolipo, o ka lipolipo
O ka lipo o ka la, o ka lipo o ka po
Po wale ho-ʻi.

Hanau ka po
Hanau Kumulipo i ka po, he kane
Hanau Poʻele i ka po, he wahine
Hanau ka ʻUku-koʻakoʻa, hanau kana, he ʻAkoʻakoʻa, puka
Hanau ke Koʻe-enuhe ʻeli hoʻopuʻu honua
Hanau kana, he Koʻe, puka
Hanau ka Peʻa, ka Peʻapeʻa kana keiki, puka
Hanau ka Weli, he Weliweli kana keiki, puka . . .

From the Kumulipo, Kalakaua text

At the time when the earth became hot
At the time when the heavens turned about
At the time when the sun was darkened
To cause the moon to shine
The time of the rise of the Pleiades
The slime, this was the source of the earth
The source of the darkness that made darkness
The source of the night that made night

The intense darkness, the deep darkness
Darkness of the sun, darkness of the night
Nothing but night.

The night gave birth
Born was Kumulipo in the night, a male
Born was Po'ele in the night, a female
Born was the coral polyp, born was the coral, came forth
Born was the grub that digs and heaps up the earth, came
    forth
Born was his [child], an earthworm, came forth
Born was the starfish, his child the small starfish came forth
Born was the sea cucumber, his child the small sea
    cucumber came forth . . .

> From the Kumulipo chant translated by Martha W.
> Beckwith[1]

Although Hawaii's story is well known, some of its lessons concerning the nature of culture and cultural influences may elude us.[2] I was born in the islands at a time when Hawaii was truly a frontier. A couple of decades earlier in 1893, some foreigners and discontented natives had seized the government from the Hawaiian aristocratic dynasty that ruled the sovereign Hawaiian kingdom. In 1898 Hawaii, by its own request, was annexed to the United States by President William McKinley.

On the volcanic slopes of Punchbowl my parents' home commanded a sweeping view of the harbor, the waterfront, the city of Honolulu, and Diamond Head. In fact, from an upstairs window my mother much later observed the attack on Pearl Harbor. The house also offered a telescopic view of Hawaii's ethnic complexity.

From a west window we could look into the backyard of an old Hawaiian homestead where, in a house with several adjoining cottages, lived a Hawaiian extended family. It included a husband and wife, their numerous children, an aged grandmother—who, to our delight, used to smoke her pipe on the back porch—and a couple of *haole* (white) sons-in-law. On feast days, amid much excitement, a squealing pig would be caught and killed. A shallow pit was dug in a corner of the yard. Wrapped in ti leaves, the pig would be placed on hot stones in the leaf-lined pit and steamed for hours. Relatives from near and far would gather for a luau. The menu also included steamed fish and poi, the baked and pounded root of the taro plant mixed with water.

About half a mile from our house the Hawaiian settlement of Papakolea nestled on the slope of Punchbowl. Here the women raised *plumeria* flowers for making into leis, which they sold at the waterfront when a ship arrived. The men of Papakolea usually worked as stevedores. In general, Hawaiians shun work on the many sugar plantations in the islands and flatly refuse to hire out as workers in mills, factories, or canneries. They also dislike clerking in stores and are very particular about the types of work they do. They enjoy raising taro for poi, fishing, making leis, and working on the waterfront. And they make impressive policemen and legislators.

It was primarily because of the Hawaiians' resistance to the plantation system and industrialization that most of Hawaii's ethnic groups were imported. To provide laborers for the growing sugar industry, corporations began to bring in Chinese coolies under contract. When their contracts expired, these men left the plantations and became shopkeepers, merchants, and bankers. As the earliest imported laborers, the Chinese were the first to move up the social ladder and into Hawaii's business world. Many of their descendants became the islands' new millionaires.

The plantations grew and more laborers were brought in: Portuguese, Puerto Ricans, Koreans, Japanese, and finally Filipinos. As each ethnic group prospered it moved out of the lower class into the middle class, and another outside source of cheap labor had to be tapped if the plantation system was to continue.

Also part of our household was a Japanese couple, who worked as cook and housemaid, and their three children. Each year that a son was born to them a great red paper fish flew proudly from their cottage on the Day of the Carp. Then over

Honolulu, as in any Japanese city, hundreds of carp pennants could be seen against the bright blue sky. The adults spoke only Japanese and pidgin, ate Japanese food with white rice as the base, and practiced their Buddhist religion. Next door and across the street lived several American families, and two blocks away in "Pordegie Town" lived Honolulu's Portuguese immigrants.

A wealthy Chinese merchant bought a large home just below ours. As each son married, a cottage was built on the parental property to house the newlyweds. On Chinese festival days large crowds of Chinese people of all ages would gather on the spacious lawn. Firecrackers and refreshments, served under a temporary pavilion, added to the occasion.

In Honolulu, then a city of about 75,000, children were allowed a good deal of freedom that is denied the child in a modern metropolis. We lived outdoors close to nature, went barefoot, ate Hawaiian food, learned to swim before we could walk, and rode the heavy surf with body, outrigger canoe, and board. We fished, sailed, and explored the islands—their shores, reefs, mountains, caves, and craters. We even climbed down into the fire pit of Kilauea, domain of the volcano goddess Pele. Almost suffocated by hot sulfur fumes, we stood on a ledge and photographed the fiery fountains of molten lava as they bubbled up from the crater floor. Later we studied hula dancing and drumming from Mary Kawena Pukui, the great authority on Hawaiian lore. The hula is a sacred dance to the Hawaiians and one of their major forms of worship. Thus our daily life primed us for an appreciation of the Hawaiian culture.

In school we pitted our wits against the other young people of Hawaii: Chinese, Japanese, Portuguese, and Hawaiians, as well as *haole*. Chinese pupils showed exceptional accuracy and speed in arithmetic. The Japanese were medal winners in photography and other arts. The Hawaiians were the pacers in singing, guitar playing, dancing, football, surfing, and swimming. Each group had its talent and temperament, each its distinctive contribution and style.

The people of modern Hawaii, a multihybrid population now numbering some 750,000, are characterized as Neo-Hawaiian. A complex of Europeans, Polynesians, Orientals, and Filipinos, the population of Hawaii is considered to be an "outstanding laboratory situation for the study of human racial hybrids under optimum living conditions."

Geography and Geology

One of the most remote archipelagoes in the world, the islands extend for 1,600 miles in a southeasterly direction from Midway to Hawaii. They are located 2,397 miles west of San Francisco and 4,000 miles east of the Philippines and Japan. They are 1,885 miles northwest of the Marquesas Islands, the nearest group inhabited by a Polynesian people of similar culture and language. The first settlers are believed to have hailed from the Marquesas.

The islands were formed by volcanic action along a fissure in the ocean floor. Geologists have detected three periods of volcanic activity: during the Lower Miocene, when the major islands appeared above the surface of the sea; during the Pleistocene epoch, when majestic Mauna Kea and Mauna Loa were formed; and the period of vulcanism now in process. All the islands are thus constructed mainly of volcanic rocks rising to central ridges and peaks.

Offshore fishing has been handicapped in many parts of Hawaii because of poorly developed barrier reefs. To compensate, the natives built numerous fishponds by enclosing areas along the shore with stone walls of basalt (Summers 1964).

Situated in the Northern Hemisphere on the Tropic of Cancer and cooled during much of the year by the northeast trade winds, Hawaii has an equable subtropical climate. The reef formation and the location of the group in relation to the currents, winds, and tides of the area account for the long rolling breakers that pound many of Hawaii's beaches.

Before the advent of man certain species of plants and animals had found their way to this remote archipelago. Some, like spiders, drifted on air movements; others came on ocean currents; still others arrived attached to driftwood. In the course of time such indigenous types evolved into many endemic species found nowhere else in the world. About 92 percent of the 1,897 plant species and varieties, 85 percent of the 150 species of nonmigratory birds, and 95 percent of the 1,000 species of land shells are endemic.[3]

The plant and animal community of the Hawaiian archipelago was a clear-cut example of a homeostatic balance with the environment. All the organic species together formed a unique, relatively closed climax ecosystem so delicately equilibrated to the habitat that the introduction of a single alien species could initiate untold damage. An example in historic times was the introduction of the thorny lantana plant, which ran wild and soon covered much of the bush.

Prehistory

Knowledge of prehistoric Hawaiian culture has been augmented by the systematic spadework of archaeologists and the precise dating of stratified sites by radiocarbon analysis. A new method of developing chronological sequence—by comparing the location and stratification of fish-hook types—was discovered by Kenneth P. Emory (Emory, Bonk, and Sinoto 1959). Archaeologists excavated a sand dune site near the ancient canoe landing at Puu Aliʻi, Kaʻu, in the southern extremity of Hawaii island. The site yielded only notched bone fish-hook points. Attempts to date the site were not successful until 1959, when, by radiocarbon analysis, the lowest level was set at A.D. 124. At the lowest level of another site in the vicinity, in a cave shelter, similar points were found and dated from A.D. 950. Above this level was a middle stratum containing both notched and knobbed points and dated A.D. 1230. Near the surface of the cave site were found only knobbed points. Another cave site in this area yielded a two-piece hook point with knobs at the base, dated A.D. 1650. A historical sequence of fish-hook types was thus clearly revealed, from the earliest notched types, to knobbed points, to relatively modern two-piece types.

Such dating methods have pushed backward the time of the original discovery and settlement of Hawaii to the beginning of the second century A.D. We know that the first Polynesian settlers in the islands brought cultivated plants and domestic animals belonging to the Asiatic assemblage including taro, sweet potato, yam, banana, sugar cane, breadfruit, coconut, paper mulberry, gourds, ti, candlenut, pigs, chickens, and dogs.

In the nearly 1,700 years between the original discovery of the archipelago and its rediscovery by Captain Cook in 1778, the Hawaiians developed their idiosyncratic version of the Polynesian culture complex. Utilization of land and sea resources in prehistoric Hawaii was so intensive that, even within the limitations of their Neolithic technology, the islands became densely populated. Stone house foundations and archaeological remains of temples, fishponds, and fish hooks abound. It is estimated that at the time of Cook's visit there were from 200,000 to 400,000 inhabitants in Hawaii.

There is evidence of skillful farming with laboriously laid-out and irrigated taro fields and also of the cultivation of dry-land taro (Handy 1940a: 9–54). The Hawaiians used natural fertilizers, such as wild growth and young *hau* branches, to restore to the fields the favor of Laka, goddess of wild wood and growth. They believed that wild growth contained the vital essence of the land and should therefore never be wasted.

A good deal of the native technology in Hawaii was highly specialized and ritualized. Although prehistoric Hawaii apparently had relatively few endemic diseases, herb doctors served a fifteen-to-twenty-year apprenticeship and could identify and use about 300 local plants for medicinal purposes (Handy, Pukui, and Livermore 1934). Many of these plants have been found of considerable value as pharmaceuticals. For instance, *pia*, a fine powder made from Polynesian arrowroot, was used for hemorrhage of the stomach and bowel and for dysentery. 'Uhaloa, a downy weed that produces an effect similar to aspirin, was used for colds and sore throats. Kava, pounded, mixed with water, and strained, was used to induce sleep and to dry up secretions. The art of massage was carried to a high point, and doctors were also skilled in controlling pain through personal influence, including suggestion. Several methods of population control were employed, including abortion, infanticide, human sacrifice, ritual continence, and warfare.

Land Use

As in Lau, there were pie-shaped land-use divisions in Hawaii, which have been described for Ka'u district by E.S.C. Handy and Mary Kawena Pukui (1958: 4–5, fig. 19). Each chiefdom (*moku*) was sliced into districts (*ahupua'a*) and each district into sections (*'ili*). On each island or within each district of a large island a sacred high chief owned all the land of his chiefdom. Each extended family (*'ohana*) was allowed the use of an *'aina* (homeland), consisting of one section or at least two dis-continuous parcels, one called the poi bowl, on the upland slopes, and one called the meat bowl, on the seashore slopes. This type of land division gave the inhabitants of each district access to the resources of both valley and mountain forest. High production was assured by the chief's tribute collector (*konohiki*), one of whose functions was to see that each parcel of land was used to advantage. There were officials to enforce the tabus, which upheld the whole social system.[4]

The land-use system fostered a balanced protein-carbohydrate diet based on fish and poi, supplemented by greens, seaweed, yams, breadfruit, fowl, dog, and pig and seasoned with sea salt. Most food was steamed in an earth oven, separate ovens being used for men and women. The method of boiling by dropping hot stones into a wooden bowl filled with liquid food was also known. Both methods of cooking were efficient in conserving essential nutriments.

The portioning of food was an important function performed by the family or household head. High-ranking people and all males were favored by the food distribution system. Indeed, choice foods used in religious ceremonies or important as the *kino-lau* of certain high gods (see below), including pork, sea turtle, coconuts, bananas, and certain esteemed fish such as *ulua*, *kumu, niuhi*, and whale, were tabu to women. Nevertheless, it appears that a large proportion of the people, whether male or female, high or low, enjoyed a fairly adequate diet.

Social Structure and Kinship

The population of native Hawaii was divided into three classes: the *ali'i*, a sacred chiefly caste subdivided into several degrees of sanctity; the *maka'ainana* ("dwellers on the land"), who were the Land People of Hawaii; and the despised *kauwa*, outcaste of slaves. The system was upheld by a tabu that functioned to isolate both the *ali'i* because they were sacred and the *kauwa* because they were defiling.

There was a strict division of labor based on sex, and the sacred was protected from defilement by the profane. All high-prestige and ritualized work—farming, tabu fishing, cooking, navigation, housebuilding, warfare, priesthood, canoe building, and the making of implements and featherwork—was performed by men. The women, who were regarded as especially defiling during the menstrual period and childbirth, cared for children and the home, gathered shellfish offshore, and made barkcloth, mats, and baskets.

The main kinship group was the *'ohana*, or extended family, a bilateral group that reckoned descent through both the male and the female lines. The *'ohana* included relatives by blood, marriage, and adoption living in a dispersed community composed of several homesteads (*kauhale*) located on the family *'aina*. Besides living members, the *'ohana* included deceased ancestors (*na kupuna*) and family guardian spirits (*'aumakua*) (Handy and Pukui 1958: 4, 75). The extended family functioned as a major economic unit, its members cooperating in house building, fishing, feasting, reciprocal exchange of goods, and paying tribute of food, barkcloth, mats, feathers, and labor to the high chief. Tribute was collected at the Makahiki festival, to honor a chief's first-born child, and prior to making war. If a chief considered the tribute insufficient, he would order the donor's *ahupua'a* plundered (Kamakau 1964: 21).

The elder male in the senior branch of an extended family was its *haku* (master or director), who planned and directed the activities of the group, presided over family councils, divided fish catches among household groups, supervised work and family ceremonies, welcomed visiting nobles, and arranged for the entertainment of strangers (Handy and Pukui 1958: 6–7).

The *hale*, or household group, was the smallest local grouping of old Hawaii. In addition to *'ohana* it included *'ohua*, dependents and helpers not related by blood or adoption. The household was led by a *po'o*, a male member who was not necessarily its senior but who assumed responsibility and made decisions. Exchange of products of the shore and lowlands such as fish, squid, lobster, edible seaweed, coconuts, salt, and gourds for products of the uplands such as taro, bananas, paper mulberry bark, medicinal plants, and *olona* vines for making fibers was obligatory between households of an extended family living on the seaward slopes and those living on the uplands.

The dwelling place of a household group consisted of a cluster of grass houses (*kauhale*), including a sleeping house, a men's eating house tabu to women, an eating house for women and children, work huts, and a menstrual hut. The *kauhale* was located on the family land, widely separated from other household groups so as to take full advantage of the natural resources. It may be classed as an isolated farmstead. There were no villages in old Hawaii.

Kinship Terminology

Hawaiian kinship terminology, like European, is an example of the descriptive type, in which relatives are designated by describing their relationship to ego. It contrasts to the classificatory type, in which relatives are grouped together into a few named categories.

Lewis H. Morgan classified (but misunderstood) the Hawaiian system as the simplest of several basic kinship terminology types.[5] The system distinguishes only five categories of kinship (plus several categories of affines): ego's grandparents, parents, siblings, offspring, and grandchildren. In one of these categories it classifies each of ego's relatives who is a member of his extended family by birth. Sex distinctions are made by modifiers (*kane*, male; *wahine*, female) following the root word for each generational term. Within a generation all males have a single term for one another and all females another.

The Hawaiian system emphasizes generational levels and the equivalence of relatives in each, nearness of relationship being ignored. Thus, no distinction is made between siblings and cousins, male parent and uncles, female parent and aunts, grandparents and their siblings of the same sex. All members of one generation address those of the next lower one as "children."

Horizontally the family is stratified by generations, and precedence in rank is determined by genealogical seniority regardless of sex. The descendants of the senior members of a group of siblings outrank all junior branches. Vertically, sex cuts through the generations. Male children are claimed by the father's side ('ao'ao kane) and females by the mother's relatives ('ao'ao wahine).

What might be called the principle of genealogical seniority, the basic concept underlying Polynesian primogeniture, defines the Hawaiian system of ranked bloodlines. To the Hawaiians the founding of lines by remote ancestors and their perpetuation through descending generations was of paramount importance because each generation ranked such ancestors by seniority and deified them as 'aumakua. The living representatives of the high ranking 'aumakua were worshiped as sacred chiefs. The kinship system highlights the Hawaiian preferred relationship pattern, a native system of classifying and relating units of sensory experience that structured many aspects of Hawaiian culture.

Religion and World Image

Another expression of the preferred relationship pattern is found in Hawaiian creation chants (mele). The Hawaiian belief in the family's relation to the gods and to the world of nature —the heavens, night, the stars, and useful plants and animals of sea and land—is expressed in chants.[6] Probably the most famous chant is the Kumulipo, a genealogical history composed about 1700, which connects a royal family (later including King Kalakaua and his sister and successor, Queen Liliuokalani) to certain deified ancestors purported to be the founders of the line.

The totemic relationships expressed in the chants derive from the Hawaiian concept of kino-lau, or multiple forms and transformations, under which significant phenomena of the perceived universe are grouped into classes according to such external similarities as form, color, movement, and texture and such personal qualities as sex, youth, and age. Each class of phenomena is associated with a real or mythical personage in the pantheon or the social hierarchy.

Pele, the goddess of vulcanism believed to have migrated to Hawaii, is classed as an essential phenomenon, and fire forms, such as a ball of fire (*popo ahi*), and occasionally female forms, such as a beautiful young girl or an ugly old hag, are interpreted as her embodiments (Handy and Pukui 1958: 123). Similarly Kumuhea, a nature god believed to have risen from the depths of the sea, is represented by sea cucumbers, baby eels, and caterpillars that eat sweet-potato leaves.

Kamapua'a (Hog Child), the god of sweet-potato planters, is regarded as the *'aumakua* of certain families. He is believed to assume many forms, including that of a human being, of candlenut tree foliage, and of seaweed. His other forms include a hog, a small fish whose head suggests a pig's snout, and a wild grass called hog's excrement (Handy 1936: 123).

Dreams, both night dreams (*moe'uhane*) and waking visions (*akaku*), were the major source of a Hawaiian's putative knowledge of the supernatural world and of contact with his *'aumakua* and his gods. He depended on interpretation of his dreams as signs to guide his life, especially in relation to planting and fishing, house and boat construction, birth and naming, and sickness, curing and death and in affairs of war and love.

According to E.S.C. Handy (1936: 121), the *'aumakua* concept is still vital to many contemporary Hawaiians: "To be comprehended, it has to be understood as a component part of native psychological heritage which Christianization has obliterated in some but affected very little in others."

Although most of the outer forms of traditional Hawaiian culture have disappeared, many spiritual elements of old Hawaii live on, creating conflicts and anxiety. (Lucy, our Hawaiian baby sitter, once caught sight of a tiny lizard on the porch and ran screaming into the house. The lizard was apparently one of the forms of her family's guardian spirit, the *'aumakua moo*. Handy writes [1936: 123]: "Moo means literally lizard or, in legends, giant lizard; but the *aumakua moo* include also the fresh water gobi fish of one variety, several varieties of reef fish, turtles, brindle dogs, and certain human beings." Lucy attended church and professed to be a Christian, but spontaneously in her behavior she expressed native beliefs and fears.)

The relationship between essential phenomena and their external manifestations is not perceived as a spatial one in the sense that the manifestations are localized within the phenomena or peripheral to them. There may, however, be noted a sea-land distinction: units associated with the sea (*kai*) take precedence over those associated with the land (*uka*). At the same time, entities living on land are viewed as the natural guardians of entities living in the sea.

Obviously no simple superordinate-subordinate relationship is expressed here. Nor does the Hawaiian classification reflect a "contents and container" model such as figures prominently in most Western European and American classification systems (Whorf 1956: 36). The Hawaiian notion is extraspatial in terms of the Western concept of absolute space. There is a spatial dimension expressed, however, if we think of the domain of the sea as completely surrounding that of the land—on these oceanic islands of the Pacific. And a natural time dimension is expressed, of course, in the Hawaiian genealogical sequences.

Hawaiians revere not only the family deities but also each of the forms in which a deity is believed to manifest itself. They regard the power and its multiple forms as guardian spirits or ancestral deities (Kamakau 1964: 28–32) that must be treated with respect and offered food and sweet-smelling plants in return for endowing their descendants with mana. Apparently it is the act rather than the content of an offering that is primary (McAllister 1933: 37–40). These concepts form the basis of sanctions (tabus) affecting family and individual behavior and serve as determinants of descent, relationship, rank, and duty.

The Hawaiians formerly propitiated a pantheon of high gods of creation (*akua*). The high gods were ancestral to the family gods, according to the creation chants. Kane was the god of sunlight, fresh water, and forests. Lono was the god of agriculture, the harvest, medicine, clouds, and weather. (When Captain

Cook arrived in the islands, he was worshiped as one of the manifestations of Lono.) Ku was the deity for success in warfare and power for the high chief to govern securely. Craftsmen worshiped special forms of Ku. Sorcerers had Kukoae. Timber workers had eight forms of Ku. Bird catchers and feather workers had a form called Kuhuluhulumanu; cultivators of the soil had Kukaʻoʻo; and fishermen had Kuʻula, a deified ancestral hero believed to have been a great fisherman and represented by fishes carved in stone or shell. Kuʻula was supplicated with food and flowers to bring luck with the catch and offered hooks and stones at seashore shrines (Malo 1951; Buck 1957: 465, 499–502). One of Ku's manifestations was Kukailimoku, god of Kamehameha I, symbolized in an image made of wicker and lashed with brilliant red and yellow feathers.

For their major gods the Hawaiians built a raised open-air temple (*heiau*), where priests made offerings of pigs, dogs, fish, coconuts, bananas, fragrant plants, and, occasionally, a human being. At these ceremonies they sought to exchange offerings for mana, the superhuman power the deities were believed to possess and to be able to pass on to their living descendants.

Mana was conceived in ancient Hawaii as so powerful that it had to be controlled by means of an elaborate tabu system designed to prevent the defilement of the sacred domain. Everything connected with the gods, the high chief, the nobles, priests, temples, and guardian spirits was considered sacred and therefore tabu. Certain men's work, such as cooking, canoe building, and deep-sea fishing, was also under protection. As noted earlier, death, sickness, and women during the menstrual period or in childbirth were regarded as especially defiling. The tabu system expressed a sort of unwritten law code and to break it meant death either by the deity or by the chief.

Mana could also be vested in persons and things. The creation chants and life-crisis ceremonial feasts, such as those marking the birth and first birthday of a child, were apparently designed to induce power into the child. House- and canoe-building rites in Hawaii, as in the Marquesas (Handy 1923: 151 ff.), were fashioned to build mana into those objects so that they would be strong, durable, and endowed with magical efficacy.

Language

Power was also believed to be a property of certain words and word combinations. The entire Kumulipo genealogical chant was recited in order to transfer mana from the universe and ancestors to a newborn child. Many Hawaiian chants have a deeply hidden meaning called *kaona*. Mary Kawena Pukui and Samuel H. Elbert (1957: 121) define *kaona* as "Hidden meaning in Hawaiian poetry: concealed reference, as to a person, thing, or place; words with a double meaning that might bring good or bad fortune." Chants have one to three levels of meaning: an outward meaning of the words, a vulgar double meaning, and a mythological-historical-geographical meaning. Chants were carefully scrutinized by *haku mele* to excise words of secret evil omen, especially in relation to the chiefs.

The Hawaiian language, which belongs to the Polynesian family of the eastern branch of the Austronesian stock, has a vocabulary of some 25,000 words, many of which have more than one meaning. The vocabulary is rich in concrete rather than abstract terms. Note that the Kumulipo expresses concrete images of such observable natural phenomena as the Pleiades, the sea urchin, the earthworm, man, and woman. In Hawaiian grammar, propositions are independent, each one constituting a sentence, or they form compound sentences consisting of two or more independent propositions connected by conjunctions, rather than complex sentences consisting of a principal and one or more subordinate clauses (Judd 1939: 60). This construction is well illustrated in the Kumulipo, where phrases of equivalent value are juxtaposed. Many of the relationships between the natural phenomena described in the chant are such natural relationships as birth and growth processes. In old Hawaii, language, religion, and world image were thus profoundly intervolved by means of describable patterns of relationship.

Preferred Relationship Patterns

Two types of relationships seem to have been dominant in the native Hawaii: the *'aumakua* type of relationship, such as that between ancestors and their living descendants, between chiefs and their tribute-paying followers, and between sea forms and

land forms; and the *kino-lau* type of relationship, such as that
between a major deity and its multiple manifestations in sea
and on land, between a deceased chief and his bones (which
were frequently hidden in a cave), and between the chiefs of
the several islands or of the districts of a large island.

The *'aumakua* relationship may be conceived as one of ceremonial exchange in which the two parties exchange values according to a reciprocity principle. The party in the role of
'aumakua (sea form, ancestor, or chief) is considered more
powerful than the recipient (land form, descendant, or retainer)
and is expected to endow mana, protection, or guardianship in
exchange for goods, services, and respect. Solicitation of a gift
implies the expectation of a countergift; for example, mana may
be solicited from an ancestor in exchange for offerings. Today,
according to Pukui and Elbert (1957: 29), if someone is asked
to dance a hula, the term *'aumakua* is used to designate the
request and the request may not be refused without giving the
solicitor a lei or flower. Solicitation of this type implies acquies-
cence to perform a service, in this case to dance a hula, or to
deliver a return gift, even if it be merely a token. The exchange
is not correlative, that is, a swapping of equivalent but not
identical values. For the party in the role of *'aumakua* is expected to give a gift of greater value than the party in the
reciprocal role. The *'aumakua* exchange is reminiscent of the
Lauan solicitation or begging custom (*kerekere*) between persons of unequal rank.

On the other hand, the *kino-lau* relationship is correlative,
that is, the units or parties within the multibodied whole manifest a relationship of equivalent but not identical value. For
example, all the *kino-lau* of a deity were believed to share that
deity's mana. Propitiation of a deity's *kino-lau* was equivalent to
propitiation of the deity itself.

The political structure of old Hawaii, before its centralization
under a paramount chief, corresponded to a coalition model
(Davenport 1964) under which a number of independent chiefs
held power over the several small islands and districts of large
islands that constituted sovereign chiefdoms (*moku*). Although
each high chief was held in great respect and even worshiped

by his retainers, he was not considered the ultimate authority in his realm but was dependent on the power of his gods. Just as heavy tribute was paid by the people of each *ahupua'a* to the high chief, the chief himself through his priests contributed a portion of his receipts as sacrifices or gifts to his gods. He also redistributed some of the tribute to the people in the form of feasts, public works, and military protection.

The political situation constantly shifted with the changing relationships between rival chiefs, no one of whom was dominant over the rest (Handy and Pukui 1958: 2). Once a chief had firmly established himself over a *moku*, his position was threatened not only from without by invasions led by rivals, but also from within by revolt or by loss of tribute-paying farmers. The Hawaiian planter was not bound to the soil like a serf as, for example, was the farmer in Tonga, but was free to switch his affiliation to another chief. A change in local leadership brought a change in privileges. Moreover, because chiefly rules of succession could be circumvented, the death of a chief might lead to civil strife and a change of regimes (Davenport 1964).

In a way, then, the chiefly political structure of old Hawaii exemplifies a balance between the *'aumakua* and the *kino-lau* relationship principles. The many island chiefs, each independent of the others, may be thought of as conceptually equivalent to *kino-lau*, or multiple bodies of a deity, and sharing the deity's mana. Respect and propitiation shown to a chief were equivalent to respecting and propitiating the deity itself. A high chief's relation to his retainers illustrates the *'aumakua* principle, with the chief in the role of *'aumakua*.

The viability of the ancient Hawaiian political system, as well as the religious and economic systems, depended on maintaining a balance between the *'aumakua* and *kino-lau* principles. That balance could be disturbed in two ways: one chief might gain dominance over the remainder and thus destroy the balance of the *kino-lau* system by changing it into a two-party, deity-chief relationship, in other words, into an *'aumakua* type of relationship; or a chief might fail to propitiate his deity or the people might refuse to support the chief, thus disrupting the 'aumakua relationship.

Culture Change

The downfall of the native Hawaiian political system, along with its religious and economic substructure, came about by such a disturbance of balance. First there was a consolidation of political power in the hands of a paramount chief, Kamehameha I, between 1782 and 1810, which destroyed the *kino-lau* system of balance between the high chiefs. Then in 1819 King Liholiho, offended his deities by failing to honor a tabu against eating in company that included both sexes (Handy 1931: 26–34). The 'aumakua-type balance between paramount chief and his gods was thus destroyed. Other events destroyed the 'aumakua relationship between the high chief and his people, including destruction of the temples and images of the gods and, beginning in 1820 with the arrival of Congregationalist missionaries from New England, acceptance of the Gospel.

The importance of the native system of land use and population control in the Hawaiian ecocultural system was highlighted by the Land Laws, or great Mahele, in 1848, when King Kamehameha III, under pressure from land-hungry Europeans, tried to transfer much of his land to the chiefs and to the common people. Out of the million acres that were made available only 28,000 were actually allotted to the people, mainly because the natives lacked comprehension of the new land-ownership concepts (Lind 1938: 46). Soon many of these and some 972,000 remaining acres were absorbed into the foreign plantation system, while the landless natives, most of whom also had lost their fishing rights, starved, became ill, and died off rapidly.

The significance of the Hawaiian complex of practices and beliefs to native welfare is underscored by the effect of their breakdown on native morality, health, and welfare after European contact. Of course, lack of immunity to such Old World diseases as syphilis, bubonic plague, measles, smallpox, influenza, tuberculosis, and leprosy played a major role in this process.

But the sudden disruption of the rigidly upheld social system, within itself and in relation to the local ecology, apparently had a paralyzing effect on the people and inhibited restorative processes that had previously operated to engender new, favorable relationships between human communities and their environments.

Conclusion

Native Hawaiian ingenuity worked out and institutionalized a unique way of life that dealt more or less satisfactorily with the practical problems inherent in the isolated habitat. Organized into localized family systems under sacred chiefs and their deputies, the Hawaiians developed a traditional culture for two millenniums to the point where, by intensive irrigated agriculture, skillful craftsmanship, and deep-sea fishing, they produced and supported a large population. They also achieved a relatively flexible and stable cultural equilibrium within the limitations of the island ecosystem and their own technology.

Thus the findings from Hawaii suggest that the indigenous inhabitants of this isolated, entirely self-sufficient island community developed and integrated a balanced culture system, based on the limited and specialized inventory of natural and human resources available, similar in delicacy and vulnerability to isolated ecosystems in the rest of the organic world.

Notes

1. Reprinted from Martha W. Beckwith, *The Kumulipo. A Hawaiian Creation Chant*. Chicago: University of Chicago Press, 1951, p. 58, by permission from the University of Chicago Press.
2. This chapter is based on fieldwork and library research in Hawaii in 1940–1941 and 1962. The former was carried out under the auspices of the Community Survey of Education, Territory of Hawaii. Regarding the native culture of Kaʻu District, Hawaii, the basic source used was a description of the family system by E. S. C. Handy and Mary Kawena Pukui (1958). Mary Pukui was born in Kaʻu, where in 1935 the Handys did the fieldwork on which their book is based. I am especially grateful to E. S. C. Handy, E. H. Bryan, Jr., Kenneth P. Emory, Yoshito Sinoto, Amy Greenwell, and William H. Davenport for their kind assistance.

3. The endemic flora of Ka'u encountered by the colonizing Polynesians, and the use of each plant, has been described by Elizabeth Green Handy (Handy and Pukui 1958: 212–222).

4. Handy (1931: 3) defines the Polynesian tabu as *"personal and social discipline by immanent supernormal agency.* Specifically, *Kapu* [in Hawaii] is related to prohibition or restriction . . . because of sanctity, or because of defilement."

5. In describing the Hawaiian kinship terminology system, Lewis H. Morgan (1870: 451–457) made several errors. For example, in this polygamous family system in which a man might have more than one wife and a woman more than one husband, the term *punalua* was used to designate the relationship of two husbands of one woman toward each other and two wives of one man toward each other (Handy and Pukui 1958: 56–65). The term was not used, as stated by Morgan (1870: 457; 480–481), to designate a kind of group marriage.

6. Dorothy B. Barrère (1961) reports that the Kumulipo and other ancient genealogies were written in the nineteenth century to include Biblical progenitors of the Hawaiian people.

6 /

NATURE AND CULTURE

> The life of a society is planned on the basis of the tradi-
> tional arts by which animals, plants, minerals and climate
> are made to serve the purposes of its existence.
>
> Richard Thurnwald (1932: 34)

Having investigated, in geological, ecological, and historical context, the changing cultures of three traditionally isolated island
communities in Oceania, we may now compare our findings and
draw up some tentative generalizations about them. We are also
in a position to review our data for its implications regarding
two basic approaches toward the problem of the relation between
nature and culture, the approach of the extreme determinists
and that of the cultural ecologists.

It is assumed that before the advent of man balanced stable
ecosystems existed on all the island groups. On volcanic islands,
the action of water and wind truncated original conelike forms
and moved soil from uplands to lowlands and into the sea in
the form of silt. Many of the islands were also reformed by volcanic action as their surface soil was covered with lava flows,
which subsequently became subject to natural erosion and eventually broke down to new soil. The ecology of Kaʻu, Hawaii,
(Handy and Pukui 1958: Ch. 8) comes to mind. Iceland also
affords a good illustration of the process (see Chapter 9).

Coral limestone islands were constantly being undercut by
the action of wind, currents, waves, and tide, a process best
illustrated perhaps by the mushroom-shaped islets in the Fulanga
lagoon. Precipitation seeps through porous limestone formations
gouging out pits and large depressions that occasionally form a
central lake, as in Wangava.

Human immigrant groups with domestic animals—dogs, fowl, and pigs—and with cultivated plants and their planting habits disturbed the natural balances. Man's acceleration of erosion and depletion of the soil has received a good deal of attention (see, for example, Thomas 1956). In Oceania swidden (slash and burn) farming has been particularly depletive. Prehistoric soil erosion from swidden farming apparently occurred on Mothe and other volcanic islands of Lau, in Hawaii, and in south-central Guam, as well as elsewhere (Fosberg 1963a). Although swidden farming methods contribute lime to the soil, the fires used to clear brush may destroy large areas of forest, as in Guam. On the other hand, native methods of wet-rice cultivation, as in Guam, and wet-taro cultivation, as in Hawaii, may have checked some soil loss.

The raised coral limestone islands have been less vulnerable than the volcanic islands to man-made destruction of resources. Although hardwoods and other jungle products have been removed from these islands, until recently the deforestation has been selective and has operated more as a stimulus to sustained yield than as a depletion.

Since wealth-seeking Europeans and Orientals arrived in the islands the picture has changed. For example, forests of sandal-wood in Mbua, Fiji, and in Hawaii were cut clean for the Chinese market and the introduction of large mammals—goats, deer, cattle, and horses—greatly disturbed the ecological balances in Hawaii and the Marianas, as well as elsewhere in the Pacific.

Cultivation and Conservation

Analysis of data from Lau, Hawaii, and elsewhere highlight the close functional relationship between cultivation, conservation, and food storage, which suggests that the conservation of natural resources may be a primary human activity widespread among farming, fishing, collecting, and hunting groups. It is but a step, for example, from sea-turtle hunting in a reef-enclosed lagoon (Kambara) to the storing and breeding of turtles in a brackish lake (Wangava). And it is but another step from the conservation of sea life in a lagoon or lake to the construction of a fishpond by enclosing part of a lagoon with a stone wall built on a reef. In such ponds on Mothe fish are fed and stored. In Hawaii, where 200 native fishponds have been located, the tabu on harvesting certain species of fish in the sea during the spawning season, a Hawaiian conservation measure, did not apply to fishponds. Therefore fish, such as the favored mullet, which was tabu from November to April, were available year around to pond owners (Summers 1964: 1). Some ancient fishponds are still in use. The Pacific islanders have domesticated bush pigs, which are penned, fed (usually grated coconut meat), and conserved for future use.

In southern Lau the wild yam is cultivated in the bush, and the ownership of each patch is known. Only a member of the owning clan may harvest the yams, and he immediately replants a piece of the root in the spot where the plant had been growing. The same cycle of harvesting and replanting is followed for the domesticated sweet yam, except that it is cultivated in garden land that has been cleared. A similar pattern may be observed in farming the main garden crops in southern Lau, sweet potato and manioc, although manioc was imported in historic times from South America and the sweet potato arrived in prehistoric times, probably from the same source. When a root has been harvested, a stalk of the sweet-potato plant or a piece of manioc root is usually replanted immediately.

The planting pattern reminds us of the Lauan first-fruits ceremony, when the planter gives a piece of goods with the expectation of a future return of greater value than the gift. It thus fits the Lau preferred relationship pattern and may indeed have served as its model.

The problem of resources conservation should not be considered without equal attention to soil erosion and resources destruction initiated or accelerated by man. In this context the roles of the chief of crops and the master fisherman in Lau, as well as their counterparts in Hawaii and elsewhere in the Pacific, take on special significance. The chief of crops has the hereditary role of fostering and conserving the resources of the land, including fruit trees and forest growth, toward maximum productivity. In this traditionally Neolithic society he and the master fisherman represent decision-making resource conservationists.

Attitudes Toward Nature

This nurturing attitude toward nature and the life force, often verging on reverence, is characteristic of many native peoples. It is especially marked in the traditional cultures of many American Indian tribes (see Chapters 13, 14, 16), the Neolithic peoples of northern Europe (see Chapter 7), and the Lower Saxons (see Chapter 10). It is also characteristic of African groups such as the Bantu Baluba (Tempels 1959: 31), as well as Eskimos, certain Siberian groups, and others. From a broad perspective of man's cultural history, a highly exploitative attitude toward nature is exceptional. The twentieth-century resources-conservation movement may indicate that the careless, exploitative attitude toward natural resources characteristic of industrialized peoples, especially city dwellers, is on the way out.

Domestication Practices

Evidence from the case studies substantiates the hypothesis that the cultivation of animals and plants originated not once but many times. It suggests that domestication does not represent a step up the cultural ladder from a lower to a higher level, as postulated by cultural evolutionists, but should be viewed as a problem-solving device that may emerge under certain circumstances. For example, the data suggest that domestication arises by a series of technological arrangements for meeting community needs and solving problems related to the storage and conservation of natural resources. In an emergency such as a natural catastrophe or an economic recession, appropriate traditional ways may be expected to reemerge. The persistence or reemergence of traditional cultural devices for the purpose of practical problem solving may therefore be regarded as a basic cultural process.

The primary role of man in the domestication process is one of seeking and fostering a favorable environment in which the plant or animal may activate its species' biogram (mode of life), rather than one of manipulator and exploiter of nature. The organism itself—plant or animal—is always of course the active agent in the growth and development process. Maximization rather than minimization of the life process through the generations has been the strategy expressed in the cultural institutions and practices of communities that have attained a certain success toward self-actualization within the potentials and limitations of their habitats. Further evidence of such maximization of the life process will be presented in chapters that follow.

Variations in Geology and Natural Resources

It should be noted, however, that man cannot extract from land or sea what is not there. Nor can man invent metallurgy in localities where metals are absent or unobtainable under native conditions, as in most of Polynesia. He cannot develop the potter's art where potter's clay is absent, as in some Pacific islands such as Fulanga. Indeed, the presence or absence of specific natural resources such as good garden land, potter's clay, or greenstone (hard, jadelike quartzite) frequently is built into the structure of a culture.

To illustrate, potter's clay is prevalent in most of the larger islands on the Pacific continental shelf, and many Melanesians and some Micronesians practice or formerly practiced the potter's art (Chang, Solheim, and Grace 1964: 360 ff.). Indeed, pots are the base of interisland trade among many of these peoples. In Polynesia, where potter's clay is rare, the potter's art is also rare, although evidence of it has been found in archaeological sites in the Marquesas and Samoa, where the natives have not practiced the art during historic times.

Greenstone, highly valued for its beautiful color, smooth texture, and hardness that takes a high polish, is present in only three areas of Oceania, all on the shelf: New Zealand, New Caledonia, and Murua (Woodlark), an island off the southeast coast of New Guinea. In New Zealand it was fashioned into ceremonial *tiki* (figurines symbolizing male fertility) by a stone-cutting method using a sand abrasive. On Murua the natives of Suloga village shaped the stone into rough blades and exported them to the Trobriands (and probably to Misima), where the blades were ground. From there the finished blades, now highly valued ceremonial objects, were exported as far west as the Papuan Gulf (Seligmann 1910: 68, 69). In New Caledonia it was also used for adz blades. Thus, in all three localities greenstone was quarried and played a significant role in the traditional culture.

On the other hand, the presence of a natural resource does not signify that it will be used. For example, gold is present in many islands on the continental shelf, including New Guinea and Fiji, but it was not used by any native group in Oceania.

Culture Persistence

Impressive in each island-community case study is evidence of the persistence of institutions, leadership roles, and approaches toward problem solving that were developed within the traditional symbiotic relationship between man and nature. The data reveal that such cultural devices may persist in a slightly changed form after many other aspects of the traditional culture have disappeared or become dysfunctional and the symbiotic relationship itself has begun to deteriorate. Their presence, however, is frequently hidden or outside the cultural awareness of those who are not members of the native ingroup (Handy 1936). A similar phenomenon has been reported from many other parts of the world (for example, Elwin 1947; Firth 1959, 1961; Evans-Pritchard 1940).

Variations in Climate and Geography

Furthermore, the data show that climate is a basic factor that must be kept in mind if we are to understand native behavior and culture. True, with the exception of New Zealand, Easter Island, Pitcairn, and Rapa, most of the Pacific island groups are located in the torrid zone, which tends to have an equable tropical climate. But the climate of the Pacific world varies significantly in the several island groups, within each island group, and according to the side of the island, whether windward or leeward. Small-scale variations in temperature and large-scale cosmic factors, such as solar radiation, earth and ocean-bed movements, lunar influences, tidal movements, ocean currents, prevailing winds, precipitation, glaciation and sea levels, latitude, altitude, and proximity to larger landmasses affect man's behavior in countless ways, especially the routes followed in migrations across the sea, settlement patterns, pace and rhythm of biogram, and contacts with the outside world. In the case of human groups these factors affect his attitudes, values, and preferred relationship patterns.

Minute differences in climate and geography have thus had far-reaching effects on human community structures as well as those of plants and animals, a fact well documented by ecologists. They have also greatly affected the kind and degree of stresses induced by man-made influences from both the Old World and the New, to which the natives of the several island groups have been exposed. Such pressures are increasing rapidly as commercial exploitation and industrialization gain momentum in the Pacific.

Conclusion

It seems hardly necessary to reiterate the truism that man is irrevocably a part of the world of nature. As George G. Simpson (1949: 281) said, "Not only are all men brothers, all living things are brothers in the very real sense that all have arisen from one source and have been developed within the intricacies of one process."

All organisms face the same essential problem: adaptation for survival. But every viable community does much more than adapt itself to its environment for survival. It strives to actualize its species biogram and perpetuate itself in future generations. Human communities differ from those of all other species in that each has developed a unique device for dealing with the universal living problem of the species (Spuhler 1959). We call this device "culture."

Every community sketched in this volume was at the time of observation successfully implementing more than the mere survival of its members. Each had so organized itself to use its resources—natural and human—and had so styled its way of life that its members might achieve some degree of self-actualization. In other words, most of its members succeeded in obtaining a more or less adequate diet, in mating and producing children, and in spontaneously expressing themselves and transmitting their culture to future generations. All the groups except the Sioux (see Chapter 16) showed a conspicuous *joi de vivre*.

The Lau case clearly shows in detail that the members of the community have created a way of behaving, perceiving, believing, and evaluating by which they do not simply adapt themselves to the environment. They build the environment into their culture and they use their culture, including its decision-making roles and its basic skills and organized knowledge, along with their other resources as a means of developing and actualizing themselves as individuals and as a group, within the potentials of the environment and the limitations of their technology. A viable human community thus does not simply adapt itself to the environment; it builds the environment into its culture and the culture into the environment.

Obviously, the usual concept of adaptation is inadequate to pinpointing the intricate feedback processes by which, for example, the small human groups in Oceania bind themselves organically and culturally to their microenvironments. John Dewey and Arthur F. Bentley (1949: Chs. 4, 5) have moved us conceptually closer to processual reality as its effects may be observed clinically in certain favorable natural laboratories. The process, as revealed by modern scientific research, is one of "transaction" (multiway interpenetration). We need a transactional frame for studies of culture change that can accommodate multiple interpenetrating systems.

The analysis thus reveals no simple process of environmental determinism, of cultural evolution, or of social progress in the Euro-American sense. The data from Lau, Hawaii, and Guam— and also from Iceland, Lower Saxony, and selected American Indian communities (Chapters 9, 10, 13–16)—point rather to a transactive process, directed toward maximization of the life process and homeostatic balance between natural and cultural phenomena. By this process a community tends to build and organize its culture and its environment toward optimum future function as the major way of actualizing itself as an ongoing social entity.

Man can, of course, use his culture and also his environment against himself (see J. Henry 1965). In an atomic age the extinction of Homo sapiens as a species and the destruction of his environment is by no means unimaginable. Several species of the genus *Homo* failed at finding a solution to their living problems under changing environmental conditions and became extinct. If such an eventuality should occur again, it will be the first time that a species of the genus *Homo* has exterminated itself, through self-made cultural mechanisms, with the means of prevention at hand. Assessment of this and other catastrophes, such as gross worldwide overpopulation, depends on man's enlistment of his great achievement—his historically diverse cultures—toward realistically appraising the present world crisis. Prevention will depend on man's restyling his cultures within the planet's environmental limitations and potentials and using them actively to resolve the crisis not merely for today but for generations yet unborn.

PART 2

7 /

EARLY MAN IN NORTH EUROPE

> Human life, from the very first traces met with, seems to
> have this in common, that human beings strive to make
> their existence secure and to give it greater content. It was
> no different with the Scandinavians. Tensely and watch-
> fully they struggle with all the powers that can break down
> and annihilate—storm and rain, hail and harmful frost,
> plague and illness afflicting men and cattle, . . . evil and
> secretive forces. The struggle was for the future, that the
> generations might increase and add their strength, that
> the cattle might thrive and the fields yield their harvests.
>
> Hal Koch (1959: 130)

I became interested in European indigenous cultures when I
went to live in a Lower Saxon rural community after returning
from Fiji. I also traveled extensively in Germany as well as in
Switzerland, Italy, England, and Czechoslovakia. Later, hoping
to gain some perspective on Lower Saxon culture, I started systematic work on European indigenous cultures, which grew into
a specific investigation of the culture history of the Baltic–
North Sea peoples and included two field trips to Iceland and
another visit to West Germany.[1]

Before discussing the European communities selected for
study, let us consider another basic concern of anthropologists;
namely, the nature of society and the relation between society
and culture. Men have been interested in this problem since
classical times, and sociology had gained general recognition
before the discipline of anthropology emerged during the nineteenth century. Like psychology and many of the social sciences,
sociology developed out of philosophy and theology.

After the ninth century, when the concept of the infallibility of the pope gained prominence, a single immutable power image, the Roman Catholic world view, tended to dominate Western man's perception of the world except in the pagan northland. From this position it was but a step to the social determinism that characterized humanistic Renaissance and Enlightenment thinking. For example, in Auguste Comte's system (1830–1842), humanity took the role that had been played by God in medieval theology and by substance in classical metaphysics, and he replaced the concept of a divinely ascribed law of society with that of a natural predisposition. According to this "given" principle, the human mind by its nature progresses upward through three historical stages, which Comte called the theological or fictitious, the metaphysical or abstract, and the positive or scientific. He postulated a theory of unilinear social evolution in terms of these three stages, and he adhered to the pre-Darwinian classification of the organic world into fixed species (Comte 1958: 346–349).

At about the same time, Herbert Spencer attempted to replace medieval theological systems with a developmental synthesis of the fundamental principles of the sciences. Spencer explained development as a homogeneous-to-heterogeneous process suggested by his pre-Darwinian belief that biological species evolved through the inheritance of acquired abilities (Spencer 1866 [1]: 269–270). In 1859, by establishing natural selection based on accidental variations as the major mechanism in the evolution of new species, Charles Darwin upset the dominant Western belief in a single immutable order of nature and man. Soon the concept of evolution, validated as a basic process of organic nature including the human species, was extended to society. Lewis H. Morgan captured the imagination of Occidental intellectuals when he associated detailed technological sequences with the evolution of family forms. Morgan (1877: 393–515) formulated, on the basis of earlier models and on what he believed to be empirical evidence, a unilinear scheme of the "evolution" of human society. It consisted of three basic periods: "savagery," "barbarism," and "civilization." Morgan's field researches on the kinship systems of certain North American Indian tribes and other ethnic groups led him to believe that the nineteenth-century Euro-American monogamous nuclear family was the culmination of the series of social groupings through which he believed man had progressed. These included, for example, "promiscuity," the "consanguine family" founded on intermarriage of brothers and sisters in a group, the "patriarchal family," and so on. Karl Marx built Morgan's findings into his communist ideology, and soon the idea of unilinear evolution was established in the West as the basic tenet of the social universe. Indeed, the evolutionary formula was extended to embrace all of culture (Tylor 1881).

The convenience of the unilinear cultural evolutionary hypothesis as a device to rationalize and explain their own behavior helped, of course, to convert it into a fixed idea, which became deeply entrenched in the world image of most Occidentals. It afforded a ready-made justification for diverse forms of aggressive activity toward non-Western peoples, including military conquest and attempted conversion to the Christian faith, exploitation of the earth's natural resources on a global scale, and the search for new markets for commercial gain. Social Darwinism thus served as a convenient rationale for nineteenth-century imperialism, which placed most of the tribal areas of the world under the domination of a handful of European nations.

Toward the end of the nineteenth century an important new emphasis appeared in sociology. Emile Durkheim exhorted his colleagues to shun easy formulas constructed by analogy and turn their attention to a strictly empirical approach. Durkheim's polemics stimulated a shift toward investigation and statistical analysis of "social facts," like the suicide rate (Durkheim 1951), as contrasted to philosophers' armchair speculations.

Anthropologists preferred firsthand field investigations of human behavior in situational context, according to a natural-history tradition, as their major methodological tool. Under the influence of Franz Boas (for example, 1940), who emphasized the development of more precise field operations, anthropologists were overwhelmingly preoccupied with the immense task of describing the unique and rapidly changing cultures of the many traditionally nonliterate societies of the world. They believed that a case-counting, clinical study and comparison of the cultures of a number of groups were more valuable than a statistical approach, except in certain circumstances. The field work on which the Lau case study is based was done according to a modification of this natural-history tradition. Under these circumstances anthropologists were slow to develop inductive generalizations from their field findings and deductive hypotheses related to them. There was also some confusion as to what precisely should be the appropriate units of research in relation to cultural problems.

At this point A. R. Radcliffe-Brown stepped in. Influenced by Durkheim and other sociologists, he emphasized a problem-centered approach and focused on "social structures" as the fundamental units for social research. He defined a social structure as "the totality of all social relations recognized according to social usage . . . in a suitable collection of individuals," (Radcliffe-Brown 1957: 152), which he called a "natural system." In what he conceived as the interest of empiricism in research, Radcliffe-Brown (1957: 19–22; 1958) attempted conceptually to isolate such "natural systems" from their "environments," including their culture-historical antecedents. He advocated an attempt to analyze, classify, and compare them. In this way he hoped to arrive at valid sociological laws.

Thus developed a school of thought that separated the study of social structure from the study of human behavior perceived as a complex event in situational context and in historical, biological, and geographical perspective (see Fortes 1953: 21). This school is called comparative sociology or social anthropology. Out of this movement, reinforced by the earlier constructs of Marx and Morgan, the theory of sociocultural evolution was reinforced. At present several variations of this approach are fashionable among contemporary social scientists and prehistorians.[2]

On the other hand, one of the most impressive findings of

cultural anthropology relates to the application of the principle of limited possibilities of change to social order. According to this principle, derived by applying the comparative method to observed social phenomena, a social order and even its several component features tend to change not in a random manner but according to certain limited possibilities and potentialities of change inherent in the order itself. The principle is probably most clearly illustrated by linguistic phenomena viewed as an expression of human cultural behavior. The grammatical categories of any language, for example, afford the speaker a limited set of forms out of the unlimited possibilities by which experience may be classified. Otherwise there could be no grammar. These categories change, if at all, only in certain predictable ways. Alexander A. Goldenweiser (1913) explained the relevance of the principle of limited possibilities of change, which he attributed to the psychic unity of mankind, to cultural phenomena. George Peter Murdock (1949: 115 ff.) demonstrated statistically that the principle can be applied appropriately to a sample of kinship systems of the world, although perhaps this aspect of his analysis has not received the attention it deserves. Ward H. Goodenough (1957: 153–154) suggested that the potential for change and development inherent in an ancestral culture may fruitfully be studied in Oceania.

Today, besides the old-fashioned natural-history approach, there are at least two basically different theoretical approaches available to a field anthropologist. On one hand, he may choose a social-evolutionary model, by which, regardless of environment, biogenetic heritage, or culture history, a human society is assumed, on account of its inherent dynamics, to "advance" or "develop" from a simple "primitive" social system to a complex "civilized" system. On the other hand, he may select an eco-cultural model, by which a society localized in a given ecological niche is thought to change under different kinds and degrees of stress toward greater or lesser balance, according to the limitations and potentials of its structure.

By the first approach, here called sociological, the future course of the society has been built into the research model. Its prediction, therefore, is not a fruitful area for scientific inquiry. Application of the findings from research of this type toward the solution of social problems is effectuated by reinforcing and accelerating the "natural" process of social "evolutionary development" or "advancement." Such reinforcement and acceleration may be implemented either by agents from outside the group or by the group itself or by both. (Erasmus 1961, 1967).

By contrast, according to the second, far less popular approach, here called ecological, prediction of the probable behavior of the group under changing conditions is the basic scientific problem. When prediction has been successfully achieved, the research findings may be applied toward the solution of the particular society's practical problems, not directly but rather by formulating, on the basis of the scientific findings, the realistic alternatives that the group faces under changing conditions at a designated moment in its history and by predicting the probable consequences of each alternative should it be selected and implemented by group action (see Barnett 1956: 158–170; Thompson 1967b). According to this approach, effective group action may be directly implemented only by members of the group themselves, not by agents from without. These points will be elaborated in later chapters (especially Chapter 21).

The study of social order within its geographic and historical context has received strong support by recent findings from ethology, the science of animal behavior. Systematic observation of the behavior of many different species, especially anthropoid apes and other primates, has produced convincing evidence that social order is an infrahuman phenomenon. Thus the social structure of a human community is not merely a fortuitous human behavioral characteristic but a very basic component of community organization extending backward to prehuman foundations (Count 1958; Hallowell 1961).

With these problems in mind, let us now turn to the relationship between society and culture based on firsthand field investigations of northern European indigenous communities in geographical, archaeological, and historical context.

Geological and Climatic Changes

As in the Pacific, the prehistory of man in northern Europe is closely related to the geology of the area and to its changing climate and ecology, especially during the last glacial (Würm) recession (c. 14000–8000 B.C.) and the immediate postglacial period (8000–4500 B.C.). In Europe the climate became warmer and drier as the last great glaciers melted and shrank toward the arctic. Climatic change fluctuated to a high degree and recession of the ice sheets was uneven. Prehistoric mammals that had adjusted genetically to glacial conditions moved northward, and their human hunters followed. During the transition period from the ice age to recent times, many animal species were unable to adapt successfully to planetary changes and thus became extinct. Apparently several species of the genus *Homo* also died out except insofar as they mixed with more flexible types and survived in hybrid form. Physical anthropologists differ on this point.

The great ice sheet had covered most of the area of northern Europe we are discussing. Because evidences of Paleolithic man are absent or rare in this area, we shall begin our explorations with the immediate post-Pleistocene era.

Mesolithic I (c. 8300 to c. 6800 B.C.)[3]

The first postglacial human cultures of northern Europe developed during the six millenniums of the Mesolithic (8300–2500 B.C.), between the end of the glacial epoch and the Neolithic. The main sequences of climatic, ecological, and cultural changes during the Mesolithic fall into three periods, designated Mesolithic I, II, and III respectively.

About 8300 B.C. the temperature began to rise from an average of 46.4 degrees F. to an average of 53.6 degrees in July, and the climate of what is now northern Germany changed gradually from subarctic to preboreal. The dwarf birch and willow flora of the late glacial era developed into forests of birch, pine, and willow. On the rims of marshes and shallow lakes formed by glacial melt water grew cotton grass, heather, birch, and pine. Peat laid down through plant decay formed the foundation for moor development, and the first postglacial moors began to form. These low moors provided the first humus layers in the north European lowlands.

These changes occurred during the Yoldia Sea phase of the Baltic. As the rising coasts of Denmark and Baltic Germany attained a height of about 400 feet above their present elevations, the Yoldia Sea gradually changed into a large brackish lake, called the Ancylus.

Mesolithic I was also characterized by a transitional fauna. Such tundra and steppe species as reindeer, arctic fox, white grouse, arctic hare, and wild horse appeared with such forest forms as beaver, roe deer, wild pig, red deer, and aurochs, or wild ox. The obi, banded lemming, pika, and glutton of the previous era had already disappeared from northern European sites.

Intrusive Tanged-Point Culture

During Mesolithic I a homogeneous culture flourished over much of the northern European plain from Belgium to the Ukraine. Although there were minor local variations, this culture was generally characterized by flaked flint implements with tanged points and by simple forms of microliths, burins (pointed cutting tools), and scrapers. The absence of such heavy equipment as axes indicates that this culture was not geared to handle a dense forest environment. We can thus surmise that the forests were usually open and parklike.

It is believed that the Tanged-Point culture was related to certain Upper Paleolithic traditions of central and eastern Europe. Dominant in the northern European lowlands during Mesolithic I, it survived in parts of Scandinavia throughout the Mesolithic and contributed to the later megalithic civilization of the Neolithic era there (see Table 1).

Lyngby Forest Culture

Alongside the Tanged-Point culture a new tradition on the northern plain developed in response to the gradual encroachment of forests. This is called the Lyngby culture, distinguished especially for its hafted axes and adzes of reindeer antler (Childe

1931: 326). This innovation, obviously created to resolve new problems of living, is significant because it developed into the distinctive northern forest cultures of Mesolithic II and later periods.

Evidences of the Lyngby culture have been found most frequently in Denmark and southern Sweden (which were then connected by a land bridge), as well as sporadically from Poland to Haltern in Westphalia.

Mesolithic II (c. 6800 to c. 5000 B.C.)

About 6800 B.C., during the Ancylus Lake period of the Baltic, the preboreal climate of northern Europe gave way to a warmer and drier boreal phase, when the July temperature averaged 53.6 to 57.2 degrees F. Birch and pine became dominant with alder and mixed forest (elm, oak, lime) coming in. Hazel became important toward the end of the period, when the July temperature rose to an average of about 62.6 degrees F. The all-pervasiveness and density of the virgin forest in Europe at this time have been stressed by Grahame Clark (1952: 14). The forest line extended farther northward than it does today and was about 684 feet higher in the Scandinavian mountains than the present line (Shetelig and Falk 1937: 53). It was probably during this period that the great amber deposits of the Baltic and west Jutland coasts, which later became important in trade with southern Europe, were formed from resin exuded by the conifer forests and small peat bogs formed in the German lowlands.

The reindeer survived into this period. Elk and aurochs were common, as well as forest and lake animals, especially roe deer, wild pig, and beaver. The dog, man's first tame animal, appeared in northern Europe at this time.

Maglemose Lakeside Culture

The dominant northern European way of life in Mesolithic II was the Maglemose, a lake and riverside culture that developed out of the Lyngby tradition. The Maglemose was a homogeneous, widespread culture. Members of this class lived on the (by now) densely forested northern European plain from eastern

Table 1. Ecological and Cultural Sequences, North European Culture Area

| Prehistoric or Historic Period | Chronology | ECOLOGY | |
		Climatic Phase	Forest Sequence
Modern	A.D. 1930s–1940s		
Early Modern	19th c.	warmer, drier	
Reformation	16th c.	climatic nadir	moor, heath, reduced bogs form
	13th c.	climate deteriorates to damp cold	
Late Medieval			
Medieval	800	atlantic	
Early Medieval	500–600	calm seas, low tides	
Late Iron	300–450	drier, more continental	mixed oak
Early Iron	B.C. 400–300	land inundation storms, high tides	beech, pine
Bronze	850–750	rainfall increase, wet, cold	moors raised, bogs form, heather spreads, forest reduced
	1800–1500		
Neolithic	2000	dry, warm subboreal	oak climax
Mesolithic III	2500	moist, warm atlantic optimum	bogs form, alder, mixed oak, hazel
	5000	boreal	elm, oak, lime,
Mesolithic II	6800	preboreal	pine, birch
Mesolithic I	8300		
Würm recession		subarctic	dwarf birch, willow Dryas flora
Upper Paleolithic	14000	arctic	sanddune formation

	CULTURE	
Osnabrück *Northland*	*Early Northern Europe*	*Norse-Iceland*

mechanized tools Hitler regime		mechanized tools, industrialization sovereignty regained crafts disappear
World War I		
crafts disappear chemical fertilizer		nationalist movement Danish trade monopoly
Thirty Years' War free farms reemerge manors fail		Lutherans established religious strife
Black Death		famine and Black Death loss of sovereignty civil strife
feudalism, trading		Icelandic commonwealth settlement of Iceland
Frankish conquest		trading towns
Altsächische farms established		rise of Vikings, Norse Iron Age
Angles, Saxons migrate Roman threat, Goths		Danes conquer Jutland Angles, Saxons migrate Roman Iron
Teutonic conquest urnfields trade route shift		Cimbrians, Teutons, Burgundians migrate Celtic Iron (La Tène)
tumulus beakers		burial urns barrows, bronze casting
passage graves dolmens		conquest of Battle Axe People, passage graves, dolmens
	Ertebølle	
	Maglemose Lyngby	Tardenoisian Tanged Point

Britain to Poland and Estonia and from southern Norway and Sweden to central Germany, as well as on extensive lands that have since been submerged by the North Sea and the Baltic (Clark 1936: pocket map). The evidence indicates that the cradle area of the Maglemose culture was the wide land bridge between southern Sweden and Denmark that separated the then nearly dry North Sea from the Ancylus Lake. This is also the area of greatest frequency of Lyngby finds.

Maglemose sites are frequently found on slight prominences on the shores of what were then bogs, lakes, and rivers. They were mostly at or below sea level, never elevated as high as 600 feet. Because no definite traces of piles have been found, it seems probable that the sites were inhabited only during the dry season. The Duvensee site, an island in a bog, was habitable only during the dry season, for example, but five superimposed floors suggest that it was chosen as a settlement for five seasons. Apparently each season sand and clay, to accommodate a fire, were deposited on a floor of pine bark and birch laid over peat—evidence of artificial construction (Clark 1936: 91–92). The Maglemose people were freshwater fishermen, fowlers, and hunters who lived in small groups and undertook seasonal migrations. They spent the dry summer and autumn months on fen, lakeside, and river sites and apparently moved to less damp areas for the remainder of the year. They had no domestic animals except dogs and did not practice agriculture or make pottery. In contrast to most Mesolithic peoples the Maglemosians coped actively with the virgin forest by means of flint-bladed axes and adzes hafted with antler and wood. They fashioned tools from bone and antler, including barbed spearheads and barbless fish hooks, and they used flint microliths to tip arrows for hunting small game. They also decorated many objects of daily use with incised geometric patterns (linear chevrons, criss-cross lines) and with animal and anthropomorphic designs. V. Gordon Childe (1931: 329) suggests that this forest life fostered the isolation of small local communities for long intervals, particularly in winter. Such communities developed idiosyncratic cultures to cope with local conditions both through innovations and by borrowing inventions from others.

The scant evidence of Maglemose man indicates that he was tall, slight, and dolichocephalic (narrow) in head form. At least some individuals were buried in a crouching position accompanied by weapons and tools, like the arrow and chisel found with the "Archer of Barnum" near Skåne, Scania (Skovmand 1959a: 35–36).

Intrusive Tardenoisian Culture

Whereas the Maglemose folk inhabited the forested lowlands, people of quite another tradition spread to inland dunes and low hills where the forestation was sparse. These northern Tardenoisians, whose cultural counterparts have been found in southwestern Europe and north Africa, were a hunting, collecting, and fishing folk who had no heavy equipment like axes or adzes to clear forests. They lived in natural caves and rock shelters and also built windbreaks or temporary pit dwellings with branch frames covered with wattle and daub. Their culture was remarkably uniform and was characterized by a series of microliths of flint and stone. Northern Tardenoisian sites are found in eastern Britain, northern France, Belgium, Holland, the southern fringe of the north German plain (Teutoberg Forest and Bielefeld area), Franconia, Württemberg, Poland, and the western Ukraine. The sites are located mostly on sandy soils, never on loess (light fertile soil deposited by glacial winds), which attracted human settlement only after farming had been introduced. Grahame Clark (1936: 190) notes that it would be hard to find a better example of "geological control over human settlement." Because local Tardenoisian groups occupied areas of little value to Danubian farmers, who infiltrated the loess in the early Neolithic, it is likely that some of them persisted through the Neolithic into the early Bronze Age.

Mesolithic III (c. 5000 to c. 2500 B.C.)

Transgression of the North Sea bed had begun during Mesolithic II (c. 6500 B.C.) by a rapid process of land submergence. The land bar that had separated the Ancylus Lake from the North Sea became a wide strait. At the beginning of Mesolithic III, about

5000 B.C., a warm salt sea, called the Litorina, took its place. The temperature reached its maximum (62.6 degrees F. in July, 4.5 degrees above that of the present), and the boreal climate changed into a warm, moist atlantic type. Alder and mixed-oak forest became dominant. In Germany the rainfall became heavier than at present and extensive peat bogs developed. Gradually the moors grew out of reach of ground water until they could support only inconspicuous plants like bog moss.

By Mesolithic III reindeer had disappeared from the north European plain, elk were rare, and forest fauna (aurochs, red and roe deer, wild pig), as well as the dog, prevailed.

Persistence of the Maglemose Culture

Submergence of their heartland must have had a catastrophic effect on the Maglemose people. On the other hand, the isostatic rise of land nearer the center of the Scandinavian ice sheet made new lands available for settlement. In the higher latitudes, where the forest came late, the climate and ecology of Mesolithic III probably resembled that of the Maglemose culture cradle of period II. There is evidence that Maglemose populations, probably fleeing before the North Sea transgression, moved into central Sweden at this time. Furthermore, a late version of Maglemose culture developed in southwestern Norway during this period.

The semisedentary Maglemose communities apparently persisted locally through the Scandinavian Neolithic and even into the Bronze Age. Still more important, perhaps, the structure of the indigenous cultures that developed during the Mesolithic, especially the Maglemose, seem to have been the basis on which subsequent cultures in the region were built.

Ertebølle Seacoast Culture

The main cultural development in Mesolithic III was a sedentary coastal type of life that represented an adaptation of the Maglemose culture to the new living conditions created by the catastrophic Litorina marine transgression. The most vigorous development of this coastal culture, the Ertebølle, emerged south of the main inundated area, in Denmark and Schleswig-Holstein.

Whereas the Maglemosians undertook seasonal migrations, the Erteb∅lle folk were sedentary and their sites were often located on the Litorina seacoast. Abundant food supplies were apparently responsible for the more permanent settlement as well as for the rapid population growth. The Erteb∅lle people were salt-water fishermen and also gatherers of mollusks. They left quantities of kitchen middens (Clark 1936: 140). Regular burials have been found in the settlements, the body being laid in extended position and ringed by small boulders. The few new forms that appear mostly represent simple developments on inherited Maglemosian tradition, but bone combs and bracelets as well as pottery are new (Clark 1936: 153). Erteb∅lle pottery is distinguished by its coarse texture and the use of the coil technique. Large beaker shapes with pointed base and outcurved rim, as well as oval saucers with curved base, are common. Some have fingernail impressions on the rim. Erteb∅lle art is related to Maglemose art but is generally of poorer quality and occurs more rarely.

In short, archaeological evidence points to direct cultural continuity between Maglemose and Erteb∅lle despite a shift in emphasis to meet new living conditions. Coiled pottery, though unique, probably stemmed from a technique borrowed from Neolithic societies to the south and southeast.

Erteb∅lle in modified form, the so-called Dwelling Place cultures, persisted into the Neolithic era in Norway, Gotland, and East Baltic regions, especially where climatic conditions were unfavorable to agriculture. Underlying the obvious variations in the Dwelling Place cultures are "uniformities resulting (1) from the common heritage of the several groups, (2) from their constant interrelations, and (3) from their joint exposure to influence of the Ukrainian, megalithic and battle axe groups of food producers" (Childe 1931: 343).

Mesolithic Physical Types and Languages

Although skeletal material from the north European Mesolithic period is scanty, the basic physical element of the population, according to Carleton Stevens Coon (1939: 123), was probably "a long-headed Brünn-like Upper Paleolithic European survival." Possibly a brachycephalization (tendency toward broadening of the head form) of these surviving human types occurred in Europe during the Mesolithic. Toward the end of the Mesolithic a large, square-jawed brachycephalic (broad-headed with cephalic index of 81 or higher) type appeared called Borreby.[4]

Nothing is known of the languages spoken by the peoples of the northern European forest communities during the Mesolithic except that they definitely did not belong to the Indo-European stock from which most of the more recent European languages stem. The Indo-European stock apparently did not appear in Europe until the late Neolithic.

The Neolithic Period (2500 to 1500 B.C.)

During the third millennium B.C. the climate of northern Europe changed from the warm moist atlantic type, which had prevailed for the last 2,000 years of the Mesolithic, to a warm dry (drier than it is today) subboreal type. This change coincided with the beginning of a new rise in the land surface that decreased the size of the Litorina Sea. Bogs ceased to form and their surfaces dried sufficiently to allow forests to grow. In Germany bog plants were succeeded by such heath plants as cotton grass and heather. The mixed-oak forest of the previous epoch gave way to a dominant oak type. Although the elk and aurochs had virtually disappeared in Denmark, the red and roe deer and the wild boar were abundant.

Up to this time the north European forest communities had evolved an economy that yielded an abundant living without the aid of cultivated plants or domestic animals except the dog. During the third millennium, however, the significant climatic changes were paralleled by major cultural changes in indigenous communities, especially in the northern culture cradle that now centered in the Danish peninsula, southern Sweden, and Schleswig-Holstein. Herding and farming were gradually introduced into the cradle area from the south, along with new types of weapons, tools, and pottery.

Intrusive Dolmen Builders

The first permanent settlements of Dolmen (tomb) Builders in the northern cradle area were in Jutland, side by side with those of indigenous fishermen and hunters. The forebears of the Dolmen Builders are generally believed to have come from the Pyrenean region (Hawkes 1940: 170). They apparently arrived at the British Isles by way of the west coast of Europe and from there migrated to Jutland. The Dolmen Builders explored the North Sea coast and settled on or near the west coast of the Danish peninsula. They were apparently searching for small commodities of high value like copper, flint, and amber, a fossilized resin that had been exuded by the great conifer forests of the Mesolithic. Although they found no copper, the Baltic region and the west coast of Jutland were almost the only sources of amber, which became one of the main articles traded from the northern cradle to the Mediterranean.

As primitive herding agriculturalists, the Dolmen Builders were also attracted to light, dry, easily worked soils of glacial-moraine type, which were not located directly on the seacoast but on protected bays, fjords, and sandy riverbanks. Dolmen folk spread across Jutland and took firm root on its sheltered Baltic shores, in Zealand, and on adjacent islands. This area, especially Zealand, became the regional center of the Dolmen culture. Thus the geographic focus of this Neolithic development corresponded roughly to that of the Mesolithic period.

Much of our knowledge of the culture and physical type of the Dolmen people derives from their permanent megalithic tombs, many of which survive to the present as conspicuous landmarks. These giant tablelike structures composed of large stone slabs contain both skeletal material and grave goods. The findings suggest that the intrusive dolmen type of tomb was developed locally into a more complex long form with a side entrance, from a simple closed round prototype without a side entrance. The first dolmens may have been individual graves. Later, larger dolmens always accommodated several corpses. The Dolmen Builders, according to Coon (1939: 85), were tall, slender, and long-headed with moderate skull vault and face height. They are classed with the Mediterranean race.

The language of the Dolmen Builders is not known. It is believed that the peoples who spoke Indo-European did not penetrate western Europe until about 2000 B.C.

Dissemination of the megalithic people has been compared with the spread of proselyting missionaries introducing a new and powerful cult. They probably dominated native peoples of many lands not so much by conquest as by putative magical power connected with a cult that probably focused on sun worship. Furthermore, in the same way that the efficacy of the white man's technology often convinced the South Seas islanders of the superior mana of his God, the new and relatively efficient methods of food production of the newcomers may have helped convert Mesolithic man to the ideas of the Dolmen Builders.

From bones of animals found in the graves we assume that the Dolmen Builders were animal breeders who kept long-horned cattle, sheep, goats, and pigs, as well as dogs (Nordman 1935: 11). We also infer from impressions of seeds in the walls of their pots that they cultivated grain, including emmer, einkorn, wheat, and pygmy wheat. Barley was first cultivated during the Neolithic period but did not become the predominant domestic grain until the Bronze Age (Clark 1952: 108). Wool and flax, which was probably imported, are also found in dolmens. These first northern European farmers used the swidden (slash and burn) method of farming. They did not have fixed fields or fertilizer except the ash from the clearing fires and perhaps the dung dropped by herds as they grazed. Because there is no acceptable evidence for the use of the plow among the megalithic peoples of northern Europe, we assume that they cultivated the land with digging stick or hoe.

Dolmen Builders gradually spread into southern Sweden and along the northeastern German plain as far as the Oder River. They founded sporadic settlements in northwestern Germany along the lower Elbe River and the Elbe-Weser coast, in the middle Weser valley, on the Ems River and its Hase tributary (see Chapter 10), and in eastern Holland. But prehistoric farming in Europe never extended north of the deciduous forest boundary.

Development of the Northern Megalithic Culture

After their initial invasion of Jutland, the Dolmen Builders interbred with the natives. Skeletal material indicates that the
Neolithic population of southern Scandinavia was a mixed racial
type made up of both round-headed and long-headed individuals
(Coon 1939: 121–123). A cultural blend also developed that was
subsequently enriched by other exotic influences, especially the
invasion of the Battle Axe People. The development of this
blend in several subculture areas has been traced by a sequence
of megalithic tomb types and pottery styles. Megalithic tomb
types in the focal culture area of northern Europe apparently
evolved locally from the dolmen prototype to the local passage
grave form.

Passage graves are large rectangular or oval burial chambers
entered by a low narrow passageway. They were apparently
intended to be used by a family for successive burials over a
period of time. Some passage graves in Denmark and southern
Sweden contain the remains of one hundred individuals. The
contents of these graves suggest that although copper was in use
during this time it was probably imported from the British Isles
and central Europe; stone and flint still provided the basic materials for tools and weapons. Some of the forms of these implements, however, may have been borrowed from metal prototypes
found in community sites to the south. There is evidence of a
local development of dolmen-type pots, characterized by new
shapes and by subordination of decoration to form.

Two types of dwellings are associated with passage grave
finds in Jutland: small apsidal huts and two-roomed rectangular
houses built in a continuous row under an elongated gabled roof,
each house entered by a door in one long side (Childe 1950:
124).

Intrusive Battle Axe Folk

About 2000 B.C., when the Passage Grave culture was dominant
in Jutland, an abrupt break occurs in the development of pottery
types. The tombs of this period are often half-empty. Some of
them include a layer of early Passage Grave culture materials

covered by a layer containing material associated with a new culture. Earlier round and oval passage tombs are found throughout Denmark, but later types are absent in Jutland. The sudden break in cultural development coincides with the advent of invaders who came from the south and traveled down the Elbe into the Schleswig-Holstein area (Hawkes 1940: 217). These are the Battle Axe folk, also known as Corded People from the cordlike decorations on their pottery. Armed with stone battle axes, which were imitations of foreign metal axes and superior to the weapons of the Passage Grave People, these folk displaced or exterminated the population of south Jutland.

The invaders were culturally distinctive. They interred their dead in single shallow pit graves surmounted by a small bowl-shaped barrow. Each grave originally contained a single body in a contracted position, but as each subsequent burial was placed on top of the one below, a barrow represented a sequence of several generations. Besides stone battle axes, the graves of the Battle Axe People contain thick-butted flint axes with a slightly lopsided cutting edge, perforated amber disks, and a distinctive rough type of pottery decorated with cordlike lines.

It is generally assumed that Battle Axe People spoke an Indo-European language. They appear to have introduced into the northern cradle area Proto-Germanic, the speech from which all the Germanic languages developed.

Because the burials of the Battle Axe People in northern Europe were located near sources of trade commodities of small but high value, like amber, salt, and (later) tin, it seems that they were primarily adventurous traders, warriors, and herdsmen, rather than farmers. It is generally agreed that they came by several routes from the steppes of southern Russia. They probably rode horseback (Skovmand 1959b: 46).

A Late Neolithic Hybrid Culture

The Battle Axe People were also racially distinctive: tall and muscular, with long heads, long faces and prominent noses, and extremely high cranial vaults, according to Coon (1939: 85). As these invaders approached the east coast of Denmark they apparently no longer killed or drove out the Passage Grave population but rather mixed with it. A hybrid physical type and a fairly homogeneous cultural blend developed. The blend was characterized by a locally produced, precisely flaked flint dagger and by single burial in a large stone cist or grave-size dolmen that apparently stemmed from a combination of the megalithic collective stone cist and the Battle Axe single grave. Stimulated by influences from the south, this hybrid population created the brilliant civilization of the southern Scandinavian Bronze Age.

North European Bronze Age (1800–1500 to 400–300 B.C.)

No significant shift in climate marked the advent of the north European Bronze Age. The climate of the northern culture cradle in Jutland and Zealand remained mild and dry. There was little change in the species of wild fauna and flora of the area, but swidden agriculture gradually reduced the size of the oak-dominated forest zone. The proportion of such forest-feeding domestic animals as swine and oxen decreased, whereas the proportion of steppe and open-pasture domestic species, like sheep and horses, increased. Short-horned cattle probably supplanted longhorns during this time. Leaves and branches of trees, especially elm and lime, were collected for winter fodder.

Late Neolithic culture persisted into the early Bronze Age. The bronze casting process was introduced into southern Scandinavia from the Middle East about 1500 B.C. Because no copper or tin is found in this area the raw materials for making bronze were imported, tin probably from Cornwall and copper from central Europe.

The most conspicuous as well as the richest sites of the early Bronze Age in southern Scandinavia are the numerous grave mounds. Many such mounds have been preserved intact because of the veneration they inspire as dwelling places and spiritual homes of the dead. A barrow, measuring perhaps nine feet high and sixty feet across, was often located on top of a hill overlooking a wide area. It contained a body buried in a stone cist or hollowed tree trunk coffin, covered with stones and great quantities of turf. Many barrows contain several secondary burials, which consist of burned bones placed in pots or in simple holes in the sides of the mound. Grave goods include woven clothes of wool and fibers, weapons, and ornaments of bronze and gold. Occasionally complete outfits have been preserved. Bronze Age Northmen evidently believed that human life continued after death and that the dead had certain needs for their existence in the barrow. The living provided for these needs. The evidence suggests that toward the end of the Bronze Age (400–300 B.C.) cremation became the prevailing burial custom. A burial urn or cist was used as a repository for burned bones.

Objects that have been recovered from archaeological sites dated during this period reveal a very skillful development of the bronzesmith's art, which suggests wide-ranging trade relationships of communities in the northern cradle area (Piggott 1965: 239, map 134). The sensitivity and technical virtuosity of the northern craftsmen is well demonstrated by the *lur*, a musical instrument of bronze, by elegant carved decorations, and by horned helmets of bronze. Other artifacts, including cult objects suggestive of sun worship, such as the Trundholm sun chariot, have been found well preserved in bogs. Fertility in living creatures and in cultivated plants was apparently of great concern to the late Bronze Age and early Iron Age peoples of northern Europe (Klindt-Jensen 1957: 80). It is probable that specialized fertility functions associated with the Vanir gods, Njörd, Freyr, and Freyja, who figure in the early Icelandic literature, were related to religious practices of this time (see Chapter 8).

The Early Iron Age (400–300 B.C. to A.D. 300–450)

Beginning about the ninth century B.C. the climate of northern Europe underwent a rather sudden change. The warm dry subboreal climate, which had lasted throughout the Neolithic and most of the Bronze Ages, began to deteriorate to a wetter and colder subatlantic type. The change was marked by a sudden increase in rainfall about 850 B.C. (Navarro 1928: 71). A maximum tide-generating force of the sun and moon seems to have occurred during the fourth or third centuries B.C. (Pettersson

1914: 23–25), and storminess increased in the temperate regions of the Northern Hemisphere, with a maximum in the belt between Iceland, Scandinavia, and northern Germany.

The sudden climatic change and its aftermath upset the balance between nature and man in the Baltic–North Sea area. In the Emsland of northwestern Germany, where certain Old Saxon tribes eventually settled (see Chapter 10), the forests became thicker. Here and in what is now Denmark, Sweden, and Norway grain crops failed to mature because of the shortened growing season. They had to be harvested while still green (Clark 1952: 112), which reduced both the size of the crop and its nutritional value. Hardy cereals like barley, oats, and later the newly domesticated rye became dominant, and grass crops began to be cultivated for winter fodder, a practice that eventually led to the great haying industry of northern Europe. Milk products became an important part of the diet and ewes as well as cows were probably milked.

As the zone of cultivation in Europe contracted, agricultural communities situated on its northern periphery were forced either to move southward or to abandon farming altogether. Those located on small islands and peninsulas were apparently the most vulnerable. The Cimbrians and Teutons moved from the Limfjord distict in northern Jutland before 100 B.C. Somewhat later the Burgundians moved from Bornholm island in the southwestern Baltic to northern Germany. About A.D. 200 the Goths from Gotland island in the central Baltic moved across Russia toward the Black Sea. Such movements initiated the historic phenomenon known as the Teutonic migrations.

About A.D. 300, the climate of northern Europe again began to change. It became drier and more continental, approximating the present climate. Such weather conditions were a local manifestation of a widespread Eurasian climatic change. In central Asia the steppe lakes dried up and large populations who had lived on these lakeshores began to migrate. Tribe after tribe pressed westward and the Huns appeared in Europe (375). The Saxon migrations coincide with the early period of this climatic change (see Chapter 10). About 450 the Angles migrated from southern Jutland to Britain. Pushing westward along the Baltic, Slavic tribes separated Scandinavians from Germans. Danes from Zealand and nearby islands conquered Jutland and settled there (Skovmand 1959b: 67).

Conclusion

On the basis of research, which uses new, more precise dating methods, we are in a position to better understand the settlement of post-Pleistocene man in northern Europe. An examination of artifacts and skeletal material from scores of sites studied in relation to environmental changes reveals the kinds of changing situations that confronted postglacial human communities in Scandinavia and the adjacent north European coasts and lowlands. For each community the alternative to solving these practical problems more or less successfully was either to perish or to migrate. A review of this material also alerts us to the unique cultural developments that are obviously related to ecological successions based on postglacial climatic fluctuations in the region. These developments were centered in Jutland and the now-submerged land that lay between Denmark, Sweden, and adjacent areas. This region may be regarded as the cradle of the first major indigenous cultural development of northern Europe.

A description of this indigenous European culture complex has only just begun to be included in studies of world prehistory.[5] Its significance and the perspective it can give on the cultural history of Europe has not been fully appreciated, nor has its meaning been fully incorporated into sociological theory.

In Chapter 8 we shall attempt, on the basis of the available data, to reconstruct and to describe certain aspects of this northern European cradle culture at the dawn of the historical period in the early Viking age in this region.

Notes

1. The research in northern European culture history on which this chapter is based was facilitated by two grants from the Humanities Division of the Rockefeller Foundation (1950, 1951) and by a grant from the Faculty Research and Development Fund of North

Carolina State College (1960). I take this opportunity to express my gratitude to the officers and trustees of these institutions.

2. See, for example, Childe 1951; Clark 1952: 15–17, 1962; Piggott 1961, 1965; Sahlins and Service 1960; Titiev 1963; White 1959; Wolf 1966.

3. Information regarding Mesolithic, Neolithic, and Bronze Age communities of the North Sea–Baltic area is based mainly on archaeological, paleontological, and paleobotanical evidence. Cultural sequences have been reconstructed by archaeologists and cultural historians with the help of geological, climatic, and ecological background studies and of historical and other relevant written documents, so that the outline of post-Pleistocene cultural development in this region is now fairly clear. It should be understood, however, that archaeological discoveries, which may change the picture, are being made at a rapid rate. The present summary of the research of others is based on many sources. Especially useful to English-speaking readers are the following: Childe 1931, 1950; Clark 1936, 1952; Hawkes 1940; Klindt-Jensen 1957; Shetelig and Falk 1937; Sprockhoff 1938; Turville-Petre 1964.

4. According to Coon (1939: 124), this northern Borreby type differs from the brachycephalic Alpine in that "the vaults are higher, the orbits somewhat lower, the faces larger, the jaws heavier . . ." Also the northern Borreby are taller than the Alpines.

5. See, for example, Piggott 1961: Ch. 12; Clark 1962: Chs. 3, 6.

8 /

RISE OF THE VIKINGS

Better is it to die with honour, than to live in shame.

Flateyjarbók (Du Chaillu 1889 [2]: 107)

From 500–600 A.D. a climate optimum occurred in the North Sea–Baltic region. Tide-generating forces are believed to have reached a minimum. This change resulted in calm seas even in winter, according to Sven Otto Pettersson (1914: 21–22). Such tidal and climatic conditions favored sea roving and contributed to the rise of the Vikings. At this time until about 1100, Iceland and Greenland had a comparatively mild climate.

By the eighth century a distinctive Iron Age culture (Norse) and language (Old Norse) had emerged in Scandinavia.[1] Knowledge of this indigenous European development, especially its climax form—the Viking way of life—is fairly detailed due to recent archaeological research and also to relevant analyses of historical, literary, legal, and other documents.[2] For comparison with other case studies in this section, I have attempted in this chapter to present a brief description of certain aspects of early Viking social structure and values in situational context.

Geography

The map of Scandinavia reveals several striking features, including an extensive shoreline that is deeply indented by fjords, especially on the coast of Norway. A central mountainous region separating Norway from Sweden is cut by steep valleys opening in the west toward the sea. Except for glaciation in the far north this region was heavily forested. The combination of high latitude, limited resources, and seaward exposure created an environment that posed certain major problems and threats to early

Iron Age Scandinavians and set the stage for their solutions to these problems. The culture that the Northmen developed to solve these problems was based on sheep and cattle herding, farming, and fishing. They built superior wooden sailing ships (Stang 1959: 110), which they used for extensive seasonal trading and raiding.

Physical Type

Viking skeletal material has been classed into two types (Steffensen 1953: 95): an eastern type from Denmark, Sweden, and southern Norway, characterized by a high frequency of blood group A genes and long heads; and a western type from northern Norway, the British Isles, and Iceland with a high proportion of group O genes and medium head form. Both types probably had light eyes, but the easterners are presumed to have had lighter hair than the westerners, who resembled present-day Icelanders in pigmentation and blood grouping.

Settlements, Trade, and Language

Archaeological evidence reveals that during the early Viking period (sixth to eighth centuries) there were two main types of permanent settlements: isolated farmsteads and village communities (Arbman 1961: 29). An apparently self-sufficient farmstead excavated at Edsirken (Sweden) included a farmhouse, several small sheds, a smithy, a burial mound, and a burial field that seems to have been intended for slaves. As the population increased, the lighter soils—moraine and sand—were settled. By the seventh century there were farms in Norway on marginal mountain land that has since been abandoned. Although they were used for pasture, heavier clay soils were not cultivated until effective methods of drainage were developed in the eighteenth century.

During the period of Charlemagne's conquest of the Saxons (c. 800) certain Scandinavian towns, especially those located on strategic harbors where trade routes crossed, became important trading centers. A trading town site from the period has been found at Hedeby, at the root of the Jutland peninsula, and at

Birka, located in Lake Mälar on Björkön island off the east coast of Sweden. Excavations reveal that these towns were protected by hill forts and earthworks. Cemeteries were located outside the fortified areas. Such towns were apparently the homes of professional merchants (Arbman 1961: 34–42), and traders from many lands visited them (Skovmand 1959c: 111–114). There were also summer trading camps like Kaupang, in Skiringsal on the west side of Oslofjord in Norway. These seasonal marketplaces were not fortified, although they did have cemeteries. Viking trade routes eventually extended across Russia into the Mediterranean by way of the Caspian and Black Seas. The Vikings sailed along the coast of Norway westward to Iceland and Greenland, to the British Isles, and southward through the Strait of Gibraltar to the Mediterranean and North Africa.

During the Viking era and at least until the twelfth century, Old Norse, a north Germanic language of Indo-European stock, was spoken in all of Scandinavia. It was also commonly used in Viking colonies, which were located mainly in the British Isles and in Normandy, on the coasts of the Baltic, in Wendish territory east of the Elbe, and in Russian Novgorod and Kiev. The Vikings traded furs, slaves, timber, amber, woolen cloth, tallow, falcons, fish, and walrus ivory in exchange for wine, silver, fine cloth, jewelry, spices, honey, and weapons.

Young Vikings found it exciting and profitable to engage also in private plundering expeditions in the summer (the remainder of the year was devoted to farm management, rest, and recreation). Viking strategy depended on sudden stealthy attack and quick escape. Their sailing ships were designed and their boat groups were organized with an emphasis on the maneuverability such forays required.

The Local Community

A local community was called a *her*. It consisted of a group of kindreds joined together for mutual protection and welfare (Du Chaillu 1889 [1]: 478, 491). Such a group of kindreds was held together by allegiance to a popular *hersir* (leader) and by membership in a legal order centered in a *thing* (popular judicial assembly; see Grönbech 1931 [1]: 381). A *hersir* led a *her* in warfare, in the administration of justice, and in religious functions.

A *her* inhabited a tract of land called a *herad*. Such a tract was divided for purposes of land use into private property and commons. Apparently there were two major types of private property: *odal* land and *kaup* land. The latter was freehold, unattached land that could be bought or leased. The title to *odal* land was unencumbered and independent of any superior agent. *Odal* land could not be alienated from the owning family except in cases when kinsmen had the right of redemption (Du Chaillu 1889 [1] 479–482). In Norway, according to Dame Bertha S. Phillpotts (1913: 67), "*Odal* land—land which had been inherited from grandfather's grandfather—could not be alienated unless first offered to the odal-sharers, i.e. those other kinsmen who had an inherited claim to it. In default of nearer kinsmen, these might be as distant as second cousins."

The right of preemption of ancestral land by kinsmen under certain circumstances persisted all over northern Teutonic Europe until after the Middle Ages except in Iceland and England. Indeed, there are still farms legally classed as *odal* in Sweden, Norway, and Lower Saxony (see Chapter 10).

Herad lands that were not held privately as well as adjacent seacoasts and waters were called commons (*almenning*). Common land was used by members of the *her* and others by permission under the administration of the *hersir*. According to Du Chaillu (1889 [1]: 483):

> Every one had the right to make use of wood and water on these commons: to build himself [a chalet], as well as smithies and hunting-huts; to fish in the waters, hunt and trap animals; to cut timber and mow grass, observing the previous rights of an earlier user. The settler ought then to fence around his property within twelve months.

The Popular Assembly

The most famous institution of the Norse community was the popular deliberative assembly (*thing*). It had more judicial and legislative than executive duties and seems to have emerged early in the northern culture cradle. The social structure was equalitarian to the extent that it lacked hereditary monarchs, powerful and professional magistrates, a sacerdotal class, a military aristocracy, and even an organized police (Veblen 1915: 44; Shetelig and Falk 1937: 263–264). The popular deliberative assembly was obviously an institution well equipped to deal with certain community or neighborhood problems in such a society.

Roles of authority—the *hersir*, the lawspeaker (who "spoke" from memory the unwritten legal code), and the skald (Norse poet and reciter of heroic poems)—were assigned by the assembly. Such honorary titles were bestowed by the community on individuals who possessed special aptitudes, wisdom, character, or rank. Such roles carried heavy responsibilities relating to problem solving.

Judicial System

In Norse society there were traditionally no judges, magistrates, or even lawyers in the customary sense. According to Thorliefur Gudmundsson Repp (1832: 148): "In all Northern Courts the magistrates and lawmen were, at first, only *Hegemones*,—mere conductors of the process, who took care that legal forms were observed, without being judges." The Norse judicial system was thus essentially different from that of many Celtic-speaking peoples and, of course, also from the court system of Rome. But it fitted into the northern European preferred concept of society as a community that considered every freeman in good standing to have sanctity and where executive functions were not lodged in an executive officer but were diffused throughout the community in the form of social sanctions, especially regarding the responsibilities of kindreds.

The Norse wager of law developed within the Norse judicial system. This ancient institution may perhaps best be understood by a study of its linear descendant, the early Saxon wager of law that apparently closely resembled the prototype form. Trial by battle preceded both. According to Repp (1832: 38), "A man, when accused of a crime, either paid a certain fine, or if he wished to prove his innocence, he provided himself with a certain number of men, who assisted him, while he by oath cleared himself of the crime with which he was charged." The number of conjurators varied according to the seriousness of the crime. The mildest offense required the oath of three conjurators; more severe crimes, six. The most severely censored crimes required the oath of eleven conjurators plus the defendant, who had the right to choose his own jurors. Scholars believe that, unless the conjurators were in unanimous agreement, the accused was considered to be guilty (Repp 1832: 38–39, 141). No judges were employed, the functions of a judge being performed by the conjurators (Repp 1832: 40, 148).

The northern European trial by jury developed out of the wager of law. Both institutions demonstrated the power of the jury over the lawspeakers. But whereas the wager of law required unanimity of twelve or less conjurators to establish the innocence of the defendant, in a trial by jury the requirement was a majority oath of at least twelve (Repp 1832: 141–142, 146, 189–190).

The usefulness of both the wager of law and the trial by jury, without a judge, depended on the value attached to a freeman's word or oath as an expression of his personal honor. The system reflects, perhaps more sharply than any other institution, the Norse code of respect for the personal honor and integrity of the free adult male. The ancient Hebrews and early Christians valued a man because he was believed to have been created in the image of the deity. The Romans respected citizens because they were empowered by some high-ranking or dominant personage. In Norse culture a freeman was valued because he himself was considered worthy of respect, even sacrosanct. If he lost his free status, he also lost his honor. Women, minors, lunatics, criminals and outlaws, for example, could not function as jurors (Repp 1832: 183–184).

The traditional Northmen's concept of the nature of man was incompatible with that introduced by the Roman Catholic clergy. Although the foreigners adopted from the natives the use of the oath as a reflection of the personal honor of the swearer, they favored the trial by ordeal, which was dependent on the miraculously expressed will of God, as an instrument for determining a man's guilt or innocence.[3] Catholic doctrine also shifted the emphasis from the authority of the individual's own inner integrity to the authority of an externally imposed, magically expressed sign of a single, absolute, and immutable power figure. Toward the latter part of the thirteenth century there was a tendency to abolish the jury. During the eighteenth century it virtually disappeared in Scandinavia.

Social Classes

Thus, in early Viking society several social classes were distinguished. The most clearly defined status was that of freeman landowner (*bondi*). The *bondi* of a *her* administered it through a popular assembly (*thing*), where laws were made and unmade. The members of the assembly chose their leader (*hersir*), who led them in time of scarcity or war and presided over the *thing* and the *hof* (temple or sanctuary). The Vikings conferred the title of *jarl* on distinguished warriors. After the development of kingdoms in northern Europe, the members of a *thing* had the power to approve the title of *kon* (king).

There was also a low class of thralls, who were often foreigners captured in raids. Thralls were classed as property along with cattle and goods (Du Chaillu 1889 [1]: 508). They were believed to lack souls and were not held legally accountable for their deeds (Grönbech 1931 [1]: 276, 278).

The Kindred

The basic kinship unit of the Viking homeland was the kindred, which may be defined as a bilateral unit in which both sides of the family—the father's and the mother's relatives—were considered in reckoning descent. From the viewpoint of any member, such a kindred may be viewed as an overlapping set of circles or "sibs" of kin, with ego at the center of the primary circle. By this system, according to Radcliffe-Brown (Radcliffe-Brown and Forde 1950: 15):

> A man's sib were all his cognates within a certain degree. One method of arranging the sib was by reference to the human body and its "joints" (*glied*). The father and mother stand in the head, full brothers and sisters in the neck, first cousins at the shoulders,

second cousins at the elbow, third cousins at the wrists, fourth, fifth, and sixth cousins at the joints of the fingers. Finally come the nails, at which would stand the seventh cousins. On one scheme these nail kinsmen (*nagel magas*) were not included in the sib, though they were recognized as kinsmen (*magas*) if known to be such. The sib therefore included all kinsfolk up to and including sixth cousins . . .

In this ephemeral configuration each circle of kin interacted with the primary central circle. From the standpoint of ego, the circle may be viewed as composed of concentric rings of kin representing, from innermost to outermost, the degrees of kinship to ego recognized by the community. The number of such concentric rings that were recognized as kin varied among the Germanic-speaking groups up to seventh cousins.

The greatest equality of function and status between members of a kindred related through males and those related through females prevailed in Denmark, Schleswig, and southern Sweden, the cradle area that Dame Phillpotts (1913: 255–256, 260–261, 269) found to be the historical stronghold of the prototype northern kindred system. In Norway, Iceland, England, central and southern Germany, and to some extent among the Lower Saxons of northwestern Germany, on the other hand, persons related through males were favored and the kindred system tended to break down and disappear at an early date.

To grasp this kindred model we must keep a firm hold on ego, the individual from whose vantage point we are describing the kindred at any one moment, since the set-up varies according to the angle from which it is being constructed. Anthropologists and other students of man have experienced less difficulty describing unilineal types of kinship systems such as clans than describing bilateral types such as the prehistoric Teutonic kindreds. In the unilateral system ego is presumed to be in a fixed, lineal position in relation to his ancestors and descendants, and the relationships can be depicted fairly adequately by means of linear genealogical charts and diagrams. Obviously, a bilateral system cannot be so diagramed. Unilineal genealogy fits readily into contemporary Western thought patterns that reflect preferences for a linear codification of "common sense" reality (Lee

1959: 105–120) and simplistic location of objects in "absolute" space and "absolute" time (see Whitehead 1925: 74 ff., 85 ff.). A bilateral system like the kindred, on the other hand, might be rendered more accurately by a number of intervolving geometric figures, with several egos, each one at the center of his own concentric circles of kin.

A kindred in the northern cradle culture did not necessarily have a special name although it might be designated by a place-name if it were associated with a particular farmstead. In Iceland, where the patronymic system still prevails, I found that even today family lines (*aettir*), although of utmost social importance, are rarely named except when they are related to well-known ancestral farms or such eminent ancestors as the Sturlung (see Chapter 9). Some individuals in modern Iceland, following the modern Danish custom, have arbitrarily selected family names.

Viking kindreds were self-limiting as to size. Regarding this point, Dame Phillpotts (1913: 274) stated:

> . . . once kinship is reckoned through both sexes, we have to take into account the fact that the various branches of a man's kindred will no longer share a common name, will in fact, no longer be related to each other as well as to himself, and the unwieldiness of the kindred will increase in proportion to the number of unrelated groups in it.

Compared with an individual's status in unilineal descent systems, in a bilateral system it is not built irrevocably into a prototype kindred by an individual's birth, age, or generation. To a considerable extent an individual's place in life might be a function of his activities, his character, and his personality. Marriage rather than birth might be socially the most important event in his life.

In short, the indigenous kindred structure of northern Europe was an open system. Rather than perpetuating the status quo, it afforded an individual maximum mobility and flexibility to respond to environmental pressures. The Viking kindred structure allowed emergence of real leadership based on talents, charisma, and achievements rather than on formal ascription. Witness the selection of the *hersir, jarl,* and *kon.*

Kindred Solidarity and the Blood Feud

In the northern cradle culture the blood feud, as an expression of kindred solidarity, is well documented. According to Dame Phillpotts (1913: 3), by traditional kindred solidarity we imply

> that not only do individual kinsmen act on occasion so as to further a kinsman's prospects or shield him from a penalty, but that this kinsman becomes the centre of a united group of kindred, who act on his behalf, partly perhaps because they have his prospects at heart, but mainly because public opinion, the law, and their own views of life, make them guilty with him, and almost equally liable to penalty; or, in the event of his death by violence, throw the responsibility for vengeance or satisfaction upon the whole group, not only on a few near kinsmen.

The individual's next of kin were responsible for avenging him in case of injury or death inflicted by a nonmember. Vengeance took the form of retaliation on the slayer or his next of kin. The system of retaliation was a key survival device in a society whose controls were diffused throughout the community or neighborhood rather than centralized in the form of such coercive agents as a sacerdotal class or a police system. The blood feud reflected and promoted the internal cohesion and solidarity of the kindreds. It is hardly surprising, therefore, that responsibility to avenge one's kin acquired moral sanctions and became one of the main tenets of the traditional Norse moral code, discussed below. The blood feud in the early northern culture cradle was essentially an interfamily, intratribal protective device. Out of it arose conflicts of duty that, under the implicit ethical code, took the form of moral problems (see Chapter 9).

Customary Law and the Wergild

Blood vengeance was superseded in north Germanic customary law by payment, called wergild, made by the responsible party to compensate an injured person or the relatives of a slain person. Accordingly, every freeman had his *rétt*, or indemnity value due the family as redress for the slaying of a member. Exact compensation for any one individual depended on his status in the family and the position of the family in the community.

According to evidence presented by Dame Phillpotts (1913: 265–271), in its early form the wergild was apparently paid in three installments. An individual was responsible for payment, or was due payment, in proportion to his degree of kinship with the slayer or the slain, and the amount of liability of any given degree on the slayer's side usually equaled the claim of that same degree on the side of the slain. The claims and responsibility of the kindred were higher than those of the heirs, and there was no distinction in wergild payment rates between persons related through females, whether on the paternal or on the maternal side. The father's and the mother's kin were also treated exactly alike in the matter of payment. In later northern European forms, wergild indemnity rates increased according to the importance of the slain's position in the society, and the position of the slayer was not taken into account. By contrast, in many Germanic feudal societies, as well as among Celtic-speaking peoples (H. Hubert 1934b: 217), wergild rates were computed in accordance with the rank of both the slain and the slayer.

The concepts of *rétt* and wergild were based on the tenet that the person and the honor of a freeman were *fridheilag* (sacred or peace-holy) and inviolate unless he forfeited his right to peace (Du Chaillu 1889 [1]: 544). For every breach of sacredness of person, not only in deed but also in word, a freeman could claim redress according to his *rétt*. He might lose this right by neglecting to fulfill his kindred obligations, especially by failure to avenge a kinsman.

Thus, a crime within this social system was not expiated by payment to a king or other state official as Roman law required or by penance to a supreme deity through the intercession of ecclesiastical authorities as canon law demands. In Viking society a crime could only be expunged by direct compensation to the injured man and his family. In northern Europe schemes and rates of compensation were not meted out by a judge or priest as among the Romans, the Hebrews, the Roman Catholics, and the early Celtic-speaking peoples. On the contrary, they were determined by customary law.

Outlawry

Individuals who committed the ultimate offenses against society (the worst crime was a violation of the sanctity of the kindred) were removed from society by the supreme punishment. This was not physical chastisement, a reprimand that was unthinkable to a Northman in regard to a freeman (Wax 1957: 325), nor was it the capital punishment prevalent in Romanized Europe. The most severe Viking punishment was complete social ostracism or outlawry. The protection and help of the community and its laws were withheld permanently from the offending member. An outlaw forfeited his *rétt*. He was forced to leave family and kin, relinquish honor, fortune, and property, and either migrate elsewhere or withdraw into the wilderness. The institution of outlawry was thus a device that allowed the community to repudiate an offending member and thereby to protect itself against disorganization from within. (Lange 1935: Ch. 5). By eliminating those considered morally unfit, it may have operated also as a measure of genetic health and population control.

The significance of outlawry, which deprived a man not of his life but his honor and reputation, is further illuminated within the context of Norse beliefs regarding death. Unlike certain Celtic-speaking peoples, the Norse did not believe that the ego extended beyond death by transmigration (H. Hubert 1934b: 231–232; Caesar 1951: 32–33). The ancient Northmen also did not possess a concept of personal immortality like that of the Christians and that of the supposedly intrusive Odin cult.[4] Evidently the Norse believed that the spirits of ancestors continued to live in their home territories, where they might exercise a beneficent influence over the fortunes of the family. A Northman lived beyond death chiefly through the perpetuation of his record of outstanding deeds in poetry, song, and saga. To become a hero was the ultimate goal, to become an outlaw, the greatest punishment.

Devices for Strengthening the Kindred

In this society the individual with a large, strong, and able kindred had a distinct advantage. It is not surprising, therefore, that the Vikings had various institutions besides marriage that permitted a man to increase and strengthen his near of kin. Such institutions performed this function as foster kinship (by which a child belonging to one kindred was raised by a member of another, thus becoming a foster member of the family of his foster father), blood brotherhood (a symbolic exchange of blood between two men who were not brothers in order to create a strong kinship tie), and adoption or "leading into the kin." The ceremony to make an illegitimate son a rightful heir has been described as follows:

> There shall be made a banquet with three casks of ale, and slaughter a three-year-old ox and flay the skin from its right foreleg and make a shoe thereof and set it by the side of the ale tankard; then shall he first step into the shoe who leads the man into the kin, then he who is to be led into the kin, then he who has granted him the conditions of heirship, and then he that has granted the allodial impartible freehold law, and then all the other kin (Olrik 1930: 21).

These institutions functioned as group self-help mechanisms that allowed certain individuals, regardless of birth or parentage, to become part of the kindred system. But they also afforded a means by which the kindred institution might be reinforced at critical points, made more flexible, and perpetuated.

The Kindred as a Mutual Insurance Society

According to the available evidence,[5] we infer that the traditional northern kindred also functioned as a group self-help organization, a sort of mutual insurance society. It cared for its destitute orphans, widows, infirm, and aged people, and it took responsibility when natural catastrophies or accidents such as floods or fire befell its members. It was, however, a freeman's responsibility to maintain his parents, children, brothers, and sisters if they were in want or unable to work. Such devices as infanticide, abortion, widow strangling, and euthanasia were practiced, apparently functioning as population control and conservation measures, mainly at the discretion of the family.

According to northern European core values, monogamous

marriage was the ideal state for both sexes. Both spouses had rights in their joint estate. Divorce was apparently rather easily obtained by either party, but chastity before marriage and fidelity after it were the ideal, a standard by no means always honored (See Ibn Fadhlan 1948).

The vital role of these mutual insurance measures in maintaining the population balance and group health is suggested by the fact that wergild payments and certain self-help functions of the extended family survived in modified form until after the Reformation in many parts of northern Europe (Phillpotts 1913: Ch. 8). Infanticide, euthanasia, and the ideal of monogamous marriage for all adults, including the priesthood, persisted among the converted Northmen for centuries despite the proscription of these customs by the Roman Catholic church. After the Reformation, marriage of the clergy reemerged throughout the northern culture area in the doctrine and practices of the Lutheran church.

Monogamous Marriage, Key-Link in the Kindred System

In the traditional northern social system, the individual's deepest loyalties bound him primarily to his blood kin on both the father's and the mother's sides of his kindred. The balance of the social structure actually depended on the socially equivalent value of pairs of kindreds. And the connecting link between the individual's two sets of kin was, of course, the monogamous marriage of his parents. A man might have several concubines, but he had only one legal wife. Her status and her rights and privileges were clearly defined according to law. Any other type of marriage would have given ego three or more sets of kindreds. Within the context of the northern core culture, polygyny or polyandry would have critically disturbed the internal balance of the kindred structure.

The major ties of each partner in a monogamous marriage were to his own blood kin. As in Iceland today, when a woman married she did not assume the name of her husband. Traditionally there were no family names as such. Inasmuch as the strong bonds of blood kin demanded heavy obligations and privileges that tended to pull marriage partners apart, it is easy to understand why the traditional northern social system bolstered the institution of monogamous marriage with strong social sanctions.

The Viking Household

Monogamous marriage was also the foundation of the traditional northern household. Thus, the weakness of the family unit in a kindred-oriented society was to some extent alleviated by its strength as the core of an important property-owning local unit.

The Viking household group consisted of a nuclear family usually enlarged by dependent kin from both the husband's and the wife's relatives. It was also strengthened through the support of foster kin, laborers, servants, and slaves. And it included the domestic animals of the family, especially cattle, sheep, and horses, which represented its wealth. Management of the farmstead was the responsibility of the husband, the person who had the right to occupy the high seat in the hall. During his absence, however, the wife might take over the farmstead decision making.

The household, which occupied a complex of wooden buildings, including a hall or dwelling house, sheltered strangers who sought its protection. A guest, no matter what his relations to the host, occupied a special, honored place. So long as he remained under the host's roof—three days was the customary length of a visit—he was welcomed, given food and drink, and protected from harm. The strength of this hospitality custom is revealed in the Eddas, a collection of Old Norse poetry and mythology, and also, of course, in the Icelandic sagas (see Chapter 9).

Norse Deities[6]

The original Vanir gods were a "race" of specialized deities associated with fertility, peace, and plenty. Njörd (also known as Niördr) was god of the sea, ships, and wealth; Freyr, the son of Njörd, was the god of fertility, fruitful harvests, and peace; and Freyja, the amorous, seductive daughter of Njörd, was goddess of fertility and the ever recurring cycle of birth and death.

Freyja was also a witch who controlled much feared evil magic (*seid*), gold, and jewels. Horses, especially stallions, and boars were particularly venerated in Vanir sacrificial fertility rites, their flesh being eaten as part of the Freyr cult, which was especially popular in Iceland.

The Vanir lived in Vanaheimr, but they dwelled among the Aesir, another "race" of gods whose home was Ásgard. The gods were conceived as forming a community oriented toward peace and plenty and organized along the same lines as a human community. The gods, for example, were believed to meet in judiciary assemblies as humans did. Their great function, however, was to hold off the mighty "race" of giants who lived in the fearsome frozen region of the north and threatened to overwhelm both gods and men.

Thor held an honored place among the ancient Norse gods. He presided in the air and governed the elements—including thunder, lightning, winds, and rain—as well as fair weather and crops. According to Hector Munro Chadwick (1912: 396):

> Thor is represented as a middle-aged man of immense bodily strength. He is well disposed towards the human race and looked upon as their protector against harmful demons, to whom he is an implacable foe. . . . we have descriptions of Thor's adventures with giants, in which he is generally represented as breaking their skulls with his hammer. He uses no weapon except the hammer, and when he travels he either walks or drives in a car drawn by goats. When he comes to the assembly of the gods he is said to wade through certain rivers on the way. His escort never consists of more than three persons; very often he goes alone . . .

Apparently in Norway and Iceland, on the northwestern periphery of Europe, Thor was never displaced by Odin (Turville-Petre 1964: 25, 65–66, 86–90), whom many scholars believe to have originated outside the northern culture cradle. It was Thor, not Odin, who was pitted against Christ and who generated anxiety among early Christian converts in Iceland (Turville-Petre 1964: 89; Craigie 1914: 112). There Thor was considered to be the "strongest" of the gods. This meant that Thor was accorded first place among the deities according to the Northmen's concept of a leader as the first among equals. As might be expected, there was no traditional concept of a supreme, dominant deity among the ancient native peoples of Scandinavia nor even that of dominant power as such (Turville-Petre 1964: Ch. 2; Grönbech 1931 [1]: 276). Thor retained his prominent place among the native deities until the eleventh century, when he was displaced not by Odin but by Christ. After the conversion, the cross was substituted for Thor's hammer (Craigie 1914: 13).

Even in eastern Scandinavia, where Odin displaced Thor as primary deity at least among the warrior class during the Teutonic migrations, Thor remained popular among the lower classes. Chadwick (1912: 394–395) stated:

> In Iceland, for which our records are most full, there is practically no evidence for the worship of Othin. Thor is by far the most prominent figure, and after him Frey; occasionally also we hear of Niördr. References to the worship of other supernatural beings, elves and landvaettir [local spirits] are not unfrequent. In notices refering to Norway the evidence is not very different. We do indeed sometimes hear of worship paid to Othin, especially in legendary stories, relating to early times; but in references to . . . the tenth and eleventh centuries—Thor and Frey are distinctly more prominent.

Among other apparently ancient deities was Tyr, the patron of war, who was later displaced by Odin in eastern and southern peripheral areas (Craigie 1914: 4–5).

The god of war, valor, poetry, runes, wisdom, and cunning, Odin (or Wotan, as he was called in some Germanic tribes) is probably the best known of the Norse deities. Odin putatively taught his followers a new type of battle formation, the wedge; he endowed them with poems and weapons of magical potency; and he welcomed the brave to his Valhalla home, a new form of immortality graced by war maidens. Thus, Odin rephrased the dilemma that many Northmen faced during the centuries immediately preceding the birth of Christ: whether to remain in the homeland where a longer, colder winter, a shortened growing season, and marine trangression were threatening their existence or to migrate southward into the unknown territories of fearsome strangers. Both alternatives must have been perceived as evil, according to the Norse perception pattern. Odin revealed how by following him into battle they might convert their dilemma into two alternatives, both good: to live valorously fighting with Wotan's power or to die valorously and live on in Valhalla.

The Northmen also venerated tutelary goddesses (*dísir*) attached to a locality, a family, or an individual. These might be minor fertility deities; sometimes they are difficult to distinguish from another class of guardian spirits (or fetches) known as *fylgjur* if associated with an individual and *hamingjur* if attached to a kin group. Elves (*álfar*) and land spirits (*landvaettir*), closely related to the earth, also figure among their protective deities (Turville-Petre 1964, Ch. 11).

According to Chadwick (1912: 402), in Old Scandinavian religious practice relations between worshiper and deity were of a personal and intimate character. The Northman regarded his god "as a friend, counselor, and protector." In a way a Norse god was considered to be "first among equals" in relation to his human followers, and it was believed that the first among the followers, namely the chief or leader, could best intercede with the god on behalf of the group. A chief thus led the sacrificial rites on behalf of his followers.

Most of the indigenous ceremonies of north Europe involved blood sacrifices—consisting of animals and occasionally of human beings—which were apparently designed as gifts to propitiate the gods and to gain, as countergifts, their assistance in man's communal living enterprise. The gods, although not omnipotent, were thought to have certain limited powers that, if they were so disposed, they could use to protect and to assist mankind against powers of destruction. In keeping with the native preferred relationship pattern, no professional sacerdotal class emerged in pagan Scandinavia, and the local leader functioned in the role of priest.

World Image and Moral Code

The Northman viewed the world as violent and dangerous. He conceived it as the arena of constant struggle between mutually hostile forces, and its fate hung perpetually in the balance. At the center of this world, the Northman placed mankind. He believed that, if there was to be any order and peace in the world, man had actively to create and maintain it. And he believed that man had the power to create order and peace within a limited sphere through *frid*, which meant "peace," especially between kin and kindreds. Man, by being a good kinsman, presumably created a web of harmonious relationships within his circle of kin and between kin circles to the outermost boundaries of the known world. He drew other classes of phenomena into this circle by cultivating them as totemic foster brothers. These phenomena included the sun, the moon, and species of animals and plants relevant to the Northman's way of life.

The known world, Midgard, might be controlled by man only under certain circumstances and only through constant self-restraint, vigilance, craft, and wisdom. Midgard extended outward on all sides as far as the horizon of man's knowledge, and it was surrounded by a wall guarded by Thor. It was perceived as the world of the sun, the known, the sacred, and the joyful. Midgard, as a sharply bounded island, was man's sphere of power. But man could tap certain power sources outside it by totemic foster brother alliances in *frid* and other devices.

Beneath and around Midgard was Utgard, an unknown region of darkness and frost. Utgard was perceived as the unhallowed world of night, the strange, the uncanny, the horrible, and the ill-boding. It was peopled by giants, monsters, werewolves, and even luckless outcasts. The unknown held a fascination for the Northman, and he constantly tried to extend the boundaries of his known world and his sphere of power. Because he believed that such extension could be achieved through knowledge, foresight, and wisdom, he cultivated these intellectual tools to enable him to cope with his environment and bend it to his needs and purposes.

In this image of the world the vital principle—the ultimate source of man's power—was *saell, heill, hamingja*. The meaning of these terms cannot be rendered by a single English word. They express vital force, guardian spirit, luck, fortune, blessing, gift, health, wholeness (Grönbech 1931 [1]: Ch. 4, 5; Turville-Petre 1964: 69, Ch. 11). To the Norse, this vital power was not an external power capriciously exerted upon objects from above or without. On the contrary, it was an intangible quality emanating from the inner nature of the being, or manifestation, of a class of forces. As among the Bantu (Tempels 1959: 31), all effective beings—human, animal, vegetable, or inorganic—were believed to possess vital force. Such beings loved and hated in their own fashion according to unassailable immanent principles. The vital force might be manifest in a man, a bear, a wave, an oak, and so on. The Northman classified the forces of his effective environment into categories—for example, animals, trees, stones, as well as several classes of beings in semihuman form like giants, elves, dwarfs, and wave maidens.

Each representative of such a class manifested the characteristics and the entire life history of the class to which it belonged. Accordingly, each man contained within himself his luck (*hamingja*) or his ill luck, misfortune, or disaster (*óhamingja*), obtained through the honorable or dishonorable deeds of all his kinsmen, living and dead. Luck in man was manifested as the intangible power of honor. Through totemic foster brotherhood man could augment his kindred luck through that of other classes of phenomena.

In this rather tightly knit conceptual scheme, an individual's luck thus represented vital power and accrued from the honorable deeds of every member of his ingroup. Therefore, the luck of a circle of kin depended on their mutual love and harmony, viewed in terms of a historical whole, rather than at any one moment in its history. The luck of a kindred was the outward sign, at the social level, of its *frid;* honor was its equivalent at the personal level. Conversely, ill luck was the result of dishonorable behavior, on the part of a member of the ingroup, that instigated some breach of kindred solidarity. This formulation may be viewed as the Norse version of the law of immanent justice.

A basic assumption inherent in this image of the world is that the major power sources of the universe emanate from the essential nature of man and that of other classes of beings. This assumption regarding the locus of vital power may appropriately be contrasted to that of many native peoples—for example, the northern Ojibway (Hallowell 1947) and the Dakota Sioux Indians (see Chapter 16), who postulate a universal power pool outside of man himself. In this connection the beliefs of ancient Hebrews, early Christians, and Muslems may be mentioned. By contrast, documents suggest that the Northmen believed that the force and intensity of a man's inner power depended solely on his own self-selected moral behavior and that of his kindred, and not on some external sanction. It is generally agreed that the concept of personal honor was the crux of the pre-Christian Norse moral code.

Honorable behavior (*drengskapr*), conceived as the acting out of *frid* at the voluntary personal level, was the indispensable virtue of a kinsman. *Drengskapr* meant all that being a good kinsman implied—freely fulfilling all the duties, obligations, and privileges that the role of kinsman entailed. The code of honorable behavior imposed greater obligations the higher the status of the individual. A chieftain's duties and obligations were heaviest of all. Honor was most dramatically manifested in the act of personal vengeance or restitution for an injury perpetrated against a kinsman. But it was also shown in generosity, hospitality, and helpfulness to a kinsman and in readiness to take on his cause.

With the Northman there was no minimum morality. Boundaries were sharp. There was no moral compromise, no middle ground. One slip and all one's honor was lost.[7] One was thus either an honorable man or a *niding* (a villain, a traitor, an outlaw).

In this conception of a world sustained by a balance between actively conflicting forces, there was a tendency in the long run to emphasize failure rather than success (Phillpotts 1931: 145–147). Human beings were believed to cooperate with the gods and other power figures in fighting against the forces of destruction and death. But defeat and death were foreordained. The great struggle would be terminated by internal elements already active. The world was thus believed to contain within itself the seeds of its own destruction.

Conclusion

The foregoing description of certain aspects of the social structure and core values of the Norsemen is necessarily suggestive rather than definitive. However, the available evidence strongly suggests that underlying the social structure and institutions of the Vikings was an ingenious system of beliefs and attitudes that set up kindred solidarity consciously and voluntarily maintained as one of the basic goals of human life. As Hal Koch writes (1959: 130): "The Scandinavian does not piously submit to the will of the gods: he *wills*, and men and gods must join him in this willing. Gladly he invests his life; what matters is not to preserve the individual but the family." Cultural values were conceived and interrelated in order to foster social cohesiveness at the same time that the flexibility and other situational advantages of an open social system were maintained. "Strength" within the units of this social system tended to signify flexibility rather than fixity, balanced integration rather than centralization, and many constantly changing and overlapping images of similar or equivalent value rather than a single immutable dominant image.

A comparison of the findings reveals a closeness of fit and inner logical consistency between the social structure of the community, its core values, and its image of the world. Such a comparison highlights the means by which the Vikings bolstered not only sociologically but also ideologically what might otherwise have proven to be a structural weakness in their bilateral kinship system. The Northman reinforced his institutional system and his personal behavior by means of a single, internally consistent moral code ingeniously dovetailed to the social structure and keyed to the goals of the whole community.

The analysis suggests that the drama of communal life in the northern culture cradle, as reflected in the prototype social structure and its implicit conceptual reinforcements, was not essentially that of man against man. Contrary to the usual assumption, it was not primarily that of interpersonal strife or intergroup warfare. Rather, the available evidence suggests that it was the drama of man as an individual, backed by kin and reinforced by institutional sanctions and religious beliefs, in a struggle of small isolated human communities, possessing few resources and a limited technology, to maintain their balance against catastrophic natural forces. The forms of creative expression afforded by the prototype culture, including those that regulated interpersonal relations, were keyed primarily to the postglacial northern world of nature where the long winter night, fluctuations in climate and in land-sea relations, and concomitant changes in ecosystems imposed severe limitations on living conditions.

The paramount problem of small isolated human communities in the far north of Europe during the millenniums of the immediate postglacial epoch was apparently that of group survival and self-renewal (see Chapter 20). Human energies at both individual and communal levels were channeled to cope with these problems. Under such extreme conditions, flexibility and cooperation were essential for the group; knowledge, agility, foresight, and endurance, for the individual. The analysis suggests that these were the traits that the Norse kinship system, institutions, moral code, and world image tended to foster in the members of the community.

Notes

1. Part of this chapter is based on "The Bilateral Kinship Group: Basic Institution of the Ancient Germanic Social System," presented at the annual meeting of the American Anthropological Association, Chicago, 1957. I take this opportunity to thank Einar Ólafur Sveinsson, Holger Rasmussen, and William H. Davenport for reading part or all of an earlier version of the chapter and for helpful suggestions. I am grateful to Rosalie H. Wax for the use of notes and other materials on Viking culture.
2. Early Viking culture has been reconstructed by scholars on the basis of several types of source materials, including archaeological reports, historical documents, literary documents, and legal codes. Of the many references used in preparing this chapter, I mention as particularly useful to the English reader, the following: Adam of Bremen 1959; Arbman 1961; Bede 1916; Brønsted 1965; Chadwick 1899, 1912; Craigie 1914, 1933; Du Chaillu 1889; Grönbech 1931; Ibn Fadhlan 1948; Koch 1959; Olrik 1930; Phillpotts 1913, 1931; Sawyer 1962; Saxo Grammaticus 1905; Turville-Petre 1953, 1964.

3. Clerics were forbidden to participate in trials by ordeal by the Lateran Council (1215). The last such trial in Iceland was held in 1237 (Sveinsson c.1958: 64–65).

4. See Chadwick 1899: 11, 49 ff.; Craigie 1914: 6; Davidson 1964: 48 ff.; Smith 1952: 396; Turville-Petre 1964: 66.

5. See Caesar 1951: 35–36; Chadwick 1899 (2): 39; Phillpotts 1913: 7, 43–44, 247, 275; Sumner 1906: 82, 136, 408–409, 559.

6. Major sources for information concerning the deities and religious practices of the Northmen are recorded in *The Poetic Edda* (Hollander 1962) and poetry embedded in some of the Icelandic sagas. See also note 2.

7. The traditional concept of honor in Scandinavia contrasts with that of the Mediterranean region. Among the Sarakatsani sheep herders of Greece, for example, loss of honor may be partial rather than complete. According to J. K. Campbell (1964: 273), among these mountain people "Loss of honor does not mean direct social ostracism . . . it implies the withdrawal of full recognition or response."

9 /

THE ICELANDERS

Eldr er beztr
med ýta sonum
ok sólar sýn
heilindi sitt
ef madr hafa náir,
án vid löst at lifa.

Deyr fé,
deyja fraendr,
deyr sjálfr it sama,
en ordstírr
deyr aldregi
hveim, er sér gódan getr.

Fire is the best
boon among men,
and sight of the sun,
man's health as well
if he have it may,
and living life unblemished.

Cattle die,
kinsmen die,
dies one's self the same,
but a good renown
will never die
for any one who earns it.

> *Hávamál* (stanzas 68 and 76), translated by Vilhjál-
> mur Bjarnar[1]

I discovered Iceland in a roundabout way. Investigating the culture history of the Osnabrück Northland in the lowlands of West Germany, I was baffled by discrepancies in the rather meager written reports about the region. The problem did not yield to the usual research tools. I could not reconcile historical accounts that seemed to reflect obscure partisan biases.

Because the Lower Saxon culture of West Germany appeared to represent a southern variation of the prototype north European cradle culture discussed in Chapter 7 and because the culture of Iceland represented another version of the same ancestral stock, but was better documented and easier to control on account of the geographic isolation of the island and its relatively recent settlement, I decided to investigate Iceland.[2] The Icelanders themselves, as well as many other investigators, have studied meticulously virtually every phase of the history, prehistory, literature, and changing modern life of the nation, as well as the changing environment of the island.[3] By studying the culture history of Iceland and by visiting some of her rural communities, I hoped to gain perspective on the northern European core culture as a whole and thus to be in a better position to evaluate the Old Saxon sources.

Eventually I made two summer expeditions to Iceland.[4] With the help of Icelandic administrators, colleagues, and friends, I visited three rural communities there in 1952: Skútustadahreppur, in the northern part of the island; Breiddallur, on the remote east coast; and Hruni, in the southwest. In 1960 I had the unforgettable experience of visiting Öraefi (Hofshreppur), nestled between the spurs of Vatnajökull, the great glacier on the southeast coast. These experiences opened the door to one of the richest cultural adventures of my life.

Geography and Changing Resources

Rising out of the Atlantic 178 miles east of Greenland and some 500 miles northwest of Scotland, Iceland (population about 200,000) lies just below the arctic circle. The island (39,700 square miles) is of volcanic origin. The western, northwestern, and eastern portions are composed of Eocene basalts, whereas the remainder is formed of Pleistocene and post-Pleistocene tuff and other volcanic materials (Malmström 1958: 9–11). One-tenth of the island's surface is covered by these postglacial lava flows.

Since Iceland was settled, there have been nearly 150 volcanic eruptions. Earthquakes are common. Thermal activity is widespread; hot springs, for example, are found in 250 localities. Like Hawaii and the Marianas, Iceland is still in process of formation. A new islet, Surtsey, emerged during an eruption off the south coast in 1963.

The island lacks many minerals found only in continental formations, but some iron ore of poor quality and a few coal deposits have been found. Sulfur and lime are also present. The Icelanders use their thermal activity to compensate for other resources deficiencies. On thermally heated ground they raise white potatoes. In thermally heated greenhouses they raise fruits, vegetables, and flowers. The capital city of Reykjavík is heated entirely by hot water from subterranean sources.

Iceland's spectacular landscape is dominated by glaciers—the shrinking relics of the Würm ice sheet that had covered the entire island except for a few barren peaks. More than 11 percent of the island's surface is still glaciated. Vatnajökull, the largest glacier in Europe, covers over 3,000 square miles. I had the thrill of flying over this huge ice mass, whose scalloped margins look from above like the blue-white waves of a deep frozen sea. Our plane also swung directly over the peak of an active volcano so that the passengers could peer into its smoking cones.

Iceland is located in the North Atlantic storm track and her glaciers form storm centers. These facts account partly for the uncertain weather that characterizes the island. The climate of the southwestern and southern parts of the island is mitigated by the influence of the warm Irminger current, a branch of the Gulf Stream. The northwestern, northern, and eastern portions of the island, however, are skirted by the cold East Greenland current. In winter this current is responsible for the massing of block ice that, during years of climatic deterioration, closes the northern fjords. Block ice may persist well into the spring and ruin the hay harvest, or it may, in very bad years, last throughout the summer. Block ice has not presented a problem since 1919 (Malmström 1958: 44–45).

The junction of cold and warm currents off the coast of Iceland affords the best fishing banks of Europe. Fishing is modern Iceland's major natural resource. The Icelanders began to export dried fish to Europe during the thirteenth century. Iceland's controversies with other nations usually stem from her claims that foreign fishermen are encroaching on her fishing rights.

The present climate, although subject to frequent cyclonic disturbances, is of the oceanic type, warmer than might be expected at this latitude. The northern part of the island is colder and drier than the southern part. Average temperatures range from 53 to 46 degrees F. in July and from 34 to 20 degrees F. in January. Average precipitation varies from about 80 inches in the south to about 30 inches in the north. The short days and long dark nights of winter, as well as the long bright days of summer, must be kept in mind if one is to understand the lifeways of a human community in the far north.

Except on the south coast, Iceland's shoreline is indented by deep fjords that give a distinctive quality to the landscape. Classed mainly as either loess or peat soil, Icelandic soils are constantly changing, as they are subject to erosion by wind and frost. It should be noted that, although today about 87 percent of the island consists of mountain wasteland, lava flows, and glaciers, considerably more of the island was covered by vegetation toward the end of the post-Pleistocene warm maximum (c. 5500–3000 B.C.).

Iceland was settled in the late ninth and early tenth centuries, when the climate of the North Sea region was comparatively mild and the seas were relatively calm. The island is reputed to have been warmer than Norway at that time. According to the Book of Settlement (Landnámabók), the mountain slopes were covered with woods and the plains were green with grass. The sparse indigenous flora and fauna were mostly of the post-Pleistocene variety that was found in the far north of the European and North American continents. Such edible plants as Icelandic moss, dulse, and seaweed were used for food by the people, especially in times of famine. The arctic fox and the long-tailed European field mouse were the only land mammals. There were over 100 species of birds nesting on the island, including the eider duck, valued for its down and the white falcon, highly prized by European clergy in the Middle Ages for use in hunting. Doubtless every fjord was teeming with fish, and many rivers were well stocked.

Physical Type

In the absence of modern population genetics studies, we note that, according to Joyce A. Donegani, *et al.* (1950: 147–148, 150, 151, Table 2), over 200 unselected individuals of Icelandic stock showed the following approximate gene frequencies: blood group O, 75 percent; blood group B, 7 percent; in the M-N series, M, 58 percent; N, 42 percent. A conclusion reached from the available research was that "The people of Iceland have a high group O frequency similar to that found in Scotland and Ireland and considerably lower than in Norway. Their Rh [Rhesus] groups are of similar frequencies to the rest of western Europe . . . Their M frequency is somewhat higher than usually found in western Europe."

As might be expected in an isolated island, inbreeding has been characteristic of the mating patterns of Iceland. The nation affords one of the most favorable and little-explored human genetics laboratories in the world (see Hannesson 1925; Seltzer 1933; Steffensen 1953). A local microrace has apparently evolved during the millennium since Iceland was settled.

An extraordinary example of an isolated breeding population is found at Öraefi, which is situated between the southern spurs of Vatnajökull, the great glacier in the southeastern portion of the island. Öraefi was the home of Ljót, who figures in Njal's saga. Concealed beneath the dazzling white mantle of the glacier sleeps Öraefajökull, the giant of Iceland's volcanoes (elevation 6,950 feet). The people still tell of its devastating eruptions. Floods of glacial melt water and red-hot pumice boulders rained down on the community killing people, sheep, and horses, destroying farms, and darkening the day. The accounts are substantiated by archaeological evidence.[5]

Until 1945, when a biweekly plane service connected Öraefi with Reykjavík, the area could be reached only by horseback. The mounted traveler had to ford countless swift-moving icy streams draining the glacier. An informant in northern Iceland told me about a journey on horseback he had made to Öraefi as a young man. He said that it took him an hour and a half to cross one of the glacial rivers. When he was ready to leave the community, he was told that the postman was expected any day. So he decided to delay his return and travel with the postman. He waited but the letter carrier did not arrive. Several years later postman with mount and mail pouch completely preserved in ice were ejected by the glacier. The Icelanders say that the glacier always gives back what it takes. Vatnajökull is currently shrinking because the climate of the Northern Hemisphere is gradually warming. Middle-aged informants showed me the extent of the glacial retreat during their lifetime. There are still no roads or bridges here, but a bridge is reported under construction.

In 1960 Öraefi included eight farms of twenty-six farmsteads and had a population of about 156. The farmers depend for their livelihood on a narrow steep strip of glacial moraine that lies between the glittering glacier and a blue-black sandy waste, which is furrowed by melt rivers that flow to the treacherous southeastern coast of the island. The farmers cultivate their fields and pasture their sheep on this fertile strip. Each autumn they slaughter 2,000 to 3,000 lambs, mostly for market. Each farmer also combs the section of the distant seacoast attached to his farmstead for driftwood, which is the only locally available building material except sod. There is no harbor within sixty-two miles, and, before there was access by air, people took their goods by horseback across the glacial streams all the way to Eyrrabakki on the southwest coast.

I was a guest at the Skaftafell farm, considered the best in Öraefi for raising sheep. The place was owned by two brothers said to represent the fourteenth generation consecutively to work the land. One was sixty-two years old, the other forty-six. The older brother was married but had no children. The summer haying was done with the help of three boys and three girls, aged eight to seventeen years, from Reykjavík.

I was told that all the residents of Öraefi are related. Women who are not from Öraefi rarely marry into the community. Many of the residents are counted with the Skaftafell *aett* (family line), which is mentioned in records of the thirteenth century.

The Settlers

Iceland was settled by chieftains and yeomen, mainly from western Norway and from Viking colonies in the British Isles. The colonists left their homelands in the late ninth and early tenth centuries. At the time Iceland was uninhabited except for a few Gaelic-speaking Catholic monks, who avoided the heathen newcomers and in time either perished or returned to their homeland.

The settlers were seeking new lands and resources, greater personal freedom, fame, and wealth. Many freemen from Norway wished to escape payment of tribute to Harold Fairhair, a petty chieftain who, influenced by the concept of kingship that was infiltrating from southern and central Europe, was imposing his authority over the whole of Norway.

The Vikings did not sail empty-handed from their homes. They took weapons, tools, silver, domestic animals and seeds, and images of their gods. Some even carried the carved high seat pillars that symbolized their family lines. The Vikings also possessed the skills that had been appropriate to the local division of labor by sex, talent, and experience in Norway. Such skills included seamanship based on celestial observations; a mode of warfare dependent upon mobility and agility; the cultivation of certain hardy field crops like barley; the care of sheep, cattle, and horses; the art of spinning and weaving woolen cloth; and iron-ore metallurgy. The settlers also brought an organized system of meanings, of reckoning time, and of communication in the old Norse language, their oral literature, and their productions—designs on tools, house forms, and land-use patterns. In their memories they had stored certain customs, the beliefs of their Norse religion, and a knowledge of their poems and poetic forms. Among the migrants were individuals with craft skills, the gift of poetry, and a knowledge of runes. Runes were signs borrowed from the alphabet by Germanic peoples about the third century, before they had developed a written language, and used as magical symbols as well as in written communication.

Settlements

The small Viking ships imposed an almost automatic control on the size of the migrating units. In general, only his immediate family and household (including house servants and thralls who generally were Gaelic-speaking Catholics from the British Isles) accompanied a leader. A few unrelated individuals also attached themselves to the group. For practical purposes, a migrant household head thus cut himself off from most of his kindred in the homeland.

In Iceland each leader staked a limited freehold claim from shore to mountains. This was usually no larger than a man and his crew carrying fire or a woman leading a "two-winter-old" heifer could circle in a day. The isolated farmstead pattern of land use was thus established in Iceland by the first Northmen as early as the ninth century. In Iceland, freeholds were not considered inalienable, as they were in Norway and Lower Saxony.

The early Icelanders raised their stock on the fine wild grasses that grew abundantly in the valleys and along the seacoast. They also cultivated grains. In summer, they ran their sheep without shepherds on the rugged upland pastures that were shared, as commons, by neighboring farms. They also fished. They found it easy to hunt birds and seals because these creatures were unaccustomed to men.

Wood soon became scarce as foraging of livestock including goats, clearing for cultivation, burning for charcoal, and fires depleted the virgin forests. Natural soil-erosion processes by the action of wind, frost, and water were accelerated. As in Hawaii and the Marianas, the advent of man and his large herbivorous quadrupeds upset the delicate ecological balance in this isolated island community.

As far as possible within the limitations of the resources available to them, the settlers followed Norwegian models when they built their houses. In Norway, as in Hawaii, a farmstead consisted of several separate houses built of wood, each with a special function. One long house was used for living and dining, a smaller one for sleeping, another for cooking. There were also storehouses and stables for cattle and sheep.

Expeditions and Trade

The early settlers in Iceland were heirs to the traditions of the early Iron Age that emphasized excellent craftsmanship and intricate design in wood carving, metal work, and tapestry. The upper classes liked to wear showy clothes and ornaments of silver and bronze.

But after they had settled in Iceland, where wood rapidly became scarce, we would not expect the Icelanders to stress woodcarving, nor would we look for a continuing tradition of metal work where virtually no appropriate metals were found. As noted by E. O. Gabriel Turville-Petre (1953: 7), the medieval Icelanders showed little talent in these arts. From the beginning, precious objects had to be imported. The desire to possess them doubtless played a role in motivating Viking expeditions from Iceland during the early years of settlement.

In summer the young Vikings of Iceland sailed on expeditions to the coasts of Europe. Later they went to Greenland, which Eric the Red, outlawed from both Norway and Iceland, discovered in 985–986. They also sailed to America, which Eric's son Leif, a resident of Greenland, discovered about 1000 and called Vinland.

The discovery and colonization of Vinland, recorded in the Icelandic sagas and by Adam of Bremen (1959: 219), has long been a subject of dispute. Now, however, the first acceptable archaeological evidence of the event has been reported by

Helge Ingstad. At L'Anse au Meadow on the tip of Newfoundland, Ingstad excavated the remains of several house sites that had the ember pits characteristic of the Icelandic homes found in Greenland. The charcoal yielded radiocarbon dates of about 1000; Ingstad also found the remains of a primitive smithy. There are iron-ore deposits in nearby bogs that were unknown to the Eskimos and Indians. They suggest that the search for natural resources, especially for metals that were absent or scarce in Iceland, motivated Viking explorations into the New World (*Scientific American* 1964: 56). The discovery of an early map of Vinland (Skelton, Marston, and Painter 1965) may substantiate the archaeological evidence, although its authenticity has been questioned. Specimens of a European species of shell, dated about 1000 and associated with a campsite at Halifax, Nova Scotia, have been found (Spjeldnaes and Henningsmoen 1963) but there is some question as to how the species reached America (Bird 1968). The Norsemen probably explored Labrador as far as Hudson Bay. They also seem to have sailed up the St. Lawrence River and along the shores of Nova Scotia and New England.

The Icelanders thus supplemented the limited natural resources of their island by exploring, foraging, trading, and raiding. Indeed, from the time of the earliest settlement, the Icelanders depended for their well-being and even for their very survival on the importation of such goods as wood, tools, weapons, iron, copper, wine, beer, wax, and honey. Fine clothes, jewelry, and other luxuries were also imported. For many centuries homespun woolen cloth was the chief Viking export trade article.

Beliefs, Arts and Literature

Archaeological research suggests that many settlers built temples dedicated to their traditional deities, especially Thor. No traces have been found of Christian churches built during this period, despite the fact that some settlers and many of their thralls were Celtic Catholics. Many gods, especially Thor, Freyr, and Njörd were worshiped by the Icelanders with sacrificial rites. The people also propitiated spirits in the heavens and in the atmosphere, in the earth and in the sea, and in the waters of springs and rivers. The Icelanders evidently retained the ancient Norse belief in tutelary spirits, both of individuals (*fylgjur*) and of family lineages (*aettarfylgjur*). They also followed the Northman's concept of good fortune, contrasted with ill fortune, as a kind of inborn force.

The Icelanders liked to have their boats, houses, shields, and jewelry decorated with strange animal figures coiled and twisted into elaborate but carefully confined designs. Many of these designs had magical significance that was frequently expressed in runes. Indeed, it was believed that a supernatural power could be built into such objects during construction. We found a similar concept in native Hawaii, the Marquesas islands, and other parts of the Pacific, where mana could be built into a person or thing.

The people also believed that magician-poets could influence the elements and with a verse bring good or ill fortune. There were, however, very strong sanctions (even outlawry) against making libelous, execrative verses about men and erotic poetry about women. *Ordheill* means words charged with power for good or ill. The potency of words, as a means of perpetuating the ego through fame, provided a strong motivation to poets. This is well illustrated in the heroic lay designed to eulogize a hero.

Poetry and storytelling flourished in Iceland. Indeed, oral literature became an important medium of cultural innovation. Early Icelandic court poets (skalds), for example, outdid those of other Scandinavian lands in the composition and recitation of verses. They took pleasure in fitting precise meaning into an incredibly rigid and limiting medium such as the court meter (*dróttkvaett*), an outgrowth of the heroic lay that was highly complex in detail within an overall unity of structure. Because of their desire to be immortalized in this manner, kings in Norway, Sweden, Denmark, and even England attached gifted Icelanders to their courts.

Sagas[6]

The Icelandic sagas were a local development based on the Old Norse epic. Like the heroic lay and court poetry, the sagas spread and perpetuated the fame of men and women whose lives and deaths embodied the Viking ideal. Unlike the poetic forms eulogizing kings and nobles, however, many of the sagas told the life stories of ordinary men and women and illustrated the intrinsic importance of each individual in the freeman tradition. The sagas were designed to hold the interest of a group of listeners through the long dark winter nights. The narrator let a description of actions and physical appearance reveal the characters' feelings, thoughts, motivations, and conflicts. Far from explicitly pointing to a moral, storytellers arranged their materials so that the listener might draw his own conclusions, especially about the inexorable workings of fate (Lange 1935: 127; Phillpotts 1931: 171–181).

The role of observer positioned outside of the event he is describing is still congenial to the Icelanders. When I asked a question, whether in town or in the country, I noticed that my informant never quibbled. If he did not know the answer, he said so. Otherwise, he gave a well-organized verbal description of an event or artifact based on his own observations and knowledge. This objectivity contrasts markedly with the habitual responses of informants in most communities where I have worked professionally.

Family System

The settlers, cut off from their kindreds in the homeland, founded family lines (*aettir*) of their own. Many prominent persons in present-day Iceland trace their descent to a Viking founding father or mother. In Iceland, a stem-family system developed in which, although both lines were acknowledged, the male line was favored. Icelandic *aettir* were ranked according to the ancestry, class, wealth, personality, exploits, and fame of the founding pair and their descendants. In other words, they were ranked according to the "honor" or "luck" of their kindred.

Family lines remained nameless, however, except in the case of lines that were attached to farmsteads or localities and associated with local place-names. A boy was given a male personal name, often that of a prominent ancestor, followed by his father's given name with the male offspring kinship designator, *son*, attached as a suffix. A girl was given a female personal name also followed by her father's name, but with the female child designator, *dóttir*, added. She kept this entire name even after her marriage. Individuals were known by their given names, often followed by a descriptive nickname. Even today the traditional system of naming is followed.

After the Icelandic commonwealth was established in 930, marriage among members of the upper class was arranged by contract. An attempt was made to match the two sides of the union in rank and wealth. The contract stipulated the dowry that the parents of the bride promised to give her. It had to be matched by the groom's gift to the bride. These properties, as well as her own name, belonged legally to the bride. They were retained by her in case of divorce, a rare occurrence.

The Blood Feud

An extended family held together, especially in times of trouble when wrongs committed against a member were either avenged by blood or settled through wergild payments in silver or woolen homespun. The blood feud was never recognized legally in Iceland, and from the viewpoint of Viking culture as a whole, the Icelandic form was atypical. For example, the blood feud was not carried on between kindreds, as in the Norwegian homeland. Instead, agnates predominated over cognates and class distinctions were paramount. A leader with a grievance—for example, the next of male kin in a manslaughter case—was supported in arms by his near male relatives: first by his brothers and father, his brothers-in-law and father-in-law; then by his foster brothers and cousins; and finally by his house servants and thralls. The slayer's next of kin with his supporters would oppose this grouping.

Thus in Icelandic blood feuds, conflicts of duty arose that, under the implicit Icelandic ethical code, took the form of moral problems. For example, a man might have to decide whether to support his blood kin against his foster kin or his blood kin against his in-laws. In a manslaughter case, however, an Icelander did not actually have a free choice. He could not remain neutral lest he incur the wrath of a leader who wished his support. Failing to obtain his support, such a leader might turn on him with manslaughter.

Whether to take blood vengeance, a path upheld by the highest moral sanctions, or to have recourse to the law through payment of wergild, was a matter of choice on the part of the slain's next of kin. If a lawsuit was chosen, full atonement satisfactory to both sides might be achieved under certain conditions. But winning a lawsuit, according to the early Icelandic jury system, which functioned without a judge, also involved obtaining the support of many men as witnesses, including neighbors. Nonrelatives were drawn into the jury if needed (Repp 1832: 184). Success, however, was partly a matter of getting a good lawyer to present the case. Because it was illegal to hire a lawyer, he was usually a member of the family. In addition, because there existed no central law-enforcement agency, a court judgment was executed by the winner with the help of his chief (*godi*) and supporters.

The *Godord*

The strongest and wealthiest chiefs attracted personal followers among the farmers of the neighborhood. They led the local assemblies, where matters of common interest were discussed and disputes were settled. The personal association between such chiefs (*godar*) and their followers (*thingmenn*) was called a *godord*. A farmer was free to choose his *godi*, but after he had made a selection his whole household went along with him. He paid a *thing* tax to his *godi* and thus created far-reaching moral obligations between himself and his chief. The *godi* preserved order, protected his *thingmenn*, settled disputes between them, aided them in gaining their rights, and provided leadership in times of danger and in dealing with foreigners. Fulfillment of these mutual responsibilities depended solely on one's personal honorable behavior.

It is clear that *godi* and *thingmenn* were not united primarily by kinship or territorial ties. Rather, they were joined in a voluntary personal bond of mutual advantage and mutual responsibility that could be dissolved at will by either party. There was no superior power over the holders of *godord*, who were limited only by the laws that the *godar* might make for themselves. They treated the *godord* as a hereditary possession that usually passed from father to son but also could be bought and sold. A *godord*, therefore, should be classed neither as a kinship group nor as a territorial unit. Rather, it was a voluntary contractual association.

Scholars formerly assumed that powerful settlers erected temples on their farms in which they held sacrificial feasts that attracted people from the neighborhood. Judiciary assemblies were also supposedly held at the temples. This assumption was used to explain the power of the *godar*. It now appears from archaeological evidence that the number of temples in Iceland before the establishment of the commonwealth was much greater than the number of *godord*. But the traditional Icelandic code stipulated that there should be a principal temple associated with each *godord* that would be presided over by its *godi* during certain annual festivals, such as those that marked the beginning of winter (October 14), midwinter (January 12), and the beginning of summer (April 14). Each *thingmenn* was required to pay a temple toll. The *godi's* priestly functions naturally enhanced his power. They are now believed, however, to have been a consequence, rather than a cause, of his power, which stemmed basically from his prestige and his authority over his followers (Nordal 1942: 123).

This relationship reminds us of an old Norse prototype. As has been noted, it was believed that persons of authority were the most effective interceders with the gods. The pattern also suggests the bond between the early Germanic *princeps* and his *comitatus*.

The Commonwealth

By 930, when the estimated population of the island numbered about 30,000, there were thirty-six *godord* units (increased to thirty-nine after 965). Nine *thing* formed a judiciary district (or quarter), and four judiciary districts formed the original commonwealth. These *godord* were made the local units through which each community was represented in a central judiciary assembly called the Althing, which met annually at Thingvellir in southwestern Iceland during the summer solstice. The Icelandic Althing is reputed to be the oldest parliamentary governing body in Europe. The *godord* were thus the political units that together constituted the commonwealth. The commonwealth represented in actuality not one state but rather a confederation of independent, politically equal *godord* associations.

It should be noted that none of the Icelandic *thing*, including the Althing, functioned as executive bodies. Rather, they were voluntary judiciary assemblies of freemen led by their *godar*, where mutual problems were discussed according to orderly traditional procedures. Here disputes were settled if possible, according to an unwritten legal code, which could be amended. The Althing differed from all other *thing* first in its nationwide representation. Second, it was the repository of the law through the institution of the lawspeaker (*lögsögumadr*) and a medium by which the law could be changed.

The lawspeaker was the official enunciator of the traditional law code. He recited the entire code at the meetings of the Althing every three years and he explained points of the law on request. The lawspeaker was the personal repository of the unwritten legal charter of the commonwealth. He was not its implementor, administrator, or executor. Indeed, the concept of a single dominant authority image expressed, for example, in the roles of monarch, professional judge, magistrate, policeman, or professional priest was shunned by the settlers. It was partly to avoid the imposition of a dominant authority on the Norwegian freemen and chieftains that the Vikings originally settled in Iceland. The introduction of such concepts (from southern Europe and the Near East through Denmark and Norway) was resisted with great energy by the independent, freedom-loving Icelanders.

The lawspeaker also presided over the Lögretta (law amending body). This was an official group composed of 144 persons, 48 of whom (that is, the 39 *godar* and 9 of their nominees) formed the voting core. The Lögretta constituted the formal deliberative body within the Althing, and its voting core held the decision-making power to amend or change the law. Decisions were made according to the principle of unanimity.

In sum, the basic grass-roots unit of early Icelandic society, the *godord*, was not the ephemeral fluctuating kindred characteristic of Norse social structure. Rather, it was a voluntary, personal association of freemen with their chieftain, based on practical considerations and upheld by indigenous legal and moral codes. Prehistoric Norse society in Norway, Sweden, and Denmark also functioned without central executive authority or police, but a man's kindred helped him in time of need and protected him against his enemies by means of the blood feud and wergild. The physical separation of Iceland's settlers from their homeland kindreds, which had played such a strong sustaining role in traditional Norse society, accentuated personal ties. It was thus a significant factor in the development of the new type of independent voluntary association of freemen that the Icelanders forged out of traditional Norse prototypes to solve their practical living problems in a new environment.

The Icelandic commonwealth emerged as a coalition type of political system. It derived its strength not from a single dominant authority, unchanging and absolute, but rather from a delicate balance between many changing power units, of which none was perceived as having a permanently superior power position vis-à-vis the others. Each unit was a complex microcosm in itself. Each was a decision-making group relatively independent of the others politically, economically, and religiously. Each was headed by a leader whose power stemmed not only from his wealth in land and livestock, but also from his personal leadership qualities; his legal role at *thing* and Althing; his putative power to intercede with the gods; his honorable behavior as a freeman and a nobleman; the prestige of his family line; and the strength, number, and loyalty of his *thingmenn*. This type of decentralized system, deeply rooted in communal experience, embodied the preferred relationship pattern of the Icelanders.

Formal Acceptance of Christianity

Located beyond the northern margin of the so-called civilized world, Iceland at the end of the first millennium represented one of the last refuges of European paganism. Celtic-speaking peoples of the British Isles had long been converted. Indeed, after Saint Patrick's success in the fifth century, the Irish had played an active role in proselytizing not only among the Angles and Saxons of England but also among many of the Germanic tribes of the European mainland. After Charlemagne's victory in the early ninth century, even the Old Saxons had succumbed (see Chapter 10). By the end of the first millennium, a Saxon missionary, along with other Catholics, was working for converts in Iceland. Denmark and Norway were converted in the late ninth and tenth centuries, but parts of Sweden held out until the twelfth.

Under these circumstances it is not difficult to imagine the strong pressures that were exerted to bring the Icelanders into the Christian fold. There was a division of opinion among Icelandic leaders on this crucial question that almost disrupted the organization of the commonwealth. The people felt particularly threatened by the recently unified and Christianized Norwegian kingdom. Indeed, fear of loss of sovereignty to Norway must have been a major factor influencing the Icelandic leaders. From this perspective the decision in favor of official conversion must have been viewed, according to the Norse perception pattern, as a choice between two alternatives—both distasteful: loss of religious independence or loss of political sovereignty.

Some scholars believe that under the impact of medieval Catholic influences and the broadening experiences afforded by the Viking way of life, belief in the traditional gods and their worship had already begun to weaken. A kind of heathen agnosticism may be detected in the literature of the time, especially in the poem *Völuspá*. The traditional Norse world view had evolved into one of mature fatalism. Fate had become an inscrutable, incomprehensible, and impersonal power that controlled gods as well as men (Nordal 1942: 179). But the people still believed that the power of magic and fate could not reach the innermost core of a man's being to overwhelm his courage and will. Although man could not conquer his fate, he could thus conquer life and even death, by the triumph of his own inner spiritual strength (Phillpotts 1931: 93–94).

At any rate, the lawspeaker of the Althing, after an agonizing decision, advised the people officially to accept the new religion. In 1000 the commonwealth, by vote of the Althing, formally accepted Catholicism with certain reservations. The Icelanders agreed to discontinue public sacrificial ceremonies to their traditional gods and to destroy their images. They submitted to the Catholic ritual of the time, including baptism. But they insisted on reserving the right to practice their ancient ceremonies in private, to eat the sacred flesh of the horse, and to practice infanticide. They also rejected the idea of priestly celibacy.

Effects of Conversion

The full effect of the official acceptance of Christianity on the tenets of Icelandic constitutional law and on the official value system was not immediately apparent. Within two decades, however, the church was beginning to retract from its lenient position regarding certain pagan practices. The church ban was used to punish disobedience of the new ecclesiastical canons (Sveinsson 1953: 113). Two centuries after the formal conversion Iceland had become outwardly a relatively orthodox Catholic country. The clergy, in contrast to the monks, continued to marry far into the thirteenth century. By 1200, however, family ties had weakened and there was a general breakdown of family honor and loyalty as conceived according to traditional standards in pagan Iceland.

After the conversion, the number of *godord* was fixed by law. New power centers, concentrated in two competing bishoprics, Skálholt and Hólar, upset the balance of power between *godar*. Inasmuch as *godord* could be bought and sold, a few wealthy families, such as the Sturlung, by a gradual process of accumulation, got possession of them all. Arrogant chieftains defied the law. Civil war broke out and before long Iceland lost her political sovereignty, first to the Norwegian king (1262–1264) and later, when Denmark conquered Norway, to the Danish king (1380). Thus Iceland's formal acceptance of an alien faith merely delayed, but did not avert, loss of her political sovereignty. It is important to note, however, that the Icelanders never accepted national political dependency. They always insisted that they had a personal tributary relationship directly with the king, whether Norwegian or Danish.

Because much of early Icelandic poetry was heavily involved with the native belief system and mythology, after the conversion many verses became incomprehensible. The increasing obscurity was significant in the decline of skaldic poetry during the eleventh century. The advent of written literature in the vernacular and other forms of entertainment and the subsequent loss of interest in the recitation of poems and sagas also played a role in the decline of skaldic poetry. Moreover, the Catholic belief in immortality afforded a new medium for extension of the ego beyond death, and thus much of the native literature was deprived of its main function. During the thirteenth and fourteenth centuries oft-told sagas were developed by anonymous writers in the vernacular into written works of art. Doubtless we should not accept as factually correct all statements about early Icelandic culture found in the sagas (Sveinsson 1954, 1957–1958), but exceptions may be found. For example, conflicts of personal loyalty and honorable behavior within the family and the neighborhood group probably expressed conflicts of role inherent in the social system.

The formal introduction of Roman Catholicism into Iceland seems to have marked the abandonment of native religious practices rather than the full acceptance of Christianity. Actually, propitiation of Thor especially by fishermen continued for many years. Sigurdur Nordal perceptively suggests that Scandinavian heathenism is expressed most abundantly in Icelandic sagas created *after* the introduction of Christianity. Indeed, modern appreciation of the cultural value of the Old Icelandic literature may perhaps be proportional to its revelation of the heathen outlook on life. Even today Icelanders, along with other Scandinavians, do not accept so much of Christianity as other Europeans or regard it so seriously.

The Long Dark Night (1300 to 1900)

A marked deterioration of the climate of the Northern Hemisphere began toward the end of the thirteenth century. This phenomenon was manifested in Iceland not by desiccation and drought, as in Hopiland (see Chapter 14) and Papagoland (see Chapter 13), but, as among the Lower Saxons (see Chapter 10), by increasing dampness and a lowering of the mean temperature. The glaciers advanced and pack ice frequently blocked the fjords of the northern and eastern coasts of Iceland even in summer. The worsening climate made practical living problems even more difficult to resolve. It especially hindered and even prevented the importation of such foreign goods as grains, fuel, and building materials, which were indispensable to the welfare of the people. In time the Icelandic colonists in Greenland, cut off from the homeland by pack ice, either perished or mixed with Eskimos. In Iceland a period of natural catastrophies set in. Volcanic eruptions, glacial invasions, and earthquakes destroyed or damaged large areas of farm and pasture land. Crops failed, sheep and cattle died, and the people suffered from exposure, severe epidemics, and starvation.

By the middle of the sixteenth century, when the climatic deterioration in Iceland had reached its low point, all farming on the island had been abandoned except for the cultivation of hay. The Protestant Reformation, which occurred during the mid-sixteenth century, engendered further stress and also bloodshed. One significant effect of the Reformation was to enhance the power of the Danish king, which had been inhibited on the island by that of the Catholic bishops. Since the Reformation, the Icelanders have officially supported the Lutheran faith.

Because timber for construction was lacking, the Icelanders

had long since lost the art of shipbuilding. Dependent on outsiders for the importation of necessities, they had also lost
their navigational skill. They were therefore unable to escape
exploitation when the Danes imposed a monopoly on island
trade (1602–1787) and thus intensified the already critical economic situation of the population. Climaxing this desperate
plight, the greatest volcanic devastation on record in Iceland
occurred in 1783, when eruptions covered much of the island
with ashes, and lava ruined many farms.

These events were associated with great changes in the mode
of life, size, and number of the Icelandic communities. All
communities were rural until a few seaports began to attract
fishermen and sailors during the nineteenth century. Most of
the farmers lost their freeholds during the economic crisis. There
was a general leveling of social classes in tributary relationship to church and king. The spacious wooden longhouse gave
way to a row of small connected rooms built of stone and turf.
Even furniture, especially beds, became shorter, reflecting not
only the scarcity of wood but also the fact that the Icelanders
themselves had diminished appreciably in stature. As Coon remarks (1939: 10):

> During the Dark Ages the Icelanders, originally as tall as their
> Norwegian ancestors, shrank in stature to the size of southern
> Italians. Climatologists now tell us that this shrinking accom-
> panied a lowering of mean annual temperature, and an increased
> dampness. Icelandic history adds that it was a period of near
> starvation . . . Yet the Icelanders who survived this depression
> grew rapidly once it was over, until at present they comprise
> one of the tallest groups in Europe.

By 1702–1703, when the first modern census was taken on the
island, over 3,000 farms had been abandoned, and some 4,000
were still being worked by a population of about 50,000. During
the next century the population declined to 47,000. The introduction of the white potato in 1759 had brought some relief
from starvation, but even this hardy Andean plant did not grow
well in northern Iceland except in thermally heated ground. The
low point of the population (about 38,000) was reached in 1786.

The climate of Iceland did not improve markedly until the end of the nineteenth century, when all of northern Europe became drier and warmer than it had been for more than 500 years. Today the climate is almost as warm as it was during the period of original settlement. However, grains are not yet grown on the island to any extent, although experiments are being made in their cultivation as field crops.

Culture Change and Persistence in Modern Iceland

During the nineteenth century many changes began to occur in Icelandic culture. To fill the hiatus left by the abolition of the Danish trade monopoly, which had encompassed not only external but also internal trade, the farmers of the Husivík district in the northeast organized themselves into a producer-consumer cooperative, which after 1880 proved so successful that the voluntary-cooperative idea spread to all the farmers on the island. The use of trawlers, which superseded small fishing boats, greatly augmented the size of the catch. Contacts with the outside world increased, and a few crafts, such as spinning and weaving, began to be mechanized.

The nationalist movement, spurred by the efforts of the national hero Jón Sigurdsson, led directly to the Act of Union in 1918, when the Danes technically recognized Iceland's change of political status from colony to independence. Iceland formally became a sovereign nation again in 1944.

Now citizens over twenty-one years of age may vote directly for the president of Iceland and for representatives in both houses of the Althing. Iceland's president appoints the prime minister, who then selects a cabinet. The prime minister has responsibility for basic political decisions. Although the cabinet is Iceland's executive authority, it is extremely sensitive to the will of the people and may stand or fall on the basis of no confidence.

The members of the Althing, also elected by direct popular vote, initiate and enact legislation. The president technically may veto a bill, but his veto may be overridden by popular plebiscite. So far as I am aware, he has never exercised this prerogative, and his role remains chiefly social and ceremonial.

Language

Icelandic, a modern version of Old Norse, is the official language of the nation. Local dialect differences are less pronounced than might be expected on the basis of the isolation of the rural districts.

Norwegian, Danish, and Swedish are modern languages that represent simplified forms of Old Norse. Modern Icelandic, on the other hand, has changed little from the parent stock. Latin, although introduced into Iceland with Catholicism, never gained a foothold on the island except among the pre-Reformation priesthood. Icelandic retains most of the morphological complexity of Old Norse, as well as its accent on the first or root syllable of a word, a feature that has been lost in the other Scandinavian languages as well as in High German. This makes it possible for modern Icelanders to compose poetry according to traditional rules that depend on stressing the first syllable. Contemporary Icelanders also can read in the original their medieval literature, most of which has been preserved in manuscripts dating from the thirteenth and fourteenth centuries. They can also understand and read modern Danish, Norwegian, and Swedish with little difficulty.

Icelanders love their language and strongly resist any tendencies to change it. They have even set up a committee to find Icelandic words that may be substituted for those that have been borrowed from abroad. A list of such words is publicized for use by writers and journalists.

The Icelanders are one of the most literate and literary nations in the world. Half a dozen daily newspapers and several weeklies are published in Reykjavík, and the output of books per capita is many times that in the United States, for example. Every urban home and many a rural one has its booklined library. I have seen an Icelander trying to illustrate a point, jump up from the dinner table, quickly locate a volume of poetry in his collection, and read a poem to the delight of his guests. The Icelanders have even produced a Nobel prize winner, Haldor K. Laxness, who received the award for literature in 1955.

The Farmstead

Despite changes that have occurred through the centuries, the isolated farmstead persists as the basic rural population unit in modern Iceland. Many farmsteads mentioned in the sagas still exist and are known by their saga names; for example, Bergthórshvoll in Njál's saga.

Many farms have been in the same family for generations. There are no inflexible rules of inheritance except that the widow gets at least half of the estate. A farm customarily is taken over intact by the son whom the family as a whole considers to be the best potential farmer. The heir then pays each of his siblings a share of the inheritance. Sometimes two or even three sons take over.

In 1960 some 62 percent of Icelandic farms were freeholds; 7.5 percent were partly freehold. The remainder were leaseholds or partly leased. At least one farm in each rural community is a church farm, which is owned by the government and supervised by a Lutheran pastor who receives the proceeds for his "living." Each church farm has a chapel that serves the neighboring farmers and their families, and some farms have chapels without resident pastors.

A farmstead consists of "homefields" (averaging 28.5 acres) located near the farmhouse, meadowlands (averaging 31.5 acres), and unimproved pasture. The homefields are drained, leveled, manured, and planted with rich grasses, which are dried and stored for winter fodder. A similar type of hay farming adapted to northern latitudes, called crofting, is found in the west Highlands and the islands of Scotland (see Darling 1955: 208 ff.). Before the turn of the century hay was cultivated entirely with hand tools. Indeed, scythes are still used to cut wild hay from the meadowlands. Since the advent of mechanized equipment, the number of homefields per farm and their size have been increasing.

Although formerly each Icelandic farm required an average of two dozen hands, today a farm may be worked by one family with the assistance of one or more helpers, who are supplemented during the summer haying season by young people of both sexes (often schoolchildren over seven years of age). Most

Icelandic farms now have new living quarters constructed of concrete with roofs of tile or corrugated iron. The people, however, say that these new buildings do not keep out the cold so well as the old, multigabled stone and turf houses did. Sometimes a new front wing is added to an old stone and turf house, but only on special occasions are such elegant front rooms heated and used.

The Rural Community

A number of farms make up a rural municipality (*hreppur*). The farmers of the municipality may jointly own a tract of upland waste. According to customary law, every farmer in the *hreppur* has the right to run his flocks without a shepherd on this communal pasture during the summer months provided he sends, to help with the annual roundup, the requisite number of able-bodied men in proportion to the stock he has pastured. At roundup time in September the sheep are herded into a communal corral, which is divided into rectangular sections, one for each farm in the municipality. The sheep are sorted according to the individual owner's earmark. The owner calculates how many sheep he will be able to feed through the coming winter, and the remainder are slaughtered and sold.

An exceptional arrangement is found in Skútustadahreppur, a rural community in northeastern Iceland that I visited briefly in 1952. In this community there were 26 farms, 58 farmers, and a total population of 330. The area of the municipality is about 2,521 square miles, which consists mainly of upland pasture owned by the two church farms of the community, but every farmer in the *hreppur* is allowed to run his sheep there. Technically, this privilege costs a small fee, but I was told that the fee was not collected.

The farmers of a municipality may also jointly possess certain rights of access to other natural resources. The fishing rights in Mývatn, a lake in northeastern Iceland, are jointly owned, for example. The rights to collect driftwood and other debris from a beach or to gather eiderdown from the nesting places of the eider duck, however, are privately owned.

Most Icelandic rural communities have built a modern community center that serves as an adult education locale, a dance hall, and a theater for films and visiting players from the capital. Frequently the center also is used as a meeting place for community associations such as athletic and women's clubs. The center is usually built of concrete and up to 40 percent of the cost of construction is subsidized by the federal government through an entertainment tax. The community usually pays the remainder, partly in the form of voluntary labor. In addition, many rural communities own a library, which may be housed in its own building.

Children are taught to read and write at home but practically every rural community in Iceland has its own school for children aged ten to thirteen years. Farmers take turns boarding the teacher, whose salary is paid partly by the community tax and partly by the government.

Each municipality manages its own affairs through a council of five, called the *hreppsnefnd*. The council members are elected every four years by direct vole of those residents of the community who are twenty-one years or older. The council has charge of building and maintaining its center and its local roads. It is partially responsible for the support of the school and contributes to the government's efforts to conserve natural resources, for example, by exterminating foxes. It partially cares for the local poor, aged, orphans, illegitimate children, and mentally ill. In some municipalities the council also checks each constituent farmer's supply of winter fodder to ensure that none of the livestock will become a community liability.

The council finances its efforts through a municipal tax (*útsvar*). Certain of its responsibilities have been reduced since the inauguration of the Icelandic social security system. Like other Scandinavian systems, this has relatively high coverage.

The council elects its chairman, called the *oddviti*, from among its members. The Icelanders say that the *oddviti* is the odd man with the deciding vote. He functions as the council's executive officer as well as its treasurer, bookkeeper, and municipal tax collector. The community's records and book of laws are kept by the *oddviti*. He represents the municipality with the federal government.

The municipal council sends an elected representative, often the chairman, to the county council, called the *sýslunefnd*. This council supervises the affairs of the municipalities within its jurisdiction. A magistrate (*sýslumadur*), who is appointed by the Icelandic minister of justice, chairs the county council. Fourteen town units and eighteen counties form the basic local units of the federal government.

A rural community also has a federally paid bailiff (*hreppstjóri*). The bailiff is directly responsible to the county magistrate. The bailiff's duties include collecting federal income and property taxes for the county magistrate and keeping municipality census statistics on the size of the population, the numbers of livestock, and the amounts of other property, production, and exports. The bailiff also assumes leadership in case of such emergencies as shipwrecks. If a crime is committed, a rare event in Iceland, the bailiff may serve as agent for the county magistrate. In some Icelandic rural communities, however, no crimes are committed.

Trade Districts and Agricultural Societies

Iceland is also divided into trade districts that do not coincide with municipalities or counties. The trade districts are organized into cooperatives on the basis of economic resources and functions, as well as on the basis of existing transportation and communication facilities. Such voluntary societies now handle most of Iceland's farm products from the delivery of raw farm produce by individual farmer members through all the steps of processing, shipping, exporting, and marketing. They operate like corporations and function as purchasing agents, banks, and credit sources for their members. Cooperatives manage much of the manufacturing on the island, including the production of leather goods, woolen cloth, soap, and tallow. Home production has been superseded to a considerable extent by the factory system. The fishing industry, however, remains largely in private hands.

Every Icelandic farmer also belongs to a quasi-governmental

agricultural society, which exercises a limited lobbying influence on relevant legislation in the Althing and furnishes certain indispensable services to the rural districts.

Iceland must import all the wood used for houses and furniture (except driftwood), as well as other construction material, grains, tools, fuel, clothing, and other products. Fish products constitute about 95 percent of the country's total exports. Fishing, the most lucrative industry, triggered an economic boom during the past decade, but the nation is presently suffering from a severe depression due to migration of herring from the Icelandic banks to feeding grounds far to the northeast and also to a decrease in demand for herring and fish meal in the international market. Iceland's dependence on imports and her essentially one-crop export economy thus render her economically vulnerable.

Conclusion

We have briefly surveyed some of the major problems faced by Icelandic communities since their founding over 1,000 years ago. We have noted how local groups have resolved these problems in relation to their natural and human resources. Our findings suggest that the *godi-thingmenn* association, which the Icelanders on the basis of traditions from the Scandinavian homeland developed to resolve their group living problems, established a pattern of human relations, status roles, and land use in response to the resources of the island.

The *godi-thingmenn* relationship may be described abstractly as an arrangement of parts into a complex decentralized whole. The group thus formed is characterized by balance, flexibility, the mutual responsibility and advantage of the several parts to one another, and the absence of strong dominance of any one part over the remainder. Two statuses are recognized, *godi* and *thingmenn*. Each has its own responsibilities and privileges, but the two are perceived as correlative and complementary, and the superordinate (*godi*) relates to the subordinate (*thingmenn*) as the first among equals. Thus the system tends to be egalitarian rather than authoritarian. Key parts in this system are autonomous units conceived as organically balanced rather than mechanistic in character, and they rather than the system as a whole are dynamic centers of power. Thus the parts are intrinsic to the whole. They are nonexpendable. They are the raison d'être for its existence.

This preferred relationship pattern has either persisted in many guises or reemerged in slightly changed form to the present despite significant changes in climate, resources, population size, political organization, religion, economy, and other fundamental aspects of the native culture and environment. A historical perspective reveals that in the early Icelandic commonwealth the *godar* assumed a *thingmenn*-type role in relation to one another. Similarly, the lawspeaker took a *godi*-type role and merely recited the law and advised regarding facts of law upon request. He did not decide legal cases like a judge or implement decisions like an executive. The Icelandic nation's phrasing of its loss of sovereignty as the personal tributary relationship of a freeman (*thingmenn*-type role) to a responsible local leader (*godi*-type role), rather than that of a subject or colonial people to an alien king, conforms to the same conceptual model.

The preferred form of association is also reflected in the Icelandic cooperatives and in the structures of both the municipal organization and the national government of the modern republic of Iceland. Relations between such traditional units as chieftains and freemen have been institutionalized into a complex sociopolitical system that affords much of the balance, flexibility, and local independence that characterized traditional forms. Responsible, face-to-face leadership roles and local group decision-making prerogatives have been legally safeguarded. The modern rural communities of Iceland thus exemplify the persistence or the reemergence of social units, including status roles, institutions, man-nature relationship patterns, and values, that formerly characterized a prehistoric form of tribal organization. Such units have been built as foundation stones into the structure of the modern nation. In this sovereign state an elected president, whose duties are largely ceremonial; a prime minister, whose cabinet holds office by confidence; and a reconstituted Althing, whose members are elected by popular vote, all reflect a political pattern that legally soft-pedals authoritarianism and fosters decentralized egalitarianism.

This example of development, persistence, and reemergence of a preferred pattern suggests that the Icelandic nation, with its fully documented history, prehistory, and archaeology, may offer the student of culture an unusually favorable natural laboratory. Among the cases described in this volume, Iceland represents the only relatively isolated island community that is located in the far north. Chiefly on account of the industry, historical interest, and literary skill of its people, the Icelandic case affords data for an investigation of cultural process in the context not only of difficult and fluctuating climatic conditions but also of an environment with limited natural resources. It thus affords an opportunity to test, over a significant time span, certain hypotheses, such as the theory of unilinear sociocultural evolution, and the principle of limited possibilities, including the role of ecological factors in cultural development and change (see Chapter 11).

Furthermore, Iceland furnishes an opportunity to study the relation between the development of a culture and the development of a microrace by a population that had been relatively isolated for 1,000 years until World War II. Indeed, it still contains many small, relatively isolated subgroups. Investigations in population genetics are urgently needed before the laboratory situation deteriorates further due to the influx of new gene frequencies by migration, and other changes.

Notes

1. I am indebted to Vilhjálmur Bjarnar for permission to use this quote.
2. Our knowledge of early Icelandic culture has been refined recently by the scholarly analyses of written sources by Einar Ólafur Sveinsson (for example, 1953, 1954, 1957–1958), Sigurdur Jóhannesson Nordal (for example, 1942), E. O. Gabriel Turville-Petre (1953, 1964), and other scholars. In the area of social structure the earlier meticulous work of Dame Phillpotts (1913), based on records of wergild payments in Germanic-speaking countries, is invaluable. Many of the important documents have been translated

into English by the tireless efforts of Halldór Hermannson (for example, 1930) and others.

3. Only a few of the many source materials used in this chapter have been noted. Mention should be made of the work of Saemund Sigfússon (1056–1133), Ari Thorgilsson (1067–1148), and Snorri Sturluson (1179–1241). There is also the anonymous *Elder Edda,* a record of early Norse poetry and mythology (Hollander 1962). Most of the Icelandic sagas, written in Icelandic during the twelfth and thirteenth centuries, have been translated into other languages, including English. For a modern history of Icelandic literature, see Stefán Einarsson (1957). The Icelandic annals are a priceless source of facts bridging the gap between ancient and modern Iceland. The work of modern scholars, such as the recently elected President of Iceland. Dr. Kristján Eldjárn (for example, 1957), who is a professional archaeologist, the geologist Sigurdur Thorarinsson (for example, 1956, 1958), and others help to relate present-day events to history and prehistory.

4. The brief field studies (1952, 1960) that have contributed to this chapter were financed in part by grants, here gratefully acknowledged, from the Humanities Division of the Rockefeller Foundation and from the Faculty Research and Development Fund of North Carolina State University. I take this opportunity to thank all the Icelanders who aided me in the research for their kindness and help, especially Einar Ólafur Sveinsson and Stefán Einarsson. I am deeply indebted to Anna Gudmundsdóttir for her hospitality and generous assistance in the field work. I thank Vilhjálmur Bjarnar for reading the chapter in an earlier draft and for very helpful comments, as well as for permission to read the manuscript of his translation of S. J. Nordal's important book on Icelandic culture (1942), to be published by Cornell University Press. I am grateful to Helen Codere for the use of her field notes on Iceland. I have incorporated into this chapter some material already published (Thompson 1960b, 1963).

5. During the 1727 eruption two small farms were evacuated (Thorarinsson 1956: 46).

6. Hallburg 1963. See, for example, Njáls saga (Magnusson and Pálsson 1960), Egil's saga (Jones 1960), and Laxdoela saga (Arent 1964).

10 /

SAXONS OF THE
OSNABRÜCK NORTHLAND

Mien Vader sien Land is mi nöger as den Konig sien Riek.

My father's land is dearer to me than his kingdom is to
a king.

Lower Saxon folk saying[1]

It has been thirty-five years since I first visited the Osnabrück
Northland in the lowlands of West Germany. I lived for twelve
months over a period of three years as a family member in a
remote Lower Saxon farmstead. This was no ordinary *Hof*. Situated in beautiful rolling country of woods and meadows interspersed with plowed fields, it had been in the same family for a
thousand years. I had the unique opportunity of participating
in the tradition-bound life-way during the entire round of the
agricultural year.

The farmstead is located about a half-mile from Ankum
(population 2,522 in 1956), an Old Saxon market town that is
the center of a Roman Catholic parish in the former province of
Hanover. Ankum belongs to the bishopric of Osnabrück, and
Osnabrück itself is a historic cathedral city some fifteen miles
to the southeast. Such facts, however, give no idea of the cultural distance that separates the population of Ankum from
the modern world.

The people with whom I associated valued their way of life
in a proud and tenacious way. Living in closely knit family
and neighborhood groups, they were unusually clannish and
suspicious of outsiders. While at the farmstead, I did not observe
that a single visitor was invited into the family living quarters
except relatives, neighbors, and (once) a priest. Only two

182

Lutheran families and no Jews, gypsies, or foreigners lived in the parish. No tourists visited the area. Even the Germans themselves were unacquainted with the local culture, as I discovered when I spent a winter in Berlin.

Ankum, near the Hase tributary of the Ems River, was marginally located in relationship to railroads, trade routes, and large industrial centers, and it was peripheral to the mainstream of European political events. Not until the construction of superhighways and factories in the area during World War II was Ankum brought into closer contact with world affairs. In 1946, as part of Bersenbrück county, it was incorporated into the state of Niedersachsen in the Federal Republic of Germany. Low German (Plattdeutsch), the language in daily use in the region, has never been popular in written form, and every rural community has its own version. Modern accounts of the local lifeway are scarce,[2] and the area remains one of the least known in the nation.

Looking back, I believe that this community has been the most difficult that I have tried to understand. An aura of nationalistic romance envelops the Lower Saxons—the historical sources contrasting in this respect with those of Iceland.[3] During the Nazi regime, the Lower Saxons were believed to represent the German nationalistic concept of *Blut und Boden* (Blood and Soil); that is, they were supposed to embody the true German race and tradition. But the rural inhabitants of Ankum were much more attached to their fathers' land than to the Fatherland. Despite these obstacles to objective study, the inherently interesting life-way of the Northlanders and its close relationship with the distinctive geology of the area, especially small differences in soil type, as well as the relevance of the analysis to sociological theory, were persuasive in the decision to include the Saxon case study in this series.[4]

Climate

The present climate of Bersenbrück county (elevation, 66 to 665 feet; area, 41 square miles) is moist, cloudy, and windy. It is mitigated by nearness to the North Sea, which is influenced by the Gulf Stream. The average annual temperature varies from 52 degrees F. in summer to 39.5 degrees F. in winter, the frost-free growing season extending only from June to October. The average annual precipitation varies from 26.5 to 30 inches.

Geology and Geography

During the Middle Pleistocene, the German lowlands between the contemporary beds of the Weser and Ems Rivers were covered by a southern extension of the Riss ice sheet. As the glacier melted, moraines were deposited over previous formations. Ankum is located on one of the glacial end moraines that is now called the Ankum-Lingen hills. Melt water ran off in glacial rivers that formed broad prehistoric valleys. One such river, flowing southward, cut a channel through the end moraine to form a prehistoric stream valley to the south. Winds blowing off the ice sheet during its recession facilitated the accumulation of flying sand. In time, much of the ground moraine was overlaid by sand, forming a characteristically dry, flat land called *Geest*. The Cloppenburger Geestplatte, located north of Bersenbrück county, exemplifies such a formation. Sand also massed below the end moraines in long flat dunes and to some extent overlay the prehistoric valley and hill formations. On the other hand, loess, a fertile windlaid glacial loam, is virtually absent in the region except for a few acres between Ankum, Bersenbrück, and Tütingen.

In post-Pleistocene times the drainage system reversed itself in this area. Recent river systems cut channels through the sand formations, obliterating them in some places. For example, the Hase River flows northward and westward to join the Ems, cutting through the prehistoric glacial stream valley between the villages of Bersenbrück and Neuenkirchen to form a fertile alluvial delta known as the Artland (ard or plowland).

Early Human Settlement

Although traces of Paleolithic and Mesolithic hunting peoples have been discovered fairly near the Ankum area, signs of extensive human occupation begin with Neolithic finds.[5] A few sites of Dolmen Builders have been reported in this region, but their distribution suggests that they were the temporary habitations of a group of Dolmen Builders who passed near Ankum en route up the Hase to a site near Tecklenburg.

More numerous in the Hase locality are the famous *Hünengräber* (giants' graves). These are collective passage graves that have a rectangular or oval ground-plan and an entrance in one of the long sides. These graves were apparently built by refugees from southern Jutland who were expelled by Battle Axe invaders about 2000 B.C. (see Chapter 7). Seeking a habitat suited to their herder-farmer way of life, they avoided the swampy North Sea coast favored by trading peoples and settled in slightly higher, dry places that had light, easily worked soil. Such sites are found on the Ankum-Lingen hills, as well as on sanddunes and in prehistoric stream valleys. As in Jutland, these Passage Grave People used the slash-and-burn method to cultivate such cereals as club millet. They raised long-horned cattle and probably also pigs, sheep, and goats. In the dense oak forests they doubtless hunted roe deer, wild pig, red deer, and wild oxen. In time they apparently mixed with an indigenous Mesolithic population and with intrusive Dolmen Builders.

The Bronze Age

The types and distribution of archaeological sites suggest that during the Bronze Age (c. 1800–750 B.C.) the Ems-Hase region became a backwash area for cultural influences and population overflow from the lower Rhine valley.[6] Major terminal points for this population movement were the Netherlands and southern England. In the Ems-Hase region there are evidences of a Beaker culture, especially in stone circle sites, and later Tumulus culture sites of the cremation mound type as well as urnfields. Also Hallstatt culture finds suggest some penetration by Hallstatt goods. Iron does not appear in the urns until about 750 B.C.

There is widespread evidence of Bronze Age population increase. The forested areas decreased in size as cultivation spread to include not only light dry soils that were the focus of primary Neolithic settlement but also intermediate soils and the heavier soils such as the Artland. Slash-and-burn cultivation of club millet gave way to the use of square, fixed fields (Celtic type) bounded by ditches and hedges. They were plowed by means of an ard (primitive plow) drawn by oxen and were planted with millet and oats. It is likely that the use of manure as fertilizer began at this time. Pastoral activities also increased during the Bronze Age. Long-horned cattle were displaced by short-horns, and sheep and the domesticated horse became important in the local economy.

The Osnabrück Northland offered none of the natural resources that Bronze Age men valued as trade commodities—precious amber, copper, and tin. (Nor was it rich in loess soil favored by Neolithic Danubian farmers.) The region was bypassed by the main Bronze Age trade routes between northern and southern Europe, which included the Elbe-Weser amber route over the Brenner Pass from the Adriatic and Mycenae; the Atlantic coast route; and the west Mediterranean-Rhone-Rhine route. Not until the latter part of the Bronze Age, according to Ernst Sprockhoff (1930: plate 45), did a main trade route connect Emsland with the north European culture cradle via the Elbe and with central Europe via the valley of the Saale. The route passed through what is now Bersenbrück county, fording the Hase at about the middle of the east-west bend. An important market, which attracted traders from the Bremen region and from even more remote points, is reported to have been held annually at Walsum in the Rüssel community of Ankum parish (Hardebeck 1902: 11, after Hartmann) and was evidently located on the route. In the late Bronze Age the Ems-Hase region was thus connected directly to the Netherlands and to Jutland and indirectly by the Weser route to central Germany, which was then a main source of copper.

The late Bronze Age population of the Osnabrück Northland may have spoken a language belonging to the Celtic stock.[7] Such a conclusion is based on the assumption that the lower Rhine Tumulus Builders spoke a Celtic language and that some Urnfield people belonged to the Celtic culture complex. The hypothesis is reinforced by river names in the region that have a Celtic derivation and by the distribution of a Celtic type of house and land-use pattern in northern Germany west of the Weser. In addition, lighting Easter fires is a Celtic custom that has continued to be practiced in this region until the present. The warmth of fire, like that of the sun, was believed to give strength and protection against evil forces (Plath 1955: 119).

Conquest by German-Speaking Groups

As has been noted, no major change occurred in the climate of northern Europe from the end of the Mesolithic (c. 2500 B.C.) until the latter part of the Bronze Age (from c. 850 B.C.). The warm dry subboreal phase of the post-Pleistocene, with its dense forests dominated by oak, lasted almost two millenniums. A marked deterioration of climate occurred in northern Europe and in Asia beginning about the ninth century B.C. The climatic change was accompanied by a shift of the southward amber trade (about 700 B.C.) to the Vistula route from the Bronze Age Elbe-Weser route. In the northern German lowlands bogs formed and plant growth raised the moors higher. In the vicinity of Bersenbrück, for example, the heather-clad Hahnen and Vinter moors became important features of the landscape. Gradually beech forest replaced oak until a beech ecological climax was reached.

During this climatic crisis groups of Germanic-speaking farmer-herders, some of whom (for example, Urnfield folk) probably infiltrated the Elbe-Weser lowlands during the Bronze Age, began to cross the Weser and to penetrate the Ems-Hase region of northwestern Germany. It is generally accepted that the core of the migratory fighting unit characteristic of these Germanic-speaking tribes was a voluntary group composed of a charismatic war leader (*princeps*) who was the "first among equals" and his followers (*comitatus*), united by mutual loyalty and personal honor.[8]

Although some Celtic-speaking peoples seem to have retreated before the invaders, the available evidence suggests that generally the Germanic tribes conquered but did not displace resident populations (H. Hubert 1934b: 94, 96). Some time before the birth of Christ the Chasuarier had apparently established themselves in the Hase region and the Frisians had settled in marshlands on the north coast (from the Elbe westward to the Zuider Zee). The Angriwaren seem to have settled on the lower Weser, the Cherusker in the hills to the south, and the Brukterer in the upper Ems drainage. The Chauken are believed to have pushed into the Hase drainage in 58 B.C. (Brüning 1950: map 148c).

These and other Germanic peoples were apparently a mixed racial type. Coon (1939: 207–208, 535–542) derived them from Upper Paleolithic forebears amalgamated with megalithic types and with strong Battle Axe and Nordic ingredients. They interbred with the natives of the territories where they settled, which reinforced the blond and reddish hair-color elements probably already present in some Urnfield and Hallstatt folk. This early Iron Age blend apparently formed the basis for the evolution of a local race. Enriched by genes from other Germanic tribes during the early centuries of the Christian era and from Frankish infiltration after the Saxon conquest, this local race has evolved into a distinctive type called Falish (Schwidetzky and Walter 1967). The *fälische* race is characterized by slightly rounder heads with somewhat shorter, broader faces than the Nordics to the east, whom they resemble. Individuals belonging to this type tend to be somewhat blonder and a little more slender. They show less blood group B and a high ratio of Rh negative. According to Coon (1968), their blood groups are: O—41.7 percent; A—44.7 percent; B—9.9 percent; AB—3.7 percent; MN—49.7 percent; MM—26.6 percent; NN—20.7 percent.

Clash with Rome

About A.D. 100, when this region was threatened by legions of the expanding Roman empire, most of the tribes east of the Rhine seemed to manifest not only a distinctive race but also a unique culture, according to the first historical records (Tacitus 1942: 710 ff.). The Germanized populations had cultures that differed in basic structure from contemporary Roman culture.[9] For example, the bilaterally balanced Teutonic kindreds and the high position accorded to women in German customary law contrasted sharply with the patriarchal Roman family dominated by its legally powerful *pater familias*. The decentralized Germanic authority pattern, depending for its "strength" on a balance of power based on personal honor and mutual loyalty between many local chieftains with their followers, contrasted significantly with the pattern of centralized political and military authority characteristic of Rome.

In A.D. 9, deep in the Teutoberg forest south of Osnabrück, the Cherusker, led by Hermann Arminius, decisively destroyed three Roman legions led by Varus and ended the Roman push toward the north. The Germans were aided, of course, by climatic and ecological factors (dense forests, swamps and bogs, heavy rainfall, and penetrating cold) adverse to their southern attackers. According to Tacitus (1942: 666, 710–712, 718), the Germans had an advantage over the Romans because, besides their superior numbers, they were not handicapped by heavy clothing and arms, could swim well, run swiftly, fight in rivers and swamps on account of their tall robust frames, and could withstand cold and hunger.

Although Roman objects have been found in the Northland, the inhabitants were not Romanized. The Cheruskers' successful resistance to Roman conquest allowed indigenous communities of the North Sea–Baltic region to continue their unique cultural development for another 750 years without critical disturbances due to alien cultural pressures from southern or central Europe. They were so isolated that we must rely on archaeological findings for most of our information about them during this period.

Saxon Penetration of the Lowlands

The movement of the Old Saxons from their homeland, which was presumably in what is now Holstein in the neck of the Jutland peninsula,[10] coincides with an improvement of the climate of the area toward a drier, colder type beginning about the fourth century. Precipitation decreased, bogs ceased to form, and tidal generating forces subsided to a minimum, which meant that land was exposed along the North Sea and Baltic coasts. Armed with the *Sax* (a short iron sword from which they may have derived their name), long spears, helmets, and coats of mail, the Saxons rowed their curved boats along the North Sea coast and up its rivers. Their activities as pirates superseded those of the Frisians and the Chauken. They raided the Atlantic coast to the Loire River and invaded southeastern England. As deep-plow agriculturalists, the Saxons avoided the coastal marshes inhabited by Frisians and sought the slightly elevated "lowlands" with better drainage and richer soil. When historical records again became available, the Old Saxons were well established in the lowlands of northwest Germany and of the adjacent Netherlands.[11] They are reported to have conquered the Münsterland Brukterer shortly before 700 (Prinz 1934: 17, from Bede).

The Old Saxons were expert agriculturalists and dairymen. Heavier clay soils, as well as some lighter types, were cultivated. The fields were long strips, which were plowed with an iron-tipped plowshare drawn by a yoke of oxen. Rye, buckwheat, and some flax were grown but there were still no meadows. The remains of an Iron Age farmhouse has been found in an archaeological site near Groningen in the Netherlands (Clark 1952: 158–163). Judging from this find, it appears that Old Saxon houses were long and rectangular with entrances at end and side. One end of the house was apparently used as a shelter for cattle, as is still the custom. Prototypes also occur in archaeological sites from the Celtic and Roman Iron Age in Jutland.

Farmsteads were apparently organized into rural communities called *Gaue*. Ankum was the center of the Varn Gau (see Brüning 1950: map 149). Like the Scandinavian *almenning*, tracts of undivided forest, heath, and moorland belonged to the *Gau* and were regulated by the mutual agreement of its members.

The Old Saxons had a strongly developed social class system: a free warrior class, which was highest in prestige; freemen; freedmen; and bondsmen (Adam of Bremen 1959: 9–10; Ashley 1900: 129; Below 1966: 8 ff.). As in Scandinavia, a very high value was placed on the status of freeman. Breach of a freeman's sanctity was accountable by either blood or wergild. Popular assemblies or tribunals of freemen were held for defining customary law, but there were no judges (Repp 1832: 31).

In case of major crimes, wergild indemnity, varying in value according to the rank both of victim and slayer, was paid by the family of the slayer. But if the accused wished to prove his innocence, he might be cleared if he could obtain the unanimous sworn testimony of conjurators. The number of conjurators depended on the nature of the crime.

Conquest by the Franks

By the last quarter of the eighth century the Old Saxon *Gaue* comprised three major tribal divisions: the Westphalians of Ems and Lippe (the Osnabrück Northland belonged to this grouping); the Angriwarans on the west bank of the Weser; and the Eastphalians on the east Weser bank. A fourth division, the Nordalbingians of Schleswig-Holstein, is often grouped with the Old Saxons. At this time the Saxons were experiencing strong territorial pressures from all sides: from Vikings and Frisians in the north; from Slavs in the east; and, by far the most intense pressure, from Franks in the south and west.

Although both tribes were of Germanic origin, the eighth-century Saxons differed in language and culture from the Franks. The Saxons spoke Old Saxon, a west Germanic language. The Emslanders spoke the Westphalian dialect of old Saxon until 1100–1300, when they shifted to the Emsland dialect of Middle Low German. The Old High German sound shift of the accent away from the root syllable of a word (which occurred in the speech of most south German groups, including the Franks, between the fifth and seventh centuries) was rejected by the lowlanders.[12]

Because a man's ego could be extended beyond death through fame conferred on him through poetry, bards were held in high esteem. The vigor of Old Saxon poetry and the joyousness and exuberance of the lifeway it reflected has been noted by Jean I. Young (1950: 275–286), E. C. Metzenthin (1924: 535), and others. Not much is known about the Old Saxon religion in which this life way was rooted, but the evidence indicates that Thor was a major deity but many other gods, including Wotan (Odin) and Niördr (Njörd), were propitiated by means of blood sacrifices of animals and occasionally of human beings in such holy places as sacred groves and springs.[13] Abortion and euthanasia were practiced, and the dead were cremated and placed in urn cemeteries (*Urnenfriedhöfe*).

The Franks, on the other hand, spoke Old High German and practiced medieval Catholicism. They were unified under a political structure bolstered by Romanized legal practices and headed by a powerful king (later, an emperor). In addition, the Franks were skilled in a type of organized warfare, military discipline, and weaponry borrowed from southern Europe.

Between 772 and 804 Charlemagne, leader of the Franks, waged eighteen campaigns against the Saxons. On a single day (in 783) some 4,500 Saxon warriors were beheaded at Verden on the Aller River, about seventy miles northeast of Osnabrück. Although the Saxons resisted fiercely, by 804 all who lived in territories as far as the Eider River in southern Jutland had surrendered. An estimated third of the population was deported and resettled in Frankish territories while Franks were settled on Saxon lands (Seeliger 1936: 612–613). Many Saxon areas were virtually depopulated. Some Saxons fled to Denmark.

According to the conditions of surrender, the Saxons had to renounce their traditional beliefs, laws, and practices, including their public assemblies and ceremonies. They were required to embrace Catholic doctrine and practice its decrees, including baptism, extreme unction and other sacraments, and the strict observance of the Sabbath and Lent. And they were forced to honor the supreme authority of the Roman church through a priestly hierarchy. The penalty of infringement of these conditions of surrender, called capitularies, was death.

To stamp out Saxon paganism, the victors destroyed the images of the Saxon gods and desecrated the holy places. An effort was made to eliminate such practices as human sacrifice, euthanasia, and abortion. Particularly abhorrent to the Saxons was the church ban on the marriage of priests because of the Saxon's conception of the sacredness of marriage and the family. They were also repelled by the medieval clergy's interest in Mary's virginity, and they were shocked by the holy writ that

Peter, who became the first pope, betrayed Christ, because disloyalty to a leader was to them a heinous crime (Metzenthin 1924: 526). They disliked all curbs on their personal freedom such as the injunction to rest on the Sabbath.

Because such extreme regulations could not be enforced, the Saxons were later permitted to retain the right of public assembly and some traditional laws and customs. In suppressing worship of the Saxon gods, however, the capitularies undercut positive aspects of the Old Saxon religion. Failing to honor their gods, the people felt vulnerable to evil powers, and their anxiety about demons increased (Metzenthin 1924: 537). Both gods and demons were occasionally propitiated surreptitiously. According to Chadwick (1912: 414), magical practices and belief in spirits and in certain deities lasted many centuries. Heathen ceremonial centers in the Osnabrück region, including elves' hills, giants' graves, and grave mounds, are still known. Between Ankum and Druchhorn a crucifix long surmounted the Swetsberg (Animal-Blood Hill) where blood sacrifices are believed to have been offered to Wotan, who is thought to haunt the vicinity in the form of the devil (Hardebeck 1902: 3).

Of course, the struggle to bring the Saxons and other pagan Germanic tribes into the European orthodox fold had repercussions also on Catholic beliefs and practices. For example, stimulated by magical thinking and the fear of demons characteristic of pagans and Christians alike, the cult of saints' relics emerged (J. W. Thompson 1928: 172). Alleged bones or clothes of martyrs and deceased persons who had been canonized by the church, or even pieces of wood and other materials supposedly once connected with them, were used to perform such miracles as the expulsion of demons. The doctrine of the supremacy and infallibility of the pope as the unerring, sinless Holy Father, which was formulated during the reign of Charlemagne's son, Louis the Pious, may have been a defense against the decentralized preferred relationship pattern of recently conquered Germanic tribes. The resistance of the Saxons to surrender and also to feudal status takes on deeper meaning when it is viewed in the context of the Saxon concepts of the freeman and the freehold.

Advent of Feudalism

As noted in Chapter 8, Charlemagne built trading towns, including one at Wilhelmshafen in the Weser estuary that connected Saxonland with Viking trade routes. In time eight bishoprics were established in Saxon territory, including one centered at Osnabrück, a strategic location on the Hase in the Osnabrücker Hügelland. In each bishopric subsidiary churches were built, apparently including a *Tauf* (mother church) in each of the Old Saxon Gaue (Prinz 1934: 19). Varn Gau's mother church was at Ankum.

According to the Roman pattern, the seat of each bishopric became a cathedral town, a center of ecclesiastical learning where Latin was taught. Writing was thus introduced in the form of religious documents, and Latin became the only medium of literacy in the area. The Old Saxon literary tradition declined both because it was directly suppressed and because its inspiration and subject matter had been undermined. However, John George Robertson (1931: 3) has suggested that although the dominance of the ecclesiastic sphere inaugurated a renaissance of Latin thinking and writing in the eleventh century, it also crushed the beginning of a written folk literature.

An overlordship of ecclesiastical and lay nobility was set up in the Osnabrück Northland that by means of heavy tithes and tribute obligations as well as by military and tribunal services tended to exercise a substantial control over the population. Many farmers were demoted to vassal status, and if they could not meet the heavy obligations they also lost their freeholds. However, despite feudal practices that were applied to Saxon properties claimed by church and nobles, blocks of Saxon lands remained in freehold under a slightly modified ancient system of tenure.[14] Due to a combination of factors, in the territory of the Saxons feudal relations were less formal than in Swabia and Bavaria, for example, and the institution of feudalism was less intense and less persistent than in central and western Europe.

Reemergence of the Saxon Freehold

The climatic deterioration that began toward the end of the thirteenth century also affected social statuses in the conquered

Saxon lands. It was more severe in the northern than in the central and southern regions. As the climate became very cold and damp the growing season contracted. Crops failed to mature and food became scarce. Famines were frequent, and in their weakened condition the people were vulnerable to epidemics, including, of course, the Black Death (1348–1350), which took a heavy toll (Abel 1935, 1956: 14). Although relatively few farms and villages in northwestern Germany were actually deserted, compared with other regions of the country, there were significant socioeconomic changes in the Osnabrück Northland. Most large manors failed when farmers were no longer able to pay their tithes and tribute (Prinz 1940: 13). When the noble families fell, their lands were sold back into small freeholds (Provinz Hannover 1915: 74). The struggle against feudalism culminated in the Thirty Years' War (1618–1648), which occurred at the low point in the climatic cycle.

So it happened that after a relatively short feudal period in the lowlands the Old Saxon freehold reemerged in slightly altered form. According to parish records, a number of isolated farmsteads in the Northland (called *altsächsische Siedlungen*) have been in the same family for a thousand years, and their locations are known. In the Ankum parish such farms have been mapped.[15]

The evidence suggests that the Old Saxon freehold (*Besitz*) contained a full hide of land. It usually covered about seventy-four acres and included ownership of a house lot with garden and plowland and access to common forest and grazing land. In other words, a *Besitz* provided ownership or access to all the types of land and resources that a farm household needed for independent viability.

Customarily a *Besitz* was handed down intact as a stem farm (*Stammhof*). This tradition intensified the problem of a surplus population, and there were traditional devices for coping with it, including abortion, infanticide, human sacrifice, euthanasia, war, migration, and monogamy. Because many customs that had helped to control births, plan families, and eliminate nonproductive family members were proscribed by the church, conversion to Christianity affected the population balance adversely.

Cultural Persistence and Change

Although the freehold system had reappeared, it was immediately exposed to severe pressures caused by excess population and land hunger. Vital resources, including large areas of forest, had been destroyed by the armies. Although the use of manure had probably been known since the late Bronze Age, signs of soil exhaustion appeared.

Saxon conquest of the Wends and other Slavic tribes located east of the Elbe provided one outlet for surplus population. Nevertheless, during the tenth and eleventh centuries, many full-hide estates were split into two parcels. Such farms, affording a living for two heirs and their families rather than only for one, were known for tax purposes as *Halberben*. As the climate deteriorated during the first half of the thirteenth century, three-part splits, called *Drittelerben*, occurred, so that three heirs could be accommodated on a full hide.

Another device used to ease the population pressure was the settlement of hereditary cotters (*Erbkotten*) on moor and heathland. Also, a farmer's younger son might receive a parcel of land from the *Stammhof* as dowry. Using one of the houses belonging to the estate, he would work a small farming enterprise. Such a hereditary cot was considered a constituent part of the stem farm. A cotter strove to free himself legally from the estate, but if the enterprise failed, the cot was returned to the stem farm.

Some hereditary cotters, unable to succeed independently, became hereditary hirelings, stem farmer and hireling forming a complementary economic relationship. The hireling and his wife gave a traditionally fixed number of days' labor to the owner annually in return for the use of a small dwelling house and a parcel of land. This arrangement persists to the present.

The hireling system, whose roots can be found in the adjustment required after the disappearance of moor and heath wasteland in the early sixteenth century, was thus developed to meet a labor shortage. Many farm workers were killed during the Thirty Years' War, and others migrated to the Netherlands. After the war, laborers were desperately needed to help with the grain crops and to cope with the problem of finding additional sources of swine fodder, which had previously been supplied by the woodlands.

The alteration in the pattern of land use under the impact of the Reformation and the Thirty Years' War was accompanied by other changes. In the Osnabrück district, wergild was paid into the sixteenth century, but payments, usually made by the slayer to the heirs, were so small that they were generally exceeded by fines paid to the public authority. Thus, obligations to the local group began to compete with those to the kindred, and kindred solidarity of the traditional type was superseded by loyalty to the family and by neighborhood reciprocities.

As the functions of the kindred waned, those of the neighborhood increased. Families who inherited farms acquired fixed reciprocal duties. A farmstead might have a "first neighbor," a "second neighbor," and even a "third neighbor." The role of each, especially during times of illness and during such rites of passage as funerals and weddings, was fixed by custom rather than by geographic proximity. Responsibilities of the first neighbor were the heaviest. When an owner died, the first neighbor's family took charge of the deceased's household until termination of the mourning rites. Families of traditional neighbors visited with one another. Each *Stammhof* was thus related to several others by a formal system of reciprocal neighbor rights, privileges, and obligations.

The Stem Family

Concomitantly, the kindred gave way to the stem family.[16] C. C. Zimmerman and M. E. Frampton (1935: 144, 133, after Le Play) have described the northern European stem family:

> The father selects as heir one of his children judged the best fitted. He bequeaths the home-place formally to the heir. The testament carries the role of the house father with all its duties and obligations. This family type, while joining one married child to the ancestral household, establishes the remainder independently with doweries . . . It perpetuates a homebase to which

all members of the family may resort and it keeps most of the property at the paternal home while passing down tradition to future generations.

In farm-owning families of the Osnabrück Northland the father may consult the mother and the siblings regarding the choice of an heir best suited to inherit the place. A son is preferred but if there are no male children a daughter may inherit. On some ancient farms, however, the junior right (inheritance by the youngest son) prevails. This practice allows parents to care for the needs of most of their children before the youngest son brings home a wife and assumes his rights over the place. The junior right also tends to reduce discord between father and heir and thus to facilitate the smooth functioning of the patriarchal order. This system usually engenders the development of an informal family council composed of siblings, parents, and uncles who advise the youngest son when he must make major decisions.

On the farm where I lived the family unanimously agreed that, of the eight sons, the seventh was best suited to manage and inherit the estate. When this son died at the age of twenty, the father was convinced that he was being punished for breaking the junior right, which had been the custom on this farmstead for a millennium. He tried to make amends by removing his youngest son, conceded to be the "student type," from the *Gymnasium* in Osnabrück and apprenticing him at the farm as heir designate. Here we note manifestation of a belief in immanent punishment for transgressing, not a rule of canon law or a tribal custom but a tradition of the ancestral estate.

The heir is also required by the *Altenteil* (parents' share) custom to provide for his parents after they relinquish proprietorship of the farm.[17] He may turn over one or more rooms and a small piece of land as an annuity to the old couple. Upon the death of the parents, this land reverts to the *Stammhof*. If need be, the heir is also expected to provide a dowry for each sister and to pay the cost of training each brother in a trade or profession. Siblings who leave the farm receive their share of the inheritance partly from the dowry of the heir's bride. Siblings may also work as unmarried "uncles" or "aunts" on the farm.

Marriage

The heir designate seeks a girl who will bring with her a substantial dowry and he chooses a bride from a neighboring farm
of similar status and faith. The young bride should have the
social position, the physical stamina, and the exacting domestic
skills needed to fulfill the traditional role of a farm owner's
wife. Virginity and marital chastity are also expected. There
is no divorce in this Catholic parish. Formerly a farm owner's
daughter aspired to "marry horses" rather than to marry into a
place that had only cows. Lately, however, some girls from
good farms who have noted that "a farmer's wife has a hard
life" have married teachers, veterinarians, physicians, bankers,
and even shopkeepers.

Visiting

Farm-owning families carry on most of their social activities
within their own group. On the farmstead where I lived equally
close ties were maintained with the father's and the mother's
relatives, especially with those who lived within a radius of five
to ten miles. First cousins met frequently, especially for coffee
after mass on Sundays in one of the inns of the village.

Except between relatives and neighbors, visiting occurred
mainly at funerals, weddings, and such seasonal affairs as the
anniversary of the founding of the village church and the farmers'
ball. Until it was opened to the public by Nazi edict, the annual
farmers' ball was attended only by local farm-owning families.
While their elders gossiped and drank beer, schnaps, and wine,
young people danced and courted. Dating was virtually non-
existent.

Hunting

Hunting, a prestige sport, is confined to male members of the
farm-owning class. A group of perhaps a dozen hunters may
organize a club. By supplementing their privately owned forests
with rentals from the state forest, they may obtain hunting rights
to perhaps 3,000 acres. Roe deer, wild boar, fox, hare, pheasant,

quail, and rabbit constitute the prey. Club rules regarding game conservation are rigidly enforced, and poachers are severely punished.

Stalking with or without a dog is the custom, but the dangerous wild boar, now somewhat rare in the area, is the object of communal hunting. When wild boar tracks are detected the whole club is notified. Half of the hunters, with guns ready, surround the boar's hiding place while the remainder flush him out. Even then the wily animal may escape. After a hunt the hunters gather at a local inn to drink and sing, discuss the hunt, inspect the kill, and praise the marksman's skill. They use an archaic vocabulary reminiscent of the Old Germanic pagan kennings. "Sweat," for example, means "blood."

Social Classes

Justus Möser (1720–1794), the Lutheran prime minister of Osnabrück who was one of the first ethnographic historians, described the three social classes of his time as nobles, burghers, and peasants. Today in the rural Northland, where burghers and even nobles are absent or very scarce indeed, the owning families, hirelings, and farm laborers form a social hierarchy of their own.

Proprietors of entailed farms (*Erbhöfe*)[18] occupy the upper rung of the local status ladder. The social position of each family depends on the size and soil quality of its holdings and the length of time that the family has occupied the land. The earliest settlers' descendants have the highest prestige. Cotters and hirelings occupy the middle rung, and farm laborers constitute the lowest class. In Ankum such professionals as the veterinarian, the physician, bank clerks, and schoolteachers outrank small business owners and shopkeepers, who themselves are higher on the social scale than such skilled technicians as mechanics, blacksmiths, and bakers. From the viewpoint of the farm owners, however, the entire village hierarchy ranks between themselves and the cotters and hirelings. The Catholic priesthood, with a social hierarchy of its own, is considered to be outside of, and foreign to, local society. In this rural community the proud farm owners thus socially reign supreme.

The Farmhouse

A farm household inhabits a single farmhouse of the Lower Saxon type, a large well-built structure that houses human beings and domestic animals under a single long gabled roof. The entrance to the barn end of the house is surmounted by a portal of oak, an heirloom on which are carved the family name and the date of the house's construction as well as an appropriate motto. It is capped by two stylized horses' heads, an emblem of Lower Saxony symbolizing fertility. A stork's nest occasionally graces the roof. Several outbuildings are used for additional barns and storage. Although many local variations in construction type may be observed in the German lowlands (see Pessler 1906, 1955), all these farmhouses are isolated, single-unit complexes, each with its own garden, plowed fields, meadows, and woodland. This isolated farmstead (*Einzelhof*) arrangement, reminiscent of some Celtic-speaking peoples, contrasts with the village settlements of the farmers between the Weser and the Elbe Rivers where Celtic influences apparently did not penetrate.[19]

The Isolated Farmstead as a Self-Sustaining Unit

Characteristically, a farm household includes the farm owner (*Hofbesitzer*), his wife and unmarried children, the hired help, and the animals belonging to the farm. The owner is its undisputed head. He manages the farm enterprise, and his wife has complete charge of the household. The relationship between a human group and its domestic animals is close and nurturing, humans and their animals mutually exchanging services. Informants said that formerly when a farm owner died each one of his domestic animals was told, "The master is dead. The master is dead." Even the bees were notified. Men, women, and children of the household, and even its domestic animals, are expected to work hard at their respective tasks, each according to his species, sex, and age, for the good of the whole group.

Formerly each farmstead was organized as a self-sustaining economic unit. Virtually all the food consumed by the household is still produced and processed on the place, including potatoes, large quantities of smoked ham and sausage (about 2,000 pounds a year, depending on the size of the household), rye bread, butter, cream and buttermilk, eggs, sauerkraut, kale, onions, beets, turnips, apples, pears, and honey. This basically balanced diet is supplemented by wild game from the meadows and forest lands. The farm group also produces its own oats, hay, most other fodder, and all its natural fertilizer.

Even today relatively few food supplies are bought at a village store except a little salt, sugar, coffee, wine, and beer. Tobacco, soap, cloth, chemical fertilizers, and some tools are purchased in the village. Here the family goes to mass and the children go to school. The Catholic hospital is also located in the village. Although Low German is spoken as the mother tongue, literacy and fluency in High German, learned in school, is universal. The villagers furnish the farmers with certain other services. The miller grinds the home-grown rye and the baker makes the flour into large dark loaves. The veterinarian cares for the domestic animals, the doctor for the humans; and the banker, mechanic, electrician, and innkeeper also provide essential services.

Formerly many of these needs were met on the farm. Flax used to be an important crop because it supported the medieval spinning industry of the area. Sheep have also been raised in the Osnabrück Northland, but sheep herding is now mainly confined to parts of the Lüneburg heath.[20] Within the last century most traditional crafts such as spinning, weaving, and basketmaking have disappeared. Colorful homespun folk costumes are no longer worn.

During the 1930s, tractors, automobiles, and telephones appeared on a few Northland farms. Electric-power and machine-made tools began to be substituted for hand tools. The local farmers tended to use mechanized equipment only when they believed, on the basis of trial and error, that machines could do the job better than the traditional hand methods. In the 1930s, for example, most farmers rejected the McCormick harvester because they thought that it allowed too much grain to escape. Hay is still hand mown with a scythe on lands whose contour renders more modern methods inefficient from the viewpoint of a thrifty Lower Saxon farmer.

Industrialized milling and factories that produce machines, chemicals, textiles, paper, furniture, and glassware have greatly increased in Lower Saxony since World War II and are especially conspicuous in such urban centers as Hanover and Osnabrück. But in the Osnabrück Northland most of the country people are still dairy farmers. Besides butterfat, eggs, and Westphalian hams, the main farm products sold at market are rye, oats, sugar beets, potatoes, and highly bred stock.

Conclusion

In this chapter some behavior patterns of the population of a relatively isolated rural community of the Osnabrück Northland, located in the lowlands of West Germany, have been described. Here archaeological, historical, and ethnographic data may be examined in detailed changing environment. Our findings reveal that the culture of the Northland is distinguished by (1) small scattered entailed farms, some of which have been in the same family for many generations, each with its own cultivated fields, meadows, and forest and even its own hereditary hireling family established on a cot as part of the estate; (2) large farmhouses, sturdily built of brickwork according to an ancient design and sheltering a stem family, farmhands, and domestic animals under one long gabled roof; (3) irregularly clustered villages, some located at ancient crossroads and trading sites, serving as marketing, ceremonial, and recreation centers and offering basic services to the surrounding farm population such as an elementary school, a church, a flour mill and bakery, a physician, a hospital, and a veterinarian; (4) a local dialect of a distinctive language (Plattdeutsch) as the customary medium of verbal communication; (5) folkways that persist from the remote past such as distinctive rites of passage, hunting customs, and the habit of lighting Easter fires; (6) deeply rooted values such as loyalty to one's family and to one's father's land (a local variation of the freeman-freehold concept of the north European cradle culture), marital chastity, and a close supportive relationship between a family and its domestic animals. As a result of inbreeding, the Northlanders also have a unique genetic heritage that has evolved into a local race (Falish), and they have a distinctive character: they are clannish, proud, independent, stubborn, witty, pious, thrifty, and industrious.

Land-use patterns, directly reflecting the geological formation and the importance, to the ecocultural structure of the community, of minute differences in elevation, soil type, and drainage are also ancient. The first herder-agriculturalists were attracted to the dry, light, easily worked valley sand and dune soils. During the Bronze Age, as the population increased, intermediate and heavier soils were cultivated by means of an ard drawn by oxen. Much later, when the climate became drier, the deeper, richer alluvial lowland soils, formed by postglacial drainage systems, attracted the Old Saxons, who were seeking fields to cultivate with their iron-tipped plowshares. This type of fertile soil occurs sporadically in the region. Hence, in contrast to the village farm pattern traditionally found west of the Weser, the isolated farmstead pattern of land use, interspersed with common lands of heath, forest, and moor, was a workable solution for the Saxon herder-farmers.

The local hunting complex, now a highly valued sport that depends on archaic techniques and vocabulary, may stem from Mesolithic and early Neolithic practices, when animals that are still hunted today, such as the wild boar and the roe deer, first appeared in the region.

The prototype household spatial arrangement found in the area apparently developed during the early Neolithic era to solve a basic herder-farmer living problem. In the Northland, group living has depended on dealing with forests, bogs and marshes, and a damp, cloudy, and cold northern climate. Housing domestic animals and household group under one roof warmed the house, conserved manure, and reduced the unremitting daily labor involved in animal care. It also helped to protect the tame animals, which originally grazed in dense oak forests, from wild animals inhabiting those forests. By spatial arrangement and by size, the Lower Saxon farmhouse also reflected the social structure of the stem family, which apparently developed out of the bilaterally balanced northern European kindred characteristic of the Saxon homeland and adjacent parts of the northern culture cradle.

Ancient behavior patterns and institutions, in slightly changed form, continue to be used by the people of the Osnabrück Northland to solve practical living problems. New patterns have emerged as conditions have changed, especially in relation to the climatic deterioration of the late Middle Ages. These include the cotter and hireling institutions, neighbor reciprocities, and partial industrialization. The analysis suggests that these new developments, as well as the traditional behavior patterns, can be understood as well-tested, traditionally effective, problem-solving devices within a unique climatic, geographical, and culture-historical context. The findings thus suggest that certain partially isolated communities of the Ems-Hase region of Germany afford potential natural laboratories of considerable promise for the observation and analysis of rural group behavior in environmental, historical, and cultural context.

Notes

1. I am indebted to Dr. Helmut Plath, director of the Historisches Museum am Hohen Ufer, Hanover, for this folk saying.
2. I have not succeeded in finding a good modern account of the area in English. *Das Land Niedersachsen: Gegenwart und Tradition*, an official publication of the Niedersachsen Province (Hanover: Walter Kerber Verlag, 1955), may be used for orientation.
3. Due to space limitations, only a small number of the references used in this study have been listed.
4. Parts of this chapter were included in "Peasant Aristocrats of the Osnabrück Northland," a paper prepared for the Wenner-Gren Conference on Central and North-Central European Peasant Cultures, held in Chicago in January 1967 and revised as "Some Limitations of the Peasant Concept as a Tool in Investigating European Rural Communities," a chapter in *Modernization and Tradition in Central European Rural Cultures,* John Honigmann, editor, Canadian Research Centre for Anthropology (1968). The research reported in this chapter was partly funded by grants from the Humanities Division of the Rockefeller Foundation and the Faculty Research and Development Fund, North Carolina State College. These are gratefully acknowledged. I take

this opportunity also to express my appreciation to Carleton S. Coon for information regarding the Falish racial type and to Helmut Plath for reading an earlier draft of the manuscript and for help in assembling information and bibliography on the Lower Saxons.

5. Bowen 1931: 350, figs. 1, 2; Clark 1952: 109; Hardebeck 1902: 6–14; Hawkes 1940: 213, 217; Jacob-Friesen 1959: 70 ff.; Nordman 1935: 30, fig. 17; Prinz 1934: 11; Sprockhoff 1938: 18, 94–103.

6. Abel 1956; Clark 1952: 263, fig. 142; Jacob-Friesen 1955: 26; Navarro 1925; Rademacher 1925: 125–126; Reining 1931: 28. Stone circles occur in primary settlement soil (Hardebeck 1902: 38, 42). Urnfields are located both on sandy hills and on the plain. Hallstatt-type artifacts have been found in Merzen parish, Döllinghausen community (Hardebeck 1902: 36; see also Childe 1950: 221).

7. See Childe 1950: 226; H. Hubert 1934a: 150–168; Meitzen 1895 (1): 34, (2): 77 ff.; Rademacher 1925: 125–126. For a different opinion see Prinz 1934: 12.

8. See, for example, Tacitus 1942: 712, 715–716; J. W. Thompson 1928: 178.

9. For a contrast between the cultures of Rome and the Germanic-speaking tribes, see, for example, Gibbon 1932 (1): Chs. 3, 9, 10; Huebner 1918; Kisch 1941; Metzenthin 1924; Repp 1832: 21–39; Whatmough 1937: 116–117.

10. Ptolemy mentioned the Saxons as located "on the neck of the Cimbric peninsula" (Chadwick 1907: 93). On recent historical maps of the migrations of Angles and Saxons they are located in Holstein south of the Angles and on both banks of the Elbe near its mouth and just south of the Chauken (Brüning 1950: map 148d).

11. Adam of Bremen (1959: 6–7).

12. See Robertson 1931: 20.

13. See, for example, Adam of Bremen 1959: 10–11; Davidson 1964; Hardebeck 1902: 3, 14; Krüsselmann 1937: 4.

14. Krüsselmann 1937: 44; Philippi 1892; Prinz 1934, 1940; J. W. Thompson 1928: 195 ff.

15. See Krüsselmann 1937: map.

16. The stem family, in slightly altered form, is also found in Iceland (as has been noted) and in parts of Sweden, Denmark, and Norway.

17. Spiegel 1939.

18. According to the laws of May 15 and September 29, 1933, re-

garding hereditary domains, the term *Erbhof* was applied to
middle-sized farms—that is, large enough to maintain one family
(up to 309 acres) but not sufficient for large-scale exploitation.

19. Farms between the Weser and Elbe formed village settlements
(Weber 1950: 3–8, after Meitzen). At the center of each village the dwelling lots with houses were arranged irregularly.
Each lot had a garden plot located in a ring of fenced land surrounding the house lots. Beyond stretched the rich arable land,
forming a belt around the village. Communal pasture (*Almende*)
circled the fields, and the pasture was surrounded by woodland, the use of which was shared with other villages. Each freeman owned his lot and garden plot. Each originally had an equal
share in the several fields, which were plowed, by a joint effort,
in strips according to the three-field system. Each had a right to
herd an equal number of livestock on the common pasture.
Rights to woodcutting, to bedding, and to other forest resources
were divided equally among the inhabitants of the village and
other villages. House, dwelling lot, and a share in the garden
land, arable fields, pasture, and forest comprised the *Hufe* (hide),
a single self-sufficient farm unit.

20. In contrast to Icelandic practice, shepherds are used.

11 /

SOCIETY AND CULTURE

> From convergent evidence objectively descriptive of human
> persons and their behavior, emerges a concept of societal
> order and possibility. In the discovery of what man *can*
> do, the data of the biological sciences are pertinent; in
> the discovery of what man *does*, the social sciences pro-
> vide descriptive data. In practical decision as to what a
> specific individual or group of individuals *wish to do*, the
> limitations and possibilities of human nature and of social
> order are definitive.
>
> Douglas G. Haring and Mary E. Johnson (1940:
> vii–viii, after Giddings)

Having investigated, in historical and ecocultural context, the
social structure of the north European cradle culture and two
of its offshoots, the Old Saxon and the Icelandic, we are in a
position to compare them and to generalize on the basis of the
findings. We may also explore our data for the light they may
throw on two basic approaches, the sociological and the culture-
ecological, currently used by field anthropologists.

Development of a Lower Saxon Social Order

We have noted that the Old Saxons migrated from their homeland, probably in the neck of the Jutland peninsula, to bottom
lands in northwestern Germany. The vicissitudes of the migration act itself engendered significant changes in the prototype
social structure. For example, the logistics of travel by small
boats and through marshes and dense forests in unfriendly territory necessitated a reduction in the size of the migrating groups
and also their self-defense under competent leadership. The

small *princeps-comitatus* war unit, each man backed by his immediate family, seems to have evolved as a successful solution to this problem. Leader and followers formed a strong, voluntary, mobile association based on mutual loyalty and reinforced by the Teutonic concept of personal and kinfolk honor.

The Saxons who settled in the German lowlands retained many characteristics of the prototype kindred system in slightly changed form. Eventually the roles of the father's ancestors and the father's land outweighed those of the mother, and a Saxon version of the stem family emerged. Although in Saxon inheritance patterns males were favored over females, in the absence of sons a daughter might inherit the estate. And although the father's role as head of the family was strengthened, the mother retained an honored place in family decision making.

It is significant also that after the Franks defeated the Saxons the Saxon social system did not become a copy of the Romanized Frankish order despite strong pressures in that direction. The Saxons did not accept the feudalism of the Franks except as a result of military defeat. As soon as possible they rejected feudal relationships and attempted to reestablish their indigenous institutions and to implement Saxon values, especially those of the freehold and freeman. In time the independent farm owner on his privately owned holding regained his traditional economic and social self-sufficiency. He was supported by family, laborers, and hirelings and by reciprocal arrangements with neighboring farmers. By-passing city and church, the well-established farm owner became the focus of a postfeudal rural social order.

Development of the Icelandic Social Order

Vikings migrated from the western periphery of the Norse culture area to Iceland four or five centuries after the Old Saxons migrated westward from its center. Having left most of their kinsmen in the homeland, the Icelandic settlers evolved an extended family system with emphasis on the male line. They also developed the *godord*, a local association based on mutual personal loyalty between *thingmenn* and chief. The former contributed temple taxes and support in exchange for leadership in temple ceremonies, the administration of legal affairs, and protection against common enemies. Under the commonwealth, established in 930, Iceland was divided into competing *godithingmenn* groups, which, in the absence of institutionalized executive power, balanced one another as the basic sociopolitical units of the nation. After Iceland's formal conversion to Catholicism in 1000, this balance of power was disturbed by new influences centered in two competing bishoprics. During the ensuing period of intense rivalry among foreign and indigenous power units, Iceland lost her independence. A variation on the stem family emerged eventually in Iceland that, although it favors male heirs, still retains in the marriage relationship some of the bilateral balance characteristic of the kindred in the early northern culture cradle.

Social Structure and Cultural Reemergence

The evidence thus suggests that outside the cradle area the northern kindred lost much of its bilateral balance (by which ego's paternal and maternal kinsmen were treated as equivalents) in favor of the paternal line. In Iceland and Lower Saxony, the stem family in association with a specific piece of entailed land and the neighborhood as a local reciprocity grouping emerged as substitute balancing factors.

A lesson highlighted by these cases is that social structure, including kinship forms, is neither a "given" nor a fortuitous phenomenon without roots or direction. Extending back to pre-human foundations, social structure is an integral part of the complex problem-solving device—in other words, the culture—that a community shapes to its situational needs through processes of culture building and culture change. These processes involve not only a principle of limited possibilities and potentialities of cultural change but also that of cultural reemergence. Far from changing in a haphazard manner or changing arbitrarily in a fixed linear direction, like "forward" or "upward," the change movement seems to have components of self-regulation through balance, and the sequence seems to resemble an ecological succession toward homeostatic equilibrium. Ronald Frankenberg

(1966: 125) helps to clarify the process when he points out that the model of segmentation in Nuer society developed by E.E. Evans-Pritchard (1940) is one of dynamic balance rather than of progressive change. In other words, Evans-Pritchard's model of a specific social system expresses the homeostatic movement of an ecosystem rather than the social evolutionary movement of a social system as usually postulated by sociocultural evolutionists.

Bilateral and Unilateral Kinship Systems

It is significant, for example, that in neither case, Old Saxon or Icelandic, was the bilaterally balanced kindred changed into a unilineal system. To appreciate this finding we must first grasp the essential difference between unilineal—lineage and clan— systems and bilateral—family line and kindred—systems.

As Meyer Fortes (1953: 26 ff.) noted, a member of a lineage usually belongs to a fixed, named unit of reference that has recognized limits and remains relatively constant through the generations except for the death of old members and the birth of new ones. This principle is well illustrated in the native Australian, Lauan, and to some extent Hopi (see Chapter 14) systems. Each member's status and often his roles and functions are ascribed by birth, age, and generation. The lineage is characteristically believed to have a perpetual corporate existence and function, with leadership roles often inherited or ascribed— the clan headman of Lau, for example. Frequently the lineage also is related to a specific territory with well-known, marked boundaries (this is the case among the Australian aborigines, the Lauans, and probably also the prehistoric Chamorros). Usually the lineage is associated with special symbols (for example, colors, designs, heraldic devices), and its members claim totemic ties that set it apart from other such recognizable units of the society. This tendency is well illustrated among the Australians and the Lauans.

A member of a north European kindred, on the other hand, was not associated with a similar stable unit of reference. His kindred configuration was differently constituted from that of every other kinsman, with but one exception. In the case of two unmarried full brothers, A and B, as pointed out by Rad-cliffe-Brown, every individual who was kinsman to A was kins-man to B, and A and B were kinsmen of each other.

In short, the shifting, overlapping, and ephemeral nature of the kindreds differs significantly from the long-lived stable char-acter of unilineal descent groups (see Murdock 1949: 60–61; 1960).

Persistence of Social Structure

These basic types of social structure are remarkably persistent. We have noted that the social structure of Lau has remained characteristically Lauan despite almost a century of British rule. Nor have the Guamanians entirely lost their distinctive social patterns regardless of strong Spanish and American influences. Similarly, we shall note in the next section that the social struc-tures of the Hopi and the Navaho Indians have not become copies of the surrounding American society, despite a century of strong pressures toward conformity. When given the opportu-nity to reorganize, each of these tribes has developed its own form of tribal organization on the basis of its social traditions.

Even in acute crisis, it seems that a community does not com-pletely change its structure. As noted in the case of Hawaii, breakdown of the balance between the *kino-lau* and *'aumakua* relationship systems precipitated disorganization and physical extinction rather than the adoption of an alien model. We shall note (Chapter 16) that the Dakota Sioux underwent a similar change for almost half a century after their military defeat.

Social Structure and Problem Solving

Data so far presented suggest that the basic social relationships of a near-isolated community are developed by its members on the basis of traditional models as they search for available means to solve their practical living problems. Recent findings from ethology indicate that this tendency is found in communi-ties of animals as well as those of humans. Traditionally, such relationship patterns are rooted in impelling ecological realities of the habitat, in basic biosocial needs of the group for survival and self-actualization, and, in the case of human societies, in patterns of culture to which the members have become habituated.

For example, when the successful solution of their group living problems appears to be beyond their strength, ingenuity, or endurance, men frequently enlist the help of supernatural agents, whom they create to work on their behalf. The process is illustrated clearly by the religion of the Polynesian Tikopians, which the natives call "the work of the gods" (Firth 1940).

The Northmen believed that Odin helped man by his ceaseless exploratory activities. Odin even penetrated the fearsome world of the ice giants, traditional enemies of man, and outwitted them. Not only was Odin credited with giving the Northmen new magically potent weapons, a new order of battle, and a new incentive for bravery and daring, but he was also supposed to have inspired the poets who gave great warriors lasting fame and to have rephrased man's formulation of the life choices open to him. Before Odin, a dilemma was posed in terms of two alternatives, both of which were perceived as unpalatable or evil. Odin taught that a warrior still had two choices but that both of them were good.

The Hopi (Chapter 14) face extremely adverse living conditions, but they have chosen not to abandon their arid habitat or their agricultural way of life. Indeed, such a solution would run counter to all that has been observed about the persistence of cultural forms and the die-hard nature of group preferred relationship patterns. Instead, the Hopi and their forebears have developed an extremely elaborate annual ceremonial cycle by which the ancestral gods are believed to aid the living members of the tribe during every phase of the planting, growth, and maturation of the crops. During half the year, while the Hopi are busy in their fields, the ancestors are believed to carry out supportive activities (dances and other rituals believed to have magical efficacy). During the other half, they participate as masked dancers (*kachina*) in pueblo ceremonies.

Other peoples discussed in this book have used supernatural beings to aid in problem solving. After the Chamorros, for example, were decisively defeated by the Spaniards, they invented the *taotaomona*, giant headless men believed to be the ghosts of their former chiefs, to defend their local districts for them. When a Lauan chief lost his hereditary rank under the British colonial system, his ancestors told him in a dream that he could acquire a new prestige role as a medicine man and they taught him new curing methods.

The basic problem-solving role that a society assigns to its deities and other supernatural helpers may explain partially why every society with a balanced, viable culture resists with almost unbelievable energy any attempt to dislodge its nonhuman power figures. Such figures are an integral part of the relationship between man and nature that the group has established and maintained on behalf of its survival and self-activation through the generations.

Even when conversion to a new religion takes place, the intrusive deities are usually substituted for the old gods, whose problem-solving functions they then assume. They are rarely established independently in their own right as part of a new organization pattern. The native social structure is thus altered or elaborated to accommodate authority figures associated with the new gods. Usually it is not displaced by culturally alien relationship patterns. Thus, in early Iceland Christ was substituted for Thor as the god of thunder and the elements, and the Old Norse *hel*, a place of frost, darkness and eternal winter, the home of horrendous giants, persisted in place of the Christian hades or abyss. In time, of course, the Norse word *hel* was taken over by Christians from warmer southern climes and applied to their fiery hot underworld rather than to its original referent, an icy northern region.

Another example may be noted in the case of Hawaii during the nineteenth century, when the relation between nature and man was deteriorating rapidly due to critical disturbances of the isolated island group engendered by whalers, sandalwood traders, and the development of commerce. When the Hawaiian Prince Liholiho believed that the tabu system of his ancestral gods could not help him to solve the changed living problems of his realm, he renounced the old gods and accepted the Christian God, whom he believed had more power to help him.

However, many aspects of the Hawaiian religion and tabu system that are still functional for problem solving continue to be practiced to the present.

Traditional social patterns thus tend to be used as cultural models as long as they can possibly serve the community's purposes, and even longer if the people believes that they do not crucially interfere with the solution of basic practical problems. As a rule, only when the people perceives that the contemporary situation affords no alternative except to perish or critically to loose balance and tonicity does the group face the need to change, and sometimes not even then.

Under such circumstances culture change may be triggered by the appearance of an unfamiliar model, or some innovation may be made in the old model that stimulates more basic changes. Thoroughgoing changes are completely accepted only after they have been tested by trial and error in the situation in which they will be used. They can pass this pragmatic test by proving to the satisfaction of the community members involved that they are superior to traditional models in resolving a specific problematic situation. Even if they prove their value, changes of certain aspects of a familiar pattern are the rule rather than changes in the pattern itself (see Chapter 20).

A "new" trait is usually incorporated into the group's life way through its approval, acceptance, and use by prestige figures or leading members of the community (see Mead 1964). Behavior, feeling, perception, and thought patterns are thus altered as little as possible although the problematic situation that precipitated the change may be at least partially resolved.

Need for a Heuristic Theory of Social Behavior

An inquiry into the relations between society and culture, as revealed by a comparison of the social structures of several isolated communities, highlights the need for a heuristic theory of social behavior that, when translated into working hypotheses and concepts, stands a good chance of being verified by the available data. Social anthropologists who support the linear evolutionary school of thought have made valiant efforts to reconcile it with a modern ecological approach (for example, see Groves' [1963] review of Sahlins 1962) or with a culture historical approach (for example, White 1959). The observations that we have made about cultures suggest why such attempts can never be entirely successful. The multidimensional ecocultural process eludes such a simplistic model.

The present theoretical problem involves resisting the reductionism and easy arguments by analogy of the social evolutionists. It involves moving from the anxiety-ridden "shattered field" image of reality that is characteristic of the Occidental culture in transition (for example, the cultural relativity of Franz Boas; the "two cultures" described by C. P. Snow; the "structuralism" of some social anthropologists; the existentialism of some modern philosophers) to a more flexible, inductively based unified theory that relates man-made cultural developments to biogenetic processes (see, for example, Count 1958; Grinker 1967). Rather than concentrating on social structure or culture quite apart from the behavior and biology of their human components, the cultural anthropologist must relate one with the other by means of a scientific approach using heuristic, verifiable theory and relevant methodology.

Perhaps most difficult in attempting to construct heuristic theory, however, is the need to take seriously the existential nature of the human condition, as a dynamic multidimensional whole, and down to the tiniest details. We have seen how impossible it would be to understand the situation of the southern Lauans without considering the minutiae of their behavior as a structured whole in geological, ecological, and historical perspective. Otherwise we could not appreciate how through generations they not only have overcome their unpromising environment but have created in transaction with it their unique microculture with its small but significant local variations. By this means the Lauans have turned what might be truly "famine islands," unfit for human habitation, into a network of viable communities forming a self-sufficient native trade area. Without such detailed knowledge the meaning to the sciences of man of Lauan culture as a historical creation of the Lauans through the generations would escape us. We could not begin to encompass it as a complex pattern of human events in space and time.

Similarly, our understanding of the other communities studied as ongoing human groups, each with a job to do under changing conditions that are geographically, biologically, and historically unique, would have been more than impaired. It would have been decisively warped. For example, the behavior of the Icelanders throughout their thousand-year history would be meaningless without a knowledge of the changing subarctic land and offshore ecology. If we are searching for cultural understanding in depth, even the attitudes, values, and mental approach of the Icelanders toward their living problems must be considered in changing context that includes climatic shifts, volcanic eruptions, the retreat and advance of glaciers, ocean currents, soil erosion, and other processes that alter the geographic features of the island and its ocean setting. Obviously, knowledge of the interpersonal relations of Icelanders, both within their own island and with other peoples and nations, although essential to cultural understanding, would not have sufficed.

Currently fashionable theories of sociocultural "evolution" and "advancement" hardly meet this need. They represent one reaction to the current challenge confronting modern space-age man to change his perception and codification of reality from a medieval view tied to a single dominant immutable image or from a nineteenth-century view dependent on the idea of "progress" through social evolution, in the direction of a world view more compatible with the findings of modern science. If we wish to comprehend the human experiment as a whole historical phenomenon we must also perceive man and his social groupings as an integral part of the changing nature of this planet. We must, if we would understand man, take the long-range ecohistorical view. By relating observable spatial phenomena to a time dimension, we may encompass in depth the whole exploding human event as a natural process. We may understand it from the emergence of man as a unique species in the animal kingdom through more than 2 million years of genetic evolution in localized populations, each building toward its own microculture and microrace, to the present changing human condition. In a recent paper (1967a) I suggested that a start may be made in this direction by comparing geographically isolated breeding populations that have discrete boundaries in order to investigate the role of culture process in the genetic evolution of microraces.

If we develop a deep enough understanding of culture as a whole—that eons-long, planet-wide, pattern of human events—we may even hazard a guess as to mankind's probably immediate future under certain changing conditions. This, I suspect, is all that scientists interested in probability prediction may expect at present from an emerging science of mankind.

But what an important tool such a skill could give the human race! It could make available to human groups the knowledge they need to make realistic decisions regarding their own futures. It could also help each group to create and maintain an environment for innovation needed in a time of rapid change.

For an *explanatory* description of the role and history of mankind on the planet we need, of course, a clear-eyed view of the operations and relations of the basic forces in the universe—organic and inorganic, human and nonhuman—that interact and transact to form the effective external and internal environments of human groups and human individuals. In other words, if we would *explain* human behavior we may not limit the relevant factors to *social* factors alone. We must concern ourselves also with the changing natural environment and with human culture-building populations in historical perspective equally significant from the scientific viewpoint.

Conclusion

In sum, the findings indicate that if we would understand the processes and principles of cultural "evolution" or change we must study comparatively the development of specific cultural traditions through space and time rather than visualize them simply as a series of sequential stages of organization (see Bryan 1965: 97). Social structure and ecological structure tend to operate as complementary systems within a total community. The data suggest that neither one or the other system is dominant or determining. The members of the community themselves, not the ecosystem or the social system, mold and organize their own behavior according to their perception of their situation, their identification of the practical problems that the group must resolve or cease to exist as a viable biosocial entity, and the problem-solving tools available to them. The community itself constitutes the active agent that, by means of building and styling its culture in the course of centuries, has the demonstrated capacity to weld itself into a visible, balanced relationship with its particular habitat. From this viewpoint, a culture may be defined as a human group's self-selected and self-tailored problem-solving tool.

PART 3

PART 3

12 /

EARLY MAN IN AMERICA

> If we understand the differences in *perceiving*, we shall
> go far in understanding the differences in the resulting be-
> havior.
>
> Gardner Murphy (1947: 332)

> Perceptual organization is not a photographic process. It
> is fundamentally an innovative act; it is an interactive,
> adjustive relationship between the perceiver and the thing
> perceived. The two together make up a dynamic creative
> whole.
>
> Homer G. Barnett (1953: 114)

When I was studying anthropology at Radcliffe and Berkeley,
practically all my fellow graduate students were interested in
the American Indian. And why not? In the American Southwest, Canada, and Latin America, many tribes or remnants of
tribes still lived under sufficiently natural conditions to make
them suitable for field study using a natural-history approach.
Most of our instructors were specialists in Indian studies: Alfred
L. Kroeber and E. W. Gifford on the California Indians; Robert
H. Lowie on the Crow; Paul Radin on the Winnebago; Leslie
Spier on the Havasupai; Alfred Tozzer on the Maya.

But I resisted becoming involved with studies of the Indians
because I wanted to work on the peoples of the Pacific. My
first field trip convinced me, however, that to understand the
life way of a people one needs training not only in anthropology
and geography but also in the psychology of human development. The opportunity for such training did not materialize until just before World War II when I began to study at the Univer-

sity of Chicago under the auspices of the Committee on Human Development. Soon I was offered the job of coordinator of a multidiscipline research project being planned under the sponsorship of the U.S. Office of Indian Affairs.

Working in the Indian Laboratory

For several years I worked in close association with a team of psychiatrists, anthropologists, and ecologists on the Indian Education Research Project. We centered our efforts on the practical problems facing the Indians of five tribes: Papago, Hopi, Navaho, Zuni, and Sioux.

Because no model of sufficient complexity existed at the time, the staff of the Indian Education Research Project had to develop a multidisciplinary research instrument. We designed, tested, and implemented a field project aimed at gaining an understanding in depth of the educational and administrative problems of each tribe in relation to its environmental and social situation. This effort offered a unique challenge. We expected to obtain empirical data in new dimensions, especially from a psychological test battery. We hoped that findings from the tests, analyzed in relation to facts derived by more orthodox field methods, would yield significant insights regarding the so-called Indian problem. By means of community analysis and psychological tests on a representative sample of children from two or three communities in each of the five tribes, we gathered a great deal of information, processed it, analyzed it, and reduced the results to written form.[1]

Participating in this early multidisciplinary project through its six-year duration was, I believe, the most significant educational experience of my professional life. This fieldwork with American Indian tribes came after a decade of research and travel in the Pacific, the Orient, and Europe. The experience provided a broad perspective from which to study tribes that had already been investigated intensively by many professional anthropologists. Insights gleaned from fieldwork in isolated island communities in the tropics afforded the possibility of a fresh approach toward desert and semi-desert aboriginal communities of the American Southwest.

Out of this exploration emerged many of the approaches and concepts that are developed in this volume. For example, the concepts of a homeostatically balanced culture and of the community's pattern of perceiving reality in relation to its living problems are products of the Indian research. Realization of the significance of culture and its ultimate understanding in terms of tiny details expressed in behavior and symbolism is another. In this and the following section I shall try to elucidate these concepts.

The Pilot Study[2]

In order to test the adequacy of our multidiscipline field instrument, the project staff prepared a preliminary design for the fieldwork and several guides for fieldworkers.[3] With the help of our advisers from the Office of Indian Affairs, we selected the Papago Indian reservation in southern Arizona as the most promising site for a pilot field study. At Sells, Arizona, the seat of the Papago agency, I was joined by Ruth M. Underhill, an anthropologist with the Office of Indian Affairs, who had years of experience in studying Papago culture. We were aided during the three-month duration of the pilot study by the reservation superintendent and many members of his staff, and several teachers rendered invaluable service to the project by testing the tentative psychological battery in their classrooms. Through this experience we learned which of the tests under consideration were useful in the bilingual and cross-cultural situations found in federal Indian schoolrooms. Dr. Alice Joseph, the field physician for the Papago agency, contributed valuable medical and ethnographic data. We also obtained important facts concerning the nutrition pattern of the Papago from Dr. Michael Pijoan and Emma Reh, who were conducting field studies of Papago diet at the time.

By June 1942 the pilot fieldwork had been completed. The project staff and some of the consultants, together with volunteer fieldworkers from the reservations to be studied, gathered at the Indian School in Santa Fe, New Mexico. John Collier, then Commissioner of Indian Affairs, and many members of his staff also participated. For three weeks we held a fieldworkers' training seminar, which was attended by one hundred individuals. On the basis of pilot study findings and administrative considerations we finalized the field research design and the field guides. We also planned the fieldwork and its supervision. In its final form the test battery included eight psychological tests: Arthur's point performance scale (short form), Goodenough's draw-a-man test; Stewart's emotional response test (adapted); Bavelas' moral ideology test; Piaget's immanent-justice test (adapted); a free-drawing test; Murray's thematic apperception test (adapted); and Rorschach's psychodiagnostic test. We also trained about seventy-five fieldworkers, many of them schoolteachers and Indians, from the Indian communities that were to be the subjects of the study. Whenever possible the English language was used in administering the tests. If a child's knowledge of English proved inadequate, a specially trained interpreter was employed. (In the actual testing, most of the Papago and Navaho children and many younger Hopi, Zuni, and Sioux children required interpreters.)

The Testing Program

After the seminar the fieldworkers returned to the reservations that had been selected for study. First, a sample of children five to eighteen years of age, adjusted by sex and age, was drawn up for each of the communities. The list of subjects was checked for statistical validity as a representative sample by Robert J. Havighurst, a member of the research committee[4] and project statistician. Altogether almost 1,000 Indian children of school age, from eleven communities in the five tribes, were tested.

Insights Regarding Perception

When the results of the testing program and other field research had been processed and analyzed, they suggested many interesting and unexpected leads. For example, the results of the immanent-justice test revealed that, in all the communities tested, a belief in immanent justice (a belief that a system of rewards and punishments is built into the structure of the universe), which was present among the younger children in all the Indian communities tested, either increased or showed no statistically significant change with age[5] regardless of degree and kind of influences from formal schooling and from the outside world. These results contrast with those of Jean Piaget and his students, which show that although a belief in immanent justice is present among young Swiss children, it decreases significantly with age. Our finding suggests that a traditional world image rooted in immanent justice tends to persist in the Indian communities studied despite several centuries of pressures exerted by culturally alien administrators, missionaries, and neighbors.

Analysis of the Rorschach test results from the project sample of Indian children revealed, moreover, not only variations between individuals but also variations between tribal averages in typical "manner of approach" toward problems.[6] These findings, when placed in ecological and cultural context, suggest that each tribe studied has a definite and describable pattern of perceiving reality and of habitually approaching problems. Sample communities within each tribe show slight variations on the tribal pattern.

The next chapters explore these leads in reference to four tribes. Using project results with special reference to findings obtained from the immanent-justice test and the Rorschach test, we shall inquire into the relationships between group perception pattern, world image, and problem-solving behavior.[7] We turn first to the coming of man to the Americas.

Advent of Man in New World

Because there is no evidence of Lower or Middle Pleistocene forms of early man in the Americas, we surmise that man did not originate in the New World. When and how did the first modern men come to the Western Hemisphere?

Although scholars do not agree about the details, available

evidence indicates that during the Upper Pleistocene the first human groups reached the Western Hemisphere from Asia. Because a land bridge across the Bering Strait emerged during the last glacial regression (see Butzer 1961, 1964: fig. 70, 395), it has been suggested that colonization from Asia to North America took this route. There were apparently at least two major movements. The first group is thought to have traveled from eastern Asia along the shores of the Pacific and across the land bridge during the Würm glaciation. As part of their indigenous culture these migrants brought with them a tradition of working unpolished stone into choppers, bifaces, and amorphous flakes (Chard 1963). The second major group of colonists to America is believed to have begun their journey in central Siberia. They may have brought a flint working tradition and bifacial flaking. On the other hand, bifaced chipped and fluted projectile points may have been an American Indian invention, although possible prototype forms have been found in Upper Paleolithic deposits near Lake Baikal in Siberia (Clark 1962: 210–211).

None of these early migrants to America brought sharpened chopping tools, the hand ax, or the bow. They brought the dog, which was the descendant of the Asiatic wolf—domesticated in the Old World probably during the late Pleistocene. They also brought various microorganisms and such parasites as lice and fleas. Early man in America initially did not have polished stone tools, pottery, or any farming techniques. The first colonists in the New World also may have brought with them such values as a conservationist attitude toward nature common in both Asia and the Americas.

About 12,000 years ago, an ice-free trans-Canadian corridor apparently opened up from Siberia to the High Plains and what is now the Great Lakes area of North America for the first time in 15,000 years. Curiously, neither the interior of Alaska nor the low coastal land north of the Brooks Range was glaciated at the time. This phenomenon may have been due to low precipitation. Also, it is believed that these Alaskan areas and the valley of the Mackenzie River had a more temperate climate then than they have today, although the Cordilleran ice sheet covered most of Canada west of the Mackenzie River basin and the Laurentide ice sheet covered eastern America north of the St. Lawrence River and the area of Lakes Michigan and Superior. Pluvial conditions prevailed on what are now the Great Plains, which were covered with tundra and forest.

The High Plains as well as the ice-free areas farther north had become the New World habitat of the mammoth, as well as the musk ox, reindeer, and moose. The wapiti (an American elk), the Rocky Mountain goat, and the black bear were also present in North America. Thus, there was an abundance of game plus favorable conditions to attract Upper Paleolithic hunters from Asia.

Paleo-Indian Traditions of the High Plains

Recent research suggests that the first definitely identifiable culture in the New World, the Llano complex, was developed by Paleo-Indians who used a fairly large stone projectile point of the Clovis type (R. J. Mason 1962: 230) to hunt the mammoth. A Clovis fluted point, usually from three to five inches long, is characterized by the removal of several longitudinal flakes by percussion from the central part to the base of each face. There is no evidence of marginal retouching or pressure flaking and the base is usually ground. Remains of this culture that date from 11,500 to 8,500 years ago have been found south of the maximum advance of the ice during the Valdus climatic pulsation—from California to Massachusetts and into Mexico. The evidence suggests that during the Valdus recession the mammoth, unable to adapt to the rise in temperature, became extinct.

The Llano culture was superseded by the Folsom complex, which has been dated from 8820 to 7928 B.C. (Agogino 1963: 114). The Folsom culture is associated with hunters who slew prehistoric bison with a projectile tipped with a small, thin, leaf-shaped stone point from one to three inches long. Skillful pressure flaking was apparently used to produce a longitudinal flute or groove from midsection to base of each face and to retouch the edges into a sharp blade. According to C. V. Haynes (1964: 1410), "It appears that the change from Clovis points to Folsom points coincides with the relatively sudden disappearing of mammoths and the concomitant switch to hunting *Bison antiquus* in the High Plain suggests a change in the specialized hunting weapon in response to a change in game."

The ice-free Great Plains region formed a corridor to eastern as well as to western North America and to Middle and South America. Early man probably entered South America via the Isthmus of Panama, then moved up the Atrato, Magdalena, and Cauca Rivers of Columbia. He apparently traveled along the high plateaus of the Andes to the attractive hunting regions of the Chaco, the Pampas, and Patagonia.

From the standpoint of its animal life, South America is a sort of continental blind alley. The continent formed a pocket in which, usually on the basis of prehistoric migrants from Asia and North America, such unique animal types as the tapir and the armadillo evolved and persisted. In South America also roamed the dangerous saber-tooth tiger, the mastodon, the bison, and the prehistoric horse, as well as other animal species now extinct.

Paleo-Indian Races

The Ainu of Hokkaido, Japan, were formerly thought to represent the northeasternmost extension of the Australoid or Archaic-Caucasoid race. Recent research on certain Indian tribes in the Western Hemisphere, however, suggests that late Pleistocene hunters and gatherers of this race may have wandered still farther, possibly along the Pacific shore route, and eventually settled in the New World. Possible examples of this type, mixed, of course, with later arrivals, occur among the Papago, Ute, and Paiute in basin and range zones (that were formerly savannah) in the North American Southwest and among many South American hunting tribes associated with Paleo-Indian cultures. Later, according to this theory, small groups of Proto-Mongoloids entered the Western Hemisphere along the same corridor, perhaps from central Asia. They apparently interbred with the Archaic-Caucasoids and evolved a variety of local microracial types.

In general, American Indians have straight, coarse, blue-black hair and yellow-brown to red-brown skin. They have dark eyes, prominent cheek bones, and broad, as well as relatively large, faces. Stanley M. Garn (1961: 117–118) classes them as the Amerindian Geographical race, which he describes as follows:

> Serologically, the Americas are characterized by the low incidence (or virtual absence) of [blood type] B, the generally low incidence of A (and then only A_1), by the low incidence of N, and by varying frequencies of the Diego-positive gene Di^a. Morphologically, in hair form, tooth form, eyelid form, etc., there is an obvious overlapping with Asia and to some extent Polynesia.

The penetration of the North American arctic by Paleo-Eskimos from Siberia about 6500 B.C. postdates the Paleo-Indian migration (Butzer 1964: 394). Some modern geneticists class the Eskimos of Siberia, Alaska, northern Canada, and Greenland as an isolated local race. The Eskimos are broken into extremely small populations and evidence many physiological adaptations to extreme cold. According to Garn (1961: 130), American and Canadian Eskimos "differ from both Amerindians and most Asiatics in the high incidence of non-tasters,[8] in the near absence of BAIB [an amino acid frequently excreted by individuals of Asiatic origin] excretors, and in a low incidence of Di^a [Diego positive] thereby suggesting long-continued isolation and natural selection."

Cultural Sequence in North Carolina[9]

For a good archaeological sequence that illuminates the New World prehistory, let us consider some recent findings from excavations in the Uwharrie area of the North Carolina central piedmont, which were led by Joffre L. Coe (1964: figs. 1, 6). The earliest occupations that have been found in this area are located well below the present land surface. They are dated about 10000 B.C. Clovis-like projectile points are typical of the period. In this area, the blade is distinguished by fine workmanship. These blades are associated with the Hardaway culture complex of the Paleo-Indian period (10000–7000 B.C.). Arrow points and pottery are absent at this level.

In the next (Archaic) stratum in the piedmont sequence, which has been dated at about 7000 B.C., are found large thin projectile points with uniquely notched corners and chipped stone scrapers. These implements are associated with the Kirk complex, which had cultural affinities to contemporary cultures of the High Plains, the southern, southwestern, and, less conspicuously, with the northern United States.

Moving upward in geological level and forward in time, Coe and his students reached a middle Archaic period dated about 5000 B.C. Excavating the Archaic period of the Doerschuk site on the Yadkin River, they reached the fourteen-foot level of a stratified river bottom occupation on a flood plain. Here they found the famous Stanly points. The form of these points differs markedly from that of both the Hardaway and the Kirk points. The blade is wider, the stem narrow, the concave base definitely notched, and the serration distinct. As part of the Stanly complex the earliest evidence of polished stone artifacts are found in the pick type of *atlatl* (throwing stick) weight. This type is associated with stone scrapers and probably also with some form of grooved axe.

At a slightly higher level, dated about 4000 B.C., were found long thick "lanceolate" flint points characteristic of the Guilford complex. The most recent level of the late Archaic period on the piedmont, dated 2000 to 500 B.C., is represented by the Savannah River type of projectile point. This point is in the tradition of a broad-bladed, broad-stemmed point, which is associated with polished stone *atlatl* weights and grooved axes.

Following the Savannah River complex there is evidence of a sudden change in style. According to Coe (1964: 123–124), "The stemmed projectile points . . . appear to have been replaced abruptly by large triangular points and well-made cord-and-fabric-marked pottery." This cultural discontinuity marks the end of the late Archaic period and the beginning of the pre-historic Woodland tradition. Early Eastern Woodland culture probably spread into North Carolina from the north. During this period there is little evidence of contact with the south.

The recent period of North Carolina Indian history begins

with deposits of well-made potsherds and Badin points dated A.D. 500. The large triangular arrowpoints mentioned by Coe furnish the first conclusive evidence of the presence of the bow. Fabric-marked and cord-marked potsherds are also present. This type of pottery has been found elsewhere. It is reminiscent, for example, of Mariana Cordware associated with the *latte* culture.

About A.D. 1500 the Pee Dee temple and mound-building people came to the North Carolina piedmont from Georgia and South Carolina. They seem to have used the Doerschuk site as a small hunting and fishing camp, but they developed a ceremonial center at Town Creek. After 1650 the Pee Dee People retreated from North Carolina and by 1700 the cord and fabric ceramic style had disappeared from the piedmont. Several other cultural sequences in North America will be considered in the following chapters.

America Rediscovered

As previously mentioned, in their far-flung prehistoric explorations of the Pacific the Polynesians probably reached the west coast of America, perhaps more than once. At the time of the rediscovery of Polynesia by Europeans, as already noted, these daring navigators had acquired the sweet potato, which may be indigenous to South America. But the Polynesians apparently had little significant influence on American Indian and Eskimo cultures, languages, and physical types, and vice versa except for cultivated plants. Archaeological and documentary evidence reveals that the Vikings also reached the New World in prehistoric times, as we have noted. Like the Polynesians, the Vikings had little significant influence on the Indians.

When the New World was rediscovered by Columbus, the Indians had long since made it their own. No part of the two American continents had not been claimed by some tribe. Contrary to the usual assumption, there was no free land available for settlement. It is estimated that just before 1492 there were about 15.5 million Indians in the Western Hemisphere. Between 4 million and 8 million Indians lived in the Andean highlands alone. After a rapid downward trend precipitated by the European conquest, the aboriginal population began to increase—Indians in the Western Hemisphere now total over 40 million. In 1960 in the United States alone there were some 552,000 American Indians, including Eskimos and Aleut (Bureau of Indian Affairs 1963b: 2). Far from vanishing, the American Indians are now one of the fastest growing ethnic groups in the world.

Linguistic evidence also attests to the Indians' long occupation of the Americas. The Western Hemisphere has the greatest linguistic diversity in the world. Indian languages belong to about a hundred linguistic stocks, and none of the aggregates is related to any other or to any known Old World stocks, according to the findings of linguists. Many contemporary Indian languages still remain unrecorded and unclassified. As we shall see, study of Indian languages, each with its unique structure and idiosyncratic forms, as well as examination of others unrelated to those of western Europe, helps the student of cultures to develop an awareness of unfamiliar types of relationship patterns. If a student expands his awareness of relationship types, he becomes more receptive to forms that may be unfamiliar to him in the cultures of native peoples. Thus, his appreciation of structural diversity sharpens his tools for observing and describing the complex customs, tongues, attitudes, and beliefs of his contemporaries whether indigenous, rural, or urban.

The Indians invented two great agricultural systems in the New World: the culture of the seed planters of Middle and North America and that of the vegetable planters of South America and the Caribbean. These agriculturalists domesticated many useful plants, including maize, squash, beans, white and sweet potatoes, tomato, pumpkin, pineapple, manioc, gourd, cotton, kapok, chile pepper, peanut, avocado, artichoke, cacao, and cocaine. The American Indians, of course, were the original domesticators of tobacco, although most of their smoking practices had a ceremonial function.

The Indians also initiated some of the most sophisticated experiments in group living that the world has ever known (for

example, the social structure of the Incas of the Andean highlands, the Mayas of Central America, and the Aztecs of the
Mexican Plateau). Four such experiments will be described in
the following chapters. The perception patterns and world
images of these groups in situational context will be the special
subject of our scrutiny.

Conclusion

In the following chapters, we shall further explore the behavior
of a number of populations in situational context and historical
perspective to gain insight into the interrelations between nature, society, and culture. We shall present the facts in the form
of a comparison between the cultural biographies of selected
communities from a social-psychiatric viewpoint that is deeper
and more inclusive than is usually employed in community studies. These community biographies suggest that a human group
tends to seek a habitat that appears favorable for its future
survival and self-actualization (see Chapter 18). The members
of the group organize themselves to take advantage of the resources available to them within the limitations of their traditional social patterns and technology. Only if the traditional
framework proves, by trial and error, inadequate to solving the
ongoing problems of the group are pragmatic innovations sought.
Such innovations tend to be incorporated experimentally into
familiar forms in a way that allows habitual relationship patterns to persist as symbolic prototypes if possible (Barnett
1953: 259).

A major problem remains, however. We must examine the
community's mode of perceiving the external world in order to
understand its culture-building and culture-changing behavior.
In other words, unless we explicitly recognize and analyze the
group's perception of its basic living problems, a vital step in
the culture change process will be missing from the discussion.

Human beings possess only their sensory apparatus to directly sense, examine and evaluate the immediate external
world. Research suggests that several senses are available to

human beings in addition to the traditional five (for example, see Milne and Milne 1962). The sense of timing, rhythm, and vibration; the sense of direction and balance; the sense of bodily satisfaction (euphoria) and of disease are now being recognized although they have no sense organ equivalents according to the traditional view.

The relative acuity of each sense and the way each functions for the individual as well as its relative importance in his life depends on both the inherited potential of each sense and on how it has been developed and incorporated into his neuro-muscular system through use. A Lauan, for example, can see the fish he is poised to spear as it darts through a wave breaking over the reef because he has practiced this kind of visual ex-pertise since the age of six. An Eskimo can find his way across the apparently trackless tundra in winter. A Navaho can pick up the trail of an enemy in modern guerrilla warfare. A Mo-hawk can balance himself with ease and grace as he builds the scaffolding of a New York skyscraper. Since the work of Max Wertheimer and the Gestalt psychologists, most students of man accept the rather obvious conclusion that perceiving varies with circumstances and with experience. It also varies with the sen-sory endowment and with the sensory maturity of the perceiver, his psychological state, fatigue factors, health, age, and so on.

In this section we shall try to highlight the perception aspect of the culture-building and culture-styling processes. Because the Indian communities of America developed their native cul-tures for many millenniums without culturally significant con-tact with the rest of the world, many of these communities af-ford ideal natural laboratories for comparative depth studies of group perception problems in situational context.

Before man's advent in the New World, as elsewhere, micro-organisms, plant and animal species had already built bal-anced ecological communities in relation to physical resources and changing climate. The arrival of man marked the advent of a new species in the hemisphere. In this section we shall investi-gate how four tribal groups perceived their living problems in situational context and fashioned their activities, values and be-liefs accordingly.

Notes

1. For a description of the approach and methodology of the Indian Education Research Project, later called the Indian Education, Personality, and Administration Research, see Thompson 1951b: Ch. 2.
2. The pilot study is briefly described in Thompson 1951b: 15–17.
3. The following field guides were prepared: A guide for field workers describing field organization and operations; a field guide to the study of the development of interpersonal relations, for staff and consultants; and a guide to the analysis of the authority system of each tribe.
4. The research committee consisted of W. Lloyd Warner, chairman, Robert J. Havighurst, and Ralph Tylor.
5. See Havighurst and Neugarten, 1955: 150, Table 32.
6. Rorschach tests have revealed that the typical "manner of approach" (*Erfassungstyp*) toward everyday problems varies from one individual to another. This is reflected, according to Rorschach theory, in the way the subject chooses to organize the ink blot areas.
7. I presented these findings in "Perception Patterns in Three Indian Tribes," *Psychiatry* 14 (3): 255–263, 1951. I thank the Editors of *Psychiatry* for kindly granting me permission to use parts of this article in altered and rearranged form in the following three chapters.
8. Sensitivity to taste varies among populations and probably is to some extent genetically determined. The majority of American Indians are "tasters" (Garn 1961: 33–34).
9. I thank Joffre L. Coe for generously briefing me on his central piedmont finds in North Carolina and for helpful comments on an earlier draft of this section of the chapter.

13 /

PAPAGO OF ARIZONA[1]

Brown owls come here in the blue evening,
They are hooting about,
They are shaking their wings and hooting.

Papago curing song (Densmore 1929: 117)

The Papago tribe owns 4,460 square miles of land on the eastern
margin of the Lower Sonoran desert, and the southern edge of
this land extends over 60 miles along the border between Arizona and Mexico. These Indians are closely related physically
and culturally to the Mexican Papago, who occupy contiguous
territory to the south. The Papago represent a desert-dwelling
branch of the Pima Indians, who live on the banks of the Gila
and its tributaries. Of the 11,700 (1959 estimate) Papago in the
United States, only about half live on the reservation at any
one time. The rest earn their living either temporarily or permanently outside the reservation (Kelly 1963: 54–55).

Microrace

This tribe is believed to represent a contemporary manifestation of an early Archaic-Caucasoid strain in America, mixed with
later Mongoloid settlers. According to a recent study (Kelly
1963), 92 percent of the reservation population is classed as
fullblood, compared with 65 percent for the off-reservation Papago. The present trend favors greater racial mixture at younger
age levels. Papago outgroup marriage has become especially
noticeable in the age group between thirty-five and fifty-five.
Papago who marry outside the tribe tend to marry other Indians
rather than non-Indians (Papago Indian Agency 1966).

All fullblood Papago are classed in blood group O, Rh positive. Indeed, all Papago are classed as Rh positive, but a few mixed bloods have type A or A-B blood (United States Public Health Service Hospital, Sells, Arizona, 1967). The Papago are tall and heavy-boned. They have dark brown eyes, brown skin, straight coarse black hair, and a mean cephalic index of 80.52 (Gabel 1949: 27; 92–93). They are distinguished from most other American Indians by their relatively broad chests and greater body size, as well as their lower-keyed mongoloid traits, a characteristic of Archaic-Caucasoid Indians in the Americas.

Language and Song

The Papago speak six major (and several minor) dialects of the Pima language (Joseph, *et al.* 1949: 66–71; J. A. Mason 1950). The Pima language belongs to the Utaztecan stock, which also includes the languages of the Hopi Indians and of several Mexican tribes. At the time of the Indian Education Research Project fieldwork (1941–1942), less than 40 percent of the Papago spoke some English and less than 20 percent could read and write. By 1965, however, 71 percent had facility in spoken English, and 44 percent had completed seven or more years of schooling (Papago Indian Agency 1966).

The Papago are a merry, joking, and laughing people, although they express their temperament in muted key. Singing is their great means of self-expression. It is also their main device for tapping the unseen power of the universe (Underhill 1938).

Geography

Papagoland is unusually beautiful. Giant cactus, mesquite, and ocotilla bushes against a background of mauve-tinted mountains and clear blue sky make this vast arid land distinctive. Extremely dry most of the year, in spring the desert blooms with incredible brilliance.

The relative isolation of the tribe can only be understood in terms of geography. The land of the Papago is classed as basin and range topography. Elevation varies from 1,400 to 7,740 feet, and most of the area has an altitude of 1,400 to 3,000 feet. Much of the soil is productive, but the region is characterized by climatic extremes. These include torrential summer rains, prolonged droughts, and a wide range of daily (51 to 82 degrees F.) and seasonal (67 degrees F. mean annual) temperatures. There are no permanent streams. Annual precipitation averages 18 inches in the mountains and 13 inches in the valleys. Districts in the extreme west and north of the region, however, average only 7 inches or less (Kelly 1963: map 2). Most of the rain falls in July, August, and September. The frost-free season varies from 250 days in the eastern part of the reservation to 315 days in the western part. The growing season for crops cultivated by traditional arroyo-flood methods, however, lasts only about two months, from the time the fields are flooded until exhaustion of the available moisture.

Although some parts of Papagoland are true desert, much is classed as rangeland. When surveyed in 1939, the Papago range had an approved carrying capacity of only 10,304 cattle units. It was 400 percent overstocked, mainly with cattle and horses. With great effort and handicapped by their belief that the mishandling of animals may bring ill fortune and sickness, the Indians managed to reduce their stock. But the range is still more than 56 percent overstocked (Papago Indian Agency 1966; Kelly 1963: 78). There are only a few other resources, although the entire area is lightly mineralized, chiefly with copper, gold, silver, lead, and manganese. The Papago reservation was recently closed to mineral entry by those who were not members of the tribe, and the Papago tribal council has established a mining department to encourage development of minerals. A lease to develop an open-pit copper mine has been concluded and others are under consideration (Papago Indian Agency 1966).

Archaeology and Culture History

One of the most important archaeological finds in the Americas is located in Papagoland. Stratified deposits in Ventana Cave, discovered by Emil W. Haury (1950), contain quantities of stone and other artifacts. The evidence indicates that the region has been inhabited by man for 15,000 to 20,000 years. The earliest men were hunters and gatherers. Their cultures date from an era when the climate of the American Southwest was cooler and more humid than it is today. The savannah was the home of the mammoth, ancient bison, jaguar, four-horned antelope, sloth, and tapir. A chipped, leaf-shaped projectile point with concave base, of the Folsom type, found in the cave is dated about 7000 B.C. The culture associated with this instrument is classified as Paleo-Indian of the Cochise Desert type (Sayles and Antevs 1941), whereas artifacts from the early strata of the North Carolina piedmont, discussed in Chapter 12, are associated with a Paleo-Indian culture of the High Plains type.

During the fifth millennium B.C., when the climate had become warmer and drier, cultivated maize appeared, probably intrusive from the south. The first pottery unearthed at Ventana has been dated about A.D. 100. Hafted stone axes and clay ceremonial urns with painted decorations, dated A.D. 1100, have also been found. The designs on these urns are similar to those on contemporary handmade Papago baskets.

From the fifth millennium B.C. to the end of the fourteenth century Papago culture shows a continuous growth, while there is some variation in the racial stock suggesting some infiltration of non-Papago. Between 1400 and 1694, the earliest recorded history (Bolton 1960: 284–286), there is a hiatus in the archaeological deposits at Ventana Cave, which suggests that as the climate deteriorated during a long drought (see Butzer 1961: 47) the desert dwellers moved out. Continuation of the cultural style after the break indicates that the people returned to their traditional life way after the drought.

Economy and Nutrition

The Papago use the natural resources of their habitat with considerable ingenuity. They also conserve them and foster life actively and energetically (Underhill 1946: 15). Besides collecting wild edible plants and hunting game, the Papago cultivate beans, corn, and squash. Their farming methods are ingeniously designed to take advantage of the summer floods. Formerly, they built canals to spread the water (Castetter and Bell 1942:

161–165). Farmland irrigated by modern installations presently totals about 5,275 acres, but not all of it is in use (Kelly 1963: 84–93). The indigenous variety of maize cultivated by the Papago matures in about two months, before all the moisture from the summer rains has evaporated (Carter 1945: 96–108). Formerly, after the harvest had been gathered and dried, the village groups moved to their winter hunting camps in the nearby mountains, where freshwater springs or wells were available. These seasonal migrations have been discontinued because the deep wells that have been dug in the valleys have somewhat stabilized the drinking water supply for both the people and their stock.

Research into Papago nutrition suggests that the traditional diet of the Papago was quite well balanced (Reh n.d.; Pijoan, Elkin, and Eslinger 1943). It included corn, squash, beans, chile, wild plants, and small game. This diet has tended to deteriorate recently, however, under influences from American industrial civilization. Deficiencies in vitamin C are particularly noticeable.

Social Structure and Kinship in the Papago Village

The basic social unit of the Papago is the extended family. It includes a married couple, their sons with wives and children, their unmarried daughters, and their parents. The oldest active male is the leader of the group. The men of each family collectively work a section of tribal land that has been assigned to the family by the village council. Cattle and horses are owned by individuals, but the members of a village pool their stock for herding under an elected stock foreman. The women and girls of the household share the tasks of caring for the children, cooking, basket and pottery making, and gathering wild plants.

Although every individual in the family is respected and given a role in decision making, an authority pattern in terms of patrilocal residence and seniority is expressed in Papago behavior and kinship. Papago kinship usages (classed as Yuman) are characterized by emphasis on distinctions of sex and relative age according to generation and by a terminological differentiation of parents from their siblings and of siblings from one another. Males outrank females and older people outrank younger.

A number of related families with common residence form a village community. There are now about thirty-seven villages on the reservation (Kelly 1963: 37–39). Located in the many wide valleys that cut across the region, a Papago village covers a considerable area. Dwellings are constructed of wattle and daub or adobe; storehouses, of mesquite and giant cactus branches. Each dwelling has one or more *ramada* (branch-covered shelters), in which the women do most of their work. Corrals and fences of ocotilla stems, planted in the ground, form a part of the arrangement. Every spring these fences sprout bright red blossoms.

Formerly each village had a council composed of all the adult males of the group. The village council met nightly under the leadership of the elected village headman, who usually belonged to a prominent family. Its members considered village problems as they arose. They reached practical decisions not by majority rule but by a more subtle process aimed at achieving a certain unanimity of opinion (Dobyns 1952: 35). When I studied the Papago, I was impressed with this decision-making process as a mechanism for tapping the brainpower and accumulated wisdom of the whole village group of males—not just the old men or the young adults or the middle aged.

Child Development

A Papago child develops in an unusually permissive social environment. He is humored and indulged by all the members of his extended family, including his mother, grandmother, father, grandfather, aunts, sisters and brothers, and even his child nurse, a sister or cousin who takes care of him while the mother performs her household tasks.

As soon as a young Papago begins to walk (between fourteen and twenty-two months) he is taught not to handle or play with wild animals. The Papago believe that a wild animal can serve as a medium of the great power source and thus can bring sickness. These warnings apparently imbue the child with a lasting fear of animals. Owls are especially feared. Even as a little child, a Papago is taught never to pick anything—not even a blade of grass—that he does not intend to use and to use everything that he picks or hunts. Thus a succoring and conserving attitude toward nature and the resources of the tribe is instilled at an early age.

Papago children soon begin to learn the social roles and functions of their respective sexes according to tribal custom. A little boy runs errands and chops wood while his sister helps with household chores and takes care of younger children. Pressure on the child to assume the expected behavior patterns and regular duties of his sex and age group is mainly verbal. This takes the form of stories and lectures by the grandfather, who explains why a person should be industrious and wise. A child is always regarded as a person in his own right, and in many ways he is free to make his own choices. For example, until recently school attendance on American Indian reservations was not compulsory. When a Papago child reached school age, he was asked whether or not he wanted to attend school. He was not urged or constrained and his decision was respected. Only two-thirds of the Papago children of school age were enrolled in 1942, and most of those in school attended irregularly. During the past two decades education facilities for the Papago have improved. Elementary schooling is available at the consolidated school in Sells, at four village day schools, and at a boarding school in Santa Rosa. The Phoenix Indian school and several out-of-state Indian schools offer high school work. Papago children also attend public high schools in Tucson and Roman Catholic Indian high schools. Adult education is also offered in several villages by the Indian Service (Bureau of Indian Affairs 1966). In 1966 over 95 percent of the children were enrolled in grades one through eight with regular attendance.

Papago children mature at their own pace into an early adulthood. By the time they are ten years old children of both sexes have usually become working members of the family group and have already learned most of the skills required for participation in traditional Papago adult life.

Formerly a Papago youth went on a solitary vision quest, but this practice has been discontinued. A girl's first menstruation used to be marked by dancing and feasting after she had been segregated for four days in a menstrual hut and instructed by an old woman in her duties as a woman. In the 1940s the event was still celebrated by a simple rite by which a medicine man purified her with sacred eagle feathers and a drink of magical white clay mixed with water. She might be given a new name that the medicine man had dreamed. If this ceremony was omitted, the girl might bring sickness and death to any member of the group. Thereafter the girl was customarily kept under surveillance by her female relatives until her marriage, which usually did not take place until she was at least sixteen years old. This is still the custom. Marriage marks the achievement of full adult status in the community, and the couple gains prestige with the birth of each child.

Traditional Ceremonies and World Image

Some traditional ceremonies concerned with rain, like the wine ceremony, and with health, like the singers' rites (Joseph, Spicer, and Chesky 1949: 73–77), persist, and medicine men continue to follow their traditional occupation. The wine ceremony is an annual village festival held in early summer after each family has picked the ripe fruit of the giant cactus and made it into syrup. Each family contributes its quota of syrup to the village round (ceremonial) house. After it has fermented, the ceremony is held. It is oriented toward rain bringing, life renewal, and purification of mind and heart and involves singing, speech making, and ritual group intoxication.

To the Papago the world is permeated with impersonal, superhuman power. But this mana is not perceived as either good or evil in itself. To these Indians power, including sexual power, is helpful or destructive depending on the will of the medium through which it passes (Underhill 1946: 16; Joseph, Spicer, and Chesky 1949: 78, 221). A deity, an animal, or a shaman can either harm or benefit a person; it can bring him either sickness or health. It behooves man to treat such power mediums with circumspection and respect so that they may be favorably disposed toward him and use their power to further his well-being rather than his decline and death.

Perception Pattern

The main field investigations and the psychological testing program (July 1942–September 1943) of the Indian Education Research Project on the Papago reservation used a representative sample of 200 children from two Papago communities. Topawa, in the eastern part of the reservation, was chosen to represent a community relatively acculturated to influences from the outside world. Hickiwan-Guvo, in the western part, represented a less acculturated group. Alice Joseph administered the Rorschach test to 117 Papago children: 43 in Hickiwan-Guvo and 74 in Topawa. Background studies in sociocultural anthropology were made by Ruth M. Underhill in Santa Rosa, Rosamond B. Spicer in Topawa, and Jane Chesky in Hickiwan-Guvo. Ruth Underhill and I made a pilot study on the Papago reservation from February to June 1942, and I undertook follow-up research in April 1946.

Analysis of the Papago Rorschach responses revealed that the children tended to perceive the ink blots as global wholes with little or no differentiation into component parts. This tendency was strong not only among the younger children but also throughout all the age grades tested, in both sexes, and in both Papago communities studied. The results of the psychological tests revealed little or no interest on the part of the children to differentiate parts within a whole and to restructure them. In the context of all the findings on Papago personality, Dr. Joseph interpreted this response pattern as a predilection to avoid both disentangling perceptual impressions into clear-cut images and synthesizing them into more complex concepts (Joseph, Spicer, and Chesky 1949: Ch. 17). At the same time, the responses clearly showed that Papago children were quite able to differentiate and restructure. Recent analysis of the Papago noun classes reveals a similar finding (see Mathiot 1962: 348–349).

This perception pattern takes on meaning when it is considered as an integral part of Papago personality, which, according to project findings, is distinguished by its relatively simple structure. Emotional development tends to be quite limited in range but relatively spontaneous within habitual boundaries.

Control of spontaneous impulses is relatively precarious. Anxiety in its free-floating (nonspecific or detached) form and on a conscious level is inconspicuous. The main creative outlets are imaginative fantasy and songs of magical significance. Indeed, instead of attempting to control or negate his inner psychic forces systematically, the Papago child apparently allows them to function affirmatively as a kind of safety valve.

In other words, according to these findings, Papago children's personalities are distinguishable from those of the Hopi, Navaho, and Sioux by a built-in cyclic process through which an individual is able either to recognize and cope with the practical problems of everyday life or to withdraw into a timeless world of fantasy and dream. In times of stress this rhythmic psychic mechanism apparently affords a way by which fantasy and dream may function almost automatically as an inner control to behavior. It provides a flexible means by which an individual may express disturbing personal drives in day dreaming and fantasy rather than in overt behavior. Like night dreaming,[2] this mechanism apparently affords the individual a therapeutic means of intermittently working through his immediate experiences and filing them away in his unconscious. Instead of operating only during sleep, however, it operates also during waking hours on the fringes of consciousness.

Effects of Acculturation

Through a combination of circumstances, including the fact that their land was less attractive to outsiders than that of most American Indian tribes, acculturation to modern American life did not really begin until the early twentieth century. About 1915 the Indian Service began to dig the deep wells that supply water to the valley villages. The Papago subsistence problem was also influenced by deterioration of the already meager resources through the introduction of the herding industry, which, in conjunction with periodic drought cycles, contributed to critical overgrazing of the range. To meet their economic difficulties, the Papago developed a new seasonal migration pattern. Families left the reservation during the winter to pick cotton and engage in other seasonal labor. For the rest of the year they returned to their reservation villages to farm the land and herd their stock.

The Papago tribe organized itself under the Indian Reorganization Act during the years from 1935 to 1937 on the basis of nine districts based on dialect groups. Although the transition from village to tribal self-government was not entirely smooth, especially in the remote western districts, the Papago used their traditional village council system to form a link between the people and the tribal council. The communication and organizational relationships established have allowed the tribe to take advantage of current federal antipoverty funds through their tribal office of economic opportunity.[3] Tribal self-government among the Papago has generally been more successful than among other United States Indian tribes (Kelly 1963: 125, Thompson 1951b: 107).

The Papago have developed their own form of Christianity, called Sonoran Catholicism, an indigenized form of Catholicism distinguished especially by democratic village organization of ceremonials involving both men and women. In Sonoran Catholic villages, many orthodox Catholic practices are absent. The hierarchally organized, celebate priesthood, confession, celebration of the mass, and marriage and extreme unction as sacraments have never been adopted.

In 1908 Roman Catholics set up missions in the eastern part of the reservation. Presbyterians followed in 1910. Since then these orthodox denominations have competed in attempts to reconvert the Sonoran Catholic Papago. Comparing Rorschach test findings from Roman Catholic children, Presbyterian children, and Sonoran Catholic children, the two orthodox Christian missions apparently differ significantly in their effect on traditional Papago discipline patterns. The results suggest an increase in the use of conscious and internalized control among the Presbyterian Papago and a certain impulsiveness and incapacity to control their impulses among the Roman Catholic Papago (Joseph, Spicer, and Chesky 1949: 241), whereas the Sonoran Catholics retain the indigenous balance between control and expression.

Conclusion

It seems from the available evidence that Papago traditional culture represents a highly functional development of great age, inner coherence, and durability. These aborigines seem to have achieved long ago—and re-created through the centuries—a cultural balance in transaction with the climax ecocycle of Papagoland. That the traditional culture is emotionally satisfying is evidenced both by the psychological test results and by behavior; for example, in the low-keyed rippling laughter and song constantly noted by those who know and are accepted by these Indians. At the same time the culture affords a flexible mechanism by which the group has been able to resolve its difficult and changing practical problems throughout its history. Papago personality structure, especially the preference for perceiving reality in terms of vague, global wholes (as opposed to seeing it in neat two-valued packages, for example) and the avoidance of clear-cut commitments in favor of sliding scale gradual oppositions, is compatible with Papago group life viewed in the perspective of history and depth ecology.

The Papago have also proved to be better equipped than other tribes to enhance their welfare by taking advantage of opportunities offered them by the federal government and by the surrounding industrial civilization (for a different interpretation, see Hackenberg 1962). They even created their own indigenized version of Christianity. While dovetailing with the national political structure, the Papago have kept their local identity as a culturally distinctive tribe in the ancient homeland. They have managed to retain the deeper forms of Papago traditional culture and language that nourish their ethos. William H. Kelly (1967) finds that family self-reliance and flexibility are the basic qualities of the contemporary Papago. Whether or not the Papago can continue to retain their traditional culture and personality balance in the face of strong pressures from the outside world remains to be seen.

Regardless of the ultimate outcome, however, our depth study of this American Indian tribe substantiates one of the major findings of this book. When a human group occupies a congenial niche in a climax ecosystem and builds a transactive relation with the environment into the structure of its culture and its perception of the world, this cultural pattern is likely to endure as the tribe's preferred type. Some form of persistence or reemergence may be expected, despite pressures from the outside world, so long as the population is not destroyed or severed from its homeland.

Notes

1. This chapter is based mainly on firsthand observations made on the Papago reservation in 1942 and 1946 and on findings from the Indian Education Research Project, especially as presented by Joseph, Spicer, and Chesky (1949); Havighurst and Neugarten (1955); and Thompson (1951a; 1951b: Ch. 5). I am grateful to Ruth Underhill, W. Wade Head, former superintendent of the Papago agency and his staff, to Morris Burge, former superintendent, and to Calvin N. Brice, acting superintendent, for help in the fieldwork or in preparing this chapter. I am deeply indebted to all the fieldworkers on the Papago project, listed in Joseph, Spicer, and Chesky (1949: v). I also thank William H. Kelly, director of the Bureau of Ethnic Research, Department of Anthropology, University of Arizona, for reading and commenting on an earlier draft of the manuscript.
2. Regarding possible functions of dreaming and rapid-eye-movement sleep, see David Foulkes (1966) and D. R. Goodenough (1966).
3. Current federal grant programs of the Papago tribal office of economic opportunity include conduct and administration ($24,000); remedial reading ($12,000); guidance and counseling ($19,500); preschool centers ($11,500); parent-child centers ($45,000); Neighborhood Youth Corps ($35,000); VISTA (two workers) (Papago Indian Agency 1966).

14 /

HOPI OF THE SOUTHWEST MESAS

*Pai, pi, ita yep puu hakimimuy nalö nananü wo itanamui,
mumgwitui amongami yuyuha. Owi ita yep itah unangwasi
nanapangwani nap hakawat unangwasyag nalö nanaiwo
tuikaowak; put ako puma ich itamui okwatotowani yokwani.*

Now, then, here we array (decorate), those four different
ones, (somewhere in the four world quarters), our fathers,
the chiefs (deities); therefore cooperate we here with
our offerings. From somewhere, may, with their help, the
four different ones (the deities of the four world quarters)
have pity upon us quickly, and let it rain at the right time.

> A Hopi prayer (Marau ceremony); free translation
> by Henry R. Voth (1912: 27–28)

Geography

Hopiland is located on the Colorado plateau, a southern escarp-
ment of the great Rocky Mountain chain, 6,500 feet high.[1] Unless we grasp the significant differences in altitude, climate, pattern of precipitation, and ecology between the homeland of the
Papago and that of the Hopi, we shall lack some of the facts
necessary for a valid comparison between the living problems
faced by the two groups during their known history.

Precipitation in Hopiland averages only 11.5 inches annually.
What little rain there is falls in cloud bursts during the summer
months. Droughts are frequent. An uncertain supply of fresh
water is obtained from ephemeral washes of the Colorado River
drainage and from a few semipermanent springs that are fed by
the Black Mesa watershed. Sanddunes, which have formed on
and below the Hopi mesas, hold some moisture. The tablelike

formations, which are elevated several hundred feet above the plateau floor, are called First, Second, Third, and Antelope mesas.

There are about 6,000 Hopi (1967 estimate). Some 4,000 members of the tribe inhabit the 631,194 acres of the Hopi reservation, which is located in the heart of Navaho country. The Hopi have equal rights with the Navaho with respect to the rest of the old Moqui (Hopi) reservation of 1882, approximately 1.1 million acres. The dispute between the Hopi and the Navaho tribes over rights to the Moqui reservation was legally settled in 1962 and confirmed by the United States Supreme Court. A negotiating committee consisting of eight members from each tribe was set up in 1963. An equitable agreement on the management and use of area designated for joint use has not yet been worked out (Hopi Indian Agency 1966: 1). Very few Hopi have been able to obtain grazing permits in the area, which is almost exclusively occupied by Navaho (Pratt 1967).

Microrace and Language

According to the traditional classification system, the Hopi belong to the Proto-Mongoloid racial stock. Evidently they are the descendants of migrants who reached the Southwest more recently than the Proto-Caucasoid Papago. All Hopi are classed as fullblood, although about 5 percent of the tribesmen have mixed with Navaho, Pueblo, and other Indian groups. Less than 0.5 percent have mixed with non-Indians. Probably because there has been so little intermarriage between Hopi and non-Indians, there are very few B and AB blood types among members of the tribe. Approximately 80 percent of the Hopi are O, Rh positive, and the remainder are predominantly A, Rh positive (Hopi Indian Agency 1966).

These Indians speak Hopi, a Shoshonean language belonging to the Utaztecan stock. The close relation between the Hopi's language and culture structure has been revealed in classic studies by Benjamin Lee Whorf (1941, 1956). He suggested that the Hopi, through their language, conceptualize the flux of sensory experience largely in terms of happenings or events, often of a rhythmic or vibratory nature, against a background of time viewed as a duration rather than, for example, as cut up into disparate units that can be lined up and counted like bottles in a row. They do not perceive matter in the form of "objects" packaged like "contents within a container." Rather, their mass nouns refer to vague entities or imply a suitable type body or container. In these and many other ways the Hopi language adequately expresses relationships underlined by the Hopi culture and especially by the Hopi's image of the world, discussed below.

Virtually all these Indians also speak, read, and write English. Besides their intensive traditional training as members of the tribe, most Hopi have had at least an elementary school education, and many have graduated from high school. A large percentage of Hopi high school graduates attend colleges, universities, business colleges, and vocational schools. Subsequently living part-time off the reservation, they enter such professions as teaching, business administration, accounting, and nursing.

Archaeology and Cultural History

The Hopi are the cultural heirs—and probably also the living descendants—of the Anasazi, or Basketmakers. According to archaeological evidence, the Anasazi occupied a much larger area of the Southwest than the Hopi do today. The Anasazi appeared on the Colorado plateau before the third century B.C. They cultivated maize and dug pit houses. In the Modified Basketmaker period, the pits were covered by conical or truncated superstructures, each with a central smoke hole. The Basketmakers tipped their spears with Folsom-style chipped flint projectile points and hurled them with a spear thrower. They also made baskets and bags of twine.

The first pottery (Anasazi type) appears in these Basketmaker sites about A.D. 500. It was produced by pressing wet clay into a basket, which was destroyed during the firing. The early pottery was naturally limited in variety of form by the baskets that molded it. It manifests a craft skill that eventually developed into highly refined types.

Several Late Basketmaker sites have been found on or below the Hopi mesas. A few sites produced evidence that they had been occupied into what archaeologists call the Proto-Pueblo (Pueblo I) period. Pithouses during this period are marked by one or two rooms. This structure seems to be an ancestor of the kiva, a room partly hollowed out of the mesa floor. The kiva is used by the modern Hopi as a ceremonial chamber and men's club house. Pueblo architecture was also developed to take advantage of the limited surface area of the mesas. As the population increased, small flat-roofed rectangular rooms were added in terraces upward and around a central plaza, where important dances were held. Terraces and room entrances were oriented to the sun (Fewkes 1906: 88), and ladders were used to climb from one level to another.

The Classic Pueblo period reached its climax in the thirteenth century with the great drought of 1276–1299. Semipermanent springs in the cliffs, on which the mesa pueblos depended for drinking water, dried up. Arroyos changed their courses and deepened so that flash-flood farming, the traditional Indian method that uses the overflow of moisture to water the plateau floor, became less and less feasible (Hack 1942: 79–80). One by one the great pueblos were abandoned, and the Hopi took refuge in less arid habitats. When the climate began to improve, topography and moisture distribution changed. Some Hopi groups returned to Hopiland and rebuilt their pueblos near the new freshwater springs.

In 1540 the Hopi tribe was discovered by a Franciscan friar and soldiers from Coronado's expedition. The Hopi were then living in seven villages on or below all four major mesas. The tribe was cultivating maize, squash, beans, and cotton by both flash-flood and dry farming methods. They had also terraced, irrigated, and cultivated a few acres around their springs.

The Europeans were searching for gold on behalf of the Spanish king, as well as converts to Roman Catholicism. Although they found no gold, they eventually established a Franciscan mission in Hopiland. According to the Spanish pattern of conquest and colonization, the monks prevailed upon the Indians to build churches and cloisters, to plant mission gardens, and to run mission sheep on the ranges of their clans.

The Hopi, however, never fully accepted the autocratic mission rule. After about fifty years (1680), they joined with the other pueblo groups and killed the padres, burned the missions, and reclaimed their clan lands. Those who had been converted to the alien faith reverted to their ancient ceremonies. Anticipating European reprisals, they moved all their pueblos up to the mesa tops (except Antelope Mesa, which was abandoned) for protection. Although they have made many attempts, Catholics have never been able to regain a foothold in Hopiland.

In 1696, at the invitation of the Hopi, the Tewa-speaking people of Hano moved from their traditional homeland in the Rio Grande region to their present habitat on First Mesa. For more than 250 years they have resisted acculturation to the Hopi life way (Dozier 1951: 56–66; 1954; 1964: 90).

At the end of the nineteenth century, the Rev. Henry R. Voth, a Mennonite, established a mission near Old Oraibi pueblo on Third Mesa. By converting certain ceremonial leaders before they had trained their successors in the crucial winter solstice (Soyal) ceremony, Voth precipitated a breakdown in the annual ceremonial cycle at Old Oraibi. Within the next two decades the ancient pueblo had split into five factions (Titiev 1944). The conservative group founded Hotevilla, which is still the most tradition-bound Hopi pueblo. Mennonite converts built the village of New Oraibi below Third Mesa and the village of Moencopi near Tuba City.

Eventually Baptist missionaries gained a few converts at Second Mesa. In ten out of a total of twelve villages, however, the Hopi are trying to preserve the essentials of their traditional culture with a minimum of internal structural change. Their mesa-top villages are still constructed as three-storied, tiered stone or adobe sturctures built around a central plaza. They still practice their native religious ceremonies and support their aboriginal value system.

Although the climate of Hopiland has become more arid since the time of Coronado, the Hopi still cultivate maize, beans, and squash by ancient methods. They have also planted orchards of peach and apricot, fruits first brought by the Spaniards, on the sand dunes. The Hopi grow a variety of vegetables in their irrigated gardens, although the acreage is limited by the available spring water supply.

The Spaniards also introduced sheep, goats, and burros. Previously the Hopi's only domesticated animals were the dog and the turkey. As in the South Seas and Iceland, the introduction of new species upset the balance of nature. Overgrazing, combined with a natural erosion epicycle, seriously damaged the range. During the 1930s the United States government introduced a soil and moisture conservation program. In time the Hopi villagers managed to reduce their stock by 24 percent to the scientifically designated carrying capacity of the range. This capacity has now improved so that between 40 and 60 percent of the potential production of the Hopi range is realized (Hopi Indian Agency 1966).

Like the Papago, the Hopi came to terms with their semi-desert environment in prehistoric times, largely through centuries of trial and error. They utilize with considerable technical ingenuity many of the rather meager resources that the mesa country offers. They identify and name 200 wild plants of the region. In prehistoric times they mined local surface veins of soft coal and used it for firing their pots and for outdoor cooking. The Hopi's nurturing and conserving attitude toward all life is similar to that of the Papago. A Hopi child is taught never to pick anything that he does not use. Before killing a deer a Hopi hunter ritually asks permission from the "Head of the Deer People," and he uses every part of the slain animal, even the hoofs. The environment, with its high altitude and extremely limited water supply, imposes a severe discipline on the Hopi as a group and as individuals to ensure survival and self-actualization of the tribe. We shall next consider the impact this discipline has had on Hopi religion and world view.

World Image and Religion

An analysis of Hopi ceremonies in cultural context reveals that these Indians perceive their world as a unity. All natural phenomena relevant to the Hopi life way are regarded as interdependent, including human beings, useful animals and plants, the sun, moon, and clouds, the earth, the ancestors, and supernatural beings. Such phenomena are named and classed into orders and suborders of a universal scheme, which the Hopi traditionally believe to be regulated by a built-in principle of immanent justice. According to this principle, the several components of the system, including the Hopi themselves, cooperate for the good of the whole. The members of the several orders and suborders are believed to exchange equivalent but not identical services for their mutual benefit. Notice, for example, the correlative relationship between the Hopi and the Deer People implicit in Hopi hunting customs by which the Hopi ceremonially nurture the Deer People but expect a deer in return if their need is great.

Man has a special role in this universal scheme. He must actively participate in the operation of the universal correlative process by means of positive thinking, praying, and willing and by performing traditional ceremonies regularly according to an annual cycle. Through dancing, singing, impersonation, praying, making murals, and sand painting, wood carving, and many other creative acts, the participants in a major ceremony of the Hopi cycle are believed actively to reinforce the universal process and to engender its fulfillment. The winter solstice (Soyal) ceremony, for example, is keyed to promote fertility and growth in living things, to help the sun "turn back from his winter house," to bring rain, and to promote the growth of crops. When the members of the secret society that perpetuates the Soyal perform their roles, they believe that they are thereby helping to activate the universal process.

Hopi boys do not go on a vision quest as the Papago youths used to do, and individuals are not expected to contact a superhuman power source directly. Rather, in their ceremonial activities the Hopi seek power and well-being as a group for the benefit of the whole community—plant and animal species, supernaturals, and ancestors, as well as living human beings.

The correlativity principle may be difficult for outsiders to grasp, especially Westerners, who prefer to phrase relationships in terms of reciprocity (the exchange of identical values) and of superordinate-subordinate dyads. The Hopi pattern may be illustrated by the kachina society. The main purpose of this secret association seems to be to facilitate the cooperative relationship between the living members of a Hopi clan and its ancestors. In their underworld home and on periodic visits to the Hopi mesas, the ancestors are believed to carry on activities that reinforce those of the living. The putative annual visit of the Hopi ancestors to the mesas is symbolized in kachina ceremonies in which masked dancers impersonate clan ancestors (see Fewkes 1903).

Despite strong pressures by Christian missionaries, most Hopi men until recently were initiated into the traditional religion when they were about twenty years old. The Hopi annual ceremonial cycle is still enacted in the major Hopi mesa-top pueblos except Old Oraibi.

Unlike the traditional Papago village, governed by a democratic council that included all adult males, the traditional Hopi pueblo was organized on the basis of its ceremonies and headed by a chief priest, who led the major ceremony. Thus, it functioned mainly through religious mechanisms, including secret societies and ritual responsibilities, patterned according to the annual ceremonial cycle. Sanctions were, to a considerable extent, diffuse and informal.

Formerly the priests of each pueblo participated in an informal "chief's talk" under the chief priest, but no political organization with legislative or executive power existed at either the tribal or village level.

Social Structure

According to Frederick R. Eggan (1950: 291, Ch. 1), Hopi social structure, like that of the Zuni, Acoma, Laguna, and some other North American tribes, is characterized by a Crow type of kinship system. In contrast to the patriarchal extended-family system of the Papago, Hopi clans are based on matrilineal descent. A Hopi clan acknowledges relationship to a number of classes of nonhuman partners like an animal or plant species or to a class of natural or supernatural phenomena. Such totems give the clan its special quality, its power or "medicine," and its name. Clans acknowledging the same totems are related according to the Hopi kinship system. They form exogamous totemic units or phratries.

Each clan consists of one or more matrilineal lineages, which are theoretically descended from a common ancestor. The lineage focuses in a group of related females consisting of a senior member, her sisters, and their female descendants. Brothers and male descendants of these females are also members of the lineage, whereas relatives by marriage are not. A Hopi is not allowed to marry into his mother's, his father's, or his mother's father's clan. Usually when a man marries, he and his wife take up residence with or near his wife's relatives. The Hopi clan, therefore, traditionally consists of a group of closely related women living with their husbands, children, and other relatives in several contiguous or nearby households.

One household belonging to each clan is known as its "ancestral house." The female head of the family living in this house is acknowledged to be the "real head" of the clan. She has charge of the clan's sacred property, such as its fetishes, which are kept in the ancestral house. The brother of the real head is the clan's ceremonial head. He activates the ceremonies that are the property of the clan through a secret religious society that performs the rites connected with ceremony as well as curing rites. There are nine such societies in Hopiland.

Each household group traditionally occupies two adjacent rooms, one of which is used for storing maize, in the apartment-like structure that houses the whole village. A Hopi household is an independent economic unit. The women and girls cooperate in caring for the dwelling rooms and the children, in grinding corn, and in cooking for the household group. They haul water from the pueblo spring, cultivate a small irrigated garden, and also frequently make baskets and pottery.

The men of the household, with the help of their sons and maternal nephews, farm, herd, hunt, and collect fuel and timber for the group. Many of them also spin, weave, and work in leather or silver. Occasionally Hopi silversmiths work out jewelry designs inspired by the borders of Hopi handwoven woolen blankets. The development of high-quality craftwork has been encouraged by the federal government since the 1930s. Hopi men also operate trade stores and engage in wage work both on and off the reservation. In October 1966 an estimated 501 Hopi were engaged in permanent wage work, and 526 Hopi were engaged in temporary or seasonal work. The average annual income per Hopi family was estimated to be $1,800 (Hopi Indian Agency 1966). A demographic analysis and labor-force survey is being conducted on the Hopi reservation. The Hopi men run the tribal government through a nonindigenous tribal council, which will be discussed later.

Child Training

Hopi children are warmly welcomed into the family. For the first three to six months they spend much time bound to a cradle board. They are petted and protected from disturbances that might interfere with their well-being and contentment. At the same time, once off the cradle, they are given a good deal of freedom to explore their world. They are brought up sharply, however, if they wander too near the edge of the mesa cliff or do anything that threatens their safety.

The Hopi conceive the life cycle as a journey along the "road of life," which involves four phases: childhood, youth, adulthood, and old age. Each phase is regarded as part of a gradual maturation process that involves developing out of the previous stage and preparing for those to come. Passage from one phase to the next is usually marked with a ceremony. If an individual fails to make the grade within certain limits he may receive a harsh reprimand, as illustrated in the kachina initiation ceremony.

All Hopi children between eight and ten years of age undergo ceremonial initiation into the kachina society. This rite (Powamu) is designed to introduce the child to his clan ancestors. It symbolically depicts a child's close correlative relationship to his ancestors, who are represented by masked kachina dancers. According to Henry R. Voth (1901), as part of this ceremony the naked boy stands with his godfather on a sand painting. Initiate and godfather face each other, the godfather holding his godson's hands above the boy's head. The sand painting depicts symbolically the Hopi concept of the four phases of the "road of life." During the ceremony the child is whipped by two whipper kachinas with yucca switches supplied by the kachina mother, who stands by. A rebellious boy, who may be having difficulty moving from the childhood to youth according to Hopi standards, is whipped soundly. Then the kachina mother steps onto the sand painting and is whipped by the whipper kachinas. Then the whipper kachinas whip each other. The Powamu ceremony thus provides remedial treatment, Hopi-style, for laggards on the road of life. A Hopi girl, fully clothed and supported by her godaunt, undergoes a similar but less strenuous treatment. The Powamu is a ritual of exorcism "possibly against the evils of life and to promote growth and well being," according to Alexander M. Stephen (1936 1: 156). Its symbolic meaning in the context of Hopi culture will be discussed in Chapter 19.

After initiation a Hopi boy is expected to join one or more of the secret societies of the pueblo, usually those to which his godfather belongs. Similarly, a Hopi girl usually joins the society of her godaunt. Gradually the child's activities and responsibilities expand. The male world, centered in ceremonial activities, corn growing, sheep raising, hunting and craftwork, opens to the boy. Traditionally the girl becomes more confined to the house as she masters the intricacies of Hopi household chores.

The relatively recent introduction of school attendance, which is now compulsory, tends to expand the Hopi girl's activities by taking her away from home, whereas it may tend to curb those of the Hopi boy by keeping him indoors and reducing his masculine activities. The economic responsibilities of the youth increase rapidly; by the time he is fourteen years old he has mastered the traditional skills of the Hopi adult male and may even be running his own flock of sheep on the range of his clan. Before World War II virtually all Hopi youths were initiated a second time after they had passed adolescence in a rite known as the Grown Man (Wuwuchim) ceremony, but many Hopi youths of today do not go through this ceremony, which is held infrequently in all the mesa pueblos except those of Second Mesa.

Boys and girls are expected to marry when they are about twenty years old. Marriage is marked by an important ceremony closely connected in native theology with the individual's access to the underworld after death. With the Hopi, age does not automatically bring prestige as it does among the Papago. Honor is accorded only for the complete fulfillment of role as defined by the Hopi traditional code.

Perception Pattern

During the course of the Indian Education Research Project a sample of 190 children were tested from July 1942 to February 1943 in two Hopi communities—Walpi-Sichomovi-Polacca of First Mesa and the Oraibis of Third Mesa. The fieldwork was supervised by Dr. Alice Joseph and Dr. Dorothea C. Leighton and implemented by a team of fourteen fieldworkers (listed in Thompson 1950: xxiii–xxiv). Dr. Joseph administered the Rorschach test to 185 Hopi children, 80 from the First Mesa sample and 105 from the Third Mesa sample. Dr. Joseph also analyzed the Hopi records. The main field findings were processed and analyzed at the University of Chicago during the winter of 1942–1943.

Dr. Joseph (Thompson and Joseph 1944: 108–109) found that the Hopi children's responses were distinguished from those of Papago, Navaho, Sioux, and Zuni children by their subtlety of perception and by the organization of perception into clear-cut, rather elaborate concepts. Hopi children of both sexes tended to approach problems as complex integrated wholes and to carefully consider the many parts as well as the whole. This tendency was found in the records of the youngest Hopi children (five years) who were tested and persisted throughout all the age groups investigated in both Hopi communities. A Hopi potter conceives a traditionally styled, complex design as a complete whole in her mind before starting to paint it, and then she paints it on a pot freehand without benefit of any guides and measuring devices (Bunzel 1929: 49; V. Hubert 1937). This example illustrates the approach of individuals who tend to perceive a complex problem with its details in interrelationship and at the same time to visualize its solution. Characteristically, the Hopi view an event not as static but as emerging out of the past into the future.

In contrast to the Papago, the Hopi children appeared to be more concerned with the conceptual and imaginative aspects of impressions and events than with their emotional content. There was a definite, finished quality about the children's reactions to the stimulus material. When telling a story in response to the Thematic Apperception test, for example, a Hopi child usually followed a short logical plan that began with a problematic situation and ended with its resolution.

The findings of the Indian Education Research Project suggest that the Hopi children's perception pattern tends to be both subtly differentiating and synthesizing, both logical and balanced. As with the other Indian tribes studied in the project, there appears to be a close relationship between the children's habitual perception pattern as revealed by psychological tests and the world image of the tribe as revealed by the behavior and the cultural productions of its members. In the Hopi's view the world is regulated by just and immanent natural law. Each individual must engage in a high degree of emotional, intellectual, and volitional activity in order to fulfill his social and his cosmic responsibilities.

The Hopi perception pattern should be viewed in the context of the characteristic Hopi personality configuration, which is much more complex (allowing for considerable individual variation) than that of other tribes in the project sample. This relative structural complexity also stands out because it is limited within clearly defined boundaries. Spontaneous psychic forces are characteristically regulated and toned down by a well-developed and balanced control system that involves the use of both outer and inner psychic devices. The Hopi social code tends to become internalized in each child in the form of an individual conscience. So effective is this discipline pattern that it fosters a relatively precocious development of social and emotional maturity. This maturity, however, is achieved at the expense of engendering a certain amount of conscious anxiety, which in some cases develops into a definite constriction. Such anxiety may manifest itself in behavior by failure to respond appropriately and readily to new situations (Thompson and Joseph 1944: 76–82; 110–118).

Recent Changes

According to the project findings, the tendency toward constriction is accentuated under certain types of acculturation pressures, which include stresses that create both sudden freedom and sudden breakdown of the traditional ceremonial cycle. Breakdown in the male-activated ceremonial cycle tends to aggravate social disorganization, which seems to be be associated with the development of free floating anxiety among the males, at least in the Mennonite-dominated villages. When this phenomenon occurs, the group has trouble in finding and implementing an appropriate substitute organization. The group may also find it hard to replace the traditional village priests by new leaders adequate to deal with the changed situation.

For example, the Hopi tribe reorganized itself in 1935 under the Wheeler-Howard Act and attempted to develop a tribal council on the basis of existing village groupings. Traditionally each Hopi pueblo constituted a complete social entity and had no external political ties. Because there was no native tribal organization on which to base tribal reorganization, efforts on the part of the Indian Service staff to develop a formal tribal organization met with little success for about twenty years. In 1955, however, an elected tribal council was recognized by the Hopi villages as the official governing body of the tribe. Official reports state that the council has become fairly representative of the pueblo groupings and functions effectively (Hopi Indian Agency 1966: 2). It has, for example, completed one coal-development lease on the Hopi-Navaho joint-use area in conjunction with the Navaho tribal council (Hopi Indian Agency 1966). Other leasing arrangements regarding exploration for oil are pending. The Hopi tribal council also supports an action program funded by the Office of Economic Opportunity, which includes a Neighborhood Youth Corps, as well as projects in administration, health and home care, and Operation Headstart.

Conclusion

We may learn a lesson of primary importance from the Hopi case study. Although a tribe may have a relatively simple traditional technology, its native religious ceremonies and system of values may still be complex, appropriate to its life way, and emotionally satisfying. They may embody a complete set of symbolic solutions to the tribe's traditional living problems. Complex industrial technology does not necessarily produce either functional or "superior" values, and the classification and value systems of nonindustrialized peoples are not necessarily "primitive." (For a different opinion, see Durkheim and Mauss 1963). Weighed in situational context and historical depth, is a group's value system appropriate to the way of life, problems, and human potential of its members? This is the relevant question.

The Indian Education Research Project findings reveal that for centuries the Hopi have had by far the most precarious living problem of the Indian tribes studied. Of the tribes investigated in the early 1940s, the Hopi had the lowest average per capita acreage per family, the lowest average number of sheep per family, and the lowest tribal income. Farming is the traditional basis of Hopi subsistence. With only one inch less than the present average annual rainfall, however, farming by traditional methods would probably be impossible on the high Hopi plateau (Carter 1945: 84 ff.). Drought, frost, pests, loss of rangeland through outgroup encroachment, and soil erosion (natural and man-made) render such a subsistence pattern of village-dwelling farmers extremely vulnerable, and the groundwater shortage limits the usefulness of modern irrigation methods.

An environment in which no amount of individual industry, skill, and ingenuity could ensure group security seems to have cradled the development of a perception pattern and personality type that was sufficiently subtle, complex, balanced, and disciplined to cope successfully with the problems of group living and self-fulfillment. Analysis of the Indian Education Project findings suggests that, in the context of an exceptionally hazardous habitat, the Hopi's traditional culture, perception pattern, and personality organization were highly functional to the survival of the group through successive generations.

Natural and man-made pressures, however, have made the Hopi's living problem increasingly more difficult in recent years. The Hopi tribe thus faces a crisis probably more acute than those faced by the other Indian tribes studied except perhaps the Sioux. Although the Hopi's complexly structured perception pattern was highly functional in solving the tribe's traditional living problem, under certain types of acculturation pressures it may be insufficiently flexible to meet new needs quickly. It may even tend to operate against rapid adjustment to changing situations.

Notes

1. This chapter is based mainly on firsthand observations and interviews during visits to the Hopi reservation in 1942, 1943, 1947, and 1967 and on findings from the Indian Education Research Project, especially those presented in Thompson and Joseph (1944; 1947); Havighurst and Neugarten (1955); Henry (1947; 1956); and Thompson (1950; 1951a; 1951b: Ch. 6). Information supplied by Wayne T. Pratt, special representative of the Indian commissioner; Clyde W. Personeau, superintendent of the Hopi Indian reservation; Fred Kabotie; and Elizabeth White is gratefully acknowledged.

15 /

THE NAVAHO

The beauty in front of White Corn Boy shall be the
beauty before me.
The beauty at the back of Yellow Corn Girl shall be
the beauty behind me.
The beauty below Pollen Boy shall be the beauty under me.
The beauty on top of Cornbugy Girl shall be the beauty
above me.
All beauty surrounding Rainray Boy shall be the beauty
surrounding me.
All is restored again—

From the Navaho shooting chant (Newcomb and
Reichard 1937: 81)

Geography

The 110,000 members of the Navaho tribe inhabit some 24,000
square miles of land in northern Arizona, New Mexico, and
southern Utah.[1] About 13 million acres of this area belong to
the Navaho reservation proper, which surrounds the Hopi
reservation. A 1962 U.S. District Court decree reserved an additional 1.1 million acres of the 1882 Moqui reservation to be
held in trust for the joint use of both the Navaho and the Hopi,
but this joint-use area is still occupied almost exclusively by
Navaho. Some land adjacent to the reservation has been granted
by the federal government for tribal use or is simply occupied
by Navaho.

The land of the Navaho is a semiarid region of breathtak-
ing beauty and great topographical variety. In this area the
elevation of the Colorado plateau ranges from 3,500 to 10,000
feet above sea level. Half of the reservation averages eight to

twenty-two inches of rain a year. But the steppe country receives about twelve inches; the mountains, about twenty-two. The frost-free growing season is relatively short and varies with the altitude. Much reservation acreage is partly eroded and is classified as grazing land. Gas, oil, coal, timber, and such minerals as copper, uranium, and silver are present. Over 35,000 acres are under irrigation for tribal farmland use.[2] Highways, roads, bridges, and other transportation and communication facilities have also been developed (for details see Young 1961: 133–136).

Microrace and Appearance

Navaho living on the reservation are classed as fullbloods, mostly of Proto-Mongoloid stock. About 98 percent of the Navaho have Rh positive type of blood, group A or O.[3]

In the more remote districts the Navaho woman still wears the traditional costume, a long ruffled skirt of calico and a bright velvet blouse. Her black hair is tied into a knot at the nape. Little girls often dress like their mothers. Navaho men and youths usually wear blue jeans and cowboy hat. For a folk festival many don bright satin shirts with silver buttons, belts made from silver dollars, and turquoise necklaces.

Language

The Navaho language, like the Apache, belongs to the southern branch of the Athabascan stock. According to Robert W. Young and William Morgan (1943: 1), ". . . the Navaho language is essentially monosyllabic; not in the sense that its words are all of a single syllable, but rather that they are composed of grouped monosyllabic elements, each of which contributes its individual significance to the whole."

To the Navaho, words are inherently powerful and dangerous. Some attract good; others repel evil. The most important part of a word is a monosyllabic verb stem, which conveys an image that is constant and signifies an act, a state, or a quality. Monosyllabic prefixes added to this stem elaborate and limit its meaning somewhat as adverbs and pronouns modify an

English verb. Prefixes may also convert the stem into a speech element analogous to an English noun modified by adjectives and pronouns. Small differences in pronunciation, difficult for an English speaker to master, completely change the meaning of the word.

In the early 1940s less than 50 percent of the members of the tribe spoke some English. Today, although many older people speak only Navaho, most Navaho children and young adults also speak English.

Archaeology and Culture History

Although Navaho prehistory has not yet been fully researched, the Navaho seem to have settled in the Southwest more recently than any other tribe discussed in this book. The Navaho were apparently a hunting and collecting group who with other Athabascan-speaking tribes inhabited a mountainous homeland in northwestern and western Canada. Some groups moved southward, probably during the climatic deterioration that began in the latter part of the thirteenth century.

The first definite archaeological evidence of a Navaho campsite in the American Southwest is found in the vicinity of Governador, New Mexico, dating from the middle sixteenth century or earlier (Hall 1944: 99–100). There is no evidence that the Navaho practiced agriculture at this time. The climate of the Colorado plateau was less arid and richer in plant and animal life than it is today and thus more favorable for human settlement.

The early Navaho were apparently mobile hunters and collectors. On the Colorado plateau they preyed on the sedentary Pueblos of northern New Mexico and later (eighteenth century) on the Hopi. Using quickness of movement, sudden attack, and retreat, they captured food, horses, women, and other booty from the Pueblos. They also attacked Spanish expeditions that had begun venturing across the plateau.

The Spaniards feared the Navaho, who remained in control of their newly adopted homeland until they were defeated by United States troops in 1864. About 8,000 members of the tribe were held during the next four years near Fort Sumner, New Mexico. The tribe was eventually granted a reservation of 3.5 million acres and family allotments of sheep and goats. Joined by Navaho who had evaded capture, the tribe increased 400 percent during the next seventy-five years. During the same period, its lands were expanded by 464 percent. In this movement the Navaho usurped a large proportion (75 percent) of the Hopi's range.

Social Structure

As we drive through Navaholand, vast expanses appear virtually uninhabited. Here and there, we see hogans (dome-shaped earth lodges with doorway facing east and smoke hole in the center of the roof), which merge with the surrounding countryside. Near the hogan stands a corral for sheep. Since the recent construction of hard surfaced roads on the reservation there is usually a pick-up or a car parked nearby. There may be a sunshade less substantial than the Papago ramada, but usually there is no storehouse. In the past Navaho have not been noted for foresight in storing food from season to season, as is customary among the traditionally sedentary Hopi and Papago. Tools and personal effects are stored in boxes and trunks inside the surprisingly spacious hogan. The mother may be weaving a woolen blanket on an upright, pueblo-type loom, while the grandmother spins wool with a hand spindle.

Generally Navaho do not live in villages. Each hogan characteristically houses a single biological family. Two or three hogans that are built near one another usually house the families of related women, mother and daughter, or sisters, forming a relatively independent economic unit. Related matrilineal families in this living situation cooperate in farming and herding.

The community or "outfit" is a local kinship grouping that is intermediate between hogan group and tribe. An outfit occupies a single herding and farming land-use area, which may encompass as many as 12,000 to 80,000 acres. Its size depends on the wealth of its leader and his wife or wives. It is composed of several related extended families, led by the head of the most able or affluent family.

Although Navaho women have always wielded considerable power behind the scenes, decision-making powers in the tribe were traditionally vested in the leaders of the outfits and extended-family headmen, who usually operated inconspicuously. The Navaho believe that leadership power originates not only from personal effort and ability to achieve a consensus but also from ritual acts. It also derives from ability to feel the atmosphere of a group and to influence people by persuasion. Navaho leaders have no way of coercing their followers unless they play upon their fellow tribesmen's fear of witchcraft. Leaders have responsibilities, however, for the welfare of the members of their group, especially needy persons who are neglected by their relatives.

Navaho families are also grouped by kinship into large matrilineal clans. In all, there are sixty or more of these and they cut across local divisions. A Navaho is not allowed to marry within his mother's or his father's clan. Navaho clans, therefore, regulate marriage and establish an individual's circle of kinship obligations. The Navaho kinship terminology system is classed as Normal Iroquois by George P. Murdock (1949: 341). It derives such terminological classification from both the Chiricahua Apache and the Jicarilla Apache systems but in general follows the Jicarilla type. According to Morris E. Opler (1936: 620), the Navaho and the Apache tribes adhere to a single Southern Athabascan culture pattern in most facets of their social life. "In each case the basic social segment is the extended domestic family with matrilocal residence, consisting of parents and unmarried children, married daughters, their husbands and children." Southern Athabascan marriage practices reveal a marked similarity, including practice of the sororate (the custom of a man's marrying his wife's or deceased wife's sister) and the levirate (the practice of a man's marrying his brother's widow). Marriage of a man to two or more sisters (sororal polygamy) is permitted, although attempts have been made to ban it.

For administrative purposes the Navaho reservation is divided into land-management districts, which are represented in the tribal council by delegates according to population size. Members of the tribe twenty-one years or over who have registered have the right to vote for officers and delegates to the tribal council.

Borrowed Technology on a Traditional Cultural Base

Of the peoples explored in this volume, the Navaho are probably the most adept at solving their living problems by borrowing technologies and technological products from culturally alien sources and adapting them to their own purposes. They borrowed methods of dry and arroyo flood farming from the Pueblos before the seventeenth century. They also copied Pueblo weaving techniques and painted pottery making, surpassing their teachers in elaboration of design and use of color. They borrowed herding methods from the Spaniards. And they learned silversmithing from Europeans either directly or through Mexico. Most recently they have adopted many American manufactured objects that fit into their culture such as cooking utensils, trucks, men's clothing, blankets, radios, and food. Virtually all the material objects now used by Navaho, except a few ceremonial goods such as pottery and baskets, are bought at a trade store.

Traditional Child Training

A few hours after birth the infant is cradled. The child is confined to the cradleboard, decorated with magical objects to ward off evil, which is not abandoned until he is about one year old. A Navaho cradleboard is hung on the hogan wall so that the infant's head is on a level with and directly facing his family, and he is always included in the family's activities. On horseback, in wagons and pickups, and in the hogan, the cradle keeps him warm and snug and guards his head from jolts. Recent research suggests that the cradleboard provides the child with emotional security, as well as with protection to his physical safety.

As among the Papago, Hopi, and South Sea communities already described, the Navaho infant receives a great deal of affection. He is breast-fed, usually for a period of more than two years. Weaning and cleanliness training are gradual.

A single set of social and ethical standards prevails for all ages. For example, all Navaho avoid lightning-struck trees and eating fish or water animals. No Navaho may step over the reclining body of another; to do so would invite disaster. There is thus a strong tendency to include children in the world of adults, rather than to build up a child's world segregated from the rest of the community.

A Navaho child is taught a way of thinking and behaving suitable to his world. He learns the Navaho language. By the time he is six years old and ready for school he has the pragmatic Navaho orientation toward life. At this age a child may begin to help with the herding. Even very small girls effectively perform this responsible task. Children help with other adult tasks. By the early teens both sexes have learned most of the skills required for full participation in traditional Navaho adult life.

The isolated homestead pattern of settlement and the vast spaces of the Navaho reservation pose transportation difficulties and a language problem that complicate the usual language barriers in Indian education (R. Young 1961: 20). However, every year more Navaho children attend school. Out of a school-age population of 37,370, some 31,025 Navaho children were enrolled for the 1961–1962 school year. In addition, 2,406 Navaho who were not of school age were enrolled. This figure includes 420 students in college and non-Indian Bureau vocational schools (Bureau of Indian Affairs 1963a: 13). In the early 1940s the school years were not especially rewarding to Navaho because they involved experiences and values removed from their daily lives, but this situation has been gradually altered as more influences are felt from the outside world, more adequate educational facilities become available, and more economic opportunities open up.

A girl is considered to become an adult at her first menstruation, which is celebrated by a four-night ceremonial, whereas a boy is considered mature when his voice changes. Marriage is considered natural and inevitable, and unless they are attending boarding school, Navaho usually marry in their teens. The event is celebrated by an all-night ceremony that includes Blessing Way ceremonial songs and is marked by a change of residence by the bridegroom, who brings a gift of cattle and other property to the bride's family. Too frequent sexual intercourse is believed to engender bleeding of the genitals, or madness. One may even be struck by lightning on account of it. These Indians believe that the best time in life occurs between the ages of twenty-five and sixty years. Old age brings dependency, loss of authority, and ill health. Everything connected with death is regarded with horror. Navaho especially fear ghosts that are believed to be particularly malevolent toward their own relatives.

Ceremonies

Navaho ceremonies focus on curing and restoring harmony to the individual within the family group. They are conducted by a professional medicine man or singer versed in ceremonial lore. The singer is responsible for organizing and leading a ceremony appropriate to the occasion and keyed to a desired outcome, whether it be curing a specific, native-diagnosed sickness, purifying a girl during her first menstruation, or protecting a family group from the evil influences of ghosts or witches. Accordingly, he assembles from memory parts from several chants into a composite tailored for the occasion, and he combines with the chant well-known ritual acts involving such equipment as corn pollen, rattles, the bullroarer, and prayer sticks. A Navaho chant, according to Clyde Kluckhohn (Kluckhohn and Leighton 1946: 153),

> is a framework into which are fitted more or less discrete units ("ceremonies" and "acts and procedures") either as dictated by fixed associations or in accord with the practice of individual Singers, the wishes of the patient or patient's family, precise nature of the "illness," or other circumstances. The same units are used over and over again in different chants, sometimes with slight modifications.

An important part of almost every Navaho ceremony is the construction of a stylized, colorful sand painting on the floor of the hogan under the direction of the singer. Although the sand-painting (actually dry painting) technique has been borrowed from the Pueblos, the designs are distinctively Navaho. Each design illustrates symbolically the meaning of the ceremony and makes visible Navaho concepts of power. Using guidelines previously sketched on the ground, a Navaho artist, reflecting the centrifugal dynamics of his culture, begins at the center of the design and works outward. A Hopi, on the other hand, begins his ceremonial sand painting on the margin and, in a centripetal movement symbolic of his preferred relationship pattern, works inward without benefit of any measuring devices. He always leaves a break in the border of the design as a symbolic point of escape.

World Image

Navaho apparently perceive the world as an ideally harmonious but actually a dangerous and unpredictable place, peopled by countless personal entities who may be foci of vital power, including reproductive power. There are, according to Navaho belief, two classes of such personal forces: the Earth Surface People and the Holy People. Ordinary human beings, living and dead, and their very much feared ghosts conceived as the malignant part of a dead person, are classed as Earth Surface People. These also include witches, who are conceived as living beings capable of exercising power and bringing about disharmony, sickness, and death to human beings. Uneasiness and fear of witchcraft has apparently tended to increase in parts of the reservation where influences and pressures from the surrounding American civilization are strongest. According to project test results, one effect of contact with the surrounding American culture on Navaho children seems to be an increase of anxiety in the individual. Some Navaho attempt to cope with this problem according to the native way, by devoting more time to traditional religious ceremonies and especially to those rites such as the Enemy Way (called Squaw Dance) believed to counteract the evil influences of the dreaded witches and to bring about their death.

The mysterious Holy People, who belong to the domain of the sacred and travel on sunbeams, rainbows, and flashes of lightning, created the Earth Surface People and retain great power to harm or aid them. The Holy People may attack and bring sickness to humans except Changing Woman, who is always helpful and who taught the Navaho the Blessing Way ceremony. However, by using appropriate rituals and following a great many rules of behavior, man can propitiate and even compel these powers to aid him in solving personal problems. By means of compulsive words and acts he can force them to help him to overcome illness and to restore harmony within his world, within himself, and between himself and others.

To the Navaho, therefore, man is not perceived as a co-worker with vital power sources, as he is among the Hopi. Nor is he viewed as a helpless supplicant of power dispensing supernaturals, as he is among the Sioux (see Chapter 16). Furthermore, he is not envisioned as a trader for supernatural power in exchange for ceremonial gifts, as he is among the Lauans and to some extent also among the native Hawaiians. On the contrary, by following in a literal sense infinitely painstaking rituals, the Navaho tries to *coerce* the power presences by magical means into yielding the goods he seeks and into helping him to restore harmony within himself personally and within his personal world.

Our comparative approach suggests that the Navaho value structure, expressed in native religious beliefs, reflects the tribe's traditional hunting and raiding life way. The Navaho belief system tends to persist and even to gain strength and elaboration under pressures from the alien cultures that surround or impinge on the tribe (see, for example, Vogt 1960: 26–28).

Perception Pattern

For the Indian Education Research Project, a sample of 211 children was tested from three Navaho communities: Shiprock, the group most acculturated to the contemporary American way of life; Ramah, an intermediate community; and Navaho Mountain, the least acculturated. The fieldwork, which largely took place from July 1942 to September 1943, was implemented by a team of twelve fieldworkers listed in Leighton and Kluckhohn (1947: vi), under the supervision of Dr. Dorothea C. Leighton. The Rorschach test was administered to 110 Navaho children—39

from Navaho Mountain; 28 from Ramah, and 43 from Shiprock—
by Dr. Leighton, who also analyzed the results (Leighton 1957).
The main field findings were processed and analyzed at the University of Chicago in 1943.

Rorschach test responses from this sample of children differed
markedly in "manner of approach" from those of other Indian
tribes tested. The Navaho children characteristically emphasized
large, obvious details in contrast to the Zuni children's emphasis
on tiny details (Leighton and Adair 1966: 120); the Papago
children's emphasis on unorganized, global wholes; and the Hopi
children's emphasis on complex organized wholes. This tendency
was apparent even in the responses of some of the very young
Navaho children, and it was significant in both sexes and in all
three Navaho communities investigated. It was most marked
among the inhabitants of remote Navaho Mountain. The
children at Shiprock gave slightly more attention to unusual and
less obvious details than did those of Navaho Mountain and Ramah.

In the context of other findings obtained from the project
this response pattern has been interpreted as representing a
rather strong tendency toward a differentiating, matter-of-fact
type of perception pattern. Although the children habitually
singled out for attention obvious, discrete elements, the records
show that, like the Papago children, they were able to organize
these discrete elements into a whole when they perceived that
the occasion demanded it.

This perception pattern accurately fits the total picture of
Navaho personality, which, according to project findings (Leighton and Kluckhohn 1947: 176–177), is oriented to an external
world viewed in obvious, literal terms. Perceived objects are distinctive, well-delineated entities related to one another, if at all,
in an informal manner reminiscent of Navaho traditional social
structure, Navaho ceremonials, and Navaho grammar.

The entities of this world—whether living people, witches, and
ghosts or supernatural power units—are characteristically perceived as disparate, personal forces. Such vital forces are believed
to function beneficially or malevolently depending on whether
or not a man has observed the Navaho rules for living. These

rules involve two sets of activities: those that satisfy practical obligations to one's family (including one's extended family) and those that fulfill ritual obligations to supernatural power agents.

Behavior sanctions, therefore, are characteristically simple and external, and shame (an external sanction) rather than guilt (an internalized sanction) plays the role of censor. In a loosely linked world of isolated hogans, discipline tends to be relatively low pressure. The Navaho living pattern favors the development of a control system that depends almost exclusively on external, rather than internalized, regulation of psychic forces.

This type of personality organization apparently fosters the maturation of an exceedingly vigorous, relatively spontaneous, flexible adjustment to life. Although it generates fear and anxiety, it also alleviates them to a considerable extent by means of obvious familial activities of a practical or a ceremonial nature. A personal aesthetic harmony is sought between the self and the outer world. In the attempt to achieve this harmony both sensory and cognitive faculties are used but there is little or no attempt at their inner integration. The individual habitually functions according to a strictly bounded personal code, which gives him security in exchange for minimum personal responsibility and discipline and allows him free range outside the limits of well-defined family and ceremonial obligations.

Obviously, this personality type was well suited to the expansion-oriented, marauding life way that, in contrast to the pueblo peoples and to the Papago, apparently characterized the Navaho for several centuries preceding their military defeat. The same personality was also suited to the vigorous herding orientation that the Navaho adopted when their raiding pattern was outlawed.

In the context of the tribal life way the traditional perception pattern of the Navaho with its focus on large obvious details appears highly functional. Its persistence and refinement in a rapidly changing situation is not surprising, especially when one considers the project findings from Shiprock, the most acculturated Navaho community studied. These reveal that, under stress, the Navaho personality structure changes in the direction of a more balanced control system using not merely outer control devices but also, to a degree, inner ones, while spontaneity decreases and anxiety increases (Leighton and Kluckhohn 1947: 182).

Recent Changes

Like the Papago and the Hopi, the Navaho have no traditional tribal organization. Despite strenuous efforts on the part of the Indian Bureau staff during the 1930s, the Navaho resisted attempts to introduce formal tribal self-organization and strongly opposed soil conservation and range management although the reservation range was 100 percent overstocked. By the end of World War II the tribe was confronted with a critical situation that did not yield to its traditional problem-solving devices. The boundaries of the huge Navaho reservation were legally closed. There was no chance of further conquest or expansion, little chance of encroachment on the land of other groups, and little likelihood of substantial additional land grants from the federal government. The tribal population was increasing rapidly but was poorly prepared to cope with the outside world. Because of cyclic climatic change and overgrazing, the land base was fast deteriorating.

Indian Bureau surveys indicated a need for unified long-range planning in the direction of a more complex political and economic organization at both local and tribal levels, better educational and health facilities, intensive soil and resources conservation, and a more diversified economy. When tribal affairs seemed almost hopeless, Navaho leaders, with typical flexibility, developed a workable tribal organization. According to Mary Shepardson (1962: 742–743), "In the last 14 years, the Council has augmented its authority, assumed important functions formerly discharged by the Bureau of Indian Affairs, and began to offer new and valuable services. At the same time, the participation of tribal members in elections, in Council programs, and in local Chapter organizations has markedly increased." Federal educational and health services have been greatly improved, and oil, minerals, and lumber have been developed. The tribal council has been instrumental in attracting to the reservation such industries that employ Navaho workers as uranium mills, a natural gas plant, a thermoelectric generating plant, and a furniture factory. Other members of the tribe work not only at herding and farming but at tribal or government projects and at such seasonal jobs off the reservation as cotton and beet sugar picking, railroad work, and mining. By 1965 the tribal income, mainly from lease bonuses and royalties, had soared to an unprecedented $30 million a year. The tribal council reportedly spends much of this sum on tribal welfare, education, and industrial development projects.

On the other hand, Navaho resistance to stock-reduction programs and conservation measures has increased with the result that the Navaho range has become increasingly overstocked and has continued to deteriorate (Shepardson 1963: 21–22; Young 1961: 163–164).

Conclusion

Disturbed in its northern homeland, the Navaho, a traditionally mobile hunting group, sought out and settled in a new ecological niche favorable to the unique cultural style it had developed. We have investigated the rapid expansion of this group, its usurpation of the lands and resources claimed by other inhabitants of the region, and the changes it adopted when, in response to its new situation, the Navaho borrowed technologies from nearby peoples.

With characteristic flexibility, the tribe is now learning from the Americans to industrialize. In industrializing and in arranging for the exploitation of their mineral and timber resources the Navaho have shifted the focus of their exploitation pattern from their neighbors' to their own natural resources. They have responded to their current crisis by developing their planning skills along obvious practical lines in a way that reflects their traditional group perception pattern and personality structure. Navaho tribal history and present-day behavior thus reinforce the findings from multidiscipline research that indicate that these Indians are able readily to cope with practical problems arising from the changing condition of the tribe if they feel the problems are sufficiently urgent. They may be expected to favor quicker, more obvious solutions, however, rather than more difficult and long-term plans that involve foresight and provision for future needs of the tribe.

Like the behavior of the Papago and the Hopi, Navaho present-day behavior is illuminated and rendered more understandable through depth-psychology findings and multidiscipline research. Accordingly, such research offers the possibility of bringing us one step nearer to our goal of predicting the probable behavior of a group under certain changing conditions.

Notes

1. This chapter is based mainly on findings from the Indian Education Research Project and on firsthand observations during visits to the Navaho reservation in 1942, 1943, and 1967. The results of the Navaho project were formulated for publication by Clyde Kluckhohn and Dorothea C. Leighton (1946), by Dorothea C. Leighton and Clyde Kluckhohn (1947), by William E. Henry (1947; 1956), by Robert J. Havighurst and Bernice L. Neugarten (1955), and by Thompson (1951a; 1951b: Ch. 3). Information regarding the Navaho tribe supplied by Joe Watson, Jr., Navajo area tribal operation officer, and his staff is gratefully acknowledged.

2. For details, see Harold J. Boyd and Shirley A. Allison (1965).

3. For information regarding Navaho blood groups, see Spuhler and Kluckhohn (1953), Boyd and Boyd (1949), Allen and Schaeffer (1935), Kluckhohn and Griffith (1950).

16 /

SIOUX OF THE DAKOTA HIGH PLAINS

Aŋ' paö waŋ
hina'pelo
Waŋ yaŋ 'ka yo.

A dawn
appears
behold it.

Sioux song for voice and drum (Densmore 1916:
78–79)

For our last case study we move from the Colorado plateau
northeastward to the Great Plains to investigate the Teton-
Dakota.[1] This is a tribe of about 9,570 Oglala and Brulé Sioux
(1966 estimate) on the Pine Ridge Indian reservation near the
southwestern corner of South Dakota. An additional 4,460 members of the tribe live off the reservation.

About 30 percent of the Dakota Sioux are classed as fullbloods,
whereas 63 percent are one-fourth to one-eighth Sioux. Among
blood donors at the Pine Ridge Hospital in the 1960s, 61 percent
are type O positive and 37 percent are A positive. Less than 1
percent are O negative, B positive, AB positive, and A negative.
Although figures have not been derived from statistically significant samples, they are presumably representative of the adult
Sioux population of the reservation (U.S. Public Health Service
1967). Gordon Macgregor (1946: 25–27) suggests, however, that
more than half of the Pine Ridge Sioux belong culturally to the
fullblood group; in other words, they behave like fullbloods.
Sioux are of Proto-Mongoloid stock. According to Louis Sullivan

(1920: 131–132), who measured 540 fullbloods from several Sioux tribes,

> . . . the Sioux . . . are among the very tallest of the American Indians . . . In head form they are mesocephalic with an index of 79.6. The face is very wide and high . . The nasal bridge is rather high. The hair . . . is straight and black, the eyes dark and brown, and the skin shows varying shades of brown.

The Sioux were famous warriors and to many Americans they are the prototype for all Indians. The men used to part their hair down the middle and wear it in two plaits over the ears, but most Dakota now cut their hair short. They wear dungarees like the cattlemen of the surrounding countryside. Only for ceremonies do they don a semblance of their traditional costume with feathered bonnets and buckskin garments.

A majority of these Indians speak the Lakota dialect of the Dakota language, which belongs to the Siouan linguistic stock. Most Dakota (about 95 percent) also speak English (not necessarily fluently), and 65–75 percent read English. Some 95 percent of the children of school age attend grade school regularly, and many go to high school and college (Pine Ridge Indian Agency 1966).

Like the Papago, the Sioux sing to obtain power. As explained by Frances Densmore (1926: 449), the Sioux leave

> a great deal unsaid . . . the Indian uses very few, if any, qualifying adjectives in the words of his songs. He sketches the thought and the poetic temperament of his hearers supplies the gradations of color. The Indian feels and expresses more in silence than the white man. Next to Silence comes Song, and in its rhythmic form, its beauty of thought, and its simplicity and delicacy of expression we find the True Indian.

Geography and Resources

In the very heart of the North American continent, the Pine Ridge reservation is located in a semiarid region of high rolling plains. The elevation ranges from 2,000 to 3,500 feet above sea level and the average annual rainfall is about 17 inches. The climate is definitely continental in type unmitigated by the effects of large bodies of water, with an annual temperature range from 100 degrees F. in summer to 40 degrees below zero in winter, when an icy wind sweeps across the plains. The frost-free growing season lasts about 150 days.

Approximately 80 percent of the 4,464 square-mile Pine Ridge reservation is classed as rangeland. Partly as a result of a government-sponsored stock-reduction campaign during the 1930s, 82 percent of this grassland is in good-to-excellent condition (Pine Ridge Indian Agency 1966). Part of the range is administered as an aerial gunnery range for the Corps of Engineers. The average family income of the Pine Ridge Sioux in 1964 was $2,173 per year, the median income, $1,607 (Pine Ridge Indian Agency 1966). Herding and farming, which is largely marginal and dependent on irrigation, produced only a small percentage of this income; the remainder was derived from wagework,[2] from leases and rents of land to non-Indians, and from relief.

Archaeology and Culture History

As late as 1700 the Dakota were a hunting tribe of the Eastern Woodland culture area. They lived southwest of Lake Superior in the vicinity of Mille Lacs Lake, Minnesota. During the first half of the eighteenth century they were pushed out of their homeland by Ojibway Indians who had been disturbed by white settlers. The Teton-Dakota moved westward to the High Plains with their great herds of buffalo. The acquisition of the horse accelerated the migration. As they began to use guns (about 1750), their hunting and raiding activities expanded.

Because all the land was already claimed by other tribes, the Dakota had to fight for new hunting grounds. About 1780 they reached the forested Black Hills, which somewhat resembled their homeland. They resettled in the area, displacing a number of Plains tribes, including the Pawnee, Kiowa, Crow, and Mandan. The Sioux eventually claimed much of what is now North and South Dakota as well as the northern half of Nebraska and part of Wyoming.

In their new hunting grounds the Dakota borrowed a number of traits from their Plains Indian neighbors. Their contacts with European fur traders were mutually advantageous. Hardly a generation had passed, however, before frontiersmen treking westward threatened their food supply by wantonly shooting buffalo for sport. Trouble began in earnest when discovery of gold in California (1849) tempted increasing numbers of whites to travel west. In trying to protect overland wagon trails, the United States army clashed with the Teton-Dakota. A treaty signed in 1851, prohibiting whites from trespassing on Indian territory and guaranteeing emigrants safe passage through it, was broken by both sides. Reports of the discovery of gold in the Black Hills (1875) led to the loss of that area to white men. It took thirty years of sporadic fighting—long enough to eliminate a generation of Sioux warriors and to slaughter most of the great buffalo herds—before the Dakota were defeated. The massacre of Wounded Knee (1890) was the last famous Indian stand in the West. All the lands claimed by the Dakota tribe, except about 3 million acres, were seized by the United States government, and the Teton-Dakota were forced to settle on supervised reservations, including that of Pine Ridge.

After the passage of the Indian Allotment Act (1887) another 1 million acres, including the reservation's best farmlands (which belonged by treaty to the tribe), were lost to the tribe. Like the effect of the Great Mahele on the Hawaiians (see Chapter 5), the Indian Allotment Act was the most important single factor contributing to the recent loss of tribal lands by natives. With the Sioux this loss happened chiefly through the sale, to non-Indians, of lands allotted in severalty to Indian individuals. Unallotted lands were opened to non-Indian use.

Kinship and Social Structure

The Teton-Dakota grouped themselves into seven divisions: Oglala, Blackfoot, Brulé, Hunkpapa, Sans Arcs, Minniconjou, and Two Kettle. Each division was governed by four head chiefs, and the members met annually for the great summer camp, where they celebrated the Sun Dance. During the remainder of the year each stayed in its own hunting grounds. Each division was composed of a number of bands (*tiyospaye*), and each band was an extended family headed by a band leader who had been selected for his war record and his generosity. "Each band, like each division, was an autonomous system and was, in reality, a bilaterally organized family wherein collateral and lineal relations were merged" (Hassrick 1944: 399).

The Teton-Dakota kinship system is classed with the Plains Indian "generation" type (F.R. Eggan 1937: 90 ff.). In other words, it was, according to Hassrick (1944: 338),

> really a simple familial organization emphasizing generation, thereby merging lineal and collateral relatives and creating a dispersed and amorphous family. The patterns of interaction were determined by varying intensifications of "respect" and "familiarity" dependent on sex, generation, and relationship.

When the Dakota first settled on the Pine Ridge reservation, they grouped themselves by related families, forming a great circle of tepees near the agency seat. The circular form of the encampment was symbolic of the Dakota conception of tribal life (see Mirsky 1937: 390). The Oglala chief Black Elk (Neihardt 1932: 35) expressed the concept as follows: "Then when the many little voices ceased, the great Voice said: 'Behold the circle of the nation's hoop, for it is holy, being endless, and thus all powers shall be one power in the people without end . . .'" When lands were allotted, however, the extended families spread out, each building a permanent log cabin along a cottonwoodlined creek bed. Thus the "holy circle of the nation's hoop" was broken.

The Teton-Dakota social structure also changed, but some features of the old kinship system have persisted. By the early 1940s, for example, the emphasis shifted from lineal and collateral bands to an affinal organization emphasizing relationship by marriage and the conjugal family, but cross-cousin marriage (apparently a feature of the old system) and adoption reemerged (Hassrick 1944: 338, 346–347).

Ceremonies

Formerly, according to Gordon Macgregor (1946: 94),

> At the death of an individual, his relatives and friends gathered
> at his tepee to mourn. The women spent four days in intermit-
> tent wailing. Parents often gashed themselves or severed a finger
> to express their grief. A bereaved father might wander from
> camp, singing a death song, to shoot down the first person whom
> he met and then kill himself. A give-away of the family's property
> to the mourners was part of the funeral ceremony, and another
> give-away ended the year of mourning.

Now the Indians of a neighborhood gather for the give-away.
Gifts are placed at the foot of a flagpole flying an American flag.
The Dakota still believe that, compared with human relationships, property is not important in itself (Mirsky 1937: 385–386).
Goods acquire significance only by becoming part of a social
equation. By giving away property a person or a group can pub-
licly express respect and affection for others. Besides the ceremony of giving away the family goods, a funeral ceremony may
be held in the Christian church.

Before it was prohibited by federal government regulation in
1881 as part of an official attempt to stamp out Indian religions,
the Sun Dance was performed every summer. This dramatic
ceremony, held during two periods, each lasting four days,
was designed to reward good conduct, to honor the bravest warriors, to further social solidarity and security, and to invoke the
spirit of the buffalo, on which the tribe depended for food. To
comprehend the meaning of the Sun Dance, we need to know
something about the traditional religion and world image of the
Sioux.

World Image

The Sioux traditionally have an intensely religious, reverent
orientation toward life. The Dakota believe all nature is created
and is permeated by a great supernatural power, Wakan Tanka,
and therefore is sacred. Wakan Tanka is believed to be an im-
mensely strong but relatively unstructured power source that
encompasses all aspects of the supernatural. Human beings, both

as individuals and as a group, are believed to depend on this ultimate source of vital power for life, and they are compelled to humble themselves and to supplicate Wakan Tanka if they are to live successfully. These traditionally hunting people believe that without access to the great power source man can have no success either as an individual on his own or as a member of his family and band. If man does not actively fulfill the requirements of his role in the universal scheme, he will suffer sickness or other misfortune. The Sioux's perception of the world thus embodies a principle of immanent justice.

Contacting the Power Source

The Dakota formerly had sanctioned ways, both as individuals and as a group, to contact the power source. Both personal ceremonies like the vision quest and social ceremonies like the Sun Dance were designed to prepare the individual to contact the deity and, under certain circumstances, to receive power from it. Like the Papago youth, Sioux adolescents went on a vision quest. The quest included physical hardship and self-torture, accompanied by intense and humble supplication in prayer. During the quest the youth hoped, by dreaming, to personally communicate with a messenger of the primordial power source. When the youth achieved a dreamlike state of self-hypnosis an answer might come in the form of a song. The vision might involve sacred stones, the mythical thunderbird, or an animal, which the supplicant would then take as his guardian or talisman. A Sioux described his vision as follows:

> Then I had a dream, and in my dream one of these small round stones appeared to me and told me that the maker of all was Wakan Tanka, and that in order to honor him I must honor his works in nature. The stone said that by my search I had shown myself worthy of supernatural help. It said that if I were curing a sick person I might ask its assistance, and that all the forces of nature would help me work a cure. (Densmore 1916: 77)

The dream might thus convey a specific power to the individual from the vital source (for example, power to cure sickness, to become a successful hunter, or to lead the tribe). The youth believed that if he was considered worthy he might even gain life-long access to power without the need for intermediaries, through a song with magical power or an animal guardian that had appeared in the dream (Densmore 1916: 69–77).

On the other hand, the Sun Dance was the principal medium by which the community sought and acquired strength from Wakan Tanka as a group. Prohibition of the Sun Dance severed the Sioux as a group from their traditional vital power source, but it did not deprive them of their intense, active faith in their religion. They still prayed as individuals, but they lost much of their inner security. The outlawing of their religion contributed significantly to a weakening of the ancient Sioux social system and social controls.

In 1934 the official ban against holding Indian religious ceremonies was lifted. At Pine Ridge traditional Dakota ceremonies in modified form began to be held again.

Child Training

Like Hopi and Navaho babies, Dakota infants used to be tightly wrapped in a cradle, but this custom is no longer observed at Pine Ridge. The infant is nursed whenever he cries. Weaning is gradual. Cleanliness training tends to be delayed until the child can understand its meaning. Small children are taught the approved ways of doing things by patient and kind encouragement and by ignoring, shaming, or ridiculing misbehavior. The Sioux do not approve of corporal punishment. By the time a child is five or six he has been trained in the virtues and behavior appropriate to Dakota life.

Dakota children of school age maintain a marked sex division; the sexes do not work or play together. Psychological tests revealed that although children were inclined to relatively spontaneous and outgoing behavior, before reaching puberty they began to develop a certain constriction (Macgregor 1946: 208). The personalities of adolescents, especially boys, seemed not to mature fully, and the teenagers tended to become indecisive and apathetic.

These findings are reinforced by recent research in formal

education on the Pine Ridge reservation by Murray L. Wax, Rosalie H. Wax, and Robert V. Dumont, Jr. (1964). Their study showed that the Indian children scored slightly above the usual norms in the fourth and fifth grades. In each successive grade thereafter the Indian children tended to drop below the norm. Communication between the children and the teacher deteriorated rapidly, with the children becoming progressively less responsive until they had developed a silent classroom, excluding the teacher and using their own Lakota language as a strategic weapon against her (Wax, Wax, and Dumont 1964: 8–9, 86, 98–105).

Macgregor's observations also support the results of a recent study by Luis S. Kemnitzer (1967), which suggests that, according to the Dakota code of behavior, one should not express hostility overtly. A Sioux believes that he should not discuss differences of opinion openly but should withdraw from a situation when he is confused, anxious, or angry.

Unless they attended boarding school, Dakota girls by the age of twelve years and boys by fifteen usually accepted responsibility for regular adult work in the household group. After marriage the couple might live for a short time with the parents, but most young newlyweds soon established a home of their own.

Perception Pattern

The testing program used a sample of 166 children from three Pine Ridge communities: Kyle, a community whose members are fairly representative of rural reservation Dakota; Wanblee, a moderately acculturated market village; and Pine Ridge Town, the agency seat and the most acculturated community. The fieldwork was supervised by Dr. Gordon Macgregor, who was assisted by Royal B. Hassrick. Nineteen fieldworkers, listed in Macgregor (1946: 6), carried out the testing program, mainly from August 1, 1942, to June 1, 1943. Hassrick administered the Rorschach test to a total of 154 children—81 from Kyle, 30 from Wanblee, and 43 from Pine Ridge. The results were analyzed by Hassrick and Dr. D. C. Leighton. The field findings were processed and analyzed at the University of Chicago in 1943.

The findings indicate that the traditional orientation toward the world, including belief in the principle of immanent justice, persists among the Teton-Dakota despite the fact that their religious ceremonies were banned for half a century and most members of the tribe are at least nominal Christians (Havighurst and Neugarten 1955: 150, Table 32). The Dakota view of the world has endured although the tribe has lost most of its hunting grounds and no longer has a hunting economy and although its social structure has changed drastically.

According to the psychological test results, these Indians, especially the males, seem to have suffered so much in such a sudden and disturbing way that their capacity to face and resolve problems as a group and as individuals has been inhibited (see Macgregor 1946: Ch. 14). Many of the men appeared to be quite apathetic. I was impressed by the extreme dejection expressed in the bent heads and slumped postures of idle Sioux men sitting outside reservation trading posts, reluctant to focus their attention on communal or tribal problems.

Women, on the other hand, seemed less traumatized than the men. Dakota women continued to keep house and tend the children. A few even preserved meat by drying (jerking), as they had for centuries. Females roles were less disturbed. Even if the women became schoolteachers, nurses, or household servants off the reservation, female roles did not differ fundamentally from traditional ones, for both emphasized nurturing.

Recent Changes

Many changes have occurred on the Pine Ridge reservation during the last quarter century. Each of the larger settlements has its own federal day school, mission church, store, and community center. In the town of Pine Ridge there are also a hospital, cafes, drug stores, movie houses, and even beauty shops. Present-day tensions are suggested by a dichotomy between life in the countryside and in the small towns (see Wax, Wax, and Dumont 1964: 15–17). In the towns live the mixed bloods, the whites, and a few Negroes who have recently arrived in the area. The town dwellers draw salaries as government administrators, teachers, and hospital workers. A few work in factories. The townspeople speak English and live, American style, in wooden bungalows with running water, electricity, and, in some cases, telephone service. In the country, by contrast, the "fullbloods" live in log cabins and tents that lack modern conveniences. They still practice the Indian way of life, use at least one or two traditional Indian medicines, speak Lakota, and lack fluency in English.

However, cheap radios have altered the isolation of these conservative Indians. Automobiles have, to a considerable extent, replaced horses as a means of transportation. Many roads on the reservation have been improved and a few have been paved, but the country people often lack the cash and the know-how to run their cars. Nevertheless, most of them manage to go to town from time to time for hospital services, shopping, mail, recreation, and Indian Bureau business. These Indians expect the bureau to provide school services and some medical care. They also look to it to manage their leased land and pay them the rent due, to dispense relief, and to supply them with surplus commodities.

A recent study (Malan and Schusky n.d.: 9) reported that about 53 percent of the population of Pine Ridge was unemployed. Migration of younger adult mixed-bloods out of the area has lowered the size of the middle-aged group and raised the ratio of children on the reservation. This may have reinforced the predominance of the older, more conservative, and less well-educated Sioux in tribal affairs (Wax, Wax, and Dumont 1964: 23). In his study of Indian and white medicine at Pine Ridge, Kemnitzer (1967) found two distinct sociological groups on the reservation: one "Indian" in ethnic identity and one "white." Not only was there little cross-cultural communication between the two groups, but any contacts between them served only to reinforce the incorrect stereotype each group had of the other and to increase rather than to reduce the misunderstandings between them. Although many changes have occurred on the Pine Ridge reservation in recent years, underlying tensions between Indians and whites (including culturally white Indians) persist.

Conclusion

The Pine Ridge reservation offers a good opportunity to investigate culture change, especially change aggravated by pressures from an aggressive alien civilization that exercises political dominance through conquest. There is also a possibility of discovering the effects of migration to a new homeland under pressure and the persistence of traditional attitudes and values long after many of the outward manifestations of the traditional culture have disappeared.

Our case study reveals that contacts with the white man have left a residue of bitterness among the Dakota. Indeed, the history of this tribe has been so traumatic that some Sioux suffer not only from frustration but also from a kind of emotional emaciation. The psychological wounds apparently stem from disappointment and defeat inflicted by agencies external to the tribe, especially the white man. The psychic disruption was apparently aggravated by Sioux preoccupation with the dependency behavior that was believed to aid the individual in obtaining vital power from a single ultimate power source. When the ceremonies that helped the Sioux to acquire such power were outlawed, the "pipeline" to the power source was symbolically severed. The *élan vital* of the Indians was suppressed and they appeared reluctant to face and to realistically resolve critical tribal problems.

On the other hand, the evidence suggests that, while the traditional superordinate-subordinate power structure persists as the preferred relationship pattern of the Dakota, the Great White Father has to some extent been substituted for Wakan Tanka as a power source. This shift of focus has reinforced a dependency relation between individual Indians and the Indian Bureau. The expression of frustration in the form of hostility toward the government and its representatives may be increasing on the reservation. This situation reinforces a marked failure of understanding and of communication between Indians and whites.

Notes

1. This chapter is based mainly on the findings from the Indian Education Research Project at Pine Ridge, South Dakota, in 1942–1943. The results of the Dakota Sioux project were formulated for publication by Gordon Macgregor with the collaboration of Royal B. Hassrick and William E. Henry (1946), by Robert J. Havighurst and Bernice L. Neugarten (1955), and by Thompson (1951b: Ch. 4). Information supplied by Brice H. Lay, superintendent of the Pine Ridge Indian Agency and his staff and by Aileen Maynard of the Public Health Service Hospital at Pine Ridge is gratefully acknowledged. I thank Gordon Macgregor for reading an earlier draft of the manuscript and for helpful comments.

2. Reservation employment as of October 1966 is reflected in the following table (Pine Ridge Indian Agency 1966):

Reservation Employment October 1966

Type of Employment	PERMANENT		TEMPORARY	
	Male	Female	Male	Female
Neighborhood Youth Corps	0	0	175	175
Office of Economic Opportunity	38	64	0	0
Job Corps	6	10	0	0
Ranch and farm (self-employed)	210	0	0	0
Ranch and farm (wage workers)	0	0	365	225
Industry	160	105	10	4
Clerical (BIA, tribe, PHS, state)	25	150	10	25
Construction	65	0	20	0
Professional	20	40	0	0
Services	50	25	40	30
Miscellaneous	75	25	160	110
Armed services	80	0	0	0

17 /

PERCEPTION AND CULTURE

> Although the human organism in its behavior acts as a
> result of stimuli, *these stimuli have in themselves no mean-
> ing.* The significances that are related to them in conscious-
> ness—and are experienced by the organism as sensations
> —*are derived* entirely *from the organism's prior experience,*
> *personal and inherited. . . .*
>
> The function of sensations is to disclose alternate possi-
> ble courses of action. It is the *purpose* of the organism in
> the "now" that determines which course will be followed.
>
> Adelbert Ames, Jr. (1960: 16, 17)

In seeking an explanation for persistent group perception patterns revealed by psychological tests, we have studied some of
the institutions and values of several American Indian tribes as
well as child training and other practices in situational context
and historical perspective. In this chapter we shall review the
relationship between group perception, world image, and environment and suggest a few tentative generalizations.

Communal Perception Pattern

From a comparative study of the typical way an individual or
group approaches new problems, in the context of tribal personality and culture configurations, a distinctive group perception
pattern emerged for the Papago, the Navaho, and the Hopi. This
distinctive tribal perception pattern was found in all the age
grades tested, in both sexes, and in all the communities investigated for each tribe (although these communities had been selected to represent varying degrees of acculturation to American
life ways).

The findings suggest that the more isolated communities tend over time to develop a characteristic way of perceiving reality. Members of such a group tend to perceive their basic living problems in terms of the perception pattern of their community, and they try to resolve such problems with the cultural tools available to them. The group perception pattern tends to be built into the personality of each member as a child and also into the culture structure of the community. Such a built-in group perception pattern is apparently highly resistant to change.

Perception Pattern and World Image

The tribal perception pattern of the Papago, Navaho, and Hopi, as revealed by psychological tests, was found to be structurally similar to the world image of the tribe as abstracted from tribal behavior, oral literature, and technology. With the passage of time, the members of a community apparently tend to harmonize their world image with their perception pattern, especially if the group is relatively undisturbed by influences from the outside world. Just as each individual lives in a more or less private world of his own (his idiosyncratic version of the culture of his community), so every community with a distinctive culture lives in a group world of its own, as Lawrence K. Frank (1951: Ch. 6) has shown. The structure of an individual's private world is expressed in his perception pattern, which is closely related to the way he approaches new problems; that of the group is expressed in its implicit world image.

Perception Pattern and Environment

Each tribe's perception pattern seems to fit well into the tribal culture as a whole, viewed in the perspective of changing environment and history. The findings suggest that a community's perception pattern is a function of the long-range socioeconomic response of the group to external and internal pressures and stimuli. The analysis recalls the hypothesis that perception level is a function of need. As Gardner Murphy (1947: 338–339, 351) has noted, "wherever our needs differ we literally *see* differently

. . . the perceived world pattern mirrors to a considerable degree the organized need pattern within."

Levels of Perception

Interestingly, the perception patterns of the three tribes (Hopi, Papago, Navaho) resemble closely the three levels of perception that Jean Piaget (1928: 221 ff.) found to characterize the development of the Swiss child's mental approach—the "blur" or syncretic level (to age 7–8 years); the level of differentiation and juxtaposition (to age 11–12); and the hierarchal synthesizing level (over age 12). The Indian Education Research Project data substantiate the observation that although these three levels characterize the processes of growth, development, and motor learning, they are found even when the maturation problem is not involved in any way (Murphy 1947: 343). Not only individuals but also communities, it seems, habitually function at the lowest level of perception that allows them to release tensions and to solve practical problems within their environmental circumstances.

The data also substantiate the hypothesis "that all perceptual responses are maintained as long as they *work* well, that they are shaken down only when necessary to permit a working structure, and that egocentric percepts are exactly like all others in this respect, being given up . . . only when life's demands admit no escape" (Murphy 1947: 342).

Perception Capacity

Although the tribal perception pattern apparently indicates the level of perception at which a community *habitually* functions, it does not in any way signify the group's perception *capacity*. Indeed, the data suggest that whereas only the Hopi typically function at the third or synthesizing level, the Papago and the Navaho are also able to function at this level when they are convinced that sufficient need has arisen. This point is vital to understanding the dynamics of group perception in situations of rapid change. It explains why the Papago and the Navaho, as well as the Hopi, are able to solve problems inherent in new situations. Indeed, the relatively successful adjustment of the Papago to the economic, social, and political realities of the 1940s suggests the possibility that the lower the habitual perception level, the more flexible it may be toward change based on new conditions and needs, and therefore the more responsive the group may be to new situations. Similarly, the Navaho's approach to their tribal economic problems during the postwar era and their relative effectiveness in dealing with them demonstrate their ability to face the changed situation of the tribe and to make adjustments in their traditional approach toward problem solving. Their recent behavior indicates that their manifest penchant for differentiating large obvious details and their lack of interest in complex wholes has not prevented them from perceiving and to a degree resolving their problems. Indeed, the Navaho perception pattern may even be a key factor in their success.

On the other hand, the difficulties that some Hopi communities have experienced when confronted by strong missionary or government pressures, despite their ability to perceive and synthesize complex relationships, suggest another tentative generalization. Perhaps the more complex and definitely structured the group perception pattern, the less responsive the community may be to its immediate needs. This condition may operate against its rapid adjustment to new situations.

Studies of the Zuni and the Sioux suggest how and under what circumstances a tribal perception pattern may change or break down. The Zuni was the first pueblo group discovered and conquered by the Spaniards in their exploratory trek from Mexico to the Rio Grande pueblos. For more than two centuries the Zuni tribe was the most exposed of the pueblo groups to influences from the outside world (see Leighton and Adair 1966: 18–38). The Zuni responded to these pressures by, so to say, drawing a magic circle around those secret ceremonies that they considered most sacred. Such a symbolic "line of closure" is a ritual method frequently used by pueblo Indians to restrict action. The Zuni have kept this symbolic "middle place" hidden and secret from prying outsiders. Otherwise they have adopted many foreign cultural traits. The Rorschach responses of Zuni children, which show a marked tendency to conform to a tribal norm, revealed a strong interest in tiny details. Compared with the syncretic holistic tendencies of the Hopi children, the test protocols of Zuni children revealed a "shattered field" approach suggestive of recent change in group personality pattern in a compulsive-obsessive direction. They are, however, well adjusted to their present situation, according to Dr. Dorothea C. Leighton (Leighton and Adair 1966: 120).

In the early 1940s the Dakota Sioux seemed unable to come to grips with the tribe's critical problems. The severe blockage in the Sioux's ability to perceive and resolve problems apparently stemmed from the extreme deprivation and frustration the tribe had experienced for the last 300 years.

Perception and Symbolization

A community's world image apparently depends on perceptions of the phenomenal universe that have become part of its ideology as its members for generations have tried to make sense out of life. When a poor Lutheran farmer on an isolated farmstead in northern Iceland builds his private chapel, he completes it by painting his own picture of the Sermon on the Mount. He places Jesus in a barren, tundralike landscape with glaciated mountains in the distance. The Mexicans worship the Virgin of Guadalupe, depicted as an Indian.

We have observed that a community tends to organize itself in a way that will help it solve its basic problems. We are beginning to realize that the members of the group consciously or unconsciously also organize their ceremonies and beliefs, their arts and literature, and even their language with the same purpose. The structure of a community's culture tends in time by a circular feedback process to be reflected in its literary style and art, in the grammar of the language spoken, and in the way the group perceives its world. This point, emphasized long ago by Edward Sapir (1931; Mandelbaum 1949), is clearly substantiated by Benjamin Lee Whorf's analysis of Hopi behavior in relation to the Hopi language structure (Whorf 1941), as well as by other analyses (for example, Kluckhohn and Leighton 1946: Ch. 8; Lee 1959).

We have observed that human beings tend to cling to the structure of their culture as long as possible and to change it only when all other expedients fail. If they do change, they tend to avoid altering the culture structure as a whole but rather attempt to change as few points in a culture pattern as possible. When the Papago created Sonoran Catholicism by incorporating aspects of the Roman Catholic ritual into their traditional ceremonial pattern, they exemplified this sort of partial change. In the same way the Navaho "takes over" the technology of his neighbors in a limited sense only.

It is quite understandable that a nearly isolated community's pattern of perceiving reality and its world image tend to be institutionalized, fostered, and invested with value and power. The pattern thus tends to persist even when the problematic situation that elicited it changes or when the group moves to a new habitat involving a different living problem. Consequently a group's cherished image of the world may outlive its original function and may even come to prevent the community's successful resolution of its problems, as in the case of the Dakota. Modern India with its sacred cows and burgeoning hungry population affords another well-known case. On the other hand, a major culture change or breakthrough always involves a change in perspective; in other words, a change in the structure of group perception.

A familiar example of such a breakthrough is the invention of Renaissance perspective in Europe about A.D. 1400. This development involved a change in group perception pattern on the part of southern and central Europeans from the medieval Catholic world view, involving a single immutable image, which except on the northern periphery of Europe dominated the perceptual field of Occidentals during the late Middle Ages (see Chapter 10), to one in which the perceiver observed a rigidly bounded world from a single point outside of it. The fixed relation between perceiver and perceived object is symbolized in the famous paintings of the period, designed to be framed, hung on a wall, and viewed from a frontal point. Renaissance artists resolved the major problem of the painter—the depiction of spatial depth on a flat surface—by means of a system of planes and lines originating at the eye level of the viewer and vanishing in points in the background of the painting to create the illusion of distance. This method of achieving depth perspective is so familiar to us that it is difficult to envisage it as a dated European culture trait that, since the latter part of the nineteenth century, has been displaced by new ways of perceiving, apprehending, and depicting the phenomenal world in the form of dynamic multidimensional happenings.

Renaissance perspective has become outmoded because it is incompatible with the rhythmic, circular, and spiral views of process inherent in homeostatic and other life processes as revealed by modern science. As the need for a major change in perspective was felt, Western man's image of the world became vague, as expressed, for example, in the school of Impressionism in modern art. Or it became distorted and displaced, as manifest in Dadaism and Surrealism. Or the boundaries of objects were emphasized as if to keep them from shattering into fragments and dissipating, as in the works of Georges Rouault and, occasionally, of Van Gogh. Or tiny details were emphasized at the expense of larger wholes, as exemplified in Victorian design.

Experiments with new techniques, especially in the presentation of multiple aspects of an object and the depiction of movement from many viewpoints simultaneously—from inside and outside of an object or event, from above and below, from all around it—have begun to reflect a more dynamic, transactive relationship between the perceiver and the perceived. Gradually a new perception pattern is emerging that expresses more adequately a turbulent interpenetrating space-age image of the world.

The organization of a group's perception—its patterned way of viewing the universe, the culturally structured manner in which it breaks up the flux of immediately sensed experience into units, classifies those units into categories, and organizes those categories into wholes—these processes limit man's full use of his senses in trying to understand life's dilemmas. They may hinder group members from gaining a broad, realistic view of their living problems and of mankind as a whole in the perspective of time and space. The data suggest that if the group feels that the need for successful resolution of practical issues is sufficiently urgent, it will tend to make minimal adaptations in perception over the long term. Such minimal adjustments may be reflected in changes in relevant structures of the group's culture.

PART 4

18 /

COMMUNITIES UNDER STRESS

The development of a mature science of mankind, which may be applied effectively toward the resolution of practical social problems, depends on the investigator's ability to predict probable changes in the behavior of human groups, under certain circumstances, with the degree of precision necessary to resolve significant social problems.

We have explored the behavior of nine communities in six culture areas of the world on the basis of firsthand field investigations. We have noted how each of these groups has (more or less successfully) perceived and resolved its practical living problems. These problems were found to be related to a unique living situation in a changing habitat. We have also noted how each group has reacted through the centuries under the stress of changes in its existing situation.

Our remaining task is to examine some aspects of the nine case studies and to formulate some inductive generalizations on the basis of a comparison of their cultural differences and similarities.[1] We shall consider some lessons that may be learned from comparison of the observed behaviors of several communities, each with a unique culture. These lessons may then be formulated as tentative hypotheses regarding the nature of culture to be tested by follow-up field research. Ultimately, anthropologists hope to discover universally valid principles of human behavior that may then be used to predict the probable behavior of local populations under certain changing circumstances.

Communities as Natural Laboratories

Each community in this study was selected for its high potential yield as a promising natural laboratory for the investigation of culture. Let us review our findings from this standpoint.

Four of the groups studied were relatively isolated island communities that apparently were occupied by small mobile groups of navigators seeking new sites favorable for settlement. These groups would consider as favorable unoccupied or sparsely settled habitats that provided environmental conditions comparable to the homelands where the new settlers and their forebears had developed their traditional cultures.

Guam, the Lau Islands, and Hawaii were independently discovered by seafarers, peoples probably originating in southern China, southeast Asia, and Indonesia. We infer that the natives who settled these islands were mainly bands of brothers and their families and retainers. We know that these seafarers brought with them certain basic attitudes and values, preferred perception patterns, skills, arts, and the artifacts necessary to their unique cultural life, including tools, weapons, and probably also useful plants and animals. Each of these territories was uninhabited and undeveloped. Each provided the settlers with a tropical environment whose climate and basic natural resources were familiar.

Our investigation of a fourth isolated island community, Iceland, revealed similar circumstances of settlement except that earlier settlers were present, but they soon disappeared. A majority of the founders were shaped by ninth- and early tenth-century Norwegian culture. In the climate and natural resources of Iceland the Vikings found environmental conditions similar to their homeland.

Let us check these findings with those regarding other migratory groups studied in this volume. The evidence, although somewhat controversial, suggests that the Old Saxons originally lived on or near Jutland, including the area now known as Schleswig-Holstein and probably also on adjacent land now submerged by the North Sea. The Saxons left their homeland during a period of calm seas. They found, in the lowlands of northwestern Germany, the Netherlands, northern Belgium, and southern England, ecological niches that were becoming drier and more like the homeland than they had been.

According to archaeological evidence, the Basketmaker-Anasazi People, cultural ancestors of the Hopi Indians, moved for centuries within a limited ecological zone. They established small oasis-like settlements in the American Southwest. The location and duration of a settlement depended on an uncertain supply of fresh water from semipermanent springs and on the changing depth and configuration of the Colorado River drainage system. Similarly, the Navaho presumably migrated from plateau country in the Canadian Rockies, where their linguistic relatives are still found. During the late medieval climatic deterioration they probably migrated southward to the Colorado plateau.

Even the Dakota Sioux moved to the Black Hills of South Dakota, a region that markedly resembled their Eastern Woodland base, although this new home was higher and drier than the old. The Dakota, as we have mentioned, had no choice—they were forced out of their traditional territory by the Ojibway.

The available data on the aboriginal migrations to Lau and to Guam are insufficient for comparative purposes. Both migrating groups doubtless island-hopped from west to east within the boundaries of the warm humid tropics. Both settled on the outer margins of the continental shelf. The Chamorros probably moved from the Philippines via Palau. The Lauans, according to traditional and archaeological evidence, migrated via Viti Levu, Fiji.

Culture as an Amalgam

In each of the nine communities the "native culture" thus expresses an amalgam of the traditions and practices of two or more migrations. Lauan culture reflects the life way of the aboriginal Land People and that of the prehistoric Ndaunisai conquerors, with changes introduced by two carpenter groups and the Sea People as well as the more recent Tongan and British influences. Native Hawaiian culture plainly reveals at least two basic prehistoric traditions, deriving from the aborigines from the Marquesas and from a later migration from the Society Islands. A similar dual cultural heritage is manifest in the prehistoric culture of the Chamorros. The Icelanders are descended both from the Vikings of Norway and the Western Isles and from their Celtic servants and slaves. The Lower Saxons of the Osnabrück Northland stem from Saxons and other Germanic-speaking tribes mixed perhaps with earlier settlers in the region. The Papago are also a mixed breed, and only their culture reveals long continuity with the past. The Hopi show limited cultural admixture with the Tewa-speaking people of Hano as well as with other Indian tribes such as the Navaho. The Navaho similarly have mixed genetically and culturally with various pueblo peoples, while the Sioux have borrowed from and interbred with other Plains Indians and the surrounding population.

This brief survey reveals how erroneous it is to treat a population as though it were historically "pure." Our explorations should convince us that there are no "pure" races, nor are there any "pure" cultures (see Weltfish 1960: 210).

How then do two or more traditions tend to become one culture? What do our cases of isolated communities teach us about the processes of culture creation, culture consolidation, culture persistence, and culture change?

Cultural Changes

There is a tendency among animal species to select and inhabit a specific kind of habitat favorable to the species' biogram. Similarly a human population tends, if possible, to seek out a niche favorable to its life way. When it finds and settles such a niche, the colonizing group explores the natural resources of the habitat in terms of its own needs and practical living problems and its traditional culture, including its social structure and land-use customs, technology, skills, attitudes, values, and preferred relationship patterns. In cases of resettlement, on the basis of patterns of behavior and cultural productions that they have brought from their homeland, the settlers graft cultural innovations onto their basic traditions. They attempt to restyle or recreate their culture to shape it into an adequate instrument for problem solving in relation to group survival and self-actualization in the new environment.

In the manufacture of artifacts community members tend to experiment with new raw materials and resources as a substitute for unavailable traditional ones. The community may change certain aspects of its technology. Changes even in these more superficial cultural expressions are usually not made *voluntarily*, however, unless the people have been convinced, on the basis of trial and error, that the new techniques will prove functionally superior to the old.

Even in the religious sphere voluntary changes usually are associated with a belief that an alien deity or an exotic ceremony will yield greater power than traditional ones. For example, the Lauan high chief at Lakemba accepted the Methodist faith on behalf of his domain because he believed that the white man's God had more mana than the Fijian gods inasmuch as the white man had been given gunpowder and other desirable material goods.

Individuals may be expended for the survival of the community—infants may be killed when the community is threatened by starvation or overpopulation, for example. Human beings may be sacrificed ceremonially to promote fertility and to ward off disaster, as was the custom among the ancient Hawaiians, the Vikings, and the Lower Saxons. Whole classes and generations may be expended, as illustrated by the almost universal custom of sending young warriors to defend the community against the threat of conquest by an alien tribe or nation.

Cultural Structure and Persistence

The cases studied also suggest that, once stabilized and institutionalized, the core values of a society are its most jealously guarded and fiercely defended possessions. The traditional world image of a relatively isolated population tends to mirror the effective universe as it has been perceived and conceptualized by successive generations, especially if the group has amalgamated its traditions and coped successfully with its changing situation over a long period of time. Every people's world image (which reflects their unique cultural microcosm) represents their version of reality. This generalization is as true for the nonindustrialized world as it is for the industrial peoples of Europe, Japan, and the United States. The way the components of a *Weltanschauung* are classified into categories and the pattern of relationships among the various categories reveals a people's perception of the phenomenal world. His world image structures an individual's way of relating himself to other people and to nature.

The members of each group have found their own particular explanation of the world to be pragmatically true by personal experience. Their world image is their map of the existential universe. For the group's members, it is the only guide they have to resolving their particular problems effectively. It colors their outlook and gives form to their institutions, their morality system, and their behavior. As we noted in our study of the Papago, the Hopi, the Navaho, and the Sioux, a population's core value system also is reflected in the group's unique perception pattern. It tends also to be mirrored in the organizing principles of the group's language, especially in its grammar.

Our findings suggest that if a population becomes severely disturbed, to the extent that its relationship to the environment is thrown out of balance, it still tries to preserve the structure of its core value system. It attempts to reestablish this relationship pattern in as many cultural dimensions as possible, including land-use patterns, social organization, economy, and cultural productions. The group also tries to salvage such forms of self-expression as dances, songs, poetry, ceremonies, and games. Of the nine communities studied, only among the Lower Saxons and the Guamanians have most traditional art forms disappeared. Among the Guamanians, however, the *tsamorita* refrain is still popular as a means of twitting a rival or frustrating a superior. This form may have increased in usage as the needs for circumventing authority and preserving group identity multiplied under foreign rule and military occupation.

The persistence of ancient land-use and other patterns involving the employment of resources through centuries was illustrated by the Icelandic rural community, the Lower Saxon dialect group and isolated farmstead, the Papago dialect group, the Hopi pueblo, and the Chamorro district. Eventual incorporation of such traditional units into the structure of a modern state was found in Iceland and the Marianas, as well as among the Hopi and Papago.

In no case studied have the native people given up the use of their native language entirely. None have done so even when the language of the politically dominant power is commonly learned in school and generally spoken outside the home. High German, for example, is learned as a second language by Plattdeutsch-speaking Lower Saxon children, and English is studied and used among the Guamanians, the Hawaiians, the Sioux, the Hopi, and many of the Navaho and Papago. The southern Lauans communicate in their own dialect although the islands have been a British colony for about a century. The Icelanders all speak modern Icelandic as their mother tongue. Only among the nearly extinct Hawaiians does it seem likely that the native language will shortly cease to be used as a medium of verbal expression.

It seems that the more we know about a native culture and the more accurate our knowledge, the more impressive is this principle of persistence of form. It is particularly noticeable with regard to traditional literary and art forms, as it is in the case of the Icelanders and the Hawaiians, for example. If thwarted in its tendency to reestablish its cultural focus, by either natural or man-made obstacles, the group tends to exercise considerable ingenuity to continue to move in the direction of this basic, often unconscious, objective. To illustrate, in Lau native land-use and lagoon-use patterns, traditional exchanges between islands, ceremonies, and certain leadership roles persisted although they were not endorsed and were even banned by the colonial government.

Methods and Timing of Cultural Change

A comparison of the case studies suggests again that people tend to cling as long as possible to a basic cultural pattern that has worked well in the past. Changes are thus as few, as long delayed, and as superficial as possible. The group tends to alter its traditional life way only when there is no alternative except extinction, dispersal, or an intolerable lowering of standards. The Marquesans of Polynesia and the Yapese of Micronesia, for example, apparently even preferred self-imposed genocide to intolerable change.

People thus tend to change their cultures only when they have no alternative. Of the population migration and resettlement cases studied, only the Dakota Sioux had no alternative but to emigrate from their original environment. The Dakota's Eastern Woodland culture did change to a culture similar to that of the Plains Indians. Forced migration and accompanying changes in Dakota culture seem to have operated as stimuli to new types of activity and innovation on the part of the Sioux. With the help of the white man's horses and guns, the Dakota successfully displaced many Plains tribes from their hunting grounds and borrowed many of their adaptive habits, virtually outdoing the aboriginal Plains Indians in their own territory. Such activity may be viewed as compensatory.

During the immediate post-Pleistocene period the Baltic communities of northern Europe were confronted with a sporadic warming and cooling of the climate. An ecological change from tundra through a succession of forest climaxes and reversions occurred in the region that corresponded to the climatic fluctuations. The Scandinavian populations responded by building new cultures on the traditional North Sea-Baltic prototype. These innovative cultures eventually developed into the north European forest culture complex exemplified in the Lyngby, Maglemose, Viking, and other patterns of the Mesolithic, Neolithic, Bronze and early Iron Ages. The invention of such new tools as the chopping axe was one adaptive response.

The Navaho's flexible response to the challenge of their new environment and to contact with pueblo peoples like the Hopi is another example of favorable reaction to change and stress on the part of a population. This reaction was expressed in the tribe's selective technological and cultural "borrowings," by which it developed a new cultural balance in relation to a changed environment. Recently the Navaho tribe has demonstrated a similar adaptation to the challenge of unavoidable contact with twentieth-century American culture by borrowing industrial techniques and modes of organization from the surrounding society. The tribe is now exploiting its rich resources and rangeland. It is managing its affairs on a cooperative tribal basis and stressing tribal enterprises designed to improve the welfare of the Navaho people. How long these resources will hold out, however, remains a relevant question.

The Dakota, on the other hand, no sooner had settled in an unfamiliar niche and reworked their culture into a new form that met the challenge of their environment successfully when they were again deeply disturbed. Seventy-five years later, the apathetic behavior of these Indians revealed a severe psychological wound.

Group Behavior Under Stress

These findings prompt us to hazard another tentative generalization. Certain stresses that pressure a community with a balanced mature culture in relation to its environment may have a variable effect upon its members depending on the group's capacity to recover and establish a new viable cultural balance. They suggest that thresholds of stress tolerance vary with culture type (see, for example, Howard 1966). The effect of such pressures on community members may depend on the degree of their intensity in relation to the community's defenses against stress in terms of use of its natural, cultural, and psychological resources for problem solving.

Successful Behavior Under Stress

The kind and degree of stress that requires a population to change its traditional culture merely at a superficial level and to a limited degree in order successfully to resolve a new and challenging practical problem in group living may operate as a powerful stimulus to cultural innovation and creativity. Our findings from archaeological, ethnographic, and psychological, as well as from historical, evidence document the thesis of Arnold

J. Toynbee (1957: 357–362) that challenge may serve as a stimulus to the development of civilization (in other words, culture).

This type of stress may originate from environmental change, from resettlement in a new and unfamiliar habitat, and from contact with new and alien communities that have made a successful adjustment to the environment, as well as from other stimuli. Microcultural changes elicited in response to stress situations may be relatively superficial. Adoption of new technology from relatively well-adjusted neighbors is characteristic of this kind of change. Techniques of dry farming were borrowed, for example, from the Pueblos by the Navaho. The invention of new tools is another typical response. Deep-sea fishing gear was invented by the Chamorros to handle new fishing problems.

In general, the communities studied were able to retain their perception patterns, their major conceptual orientation, and their world image. They did not change their preferred relationship patterns. Instead, they found new ways to express them.

In each case of successful readjustment—among the Lauans, the Hopi, and the Papago, for example—the community did not entirely abandon concepts concerning the nature of the world and its hidden power sources, the nature of man, animals, plants and minerals, and the relations of all these components to one another. The community was not compelled to abandon a basically nurturing and conserving relationship toward the world of nature in favor, for example, of a competitive, exploitative relationship to natural resources like that characterizes Western industrial civilization.

Unsuccessful Types of Behavior Under Stress

On the other hand, kinds and degrees of pressure that may be challenging to a community if experienced in a situation within the threshold of its stress tolerance may become culturally destructive beyond those limits, as it was in the case of the Dakota and the Hawaiians.

The disruptive effect of forced removal of a population from its homeland is shown by the behavior of the Bikini islanders. The Bikini story is well documented by the reports of trained observers beginning with official negotiations prior to removal of the island's population before the first United States atomic bomb tests in the Pacific left their homeland radioactive (L. Mason 1950). Since that time authorities have moved the Bikini natives three times. It is reported that the Bikinians have not yet accommodated successfully to any new habitat and long to return to their homeland. Whether or not they will be able to readjust to their altered homeland now that it has been made available again remains to be seen.

Roman Influences in Northern Europe

Roman influences in northern Europe offer another example of the disruptive effects of pressure acculturation. First-century Rome was the earliest modern colonizer. Rome tried to impose by force a uniform social structure and legal norm on every conquered country. By trying to implement its model of law and social organization wherever its troops went, Rome disturbed the ecocultural balances of the indigenous populations in the areas it conquered. In many northern European communities disturbances thus engendered were especially acute because the cultures of the northern cradle area and the Mediterranean culture of Rome were structurally incompatible (Piggott 1965: 229). Rome's tendency to stress the pattern of a single dominant leader (Grimal 1963: 364), for example, contrasted sharply with the preferred relationship pattern of the northern cradle cultures with their "first among equals" leadership ideal. In addition, because a subarctic environment severely limits the kinds and degrees of cultural experimentation that a community can absorb without losing recuperative powers and its identity as a group, the farther north Roman influence extended, the less a disturbance in bioculture equilibrium could be tolerated. In other words, the more uncompromising its environment, the lower the degree of a community's tolerance of arbitrarily imposed changes in its culture. This point is also illustrated by the extinction of the Icelandic colonies in Greenland when the area was subjected to severe climatic deterioration toward the end of the medieval era. Similarly, Indian communities abandoned the

Classic Pueblo sites in the American Southwest during the great twenty-three-year drought.

The death struggle that populations on the northern margin of Europe (for example, the lowland Germanic-speaking tribes) exerted to avoid the rule of Rome may be viewed appropriately in relation to their needs and problems in ecocultural and climatic context. The Germanic-speaking tribes of the North Sea–Baltic region and the Celtic-speaking peoples of the Scottish Highlands, the Hebrides, and Ireland thus escaped Roman rule. To many of these communities Roman influences came chiefly in delayed and somewhat changed form; for example, in the ecclesiastical organization and canon law of the Catholic church.

In the northern European marginal communities that did not escape direct prolonged contact of Rome, apparently only those traditional social structures, leadership roles, linguistic habits, and core values essential to group survival and self-actualization tended to persist. This cultural stability is similar to the survival in Lau of social structures, leadership roles, and preferred relationship patterns despite lack of reinforcement and even strong negative sanctions by the British colonial government. In the same way, language, land-use patterns, local divisions, house types, and many other preferred culture structures persisted in Guam despite centuries of Spanish domination and even years of American rule.

Because acculturation also involves cultural interpenetration, the persistence of northern culture cradle values in slightly changed form on the margin of the Roman realm tended to affect the Roman culture. The influence of Germanic common law, for example, modified Roman social organization and law, especially regarding the position of women and the rights of the individual. New cultural phenomena, like the cult of the saints' relics, which combined elements derived from both the early Christian and Germanic religions developed in Roman Catholic practice.

Conclusion

Comparison of findings from the nine case studies of culturally distinctive populations reveals that the unique culture of each community investigated—its organized way of living and its preferred way of problem solving—is supremely important to the group. Strong pressures to change this way of life into an alien way, if successful, tend to initiate changes that are harmful, if not highly destructive, to the community's well-being. The group's mental health may be endangered unless such pressures originate within the group itself or are whole-heartedly accepted by its members as compatible with the community's needs, problems, and habits.

Our findings also demonstrate that social scientists who employ a research model that omits the historical dimension automatically rule out the possibility of making significant discoveries on an empirical basis regarding the nature of culture and long-range sociocultural change. The phenomenon of the creation and persistence of preferred relationship patterns and of their reemergence as tools for use by a group or an individual for the solution of practical problems may elude them. Even the nature of the group problem-solving process may escape their attention. They will be prevented from understanding it as a traditionally derived, culturally structured tool that has been found functionally useful in promoting self-renewal and self-actualization through the generations. Appreciation of the persistence of pattern both in social structure and in technological design will be virtually impossible within the man-made limitations of a method that omits the historical dimension. The nature of the group creative process itself will tend to escape such scholars. Innovation will not emerge as a problem-solving device that achieves its goal if possible by bringing about change in a point or node of a well-established pattern rather than by changing the relationship between nodes. Without an empirically based detailed knowledge of the traditional culture structure in historical depth such changes at any one point in the time scale cannot be accurately assessed.

A hiatus of this sort may seem unimportant except to a social psychologist interested in the creative process. But ignorance of historical facts that explain how specific cultural innovations have occurred in situational context as a result of the behavior of historical and contemporary populations allows a scholar to distort the process or to ignore it altogether. In the absence of facts that challenge its validity and even disprove it, a theory of cultural determinism that assigns little or no role to the creativity of the individual may be espoused.

Similarly, omission of the ecological dimension from the research design rules out the discovery of facts concerning the changing environmental situation of a population within which it has made decisions regarding its major living problems. A principle of limited possibilites and potentialities of cultural change cannot emerge from the findings unless they offer the researcher an opportunity to learn the ecological facts and their interrelationships. These findings regarding the importance of historical and ecological perspectives have significance in our search for an adequate, empirically based methodology by which to predict the probable behavior of a community under conditions of stress. They also prove relevant to the formulation of an adequate theory of culture that can be verified scientifically and may be used in an attempt to resolve universal social problems.

Note

1. For an amplification of some points in this chapter, see Thompson 1961: Ch. 13.

19 /

LANGUAGES OF SYMBOLISM

> Some day these stones will speak to us and tell us their story.
>
> Panchanan Mitra

The late Panchanan Mitra, who had been professor of anthropology at Calcutta University, was working at the Bishop Museum in Honolulu when I was describing the Marianas archaeological collection. Once, while we were discussing the possible use of some large stone mortars, he remarked, "Some day these stones will speak to us and tell us their story." Mitra spoke with such casual conviction that I was impressed.

Years later at a Midwestern university I was looking for some visual material to illustrate a lecture on Lauan culture. A diligent search revealed that the art department had only one appropriate slide, a photograph of a large wooden *kava* bowl. Although the slide was labeled "Tongan," I knew that the bowl originated not in Tonga but on Kambara, southern Lau. I asked myself by what process I had known, and that question started me thinking about the language of artifacts. The next day, projecting this slide on the screen, I began to explain the meaning of the bowl to a seminar. Gradually, from the form, material, decorations, and craftsmanship of this single artifact, treated functionally in situational and cultural context, the whole culture of the Kambarans emerged. Suddenly the long-forgotten incident in the Bishop Museum flashed back. I felt I had grasped the meaning of Mitra's words. Now at last I *do* understand the language of artifacts, I thought. Even stones, buried for centuries in a faraway Pacific island, speak to us if we can only understand their language.

Symbols and Signs

Students of mankind agree that a major indicator—probably *the* major indicator—that differentiates the human species from all others is the creation and use of complex symbolic systems. Signs are used by many animal species (and simple symbols are used by some perhaps), but the use of complex symbolic systems is a definitive characteristic of man.

In this context a symbol is defined as any physical phenomenon (for example, an artifact, a design, a sequence of movements or sounds) that is assigned an arbitrary meaning by the groups who use it. The key word in our definition is "arbitrary." Symbols are not meaningful in themselves. They have significance only in a cultural context. On the other hand, the meaning of a sign is conveyed by the way in which it is used.

Because the language of speech is the most complex and at the same time the most precise symbolic system and because verbal language is a universal characteristic of all human groups of which there is any available record, the language of speech is generally used as diagnostic of humanness. A moment's reflection, however, reveals that all human groups use many other symbolic "languages," some of which may be even more basic than speech.

The Language of Artifacts

Artifacts (objects that have been worked by man) express through their forms meanings that originate in the deep layers of human creativeness. A wooden *kava* bowl from Kambara may be used not only to explain the Lauan ceremony in which it figures but also to illuminate the way in which the ceremony expresses the Lauan community's social system and preferred relationship pattern. Similarly the carved high seats of the medieval Icelanders' great halls and the carved portals of Lower Saxon farmhouses symbolize features of the social systems and preferred relationship patterns of their respective cultures. The forest-cutting axe of antler, bone, or flint and the Hallstatt long sword of bronze or iron may be used to symbolize whole cultural configurations of the north European Mesolithic and the late

Bronze to early Iron Ages. A comparison of two artifacts, the Clovis projectile point and its successor, the Folsom point, reveals a change in the Paleo-Indian Great High Plains culture from mammoth to bison hunting closely related to a climatic and ecological succession.

E.S.C. Handy (1940b: 319–321) makes an excellent case that expertness in fishing is a major clue to understanding the Polynesians. These people built all their arts and industries on the pattern they developed as they mastered deep-sea fishing, where a single false move might mean death to a whole crew. Even the priesthood was perfected to meet the standard of very high level of craftsmanship developed by the fishermen. The Polynesians also projected their fishing pattern onto many activities as, for example, their raiding type of warfare. Man hunting thus appeared analogous to fishing in their thinking. In Tahiti and elsewhere the first captive in war was called the fish of Tu, their war god; in the Marquesas the body of a slain foe was slung from a tree by means of a great fish hook. The fishing pattern also appears in Polynesian cosmogony—Maui, their culture hero, created the world by fishing the islands out of the sea. Even sin is essentially looked upon as a slip in the craftsmanship and the fine artistry of living. And the same Polynesian term for such a departure from excellence, *hara,* also denotes, for example, a slip of the master carpenter's adz in building a canoe.

The Language of Ceremony

In order to understand the meaning of symbolism it is important to recognize the role played by the ceremonial system in the life way of a relatively isolated community. In reviewing the culture of the Australian aborigines, for example, we noted how the ceremonies of the Murngin express the native conception of the universe. In addition, they express symbolically a major problem in the community's life situation and also dramatically portray a solution to the problem. The solution is one that, through the millenniums, the group has found successful for that particular problem.

The ceremony thus pinpoints a basic problem at the same time that it reveals the culturally relevant solution. Thus a Navaho ceremony teaches both what dangers and evil forces to fear in the world and how to cope by cultural means with such hazards. Because both problem and solution are expressed symbolically and because the ceremonial sequence is repeated regularly, the ceremonial participant builds into his memory a pattern of events. This built-in symbolic code is subsequently at his disposal to use as needed. In other words, as the occasion demands he can recall the traditionally successful symbolic solution or denouement and translate it into appropriate action to solve practical problems that arise in the course of his daily life.

Do the ceremonial systems of all communities with integrated cultures tend to function likewise? Does the traditional ceremonial system of a community express a symbolic code developed to use in resolving certain practical problems inherent in the group's problematic situation? Does it tend to function as a group storage system to aid in decision making regarding practical problems based on the experience and wisdom of the group throughout its history? We recall that the annual ceremonial cycle of the Hopi Indians expresses dramatically the problematic situation of these village dwellers who farmed semidesert land in an area subject to spring droughts and many other crop hazards. In addition, the cycle expresses symbolically the problem's resolution. The Hopi's ceremonial activities are more complex and abstract than those of the Australian aborigines, but the similarity is clear.

The rite that initiates a Hopi child into the kachina society similarly expresses symbolically the youth's problems and how they may be resolved. In this ceremony the mother kachina may be interpreted as symbolizing the mother, the whipper kachinas as maternal uncles, the godfather as the father, and the godaunt as the father's sister. It thus

> illustrates dramatically the complementary functions of the maternal and paternal kin in steering the child along the road of life. It emphasizes especially the role of the Hopi mother as the source of order and control in the child's life, that of her brothers

as her active partners in maintaining discipline, and that of the father and his sister as the child's supporters. It also shows the difference between the treatment of boys and girls. And finally, through the discipliners' castigating of one another, it shows that the adult pattern of social control is not one in which one group, namely the adult matrilineal kin, originates action and another group, namely the children, terminate it, but one in which each adult individual is expected to exercise a certain amount of control over the others. From now on the censorship of the group, *i.e.*, public opinion, will gradually replace, to a considerable extent at least, the maternal household group as the principal negative sanction of the child's behavior. On the other hand, the positive role of his paternal kin in motivating his behavior will remain the same (Thompson and Joseph 1944: 56).

The annual Sun Dance of the Plains Indians is also relevant to this question. The Dakota Sioux believed that this ceremony was a major avenue by which they could contact their supernatural power source. The ceremony also focused their group life and reinforced their morality system; indeed, it was the heart of the traditional Sioux culture. When the Sun Dance was outlawed, the Sioux reacted as though their contact with their power source was severed. This and other externally imposed frustrations have adversely affected both Dakota social life and psychic organization, resulting in the Dakota's social disorganization and widespread emotional emaciation.

The Papago wine ceremony, designed to "pull down the clouds," affords a particularly illuminating example of the persistence of a group ceremony that was not suppressed. The wine ceremony expressed a specialized native approach to cope with a unique set of problems under very specific conditions. The reservation Papago, although they have adapted many aspects of modern American civilization to their own tribal needs and purposes, have not severed themselves as a group from their ancient homeland. Nor have they lost the focus of their world image. They still need rain and fertility. They still require periodic relief from the strains of their difficult living situation, rendered even more complex by the pressures of the surrounding intrusive culture. The wine ceremony affords a tested means of coping with these needs and strains. It is a uniquely Papago problem-solving device, still suited to the specific situation, problems, and personality configuration of the tribe. Transition into the "other" Papago world of visions, songs, and direct contact with the superhuman is an immediate benefit of the ceremony. Indeed, it accomplishes for the group what the vision quest and solitary power-seeking experiences formerly accomplished for the individual.

We have already concerned ourselves with the deeper meaning of the Lauan first-fruits rite and its vital role in Lauan social behavior and institutions. The ceremony expresses in succinct form the Lauan preferred relationship pattern of social discourse between humans, superhumans, animals, and plants as a competitive exchange of equivalent or identical values with deferred or immediate payment. Built into this ceremonial pattern there appear to be overtones of compulsive magic similar to those found in the ceremonial patterns of the Navaho, the Hopi, the Dakota, and the Papago.

Finally, we recall the Viking ceremony of "leading into the kin." This rite emphasized the significance of the basic social grouping of the Northmen, the bilateral kindred, and showed how it might be enlarged by the incorporation of new members through adoption. The ceremony thus symbolized a way by which the pressing problem of strengthening the group in a threatening environment could be solved by group action.

The Language of Settlement Patterns and Architecture

The ground plan of a community also tends to reflect the core value system of its human residents. In the traditional Hopi mesa pueblos, for example, the clear tendency was to build the dwelling and storage rooms around a central plaza as far as possible, depending on the physical limitations of the mesa top on which they were constructed. So that every dwelling may face the sun and the plaza, a three-tiered steplike arrangement of rooms and terraces has become traditional. This convention results in a roughly semicircular, theaterlike structure of rooms, which allows every member of the pueblo an unobstructed view of the plaza from the terraced roofs. The public episodes of major ceremonies expressing the values of the culture symbolically in the annual cycle are enacted in the plaza. The Hopi kivas also tend to be located in the vicinity of the dance plaza. The Marau kiva at Old Oraibi was situated in the center of the plaza (Voth 1912: plate 1). As might be expected, kivas furnish the setting in which the most sacred parts of the major ceremonies are performed. In the floor of each kiva is a circular depression (*sipapu*), which symbolizes the entrance to the underworld. According to Hopi tradition, the ancestors, thought to be a source of power and reinforcement for the living, dwell in the underworld.

The spatial arrangement of a Hopi mesa pueblo thus forms a series of concentric circles moving centripetally downward through several levels of living and storage rooms to a dance plaza and from the dance plaza underground to a focal point that symbolizes, within an underground chamber, the entrance to the underworld realm of the power-dispensing ancestors. The pueblo dwelling complex is not closed, however, but open toward the sun, which symbolizes the major life-giving Hopi deity. Thus we discover that the traditional ground and underground plan and the architecture of the Hopi symbolize spatially the traditional world image of the tribe.

On Tinian island in the Marianas the largest and most imposing *latte* structure at the Taga site is located in the center of the village. As Alexander Spoehr (1957: 74) remarks, "the village plan, with the largest house at the center, may well be a reflection of the social organization of the community." As noted in Chapter 4, the evidence suggests that the house of the paramount chief was centrally located in relation to those of lesser lineage chiefs of the same clan.

Similarly, in the Lau islands rank tends to be spelled out spatially. Each of the clans of a village occupies its own section around the central ground where such a major village ceremony as a *solevu* is held. The chief's house is located in a prominent position on the edge of ceremonial ground. Usually it stands across the plaza from a path that connects the village with a canoe landing or anchorage. The chief's house is the largest, most substantially and skillfully built house in the village. Usually it is also the highest, due to the height of its stone-faced foundation platform. The beams of a chief's house are lashed and decorated with elaborate sennit designs. Cowrie shells, which symbolize chieftainship, adorn the house platform.

A similar ground plan is manifest in the *kava* circle. Here the highest-ranking person present sits in the central place of honor in relation to the other participants, who form the two horns of a semicircle on either side of him. The ranking man sits opposite the *kava* bowl and at a distance of several yards from it. The bowl is carefully placed with its handle, a cowrie-decorated loop of sennit, stretched across the floor in the direction of the chief or ranking man.

The same general pattern is reproduced in the elliptically shaped floor plan of the chief's dwelling house. The house's rounded ends (a Tongan trait superimposed by the Lauans on the ancient Fijian rectangular dwelling), like the *kava* ceremony, accommodate and emphasize semicircular or curvilinear lines rather than straight or geometric ones characteristic of old Fiji. About one-third of the floor space farthest removed from the house's main entrance is reserved for the occupant and his family, as well as for any ranking guests that the occupant may invite to share it. Because they have helped to build the house, the villagers are entitled to use floor space just inside the main entrance, provided they observe certain customary rules. Ranking persons may sit in the middle section.

Among the Murngin of Australia each tribe occupies a well-defined collecting and hunting territory. At the approximate center of the tribal territory is a water hole or spring, around which the tribe moves in roughly circular fashion as it pursues its seminomadic way of life. As we have noted, a tribe's water hole is believed to connect the world of the living with the underworld of the dead. It symbolizes the group's close relationship to the ghosts of its ancestors and to the spirits of its yet unborn members, which are also believed to inhabit the underworld. The water hole thus relates the aborigines temporary world of everyday life to the enduring realities of the tribe's past and future.

In early Iceland members of the Althing from all four quarters of the island gathered once a year at Thingvellir during the summer solstice. Thingvellir is located in the interior of southwestern Iceland. The central portion of the island is characterized by high wastelands, glaciers, and lava flows, but Thingvellir was accessible by horseback to islanders living in all parts of Iceland at the time, especially in the populous southwest. Thingvellir afforded flat terrain spacious enough to accommodate an extensive camp on the edge of a freshwater stream where it emptied into a glacial lake. A small island in the lake served as the jousting ground for rival factions that failed to settle their differences according to the unwritten law of the commonwealth. A steep hill formed a rostrum from which the lawspeaker could recite the law code. Because of excellent natural accoustics his voice could be heard from below.

It is clear that the groups studied tend to express their preferred relationships spatially as evidenced by their architecture and by the ground plans of their communities, but it is necessary to check this finding for universality.

The native hamlets of Melanesia and aboriginal India contain many examples of the use of space to express community values. Among the Dobuans of the d'Entrecasteaux Islands off the southeast coast of New Guinea, according to Reo F. Fortune (1932: 1–3, 178), for example, each village is owned by several *susu* (that is, matrilineal lineages, each consisting of a woman and her brothers, her children, and her daughters' children, and so on). At the center of the village is a graveyard, often an elevated mound overgrown with red croton plants, in which lie buried the male and female ancestors of the several *susu*. The dwelling houses are arranged around and facing this cemetery. The ancestral ghosts of the village are believed to endow the living *susu* descendants with property rights to its soil and trees and with magical powers.

In the Trobriands, according to Bronislaw Malinowski (1935: 24–25, fig. 2, Ch. 8), the central ceremonial ground of the village is surrounded by open-slatted storage houses. Here the precious yams, pride of each household and its principal source of prestige, are stored and displayed. At the outer edge of a circular road behind the yam houses are located the dwelling houses of the gardeners who grow the yams. In hill villages of certain aboriginal tribes of India, according to W. V. Grigson (1938: 105), the center is occupied by a house in which sleep the male youth of the community, believed to be the source of its sacred generative power. The village chief's house is also located in the central area. Nearby stands a shrine symbolizing female generative power. Around these sacred primary buildings the dwelling houses of the married couples, their young children, and unmarried daughters form a protective circle.

A consideration of the Japanese garden also illuminates the discussion of the symbolic use of space. The Japanese garden truly represents a deliberate attempt to symbolize spatially the Japanese conception of the universe. As E. A. Gutkind writes (1956: 38), "For the Japanese, the garden is a microcosm consciously created out of nature's overwhelming diversity as a 'concentrated' nature within a limited space." What appears to be a spontaneous aesthetic and primarily unconscious group process in many of the examples cited above has been made explicit and reinforced conceptually by the Japanese into a preconceived plan. The plan is then implemented step by step. The result is a formal garden that represents a sophisticated spatial rendition of a national ideology.

The Language of Song and Dance

In our discussion of the community case studies, we have noted the persistence of songs, chants, and dances. A striking example is the Chamorran *tsamorita*, an indigenous refrain used to twit a rival or to ridicule and frustrate an authority figure. Among the Papago Indians singing is still used as it was in the past, as a magical device for acquiring power and warding off—or inducing—sickness and ill fortune. In Lau the *meke* enlivens most important group ceremonies and social occasions. *Meke* are even "exchanged" between the two competing parties of a *solevu* and between hosts and guests at a social occasion. Each side contributes a dance to balance and "repay" that of the other. The *meke* formula is thus used to inject many social occasions with ceremonial meaning. The technical perfection of the traditional Hawaiian hula (which is exchanged on social occasions in the same way as the Fijian *meke*) and its former sacred function suggest that this dance was also a form of aesthetic seduction, exhortation, and acted-out compulsive magic. It apparently expressed the Hawaiian pattern of deity worship as a means of obtaining mana. The function of the Hopi ceremonial cycle, including dances accompanied by traditional and newly created songs, has already been discussed. The Hopi rituals include preparatory activities and "good" (positive) thoughts (Whorf 1941). The dances represent formal rhythmical acting out of desired events to facilitate and even compel their occurrence. The performance represents an attempt on the part of the group to exercise a measure of magical control over future events. The disciplinary efforts of these activities on the individual, including the development and reinforcement of psychic controls, may be considerable.

Our findings substantiate those of modern students of music and dance who believe that these art forms express patterns of movement and feeling that underlie whole sets of human institutions, and indeed a whole culture or subculture. They also illuminate the puzzling persistence of these forms under conditions that have submerged many other aspects of a native culture. As Alan Lomax (1962: 434) states, "Whenever a special profile is attached to a body of song with a special function, this exceptional phenomenon can often be explained by the survival, the adoption, or the recrudescence of an entire style in a culture for historical reasons."

The Language of Poetry and Prose

The literature of a group—or even a single poem, chant, song, or story—may express by means of both form and content the world image of its creators and promulgators. The Hawaiian Kumulipo creation chant, for example, may be used as an introduction to the culture of the native Hawaiians. It may also be used as a manifestation of the traditional preferred relationship pattern with its stress on natural genealogically linked sequences.

Icelandic court poetry with its intricate structure confined within strict boundaries reflects the complicated problematic situation that the Icelanders appraised and attempted to resolve. Both its form and its content express, symbolically and literally, the Icelanders' perception of their living problem and its solution. In court poetry, the universal enigma of death and the possible extension of the ego afterwards is faced and resolved in a characteristic stylized manner. It reveals the Icelandic belief that man could conquer life by the triumph of the human spirit even at the moment of death. Through song and saga, a bard could extend a person's life beyond death in the form of fame.

In many of the communities studied (for example, Iceland, Hawaii, Lau, Papagoland, and Navaholand), words and phrases as well as whole poems may be used as vehicles of magical potency. A common belief is that verbal arrangements may kill or cure. The word may even be raised to a position of superordinance among the languages of symbolism as in certain cultures of the Middle East, Europe, and modern America. "In the beginning was the Word . . ." is a Judeo-Christian expression of such a belief. Its implications have not yet been fully explored.

The Function of Fantasy, Dreaming, and Myth Making

Reinterpretation of daily experiences so that they fit the culture's preferred relationship pattern is apparently the work of dreaming, of psychic activities on the fringes of consciousness, and of myth making, song, and ceremonies. New or borrowed cultural tools, both concrete and abstract, are thus fitted into the preferred traditional form by the group through the conscious and unconscious activities of its members. The group tends to change points in the traditional culture pattern rather than the pattern itself. If the pattern is suppressed, it tends to persist in the structure of dreams, ceremonies, myths, proverbs, songs, dances, and art styles. When pressures are relaxed, it tends to reemerge to the level of consciousness and overt behavior, which will approximate the traditional form as closely as the changing circumstances of group life permit. This cultural process of suppression, adaptation, and reemergence obviously has a very long time dimension, reckoned in terms of centuries and millenniums.

Once cultural phenomena have achieved a nearly optimum functional relationship with the environment and with one another, they seem to persist in such forms or not at all. It is therefore patently foolish to ignore or try to suppress the preferred culture structure of any human group. Our findings suggest that innovations introduced by external pressures may engender anxiety but will not "take" unless they are accepted and reworked by the recipients into traditional ways. Innovations cannot be effectively implemented by force except by resettling the group in a new environment with new living problems. Such change may not be possible even then, as the Bikini case suggests. The Spanish treatment of the Chamorros of Guam and the Hopi Indians and the American treatment of the Sioux are also cases in point. In each instance traditional patterns reemerged in slightly changed guise when pressures were removed. Reemergence occurred even when the population itself was almost extinguished, as were the Chamorros.

Conclusion

Much more might be gleaned about symbolic expression from our studies of the various communities. But enough has been said to indicate the variety of forms that symbolic expression may take, aside from verbal speech. A survey of our findings suggests that man has always expressed himself symbolically in many "languages." These include the direct, mainly unconscious symbolism of space and time relationships, gesture, movement, design and color, the complex structure and meaning of formal speech, and the most complicated configurations that are embodied in a group's artifacts, literature, mythology, dreams, music, dance, drama, ceremonials, architecture, settlement, and land-use customs. Contrary to the usual assumption, a broad comparative view of the history of human cultures in social and environmental context reviewed in this volume suggests that the *relationships* expressed by a group in symbolic forms are more significant as universal media of communication than the *content* that they may convey to the culturally initiated. Speech is only one of the symbolic languages habitually employed by human groups; it is not necessarily the most significant from the viewpoint of communication. On the contrary, speech may be used directly to obscure meaning or to falsify content. But the languages of form—dreams, myths, poetry, music, dances, ceremonies, architecture, and so on—do not lie. For those who can read them, they express the hidden wisdom of the unconscious.

In the apt phrase of Edward T. Hall (1959), culture is indeed the "silent language." But it is not always silent. At times it is loud and even shrill as in the language of speech, of music and song, of poetry, story telling, and mythology, of daydreams and nightmares, even of modern television and radio. Culture is also communication. But the significant question from the present viewpoint is: what information does a culture communicate and to whom? Our data suggest that the languages of a culture communicate to its proponents a community's historic perception of its impelling problems in the context of its value system and its image of the world. But that is not the whole story. The languages of symbolism also convey to those who can read them how, according to the group's experience in the course of time, those problems may be resolved.

But the information communicated by each of a culture's languages is expressed in code. Each cultural group has built such a code into its symbolic system. Our explorations also suggest that for each cultural code there is a key. And the key is buried in the group members' unconscious. To dig for such keys and translate their codes into the languages of science—that, I suggest, is a major task for students of culture and language (see also Wolf 1964: 48). Some anthropologists, following Edward Sapir (Mandelbaum 1949) as well as Emile Durkheim and Marcel Mauss (1963), have led the way in this task. Benjamin Lee Whorf (1956) and Dorothy D. Lee (1959) have already succeeded brilliantly.

The illumination that comes from attempting to understand internally integrated, non-Western cultures through firsthand experience, using the native language, thus throws a flood of light on the nature of symbolism. Such study also provides clues to the meaning of cultural expressions like dreaming. Most anthropologists consider this kind of illumination essential to the professional development of a cultural anthropologist or an ethnologist, and many believe that there can be no substitute for it. Indeed, Robert Redfield (1956: Ch. 1) to the contrary, this essential experience in the professional training of an anthropologist—and its absence in that of most sociologists and many other students of man—constitutes one of the basic differences that sets the professional anthropologist apart from other scholars. Instead of trying to reduce observations to a form that will fit mental and emotional sets already enculturated in his perception and cognition patterns, a cultural anthropologist must change his own deeply rooted ways of perceiving the phenomenal world to encompass each new observation viewed situationally if he wishes to become a true professional.

20 /

CULTURE AS A
PROBLEM-SOLVING DEVICE

> Any culture consists of the set of habitual and traditional
> ways of thinking, feeling, and reacting that are character-
> istic of the ways a particular society meets its problems at
> a particular point in time.
>
> Clyde Kluckholm and Dorothea C. Leighton (1946:
> xviii–xix)

> The development of a theory for orienting a diversity of
> community studies to common problems of uncommon
> significance is of great urgency.
>
> Albert Schafer (1966: 434)

Throughout the ages men, as members of a community, have
sought solutions to the practical living problems and basic en-
igmas of life. In the thoroughly studied historical civilizations of
Egypt, Iran, India, China, Greece, Israel, and Rome men found
satisfying answers to perennial problems of community living.
In each of the little-known communities we considered in this
book we found such a solution. We discovered it in the economy,
social structure, ceremonials, and art forms, as well as in dream,
myth, language, and literature. Strange or illogical though each
solution may seem on superficial observation, a deeper probe
reveals that it makes sense within the unique environmental
and social context in which it has been forged. Our next questions must relate to an attempt to define culture in a way that
will be consistent with our field findings. How, for example,
does a culture relate to the community that activates it and to

the specific needs and problems of the human beings who express it?

Biogenetic Adaptation[1]

Our analysis suggests that in order for a human population to complete its life cycle successfully certain basic needs must be met and certain problems solved. A human group must actively organize itself to maintain its wholeness as a structural entity within the range of human group normalcy, just as other organic communities do. It must satisfy its essential organic requirements. To do so it must inhabit an ecological niche that will allow it to fulfill its species' biogram and resolve its practical living problems. Such problems include, of course, maintenance, defense, reproduction, self-actualization, and completion of the life cycle through successive generations.

A degree of adaptation to a specific changing environment is a necessary condition to the existence of every living creature and of every organic community. The adaptive processes of human populations may involve behavioral and biological changes. Such changes are especially noticeable in extreme geographic environments like those of the Icelanders, the Hopi, and the Papago. In the long run, significant genetic changes also occur and are perpetuated in an inbreeding human population. These genetic changes then may contribute to the evolution of a unique microrace. A phenomenon of this type was especially evident in the blood groups of small, near-isolated populations (for example, among the Australian aborigines, Polynesians, Hopi, Papago, Icelanders, and Lower Saxons). A geographically isolated human population, like a plant and animal community, thus tends under certain circumstances to consolidate itself biologically, and also in time to coadapt and restructure itself genetically, in relation to the environment.

Symbolic Adaptation

Furthermore, a human community tends to relate itself to the environment in a distinctively *human* way. As we have observed in near-isolated natural laboratories, a human community tends to create a distinctively human problem-solving device; that is, a complex symbolic system. In other words, in contrast to all other living species, the human community manifests not only a biogenetic dynamic but also a uniquely *human* dynamic for use in resolving problems of group adaptation and self-actualization.

This symbolic system building in the direction of group problem solving for adaptation and self-actualization is the distinctive process in human culture creation and change. Through communal symbolizing processes the members of a near-isolated community tend, in the course of time, to consolidate its culture into a unique, emotionally tinged system. I have called this structure the group's preferred relationship pattern. Only in complex, composite, expanding cultures like that of the United States and in relatively simple but historically composite and expanding cultures like that of the Navaho Indians do such core values tend to comprise a congeries of disparate notions or an aggregation of unrelated or loosely related themes. Even in such cases, however, the tendency we have postulated as inherent in cultural process is toward balanced aesthetic and meaningful integration.

Once it has been built into the culture of a community—into its institutions, grammar, and style in music, song and dance, and artifact designs—a preferred relationship pattern tends to resist change. We have noted that unless the community is wiped out or severed from its niche (and sometimes even then), such a relationship pattern may endure for centuries with little structural alteration. We observed this process among the Australian aborigines, the Chamorros, the Papago, the traditional Hopi communities, the Icelanders, the Lower Saxons, and other groups. It appears that in culturally homogeneous communities the pattern of indigenous core values, mirroring the group's age-old perception of the world and its vital power dynamics, is rarely affected directly by man-made external pressures. Usually it is affected, if at all, only indirectly or partially.

Under certain special pressure circumstances, of course, some of which have been described by anthropologists (see especially Mead 1964; Burgher 1965), behavior patterns may be radically restyled. But when the situation stabilizes after stress a community may be expected to reactivate its traditional preferred relationship pattern in somewhat altered guise. Recall especially the behavior of the Guamanians, the Dakota Sioux, the Icelanders, and the Lower Saxons. From evidence reported in this volume, we conclude that the perspective of a decade or even a half-century of community history is not long enough to warrant valid predictions regarding expected cultural changes within it.

Basic Community Organization

In sum, from a long-range multidiscipline standpoint it is inappropriate to view a local human community as though it were *primarily* an inorganic chemical type of system. It is even incorrect to examine it as if it were *merely* a system of human relations; that is, a social system. From the standpoint of the current discussion, community processes involve both types of systems, but also much more.

Every viable human community forms part of a larger organized biological whole. It transacts with a natural ecosystem in its effective environment, whether local, regional, or global. Although the influences of cosmic processes (such as radiation and gravitation) on a human population are not yet fully understood, each year brings new knowledge. Meanwhile it would be folly to deny that such processes affect human beings, because they clearly influence not only organic processes and behavior but also the structure and composition of a human population's gene pool.

To a considerable extent the existence and welfare of a human community thus depend on the composition and organization of the natural ecosystem of which it forms one component. This point has long been recognized, at least theoretically, by ecologists like Charles C. Adams, Paul B. Sears, and Marston Bates. Using the approach and tools of modern science in order to systematically analyze the whole ecosystem, however, has proven to be unusually difficult (see Fosberg 1963b: 1).

Our findings suggest that, if an *explanatory* description of community processes for purposes of limited probability forecasting of group behavior is the aim, a human community may be viewed appropriately, first of all, as though it were basically an organismic type of organization. Such a community may be conceived as integral to an evolving ecosystem composed of many transacting species of plants, microorganisms, and animals, each species occupying its own niche in a specific changing environment.

Cultural Diversity: A Natural Condition

The variations and sporadic distribution of natural resources throughout the planet form part of the existential situation of each community, just as differences in climate and degree of isolation do. Any colonizing species, whether human, animal, or plant, must cope with such realities in resolving its living problems if the species is to survive and actualize itself in that locality. Archaeological, ecological, and historical evidence shows that otherwise the species colony either migrates or perishes.

A highly specialized ecological niche engenders complementary behavioral and plastic biological adjustments on the part of the organisms constituting the group. An isolated breeding population also adapts to its habitat by processes of natural selection, mutation, random genetic drift, and migration (Lasker 1960) and consolidates itself genetically. Each group must adapt itself functionally to its organic and physical environment. Otherwise it cannot continue to exist and reproduce. Indeed, a primary condition for the continuation of any population as a spatial, temporal, biological (including a genetic) entity is its transactive relationship with its ecological niche. I refer to its fit to a unique, more or less specialized, and changing environment. To be viable, this relationship must afford the means of satisfying the essential needs and requirements of the population throughout the life cycles of its component individuals. Thus, whatever its complexity, a community system tends toward biogenetic homeostasis (defined as, "the self-regulation of optimal conditions for maintenance and continuation"). Because the existing ecosystems and existing human groups of the planet are highly diverse, there probably will never be a culture—surely not Western industrialized urban civilization with its discontents—that will prove viable and satisfying for every human group under all circumstances where human group life is possible. Indeed, the unique propensity of a human community to build, perpetuate through learning, and express itself through a complex symbolic system in terms of its needs and problems implies that in time it will develop a degree of cultural specialization. It is therefore vital for anthropologists to continue to concern themselves with cultural diversity.

Cultural Specialization

The communities studied exhibit a wide range of variation, from relative simplicity to extreme complexity in social structure, economy, and symbolic development. Each specialized habitat requires custom-made cultural mechanisms to meet human needs for self-maintenance, reproduction, and self-actualization. Examples of such environments would be a desert like Papagoland, an archipelago like Hawaii or the Marianas, an elevated plateau like Hopiland, or a subarctic island like Iceland.

Contemporary local human communities are each of definite, describable, and unique kinds. Each has a unique history.[2] Each is culturally and socially specialized to some degree in the direction of functional adaptation to a more and less restricted local environment.

At the New York World's Fair (1964–1965), the General Motors' exhibit contained a panorama of models of future living arrangements. These were located in the desert, on Antarctica, in a tropical rain forest, under the sea, on a mountaintop, and on the moon. The exhibit showed how the members of a number of modern communities, occupying diverse ecological niches, might solve their technical living problems with the aid of space-age ingenuity and invention. It suggested how, by judiciously using the expanding resources of science, architecture and art, human populations not only in cities but in many eco-niches heretofore unavailable to human group living, might change their culture to accommodate themselves to new situations with efficiency and grace. It is becoming increasingly clear, however, that adaptations even to the industrialization process show an ethnic bias. A Japanese plan for regional and urban redevelopment in Japan, for example, differs in culturally significant ways from a comparable American plan.

Our explorations indicate that favorable conditions for human communal existence, not just for today but across the centuries, must be actively established and maintained. We therefore expect that, in the course of solving its problems, the members of a community will build and attempt to maintain its balance in terms of future prospects. They chiefly use their behavioral activities in this endeavor. In the long run plastic biological and genetic mechanisms also play a part. When its balance is disturbed by environmental pressures (for example, climatic fluctuations, natural catastrophies, or epidemics), a community tends to move toward a new biocultural homeostasis by behavioral activities, nonhereditary biological adjustments, and finally also genetic changes.

For example, consider the Icelanders. The founders adapted their land-use patterns, social organization, house types, and other aspects of their traditional heritages to the new environment through changing their behavior. When in the late Middle Ages the climate of their new home deteriorated, they starved, and many perished. They also shrank in stature, a plastic biological adaptation; when the climate improved, they recovered their height. In time through inbreeding, natural selection, random genetic drift, and coadaptation of gene frequencies, their genetic constitution consolidated into a local microrace.

Our findings suggest that a tendency toward self-recovery and self-rehabilitation on the part of the community also operates in case of interference by man-made pressures directed toward changing the community's habitual activities. Such pressures are exemplified by enemy raids that involve the loss of crops, women, and lands. Apache raiders threatened the Papago villages in this manner; encroaching Navaho, Ute, and Paiute similarly pressured the Hopi pueblos. Other pressures may derive from militant religious proselytizing. It was in this way that the communities of the Saxons and the Chamorros were disrupted by Catholic conquerors. Incompatibility of native ways with alien models of leadership and exotic organizational patterns may also cause disturbance, as it did among the Navaho and Hopi when they were confronted by the United States Indian administrators, among the Saxons opposed by the Romanized Franks, and among the Chamorros vis-à-vis the Spanish and later the American colonial governors.

On the other hand, man-made pressures may originate within the community itself. Overpopulation in relation to the water or food supply available under existing technology is a prime example. This specific problem was found among some Polynesian groups, the medieval Saxons, the Vikings, and the Icelanders. Imbalance of the sex ratio, as in the Polynesian Marquesas (Handy 1923); internal factionalism, as among the Hopi (Titiev 1944); and an increase of such types of deviancy as mental illness, delinquency, crime, sex aberrations, and drug addiction as among residents of urban centers in contemporary societies are other examples.

Our case studies suggest that every human population tends actively to seek out a congenial niche, by migration and resettlement if necessary. The group may also improve its habitat by such man-made devices as drainage systems (Lower Saxons, Icelanders), irrigation developments (Papago, Hopi, Hawaiians, Chamorros), fishponds (Lauans, Hawaiians), and the elevation of campsites (Maglemosans) and meadows (Saxons, Icelanders). The group may even create such a niche if none is available. The Aztecs, for example, found refuge in the valley of Mexico by building islands in the Texcoco lagoon (Wolf 1959: 131–132; Moriarty 1968).

Once it has a viable habitat, the group strives to maintain itself and to defend the boundaries of its territory (as did the Saxons, Chamorros, and Hopi, for example). Its members seek out food for their nutritional needs. They copy or invent means of producing and processing them. Examples are technologies for manufacturing cutting implements like the wood-chopping axe during the Mesolithic; for domesticating of plants and animals during the Neolithic; and for storing commodities against future needs such as preserving manioc in the Fulangan lagoon and stashing away a three years' supply of maize among the Hopi. Trade with neighboring groups for food and other goods also may be developed.

As noted above, the group activates a complex symbolic system, which includes several subsystems like a language and literature, characteristic rhythms, music and dance forms, and a ceremonial complex. The members use these subsystems to express a preferred pattern of values that relates the symbolic system aesthetically and logically to the culture as a whole and to the natural environment. Members of the community develop their own unique methods of rearing their young so that their idiosyncratic way of life may be perpetuated.

In all these ways and in many others every healthy human population strives to actualize itself as a viable group. We have seen that, even among so-called "primitive" and "peasant" peoples, this striving may be *consciously* purposeful and accompanied by foresight. In all societies it partially consists of directive activities at the unconscious level. Among the Lauans, the Papago, and the Dakota, for example, such activities included visions, dreams, and hallucinations. Although they are unconscious, such processes are normal, developmental, and oriented essentially toward culture building. Thus, they express what has been called the "wisdom of the unconscious."

Evolution and Cultural Homeostasis

It is generally agreed that the term "evolution" is not applicable to culture process except by analogy. But we are beginning to realize that culture process is homeostatic, rhythmic with direction, and straining toward optimum control in terms of future function. The directiveness of organic activities, now generally accepted by biologists, apparently expressed analogously at the human, symbol-building level in the process of cultural homeostasis. The active agency, of course, is always the organism. In the case of culture building, the agents are human organisms participating in group behavioral activities.

It is now recognized that man's propensity to create cultures has added a new dimension to the evolutionary process. By his use of culture as a tool to cope with his basic problems, man significantly affects the biological evolution of his own and other species. Furthermore, according to this feedback process, man's capacity for culture also tends to evolve.[3] Thus, man is learning how to control his own destiny within certain limits.

In consequence a whole new area of research has opened up, but it urgently needs clarification. We need to understand culture as a process and to understand also how cultures may be used to create and organize healthy viable communities. Furthermore, we need to understand how the culture process, keyed as we have seen to community health and balance, may overcompensate or break down and thus engender cultural crisis. For the very same process may be used by man for his benefit or his detriment, from the viewpoint of community organization and development (see, for example, M. K. Opler 1956).

Culture Power: Man's Greatest Resource

A human community's propensity to build a culture constitutes its power. Like the Papago's and the Polynesians' conception of mana, culture power is neutral, neither good nor evil in itself. Its effect, from the community welfare viewpoint, depends on how it is used. The fate of a community and indeed of its "genius," depends on how its members employ that power.

Of course the members of a community may be prevented by external interference from building their culture into an efficient problem-solving tool. Or, after they have fashioned it to their specific situation, they may be blocked from using it for this purpose. Witness the effects of colonial or feudal rule among the Guamanians, the Lower Saxons, the Icelanders, and the American Indians. Our explorations underline the need for the people themselves to retain the significant decision-making roles in their own society and to tailor and use their traditional culture structure toward a realistic solution of their problems, if improved welfare is the issue. Of course they may borrow cultural artifacts—tools, technology, ideas. But our evidence strongly indicates that the success of such borrowing, from the viewpoint of improved community development, depends on the people themselves. In each case of successful borrowing (for example, the Navaho, the Sioux) we have found that the community members have actively selected the cultural models to be copied. They themselves have worked specific alien ingredients into traditional culture structures so that the culture was strengthened and rendered more flexible as a precision instrument for successfully solving their own life problems. The analysis suggests that man's culture is his greatest resource. If we wish to successfully implement improved community development on a worldwide scale, we shall have to recognize and reinforce this priceless potential of every human group.

Significance of Decision-Making Roles

In the course of culture building a group tends to consolidate the several parts of its culture into a whole that is homeostatically balanced in relation to its ecological base. It appears that a good deal of culture processing occurs at the unconscious level. A "straining toward consistency" is implemented through dreaming, myth-making, visions, and similar mechanisms. At the same time, in every community studied we have noted decision-making roles that allow certain aspects of culture-building and culture-changing processes to be given a formal place in the social structure.

Our findings suggest that such institutionalized decision-making roles are present in every human society. Group decision making is apparently too essential a function to be left to chance. In other words, comparative community analysis indicates that fostering the decision-making process is an integral part of every viable human community system, closely related to the group's tendency to defend itself and to foster its own survival and self-actualization.

On the other hand, our case studies reveal that formal mechanisms for enforcing decisions that result from the activation of such roles may be diffuse or entirely lacking. For example, in medieval Iceland the Lögretta had the power to change the law but not to enforce it. In a Papagoan village the council's unanimous decisions were upheld only by diffuse sanctions. In southern Lau traditional decision-making powers of the master fisherman and the chief of crops have not been reinforced by the British colonial government. They were upheld to a limited extent, however, by the pressure of public opinion.

Degree of Voluntarism

Inquiring further into this problem, we note that the degree of voluntarism permitted by a society regarding individual and group behavior differs greatly among the communities studied. Even in highly authoritarian systems like that of native Hawaii, where the sacred high chief owned all the land and a limited feudalism prevailed, the common farmer was no serf. He and his family could move out of an unsatisfactory relationship (that is, one in which the high chief's tribute collector was overdemanding) by transferring his allegiance to another chief of his own choosing. This was a significant right, because if many so transferred the chief was left without followers, and therefore without manpower.

Let us compare Hawaiian feudalism with the European type. Charlemagne introduced medieval feudalism with limited success into Lower Saxony. Feudalism of this type required that a onetime free farmer fulfill all his obligations to his feudal lord, including regular payment of heavy tribute. It also demanded that he and his descendants remain in hereditary bondage to the lord. The serfs were tied to the manor land and thus lacked the decision-making power and mobility of their Hawaiian counterparts. We have noted how desperately the freedom-loving Saxons fought such serfdom and tried to circumvent it, ultimately with a certain success.

In sum, our findings suggest that, from the long-range biosocial viewpoint, formalizing the judiciary and legislative functions of a society is more widespread than formalizing those of the executive. Whereas the former tend toward a degree of institutionalization, our data reveal that there is considerable variation regarding the latter. It appears, however, as though the more the executive functions of a society are emphasized, the less voluntarism may occur among its members. If the power of the executive function outweighs the judicial and legislative, decision-making roles regarding the essential problematic situations of a society are likely to be formally restricted. Fewer members of the group participate in decision-making processes and the wisdom of the group tends to be tapped little or not at all.

Cultural Selection and Change

Theories of determinism, rooted either in natural environmental factors (such as climate and physical resources) or in human factors (like government by bureaucratic fiat, military dictatorship, or economic organization), do not wholly explain the facts that we have been considering. On the contrary, the facts suggest that externally imposed pressures on a community may set the stage for culture change and play a potentially limiting role in it. The data indicate that a group's choice of whether or not to change, how to change, and in what ways to change depends on a complex process related to the behavior and preferred perception pattern of its members. As a rule this process involves restyling traditional patterns slightly so that they continue to be useful in solving the community's basic living problems while, at the same time, they help the group to meet its changing situation.

This process utilizes the creation of new models, the borrowing and adapting of alien ones, and the reactivation of traditional models in new forms. It is a highly selective operation. The choice, adaptation, and restructuring of cultural models are accomplished by community members functioning as the "personnel" of communal institutions, in the terminology of Malinowski (1960: Ch. 6), on the basis of resources that community members perceive as available to them. The process is structured by the preferred relationship pattern or patterns implicit in the culture of the community, especially in its core value system.

Our analysis suggests that culture change is not a haphazard or mechanical process at the mercy of chance events and external pressures (see also Spoehr 1956: 96). In other words, far from being a meaningless, unpredictable, or erratic movement, culture change proceeds in a given community according to a discoverable code within a describable context, both social and natural.

These findings emphasize the importance to balanced, healthy functioning of communal decision-making processes involving both groups and individuals. They also highlight the significance of institutionalizing such processes rather than leaving them to chance circumstances.

Conclusion

We have studied the development of human communities in a wide variety of physical environments. In considering our findings, we note enormous differences in the problematic situations that have confronted human communities throughout the history and prehistory of mankind. But the practical problems that a human population must solve or cease to exist as a viable group remain more or less constant.

Many of these basic problems are shared, to a considerable extent, by all organic species, especially higher mammalian forms. But whereas other species resolve them mainly by means of sensory and genetically determined behavior, a human population works them out also by creating, tailoring, and integrating a culture. Using its culture as a glorified artifact transmitted from generation to generation by nurture rather than by nature, a human group solves its problems more or less successfully from a long-range viewpoint or ceases to exist *in situ* as an organized entity.

Once institutionalized and embodied in the social structure and symbolic system of the group, the fundamental patterns of a culture tend to persist. If outlawed they tend to go underground (for example, into the unconscious psyches of its members) and to reemerge in slightly changed form when circumstances become more auspicious. This illuminates the phenomenon of cultural stability and the tenacity of the group's preferred relationship pattern.

A culture thus represents the way of life that a human community creates, builds, balances, and repeatedly re-creates and tries to rebalance in order to resolve its group living problems in its particular habitat. A community—even the most isolated —is constantly changing its culture. It does this in response to its changing group life situation, due to limitations and possibilities imposed both from without and from within. It accomplishes such change *formally* by means of such culture-changing devices as institutionalized decision making and planned change and *informally* by means of individual creativity as well as through traditional child-rearing practices.

Such changes are never haphazard. They follow general principles of culture pattern change. Such culture patterns are structured and balanced according to a principle of limited possibilities and potentialities of culture and personality change, including social structure and language.

An anthropologist tries to discover and master these principles. He hopes to understand, and to place in true perspective, the culture-change pattern of a specific community in a given habitat. He thus strives to develop skill in predicting group behavior under certain changing conditions with the degree of precision needed to help to resolve practical living problems.

Notes

1. Parts of this chapter in different form were presented in a paper at the first meeting of the Unity Seminar, Michael Reese Hospital, Chicago, October 1951, and appeared in *Toward a Unified Theory of Human Behavior* (1967: 70–77), Roy R. Grinker, M.D., editor. I thank Dr. Grinker, chairman, and the members of the seminar for their stimulating discussion, which helped in developing the present version.

2. From the present viewpoint, therefore, contemporary sociological theories that focus on structural similarities "that make all societies in a sense alike" rather than on the differences such societies exhibit are of limited usefulness, unless, of course, the generalizations they achieve are based on all known societies.

3. A good deal of attention is now being paid to the problem of relating cultural process to genetic adaptation (see, for example, Dobzhansky 1962; Spuhler 1959; Washburn 1961). Although I have presented certain readily available facts regarding the microracial constitution of the communities under discussion, it has not been my intention to include a full discussion of this problem here.

21 /

COMMUNITY DEVELOPMENT
AND CULTURE

> The interdependencies in the intricate web of relationships within the individual organism, the intraspecific population, and the interspecific community point rather clearly to the evolutionary trend toward a balanced integration, toleration, co-existence, and comparative mutualism between the parts of all coordinated levels of organization, from the smallest gene and enzyme units of life to the largest global ecosystem.
>
> Alfred E. Emerson (1965: 63)

The question that interests us in this last chapter of our explorations is a very basic one. Of course, we need to know what human populations do, when, and under what circumstances. But more especially we need to discover what human populations do that ensures or contributes to their functional adaptation and optimum self-actualization. In other words, we are interested in learning how we can live in groups and resolve our sociocultural problems so as to maximize our long-term self-fulfilling behavior within the potentialities and limitations of our human situation.[1]

Culture as a Problem-Solving Tool

Our findings indicate that each natural process, including the distinctively human symbolizing process, operates within its own field or orbit, according to rules, potentialities, and limitations that have been built by nature into that orbit. If men wish to play the game of life with maximum success as human beings— indeed, if they wish only to avoid extinction as a species—they must discover the rules of their orbit and learn to operate in terms of them.

The time is running out when human populations may depend on trial and error as a modus vivendi. Man-made changes in our technologies and in our environments have altered the problematic situations we now face as viable communities and as individual members of such social entities. Rates of change are accelerating. The hit-or-miss approach of traditionally non-industrialized communities can no longer be expected to serve the problem-solving imperatives of modern man. Circumstances indicate that, whether or not we seek it, we need a more precise tool if we would effectively resolve our urgent social problems.

Explorations recorded in this volume suggest that this tool is already within our grasp. Like the rough implements made by Old Stone Age man, it may be crude and inefficient compared to its ultimate potential. Nonetheless a move in the appropriate direction has been made. A design has emerged that men living in modern societies may use to discover, formulate, and resolve effectively their essentially human problems.

I refer, of course, to the systematic situational approach toward problem solving by means of culture-building and culture-changing devices that has been illustrated in the behavior of communities throughout this volume. I emphasize again that this is a group process. Its success depends on the effectiveness with which community members are able to tap and utilize, for long-range biosocial purposes, the conscious and unconscious wisdom of the group. It hinges on how ingeniously a community is able to foster and focus in appropriate long-range directions the roles, talents, and creativity of its individual members.

Evaluating the Culture of a Community

Have our explorations revealed any leads that might help a community seeking guidance toward wise choices favoring its own optimal development? The evidence suggests that, if we wish to evaluate human cultures in a way that will further our interests, we need to divest ourselves of the idea that ancient man was inferior to medieval and contemporary peoples because he seems to have had a simpler (or more "primitive") culture. Discoveries regarding Stonehenge (Hawkins 1965), the Teotihuacan pyramids (Gamio, *et al.* 1922), and many other archaeological sites (Heizer 1966) reveal the complex mathematical and technological basis of many early civilizations. Evidence of the acute powers of observation of hunting, fishing, and early agricultural peoples is widespread. We have already noted the skill with which Polynesian navigators sailed over vast stretches of open ocean and discovered remote island groups. And we may cite also the observational perspicuity of Upper Paleolithic hunters as revealed by cave paintings of animals in motion. Our study of the natives of Australia and other tribal groups demonstrates that a simple technology does not preclude an elaborate social structure. Moreover, Whorf's analysis of the Hopi grammar reveals that they have a vehicle of abstract expression "often far beyond our power to follow."

Obviously contemporary man has no monopoly in ingenuity or talent. In other words, empirical evidence reveals that neither the ancient classical cultures nor modern industrial technologies are necessarily the only roads to "civilization," nor even the most effective ways to achieve that end. Comparison of the cultures of our selected communities, perceived situationally, suggests that the concept of homeostasis, borrowed from ecology and applied to the culture of a human community, affords a more reliable and universally applicable measuring device if we wish to evaluate the culture of a community. Not only may we begin to apply such a measuring device to the cultures of contemporary populations, but with the help of history, archaeology, literature, folklore, linguistics, values analysis, and other approaches, we may use it to determine the relative cultural status of historic and prehistoric groups. (For a different approach to this problem, see Naroll 1956.)

A "Genuine" Culture

A promising guideline in this direction, and one that has not yet been exploited, is Edward Sapir's concept of the "genuine" culture. Edward Sapir used this term to designate a mature culture designed to fulfill the needs of its component individuals. In other words, he referred to the organized living pattern of a society whose institutions foster growth, development, and self-fulfillment in its members as *human beings* rather than tailoring them to an arbitrary stereotype such as the traditional concept of "progress." In Sapir's words (Mandelbaum 1949: 314–316):

> The genuine culture is not of necessity either high or low; it is merely inherently harmonious, balanced, self-satisfactory. It is the expression of a richly varied and yet somehow unified and consistent attitude toward life, an attitude which sees the significance of any one element of civilization in its relation to all others. It is, ideally speaking, a culture in which nothing is spiritually meaningless, in which no important part of the general functioning brings with it a sense of frustration, of misdirected or unsympathetic effort. It is not a spiritual hybrid of contradictory patches, of water-tight compartments of consciousness that avoid participation in a harmonious synthesis. . . . A genuine culture cannot be defined as a sum of abstractly desirable ends, as a mechanism. It must be looked upon as a sturdy plant growth, each remotest leaf and twig of which is organically fed by the sap at the core. . . . A culture that does not build itself out of the central interests and desires of its bearers, that works from general ends to the individual, is an external culture. . . . The genuine culture is internal, it works from the individual to ends.

John W. Gardner (1961) offers a suggestion regarding institutions that may contribute to the fulfillment of the individual. Each has its own purposes and preoccupations, but above all, an institution should foster the development toward excellence and self-renewal of the individuals that compose it. Does our comparative situational analysis of several cultures reinforce or contribute to this approach?

A New Concept of Culture and Community Welfare

Our findings and others suggest a new concept of community welfare from a long-range point of view. Human welfare in its manifold expressions may be conceived as a total problem in the context of the local community's changing situation, as the group tries to organize its culture toward improved function as a problem-solving device.

This clinical approach to the community welfare problem as a whole supersedes the approach that treats community welfare as a series of disparate or loosely related problems, each to be treated separately. I have in mind problems referred to by such catch words as poverty, overpopulation, integration, crime, and conservation. By contrast, the emerging concept of community welfare emphasizes the dynamic interrelatedness, in space and through time, of the many aspects of group and individual living usually treated as separate welfare problems.

According to the new approach, community development may be perceived as a homeostatic cultural process involving the whole community and geared toward improved future function. Its trend may be explicitly stated as movement in the direction of optimum self-activation and self-renewal of the whole society in geographical and historical context. It underlines the genius of man as an evolving, problem-solving organism. It emphasizes the dynamic wholeness of an evolving local population, composed of groups of human beings uniquely related to one another through genetic, biosocial, psychological, and cultural ties.

A culture is thus not conceived here as something "given" or something that merely *happens* to people. Essentially a culture is conceived as the product of the teleonomic behavior of a human group in the context of the biologically based human need for self-fulfillment, not merely for survival. The trend is toward ordered resolution of the group's major living problems in situational context as these problems are perceived by the group. The situational context includes the whole effective environment of group behavior in historical context, geoecological as well as biosocial. Similarly, a human community may be conceived as uniquely related, by means of its culture, to its changing local setting viewed as a unique combination of natural resources idiosyncratically perceived, interpreted, and used (see, for example, Spoehr 1956: 93–102).

Role of the Common Man

Our researches indicate that if we would understand the cultures of mankind, viewed singly or as a total glorious human creation, we need to give more credit to the common sense and creativity—the problem-solving ability—of the common man. Time and time again the findings of archaeology and history, as well as the ethnography of contemporary peoples, document this point. Culture building, tailoring, consolidation, and styling to resolve group situational problems is a human community's most fundamental task. The penalty for bungling this business is dissolution of the society as an organized entity.

Our findings do not substantiate extreme diffusionist hypotheses that emphasize the rarity of human creativity and the spread of innovations from one or a few cultural centers. Nor do they document any of the determinist theories of culture from Marx through Huntington and Durkheim. To be sure, cultural creativity and change must operate within definite boundaries. But such checks are not set by the environment alone. Nor are they engendered by the socioeconomic structure alone, nor by the human biology and psyche in itself. They grow out of the nature and dynamics of culture—a process that always operates within the context of community action and setting, according to describable limitations and potentialities.

These findings are not new. They are the product of the inquiries of many scientists and scholars and the actions of technologists and administrators cooperating on common problems over a long period of time. Such workers also include colonial administrators, medical and public health workers, agricultural extensionists, nutritionists, Peace Corps and social workers. But these findings are by no means commonly accepted (see, for example, Erasmus 1967). Nor are their widespread implications at the practical or applied levels fully grasped and implemented.

Genuine Culture for a Price

We may now seriously consider a significant question: According to the findings of modern science, how may we define op-

erationally a healthy, viable community from a long-range remedial point of view?

Our researches suggest that every community has a job to do.
We have found that, from the culture-historical perspective, the
behavior of its members may be understood to a considerable
extent in terms of that job. The reward for doing a good job in
community terms is the establishment of a condition of balance
toward optimum group functioning—not for today or for the
presently living members only, but also for their children and
grandchildren. Accordingly, such a group would demonstrate a
marked tendency toward self-renewal under stress. The penalty
for doing a really bad job, let us say, is extinction—that is,
dispersal from its traditional habitat or death of the group as a
social entity. In such a case the group has not managed successfully its own self-actualization processes in relation to its life
situation.

For partial failure the community members pay in various
ways that spell minimal or partial fulfillment as a group. The
community survives but in a disturbed state (M. K. Opler 1956:
53; Fosberg 1963b: 264; J. Henry 1965). It cannot reestablish a
healthy equilibrium after stress and it remains off balance. Most
modern urban communities illustrate this type of disturbance.

As we have noted, each disturbed community has its own
unique way of expressing social malaise. The particular form
of expression depends on a complex of factors. Such factors include the community's relations to its environment, to other
communities, to its biologic and genetic endowment, and to its
culture. In attempting to evaluate a community's state of
"health" or "nonhealth," many interrelated factors have thus
been found relevant.

For example, if cultural understanding is the goal, the free-
floating anxiety among Hopi males, revealed by projective test
findings as well as by dream recordings and observations of behavior, should be considered in the context of the almost insolu-
ble living problem that Hopi men face as village-dwelling farmers in a high, semiarid environment. Hopiland not only suffers
from insufficient average annual precipitation but from the fact
that what rain there may be falls in summer rather than in

spring, when it is needed for germination of the crops. Moreover, precipitation is decreasing in quantity as a consequence of a natural desiccation cycle presently manifest throughout the American Southwest.

Perhaps such anxiety is the price that the Hopi pay, and choose to pay, for their preferred style of communal living. According to the index of community health suggested above, the traditional Hopi pueblos warrant a high rating. For more than fifteen centuries they have succeeded in developing a culture wherein self-actualization and self-renewal processes have been built into the very structure of social system, economy, ceremonies, art, values, and personality. They have also managed periodically to reestablish a cultural balance within their changing situation under various kinds and degrees of stress. (For a different approach to these facts, see Dorothy Eggan 1943; Edward P. Dozier 1964: 87).

How does this process come about? Microenvironmental analyses in relation to cultural studies suggest that a community's self-actualization problem is so complex and so dependent on highly specialized, detailed, esoteric, and even unconscious knowledge that only members themselves are in a favorable position to formulate their alternatives realistically and choose between them in order to resolve it. (For a different viewpoint, see Arensberg and Niehoff 1964.)

Recall the specialized knowledge and skills needed by the Lauan master fisherman and crop chief. All specialized leadership roles require training, detailed localized knowledge, and special skills for their successful activation, including notable feats of memory in nonliterate cultures.

The profit motive, cultural breakdown, emotional stress, and other factors have tended to divert the people of modern industrialized communities from an age-old concentration, as localized human groups, on successfully coping with their communal problematic situations. These problems involve group maintenance, reproduction, and ongoing self-actualization. The profit motive has engendered a certain concentration, as individuals or as small biological families, on successfully functioning in one of many industrial associations. Such institutions are organized on a regional, national, or global scale. Each corporation attempts to increase its efficiency and productiveness in relation to the modern international self-regulating market in order to report annually a "growing net profit."

This process is accepted unquestionably as inevitable and "good" by most western Europeans. Without scientific validation of its effects in terms of group welfare, billions of dollars are appropriated annually toward its promotion and acceleration in so-called underdeveloped countries by the United Nations, the United States, and other nations. Many community-development workers and social scientists are employed to implement and facilitate it, however unsuccessfully, at the village and rural community level.

A "Healthy" Community

Notable progress has been made in our understanding of a healthy *individual* from the medical and the psychiatric viewpoints. But because man is by nature a social, culture-creating animal, our answers to questions of health and welfare are incomplete unless they also encompass sociocultural facts and processes. Under these circumstances what may be used as a scientifically relevant index of community health?

Recent experiments in community welfare research indicate the direction in which a scientifically acceptable answer to this question may be found. These studies suggest that an adequate definition of a healthy, viable community should not be formulated in terms of a sum total of points scored along a number of unrelated scales. I refer, for example, to population censuses, educational status, public health scales, nutrition and standard-of-living indexes, alcoholism and drug addiction, crime and delinquency, and psychological-test findings. These researches suggest that a scientifically relevant concept of community health, when it emerges, may be phrased rather in terms of balance and order of interrelated processes. It will involve a cultural homeostasis in which individuals are considered in transactive relationship to one another and to a genetically sound, evolving population in its changing environment.

This emerging view of community welfare as a total process reinforces the concept of man as an evolving social organism who can find fulfillment as a human being only through tailoring his culture to healthy community living perceived situationally. Accordingly, social man may be viewed as comprising the dominant species in a community composed of many species of animals, plants, and microorganisms transacting with one another and with a changing environment specific to a unique area and region of the earth. Man is not divorced from nature. He is a member of a species that forms an integral part of an evolving ecosystem.

Standards of Community Health

In this context applied ecology affords a lead that has been found useful by applied social scientists working on community welfare problems. This clue is the concept of natural-resources conservation and development. Sustained-yield forestry is a method of tree cultivation by which all parts of a forest, perceived as an ecological community, are subordinated in the direction of long-range production of healthy timber. In cutting, pruning, and lumbering, the sustained optimum health and yield of the whole forest are primary considerations. A similar approach underlies soil- and moisture-conservation practices, which, during the last forty years, have proven markedly successful in increasing the long-range fertility and potential yield of thousands of soil conservation districts in the United States and elsewhere.

Extending the natural-resources conservation idea to include *human* resources, we may pinpoint a conceptual tool of considerable promise. Accordingly, a healthy, viable community would be viewed as one in which long-range community living would be perceived and sought, not for the *greatest* possible *number* of human beings, but rather for the *optimal number* that in the long run would foster balanced healthy group life (that is, a "genuine" culture) in transaction with its effective environment. Within this context the problem of family planning and population control might be regarded as a community's responsibility to itself rather than a strictly family or religious concern. Today's runaway population problem might thus be broken down into a multitude of local practical problems in community development and welfare, to be perceived by each group as an integral part of its long-range communal health picture.

Within this conceptual frame, as John W. Gardner (1961), Harry A. Overstreet (1949), E. A. Gutkind (1956), Lawrence K. Frank (1951), and others have emphasized, community health demands that the social institutions, accepted behavior patterns, attitudes, and values of a community pass a test of their fitness for human beings as evolving, culture-creating organisms in community context—and not vice versa. It demands that a culture be recognized explicitly as *man-made*. Culture is constantly in process of being critically reviewed, revamped, and re-created by community members according to their perception of their world. This process may be manipulated by the group itself in the direction of greater fitness for healthy community living.

Tentative Rules for Community Problem Solving

Our findings suggest a few general principles for use by a local community that is genuinely interested in achieving successful long-range practical solutions to its living problems. I do not have in mind those groups with other interests, such as the propagation of dated ideologies perceived as universal in scope or in implementing dated political structures on a worldwide scale. The emerging rules apply only to flexible community decision making in the direction of optimal group function. Such group action would be keyed to implement practical solutions designed to resolve local problematic situations related to universal social problems. Some of these rules might be:

1. A community might consider using its traditional decision-making devices and its culture as tools to resolve its changing problematic situation in relation to its universal social problems as common to the human species.

2. In choosing a course of action to follow, especially in times of rapid change, the members might aim to discover and formulate as many of the possible alternatives and the available community resources, natural and human, as possible. It would thus be in an advantageous position to select, on the basis of factual knowledge, one or more courses most likely to engender improved organization in the direction of probable future function.

3. The group might try to develop and use more effectively its human resources, including hereditary talents of all its subgroups, in appropriate decision-making and leadership roles.

4. In considering the development of all its human resources, especially in a time of rapid change and technological development, the members of a community might try to realize that no one can predict with complete confidence the range of problematic situations that the next generation will have to face and resolve in the interests of successful community living. Accordingly, training in problem solving under changing conditions might be considered an appropriate type of educational experience on which to build a curriculum.

5. A lesson that our comparative ecohistorical study of a number of communities in various parts of the world reveals is this: A "genuine" culture is an ordered human way of life built locally by a human group to unique situational specifications. It is also a sharp problem-solving tool. Therefore, if practical, flexible solutions are to be achieved, decision making and problem solving regarding focal community problems must remain an active voluntary function of the group itself, responsive to its daily changing situations. Attempts to remove such roles and functions out of the local group are doomed in the long run to failure. Such failure may be experienced in terms of community disorganization and breakdown of the cultural developmental process. It may also be expressed in retardation or disturbance of the personality maturation processes.

6. Thus, a lesson that comparative culture history teaches is this: The community may import such specialists as technicians, scientists and teachers to supplement and augment its own re-

sources. The basic decision-making roles, institutions, and culture-changing devices, however, should be homemade and built into the community's own culture if community development toward an optimal, self-renewing life way in situational context be the aim.

Our findings suggest that a "healthy" community is a community that uses its culture as a problem-solving medium and implements culture process to function according to its own dynamic. A "healthy" community habitually applies its traditional culture patterns to new situations and changes them realistically in order to activate its species biogram and to resolve its changing problematic situations appropriately.

Conclusion

Above all, our findings suggest that "genuine" mature cultures do not evolve along any single line of development. Neither do they "advance" by universal stages toward a predetermined state. Each and every one has been built, tailored, and consolidated actively and purposively by a human group. A culture is essentially a complex tool by which a human group attempts to resolve its universal human problems. These involve survival and self-actualization through the generations by perceiving, facing, and resolving the group's changing problematic situations.

It matters not how enchanted we may be with the ways and relationship patterns of our own cultures. It matters not how much we may wish to bestow them on other societies that we perceive as culturally "deprived" or "underprivileged" because they do not have what we have. In the business of systematically applying the findings from comparative culture history to urgent social problems, all such considerations prove to be irrelevant. Culture history teaches us that each human population has by nature the built-in resources and the ultimate responsibility for perceiving its problems and building its own culture. Only its members themselves may orient the culture, whether for or against their own interests and welfare. In the long run only the community itself—whether local, regional, or world-wide—has the real power to choose for better or worse and to act out of its own choice in terms of its culture.

Note

1. Some of the ideas in this chapter were presented at the Fifth International Congress of Anthropological and Ethnological Sciences in Philadelphia, September 1956 (see Thompson 1960a: 769–774).

REFERENCES

Abel, Wilhelm. *Agrarkrisen und Agrarkonjunktur in Mitteleuropa vom 13. bis zum 19. Jahrhundert.* Berlin: P. Parey, 1935.
———. "Kurze Geschichte der Agrarverfassung," *Schriftenreihe der Landeszentrale für Heimatdienst in Niedersachsen.* Hanover: Rock & Co., 1956.
Adam of Bremen. *History of the Archbishops of Hamburg-Bremen.* Trans. Francis J. Tschan. New York: Columbia University Press, 1959.
Agogino, George A. "New Radiocarbon Date for the Folsom Complex," *Current Anthropology,* 4(1):113–114, 1963.
Allen, F. W., and W. Schaeffer. "The Distribution of the Human Blood Groups Among the Navajos and Pueblo Indians of the Southwest," *University of New Mexico Bulletin,* 4:1–29, 1935.
Ames, Adelbert, Jr. *The Morning Notes . . .* Ed. Hadley Cantril. New Brunswick, N. J.: Rutgers University Press, 1960.
Anson, George. *A Voyage Round the World, in the Years 1740, 1, 2, 3, 4.* Comp. Richard Walter. London: John and Paul Knapton, 1748.
Arbman, Holger. *The Vikings.* Trans. A. Binns. Ed. Glyn Daniel. New York: Praeger, 1961.
Arensberg, Conrad M., and Solon T. Kimball. *Culture and Community.* New York: Harcourt, Brace & World, 1965.
———, and Arthur H. Niehoff. *Introducing Social Change: A Manual for Americans Overseas.* Chicago: Aldine, 1964.
Arent, A. Margaret, trans. *The Laxdoela Saga.* Seattle: University of Washington Press, 1964.

Ashley, William James. *Surveys, Historic and Economic.* London: Longmans, 1900.

Barnett, Homer G. *Palauan Society: A Study of Contemporary Native Life in the Palau Islands.* Eugene: University of Oregon Press, 1949.

————. *Innovation: The Basis of Cultural Change.* New York: McGraw-Hill, 1953.

————. *Anthropology in Administration.* New York: Harper & Row, 1956.

Barrère, Dorothy B. "Cosmogonic Genealogies of Hawaii," *Journal of the Polynesian Society,* 70(4):419–428, 1961.

Bates, Marston. *The Forest and the Sea: A Look at the Economy of Nature and the Ecology of Man.* New York: Random House, 1960.

Beckwith, Martha W., trans. and ed. *The Kumulipo: A Hawaiian Creation Chant.* Chicago: University of Chicago Press, 1951.

Bede, the Honorable. *The Ecclesiastical History of the English Nation.* Ernest Rhys, ed. New York: Dutton, Everyman's Library, 1916.

Below, Georg Anton Hugo von. "Geschichte der deutschen Landwirtschaft des Mittelalters in ihren Grundzügen," *Quellen und Forschungen zur Agrargeschichte.* Bd. 18. Stuttgart: Gustav Fischer, 1966.

Bird, Junius B. "Littorina Littorea: Occurrence in a Northern Newfoundland Beach Terrace, Predating Norse Settlements" *Science,* 159(3810):114, 1968.

Boas, Franz. "The Aims of Anthropological Research," *Race, Language and Culture.* New York: Macmillan, 1940.

Bolton, Herbert Eugene. *Rim of Christendom: A Biography of Eusebio Francisco Kino, Pacific Coast Pioneer.* New York: Russell and Russell, 1960.

Bowen, E. G. "The Racial Geography of Europe at the Dawn of the Age of Metal," *Journal of the Royal Anthropological Institute of Great Britain and Ireland,* 61:349–356, 1931.

Boyd, Harold J., and Shirley A. Allison. "Irrigation to the Navajo Tribe," *Reclamation Era.* Washington, D. C.: Department of the Interior, 1965.

Boyd, William C., and Lyle G. Boyd. "Blood Groups of the Ramah Navahos," *American Journal of Physical Anthropology,* 7:569–574, 1949.

Brace, C. Loring. "The Fate of the 'Classic' Neanderthals: A Consideration of Hominid Catastrophism," *Current Anthropology,* 5(1): 3–43, 1964.

Bronsted, Johannes. *The Vikings*. Kalle Skov, trans. Baltimore: Penguin Books, 1965.

Brüning, Kurt. *Atlas Niedersachsen. Deutscher Planungsatlas gegliedert nach den deutschen Ländern*. Bd. 2 (Niedersächsisches Amt für Landesplanung und Statistik. Reihe K, Bd. nr. 9). Bremen: Walter Dorn, 1950.

Bryan, Alan Lyle. "Paleo-American Prehistory," *Occasional Papers of the Idaho State University Museum* No. 16, Pocatello, Idaho, 1965.

Buck, Peter H. (*Te Rangi Hiroa*) *Vikings of the Sunrise*. New York: Stokes, 1938.

———. "Arts and Crafts of Hawaii," *Bishop Museum Special Publication* 45, Honolulu, 1957.

Bulmer, S. "Radiocarbon Dates from New Guinea," *Journal of the Polynesian Society*, 73:327–328, 1964.

Bunzel, Ruth L. "The Pueblo Potter: A Study of Creative Imagination in Primitive Art," *Columbia University Contributions to Anthropology* 8, New York, 1929.

Bureau of Indian Affairs. *The Navajo*. Washington, D. C.: Department of the Interior, 1963a.

———. *U. S. Indian Population* (1962) and *Land* (1963). Washington, D. C.: Department of the Interior, 1963b.

———. *Information Concerning the Papago Indian Tribe*. Washington, D. C.: Department of the Interior, 1966. (Mimeo.)

Burger, Henry G. "Directed Change of the Culture Core," *American Anthropologist*, 67: 489–494, 1965.

Butzer, Karl W. "Climatic Change in Arid Regions Since the Pliocene," *A History of Land Use in Arid Regions*. Paris: UNESCO, 1961.

———. *Environment and Archeology: An Introduction to Pleistocene Geography*. Chicago: Aldine, 1964.

Caesar, Julius. *The Conquest of Gaul*. Trans. S. A. Handford. Baltimore: Penguin Books, 1951.

Campbell, J. K. *Honour, Family, and Patronage: A Study of Institutions and Moral Values in a Greek Mountain Community*. Oxford: Clarendon Press, 1964.

Capell, A., and R. H. Lester. "Local Divisions and Movements in Fiji," *Oceania*, 11:313–341; 12:21–48, 1941–1942.

———. "Kinship in Fiji," *Oceania*, 15:171–200; 16:109–143, 234–253, 297–318, 1945–1946.

Carter, George Francis. "Plant Geography and Culture History in the American Southwest," *Viking Fund Publications in Anthropology* 5, New York, 1945.

Castetter, Edward F., and Willis H. Bell. *Pima and Papago Indian Agriculture.* Albuquerque: University of New Mexico Press, 1942.

Chadwick, Hector Munro. *The Cult of Othin: An Essay in the Ancient Religion of the North.* London: Clay, 1899.

———. *The Origin of the English Nation.* Cambridge, England: Cambridge University Press, 1907.

———. *The Heroic Age.* Cambridge, England: Cambridge University Press, 1912.

Chang, Kwang-chih, Wilhelm G. Solheim II, and George W. Grace. "Movements of the Malayo-Polynesians: 1500 B.C. to A.D. 500," *Current Anthropology,* 5(5):359–406, 1964.

Chard, C. S. "Wurzeln der amerikanischen Frühkulturen," *Saeculum,* 14:170–178, 1963.

Childe, V. Gordon. "The Forest Cultures of Northern Europe," *Journal of the Royal Anthropological Institute of Great Britain and Ireland,* 61:325–348, 1931.

———. "Prehistoric Migrations in Europe," Instituttet for Sammenlignende Kulturforskning Publikationer. Serie A: Forelesninger. 20. Oslo: H. Aschehoug, 1950.

———. *Social Evolution.* New York: Schuman, 1951.

Clark, John Grahame Douglas. *The Mesolithic Settlement of Northern Europe.* Cambridge, England: Cambridge University Press, 1936.

———. *Prehistoric Europe: The Economic Basis.* New York: Philosophical Library, 1952.

———. *World Prehistory: An Outline.* Cambridge, England: Cambridge University Press, 1962.

Coe, Joffre L. "The Formative Cultures of the Carolina Piedmont," *Transactions of the American Philosophical Society,* 54(5), 1964.

Colony of Fiji. *Report on the Census of the Population,* 1956. Legislative Council Paper No. 1. Suva Fiji: Government Press, 1958.

Comte, Auguste. *The Positive Philosophy of Auguste Comte.* Trans. Harriet Martineau. New York: Blanchard, 1958.

Coon, Carleton Stevens. *The Races of Europe.* New York: Macmillan, 1939.

———. *The Origin of Races.* New York: Knopf, 1962.

———. Personal correspondence. 1968.

Count, Earl. "The Biological Basis of Human Sociality," *American Anthropologist,* 60:1049–1085, 1958.

Craigie, Sir William A. *The Religion of Ancient Scandinavia.* London: Constable, 1914.

———. *The Icelandic Sagas.* Cambridge, England: Cambridge University Press, 1933.

Darling, Frank Fraser. *West Highland Survey: An Essay in Human Ecology.* Oxford: Oxford University Press, 1955.

Davenport, William H. "Political Consequences of the 'Hawaiian Cultural Revolution.'" Paper presented at the annual meeting of the American Anthropological Association, 1964.

Davidson, H. R. Ellis. *Gods and Myths of Northern Europe.* Baltimore: Penguin Books, 1964.

Densmore, Frances. "Music in Its Relation to the Religious Thought of the Teton Sioux," *Holmes Anniversary Volume: Anthropological Essays Presented to William Henry Holmes.* Washington, D.C.: Bryan Press, 1916. Pp. 67–79.

————. "American Indian Poetry," *American Anthropologist,* 28: 447–449, 1926.

————. "Papago Music," *Smithsonian Institution: Bureau of American Ethnology Bulletin* 90, 1929.

Dewey, John, and Arthur F. Bentley. *Knowing and the Known.* Boston: Beacon Press, 1949.

Dobyns, Henry F. "Thirsty Indians: Introduction of Wells Among People of an Arid Region," *Human Organization,* 11:33–36, 1952.

Dobzhansky, Theodosius. *Mankind Evolving: The Evolution of the Human Species.* New Haven, Conn: Yale University Press, 1962.

Donegani, Joyce A., N. Dungal, Elizabeth W. Ikin, and A. E. Mourant. "Blood Groups of the Icelanders," *Annals of Eugenics,* 15:147–152, 1950.

Dozier, Edward P. "Resistance to Acculturation and Assimilation in an Indian Pueblo," *American Anthropologist,* 53:56–66, 1951.

————. "The Hopi-Tewa of Arizona," *University of California Publications in American Archaeology and Ethnology,* 44(3):259–376, 1954.

————. "The Pueblo Indians of the Southwest," *Current Anthropology,* 5(2):79–97, 1964.

Du Chaillu, Paul Belloni. *The Viking Age: The Early History, Manners, and Customs of the Ancestors of the English-Speaking Nations.* New York: Scribner, 1889.

Durkheim, Emile. *Suicide: A Study in Sociology.* Trans. John A. Spaulding and George Simpson. Glencoe, Illinois: Free Press, 1951.

————, and Marcel Mauss. *Primitive Classification.* Trans. and ed. Rodney Needham. Chicago: University of Chicago Press, 1963.

Eggan, Dorothy. "The General Problem of Hopi Adjustment," *American Anthropologist,* 45:357–373, 1943.

Eggan, Frederick R., ed. *Social Anthropology of North American Tribes.* Chicago: University of Chicago Press, 1937.

————. *Social Organization of the Western Pueblos*. Chicago: University of Chicago Press, 1950.

Einarsson, Stéfan. *A History of Icelandic Literature*. Baltimore: Johns Hopkins, 1957.

Eldjárn, Kristján. *Ancient Icelandic Art*. Munich: Hanns Reich, 1957.

Elkin, A. P. *The Australian Aborigines*. Garden City, N.Y.: Anchor Books, 1964.

Elwin, Verrier. *The Muria and Their Ghotul*. Bombay: Oxford University Press, 1947.

————. *The Religion of an Indian Tribe*. Bombay: Oxford University Press, 1955.

Emerson, Alfred E. "Human Cultural Evolution and Its Relation to Organic Evolution of Insect Societies," *Social Change in Developing Areas*. Eds. H. R. Barringer, G. I. Blanksten, and R. W. Mack. Cambridge, Massachusetts: Schenkman, 1965.

Emory, Kenneth P., W. J. Bonk, and Y. H. Sinoto. "Hawaiian Archaeology: Fishhooks," *Bishop Museum Special Publication 47*, Honolulu, 1959.

Erasmus, Charles J. *Man Takes Control: Cultural Development and American Aid*. Minneapolis: University of Minnesota Press, 1961.

————. "Review of *Social Change in Developing Areas: A Reinterpretation of Evolutionary Theory*. Barringer, Blanksten, and Mack, eds. (1965)," *American Anthropologist*, 69:416–417, 1967.

Evans-Pritchard, E. E. *The Nuer*. Oxford: Clarendon Press, 1940.

Fewkes, J. Walter. "Hopi Katchinas," *Annual Report of the Bureau of American Ethnology*, 21:3–126, 1903.

————. "The Sun's Influence on the Form of Hopi Pueblos," *American Anthropologist*, 8:88–100, 1906.

Firth, Raymond W. "The Work of the Gods in Tikopia," *London School of Economics Monographs on Social Anthropology 1–2*. London: Lund, Humphries, 1940.

————. *Social Change in Tikopia: Re-study of a Polynesian Community After a Generation*. New York: Macmillan, 1959.

————. *We, the Tikopia: A Sociological Study of Kinship in Primitive Polynesia*. London: G. Allen, 1961.

Fortes, Meyer. "The Structure of Unilineal Descent Groups," *American Anthropologist*, 55:17–59, 1953.

Fortune, Reo F. *Sorcerers of Dobu*. Introduction, B. Malinowski. New York: Dutton, 1932.

Fosberg, F. Raymond. "Disturbance in Island Ecosystems," *Pacific Basin Biogeography: A Symposium*. Ed. J. L. Grassett. Honolulu: Bishop Museum, 1963a.

————. "The Island Ecosystem," *Man's Place in the Island Ecosystem.* Ed. F. R. Fosberg. Honolulu: Bishop Museum, 1963b.

Foulkes, David. *The Psychology of Sleep.* New York: Scribner, 1966.

Frank, Lawrence K. *Nature and Human Nature: Man's New Image of Himself.* New Brunswick, N.J.: Rutgers University Press, 1951.

Frankenberg, Ronald. *The Social Anthropology of Complex Societies.* Ed. Michael Banton. New York: Praeger, 1966.

Freeman, Otis W., ed. *Geography of the Pacific.* New York: Wiley, 1951.

Freycinet, Louis de. *Voyage autour du monde.* Paris: Imprimerie Royale, Vol. 2, 1829.

Gabel, Norman E. "A Comparative Racial Study of the Papago," *University of New Mexico Publications in Anthropology* 4, Albuquerque, 1949.

————. "A Racial Study of the Fijians," *Anthropological Records, University of California,* 20(1):1–44, 1958.

Gamio, Manuel, *et al. La población del Valle de Teotihuacán.* México D.F.: Talleres Gráficos de la Secretaria de Educación Pública, 1922.

Garcia, Francisco. "Vida y martirio de el venerable Padre Diego Luis de Sanvitores" (Madrid, 1683), *Guam Recorder.* Trans. Margaret Higgins. Agaña, Guam, 14:1 (April), 1937.

Gardner, John W. *Excellence: Can We Be Equal and Excellent Too?* New York: Harper & Row, 1961.

Garn, Stanley M. *Human Races.* Springfield, Ill.: Thomas, 1961.

Geddes, W. R. "Fijian Social Structure in a Period of Transition," *Anthropology in the South Seas.* Eds. J. D. Freeman and W. R. Geddes. New Plymouth, New Zealand: Thomas Avery, 1959.

Gibbon, Edward. *The Decline and Fall of the Roman Empire.* New York: Modern Library, 1932.

Gifford, E. W. "Anthropological Problems in Fiji," *Journal of the Polynesian Society,* 60:122–129, 1951a.

————. "Archaeological Excavations in Fiji," *Anthropological Records, University of California,* 13(3), 1951b.

Goldenweiser, Alexander A. "The Principle of Limited Possibilities in the Development of Culture," *Journal of American Folklore,* 26:259–290, 1913.

————. *Anthropology: An Introduction to Primitive Culture.* New York: F. S. Crofts, 1937.

Goodenough, Donald R. "The Nature and Functions of Sleep," *Science,* 153(3738):854–855, 1966.

Goodenough, Ward H. "Oceania and the Problem of Controls in the

Study of Cultural and Human Evolution," *Journal of the Polynesian Society*, 66(2):146–155, 1957.

Grigson, W. V. *The Maria Gonds of Bastar*. London: Oxford University Press, 1938.

Grimal, Pierre. *The Civilization of Rome*. Trans. W. S. Maguinness. New York: Simon and Schuster, 1963.

Grinker, Roy R., ed. *Toward a Unified Theory of Human Behavior*. New York: Basic Books, 1967.

Grönbech, Vilhelm Peter. *The Culture of the Teutons*. Trans. William Worster. London: H. Milford, 1931.

Groves, Murray. "The Nature of Fijian Society: A Review Article," *Journal of the Polynesian Society*, 72:272–291, 1963.

Gutkind, E. A. "Our World From the Air: Conflict and Adaptation," *Man's Role in Changing the Face of the Earth*. Ed. William L. Thomas, Jr. Chicago: University of Chicago Press, 1956. Pp. 1–44.

Hack, J. T. "The Changing Physical Environment of the Hopi Indians," *Peabody Museum Papers*, 35. *Reports of the Awatovi Expedition* 2: Harvard University, 1942.

Hackenberg, Robert A. "Economic Alternatives in Arid Lands: A Case Study of the Pima and Papago Indians," *Ethnology*, 1(2): 186–196, 1962.

Hall, Edward T., Jr. "Recent Clues to Athapascan Prehistory in the Southwest," *American Anthropologist*, 46:98–105, 1944.

——. *The Silent Language*. Garden City, N.Y.: Doubleday, 1959.

Hallberg, Peter. *The Icelandic Saga*. Trans. Paul Schach. Lincoln: University of Nebraska Press, 1962.

Hallowell, A. Irving. "Myth, Culture and Personality," *American Anthropologist*, 49:544–556, 1947.

——. "The Precultural Foundations of Human Adaptation," *Social Life of Early Man*. Ed. Sherwood L. Washburn. Chicago: Aldine, 1961.

Handy, Edward S. C. "The Native Culture in the Marquesas," *Bishop Museum Bulletin* 9, Honolulu, 1923.

——. *Cultural Revolution in Hawaii*. New York: American Council, Institute of Pacific Relations, 1931.

——. "Dreaming in Relation to Spirit Kindred and Sickness in Hawaii," *Essays in Anthropology Presented to A. L. Kroeber*. Berkeley: University of California Press, 1936. Pp. 119–127.

——. "The Hawaiian Planter: His Plants, Methods and Areas of Cultivation," *Bishop Museum Bulletin* 161, Honolulu, 1940a. Vol. 1.

——. "Perspectives in Polynesian Religion," *Memoirs of the Polynesian Society*, 49:309–372, 1940b.

————, and Mary Kawena Pukui. *The Polynesian Family System of Ka'u, Hawaii*. Wellington, New Zealand: The Polynesian Society, 1958.

————, M. K. Pukui, and K. Livermore. "Outline of Hawaiian Physical Therapeutics," *Bishop Museum Bulletin* 126, Honolulu, 1934.

Hannesson, Gudmundur. *Körpermasze und Körperproportionen der Isländer: Beitrag zur Anthropologie Islands*. Reykjavík: Fjelagsprentsmidjan, 1925.

Hardebeck, Wilhelm. "Uebersicht und beschreibung der früh- und vorgeschichtlichen Erd- und Steindenkmäler, Leichenfelder, Urnenfriedhöfe, Landwehren, Ringwällen und Ansiedelungsplätze im Kreise Bersenbrück," *Mitteilungen des Vereins für Geschichte und Altertumskunde des Hasegaus*, Heft 1, 2 Aufl., Lingen, 1902.

Haring, Douglas G., and Mary E. Johnson. *Order and Possibility in Social Life*. New York: Smith, 1940.

Hassrick, Royal B. "Teton Dakota Kinship System," *American Anthropologist*, 46:338–347, 1944.

Haury, Emil W. *The Stratigraphy and Archaeology of Ventana Cave, Arizona*. Tucson: University of Arizona Press, 1950.

Havighurst, Robert J., and Bernice L. Neugarten. *American Indian and White Children: A Sociopsychological Investigation*. Chicago: University of Chicago Press, 1955.

Hawkes, C. F. C. *The Prehistoric Foundations of Europe to the Mycenean Age*. London: Methuen, 1940.

Hawkins, Gerald S. *Stonehenge Decoded*. Collaborator, John B. White. Garden City, N. Y.: Doubleday, 1965.

Haynes, C. V. "Fluted Projectile Points: Their Age and Dispersion," *Science*, 145(3639):1408–1413, 1964.

Heizer, Robert F. "Ancient Heavy Transport, Methods and Achievements," *Science*, 153 (3738): 821–830, 1966.

Henry, Jules. *Culture Against Man*. New York: Random House, 1965.

Henry, William E. "The Thematic Apperception Technique in the Study of Culture-Personality Relations," *Genetic Psychology Monographs*, 35:3–135, 1947.

————. *The Analysis of Fantasy: The Thematic Apperception Technique in the Study of Personality*. New York: Wiley, 1956.

Hermannsson, Halldór, ed. and trans. "*The Book of the Icelanders*, by Are Thorgilsson," *Islandica*. Ithaca: Cornell University, 1930. Vol. 20.

Hillaby, John. "Newly Found Australian Tribe Is Living in Stone Age Culture," *The New York Times*, January 8, 1965.

Hocart, A. M. "Lau Islands, Fiji," *Bishop Museum Bulletin* 62, Honolulu, 1929.

Hollander, Lee M., ed. and trans. *The Poetic Edda*. Austin: University of Texas Press, 1962.

Hopi Indian Agency. *Reservation Information for Publication Purposes*. Washington, D.C.: Department of the Interior, 1966.

Hornbostel, Hans G. "Field Notes on the Marianas Islands." Unpublished manuscript, Honolulu: Bishop Museum Library, n.d.

Howard, Alan. "Plasticity, Achievement and Adaptation in Developing Economies," *Human Organization*, 25(4):265–272, 1966.

Howells, W. W. "Anthropometry and Blood Types in Fiji and the Solomon Islands," *Anthropological Papers, American Museum of Natural History*, New York, 1933. Vol. 33, Pt. 4.

———, and W. Lloyd Warner. "Anthropometry of the Natives of Arnhem Land and the Australian Race Problem," *Papers of the Peabody Museum*, Harvard University 16(1), 1937.

Hubert, Henri. *The Rise of the Celts*. London: Routledge & Kegan Paul, 1934a.

——— *The Greatness and Decline of the Celts*. London: Routledge & Kegan Paul, 1934b.

Hubert, V. "An Introduction to Hopi Pottery Design," *Museum Notes of the Museum of Northern Arizona*, 10(1):1–4, 1937.

Huebner, Rudolf. *A History of Germanic Private Law*. Trans. F. S. Philbrick. Boston: Little Brown, 1918.

Huntington, Ellsworth. *Mainsprings of Civilization*. New York: Wiley, 1945.

Ibn Fadhlan. "The Vikings Abroad and at Home," *A Reader in General Anthropology*. Ed. Carleton S. Coon. New York: Holt, Rinehart and Winston, 1948. Pp. 410–416.

Jacob-Friesen, K. H. "Kultur und Wirtschaft in urgeschichtlicher Zeit," *Das Land Niedersachsen: Gegenwart und Tradition*. Hanover: Kerber, 1955.

———. "Einführung in niedersachsens Urgeschichte," Teil 1, *Veröffentlichungen der urgeschichtlichen Sammlungen des Landesmuseums zu Hannover*, Hildesheim 15:1–204, 1959.

Jones, Gwyn, trans. *Egil's Saga*. Syracuse, N. Y.: Syracuse University Press, 1960.

Joseph, Alice, Rosamond B. Spicer, and Jane Chesky. *The Desert People: A Study of the Papago Indians*. Chicago: University of Chicago Press, 1949.

Judd, Henry P. *The Hawaiian Language*. Honolulu: Star Bulletin, 1939.

Kamakau, Samuel M. *Ka poʿe kahiko: The People of Old* Trans. M. K. Pukui. Ed. D. B. Barrère. *Bishop Museum Special Publication* 51, Honolulu, 1964.

Kelly, William H. *The Papago Indians of Arizona: A Population and Economic Study.* Tucson: University of Arizona Bureau of Ethnic Research, 1963.

————. Personal correspondence, 1967.

Kemnitzer, Luis S. "Whiteman Medicine, Indian Medicine, and Indian Identity on Pine Ridge Reservation, South Dakota." Paper presented at the annual meeting of the Society for Applied Anthropology, Washington, D.C., May 6, 1967.

Kisch, Guido. *Sachsenspiegel and Bible: Researches in the Source History of the Sachsenspiegel and the Influence of the Bible on Mediaeval German Law.* Notre Dame, Ind.: University of Notre Dame, 1941.

Klindt-Jensen, Ole. *Denmark Before the Vikings.* Trans. Eva and David Wilson. Ed. Glyn Daniel. New York: Praeger, 1957.

Kluckhohn, Clyde, and Charles Griffith. "Population Genetics and Social Anthropology," *Cold Spring Harbor Symposium on Quantitative Biology,* 15:401–408, 1950.

————, and Dorothea C. Leighton. *The Navaho.* Cambridge, Mass.: Harvard University Press, 1946.

Kluckhohn, Florence Rockwood. "The Participant-Observer Technique in Small Communities," *American Journal of Sociology,* 46(3):331–343, 1940.

Koch, Hal. "Paganism and Christianity," *Scandinavia Past and Present.* Eds. J. Bukdahl, *et al.* Odense, Denmark: Arnkrone, 1959. Vol 1.

Kroeber, A. L., and Clyde Kluckhohn. "Culture: A Critical Review of Concepts and Definitions," *Papers of the Peabody Museum,* Harvard University, Vol. 47 (1), 1952.

Krüsselmann, Wilhelm, *Siedlungs-, Wirtschafts- und Sozialgeschichte des Kirchspiels Ankum bis zum Ausgang des 16 Jahrhunderts. Eine Beitrag zur Geschichte des Osnabrücker Landes.* Doctoral Disc. Münster, Quakenbrück: R. Kleinert, 1937.

Kubie, L. S. "Some Implications for Psychoanalysis of Modern Concepts of the Organization of the Brain," *Psychoanalytical Quarterly,* 22:21–52, 1953.

Ladd, Harry S. "Geology of Vitilevu, Fiji," *Bishop Museum Bulletin* 119, Honolulu, 1934.

————, and J. E. Hoffmeister. "Geology of Lau, Fiji," *Bishop Museum Bulletin* 181, Honolulu, 1945.

Lange, Joost de. *The Relation and Development of English and Icelandic Outlaw Traditions.* Ph.D. dissertation. Utrecht, Haarlem: H. D. T. Willink, 1935.

Lasker, Gabriel W., ed. *The Processes of Ongoing Human Evolution.* Detroit: Wayne State University Press, 1960.

Lee, Dorothy D. *Freedom and Culture.* Englewood Cliffs, N.J.: Prentice-Hall, 1959.

Leighton, Dorothea C. *Rorschachs of 107 Navaho Children.* Microcard Publications of Primary Records in Culture and Personality, Vol. 2, No. 18. Madison: Microcard Foundation, 1957.

————, and John Adair. *People of the Middle Place: A Study of the Zuni Indians.* New Haven, Conn.: Human Relations Area Files, 1966.

————, and Clyde Kluckhohn. *Children of the People.* Cambridge, Mass.: Harvard University Press, 1947.

Lind, Andrew W. *An Island Community: Ecological Succession in Hawaii,* Chicago: University of Chicago Press, 1938.

Lomax, Alan. "Song Structure and Social Structure," *Ethnology,* 1(4): 425–451, 1962.

Macgregor, Gordon. *Warriors Without Weapons. A Study of the Society and Personality Development of the Pine Ridge Sioux.* Collaborators, Royal B. Hassrick and William E. Henry. Chicago: University of Chicago Press, 1946.

Magnusson, Magnus, and Hermann Pálsson, trans. *Njal's Saga.* Baltimore: Penguin Books, 1960.

Malan, Vernon D., and Ernest L. Schusky. "The Dakota Indian Community: An Analysis of the Non-ranching Population of the Pine Ridge Reservation," *Agricultural Experiment Station Bulletin* 505. Brookings: South Dakota State College, n.d.

Malinowski, Bronislaw. *Coral Gardens and Their Magic: A Study of the Methods of Tilling the Soil and of Agricultural Rites in the Trobriand Islands.* London: Allen and Unwin, 1935. Vol. 1.

————. *A Scientific Theory of Culture and Other Essays.* New York: Oxford University Press, 1960.

Malmström, Vincent H. "A Regional Geography of Iceland," *National Research Council Publication* 584, Washington, D.C., 1958.

Malo, David. "Hawaiian Antiquities," *Bishop Museum Special Publication* 2, Honolulu, 1951.

Mandelbaum, David G., ed. *Selected Writings of Edward Sapir in Language, Culture, and Personality.* Berkeley: University of California Press, 1949.

Mason, J. Alden. "The Language of the Papago Indians of Arizona," *Museum Monographs: The University Museum*. Philadelphia: University of Pennsylvania Press, 1950.

Mason, Leonard. "The Bikinians: A Transplanted Population," *Human Organization*, 9(1):5–15, 1950.

Mason, Ronald J. "The Paleo-Indian Tradition in Eastern North America," *Current Anthropology*, 3(3)227–278, 1962.

Mathiot, Madeleine. "Noun Classes and Folk Taxonomy in Papago," *American Anthropologist*, 64(2):340–350, 1962.

McAllister, J. G. "Archaeology of Kahoolawe," *Bishop Museum Bulletin* 115, Honolulu, 1933.

Mead, Margaret. *Continuities in Cultural Evolution*. New Haven, Conn.: Yale University Press, 1964.

Meitzen, August. *Siedelung und Agrarwesen der Westgermanen und Ostgermanen, der Kelten, Römer, Finnen und Slawen*. Berlin: W. Hertz, 1895.

Metzenthin, E. C. "The Heliand: A New Approach," *Studies in Philology*, 21:502–539, 1924.

Milne, Lorus J., and Margery Milne. *The Senses of Animals and Men*. New York: Atheneum, 1962.

Mirsky, Jeannette. "The Dakota," *Cooperation and Competition Among Primitive Peoples*. Ed. Margaret Mead. New York: McGraw-Hill, 1937.

Morgan, Lewis H. "Systems of Consanguinity and Affinity of the Human Family," *Smithsonian Contributions to Knowledge*, 17(2), 1870.

———. *Ancient Society: Or, Researches in the Lines of Human Progress from Savagery, Through Barbarism to Civilization*. New York: Holt, Rinehart and Winston, 1877.

Moriarty, James Robert. "Floating Gardens (Chinampas) Agriculture in the Old Lakes of Mexico," *America Indigena*, 28(2):461–484, 1968.

Murdock, George Peter. *Social Structure*. New York: Macmillan, 1949.

Murphy, Gardner. *Personality: A Biosocial Approach to Origins and Structure*. New York: Harper & Row, 1947.

Myrianthopoulos, N. C., and S. J. L. Pieper, Jr. "The ABO and Rh Blood Groups Among the Chamorros of Guam with Reference to Anthropologic and Genetic Problems in the Area," *American Journal of Physical Anthropology*, 17:105–108, 1959.

Naroll, Raoul. "A Preliminary Index of Social Development," *American Anthropologist*, 58:687–715, 1956.

Navarro, J. M. de. "Prehistoric Routes Between Northern Europe and Italy Defined by the Amber Trade," *Geographic Journal*, 66:481–507, 1925.

———. "The Coming of the Celts," *Cambridge Ancient History*. Cambridge, England: Cambridge University Press, 1928. 7:41–74.

Nayacakalou, Rusiate R. "The Fijian System of Kinship and Marriage," *Journal of the Polynesian Society*, 64(1):44–55, 1955; 66(1):44–59, 1957.

Neihardt, John G. *Black Elk Speaks: Being the Life Story of a Holy Man of the Ogalala Sioux*. New York: Morrow, 1932.

Newcomb, Mrs. Franc J., and Gladys A. Reichard. *Sandpaintings of the Navajo Shooting Chant*. New York: J. J. Augustin, 1937.

Newman, M. T. "Geographic and Microgeographic Races," *Current Anthropology*, 4(2):189–207, 1963.

Nordal, Sigurdur Jóhannesson. *Islenzk Menning*. Reykjavík: Mál og Menning, 1942. Trans. Vilhjálmur Bjarnar. Ithaca, N.Y.: Cornell University Library. (Manuscript in preparation for publication in *Islandica*.)

Nordman, Carl Axel. "The Megalithic Culture of Northern Europe," *Suomen Muinaismuistoyhdistyksen Aikakauskirja Finska Fornminnes-Föreningens Tidskrift*, 39(3):1–137. Helsinki: Helsingfors, 1935.

Oliver, Douglas L. *The Pacific Islands*. Garden City, N.Y.: Anchor Books, 1961.

Olrik, Axel. *Viking Civilization*. New York: Norton, 1930.

Opler, Marvin K. *Culture, Psychiatry and Human Values: The Methods and Values of Social Psychiatry*. Foreword, T. A. C. Rennie. Springfield, Ill.: Thomas, 1956.

Opler, Morris E. "The Kinship Systems of the Southern Athabaskan-Speaking Tribes," *American Anthropologist*, 38:620–633, 1936.

Osborne, Douglas. "Archaeology on Guam: A Progress Report," *American Anthropologist*, 49:518–524, 1947.

Overstreet, Harry A. *The Mature Mind*. New York: Norton, 1949.

Papago Indian Agency. Correspondence, acting superintendent, 1966.

Pessler, Wilhelm, *Das altsächsische Bauernhaus in seiner geographischen Verbreitung*. Braunschweig: F. Vieweg, 1906.

———. "Bauernhaus und Bauernleben," *Das Land Niedersachsen: Gegenwart und Tradition*. Niedersächsischen Landeszentrale für Heimatdienst. Hanover: Kerber, 1955. Pp. 100–110.

Pettersson, Sven Otto. "Climatic Variations in Historic and Prehistoric

Time," *Svenska Hydrografisk-Biologiska Kommissionens Skrifter*, 5:1–26, 1914.

Philippi, F. *Osnabrücker Urkundenbuch*. Osnabrück: Verein für Geschichte und Landeskunde von Osnabrück, 1892.

Phillpotts, Bertha Surtees. *Kindred and Clan in the Middle Ages and After: A Study in the Sociology of the Teutonic Races*. Cambridge, England: Cambridge University Press, 1913.

————. *Edda and Saga*. New York: Holt, Rinehart and Winston, 1931.

Piaget, Jean. *Judgment and Reasoning in the Child*. New York: Harcourt, Brace & World, 1928.

Piggott, Stuart. *Ancient Europe from the Beginnings of Agriculture to Classical Antiquity: A Survey*. Chicago: Aldine, 1965.

————, ed. *The Dawn of Civilization: The First World Survey of Human Cultures in Early Times*. New York: McGraw-Hill, 1961.

Pijoan, Michael, C. A. Elkin, and C. O. Eslinger. "Ascorbic Acid Deficiency Among Papago Indians," *Journal of Nutrition*, 25(5):491–496, 1943.

Pine Ridge Indian Agency. Correspondence of the superintendent, 1966.

Pittendrigh, Colin S. "Adaptation, Natural Selection, and Behavior," *Behavior and Evolution*. Eds. Anne Roe and G. G. Simpson. New Haven, Conn.: Yale University Press, 1958. Pp. 390–416.

Plath, Helmut. "Brauchtum in Niedersachsen," *Das Land Niedersachsen: Gegenwart und Tradition*. Hanover: Kerber, 1955, Pp. 117–120.

Plato, Chris C., D. L. Rucknagel, and L. T. Kurland. "Blood Group Investigations on the Carolinians and Chamorros of Saipan," *American Journal of Physical Anthropology*, 24:147–154, 1966.

Powdermaker, Hortense. *Stranger to Friend*. New York: Norton, 1966.

Pratt, Wayne T. Correspondence, 1967.

Prinz, Joseph. "Das Territorium des Bistums Osnabrück," *Historische Kommission für Hannover, Oldenburg, Braunschweig, Schaumburg-Lippe und Bremen. Veröffentlichungen* 2(15). Göttingen: Vandenhoeck und Ruprecht, 1934.

————. "Das Lehnregister des Grafen Otto von Bentheim (1346–64)," *Mitteilungen des Vereins für Geschichte und Landeskunde von Osnabrück*, 60:1–132, 1940.

Provinz Hannover. *Provinzial-Kommission zur Erforschung und Erhaltung der Denkmäler in der Provinz Hannover. 4. Regierungsbezirk Osnabrück*. Hanover: Provinzial-verwaltung, 1915.

Pukui, Mary Kawena, and Samuel H. Elbert. *Hawaiian-English Dictionary*. Honolulu: University of Hawaii, 1957.

Radcliffe-Brown, A. R. *A Natural Science of Society*. Foreword, Fred Eggan. New York: Free Press, 1957.

———. *Method in Social Anthropology*. Ed. M. N. Srinivas. Preface, Fred Eggan. Chicago: University of Chicago Press, 1958.

———, and C. Daryll Forde, eds. *African Systems of Kinship and Marriage*. New York: Oxford University Press, 1950.

Rademacher, E. "Die niederrheinische Hügelgräberkultur von der Spätsteinzeit bis zum Ende der Hallstattzeit," *Mannus: Zeitschrift für Vorgeschichte:* Ergänzungsband, 4:112–140, 1925.

Ratzel, Friedrich. *Anthropogeographie*. Stuttgart: J. Engelhorn, 1899.

Redfield, Robert. *Peasant Society and Culture: An Anthropological Approach to Civilization*. Chicago: University of Chicago Press, 1956.

Reed, Erik K. *Archaeology and History of Guam*. Washington, D.C.: Department of the Interior, National Park Service, 1952.

Reh, Emma. "Papago Diet." Unpublished manuscript, n.d.

Reining, Elisab. "Das südliche hannoverische Emsland, Landschaft und Wirtschaft im Kreise Lingen sowie den angrenzenden Kreisen Grafschaft Bentheim und Bersenbrück," Wirtschaftswissenschaftliche Gesellschaft zum Studium Niedersachsens. E. V. Veröffentlichungen: Reihe A Beiträge, Heft 18. Bad Pyrmont: Karl Bäkmann, 1931.

Reinman, Fred M. *Notes on an Archaeological Survey of Guam, Marianas Islands, 1965–66. Preliminary Report*. Washington, D.C.: National Science Foundation, n.d. (Mimeo.)

Repp, Thorliefur Gudmundsson. *A Historical Treatise on Trial by Jury, Wager of Law, and Other Co-ordinate Forensic Institutions, Formerly in Use in Scandinavia and in Iceland*. Edinburgh: Thomas Clark, 1832.

Robertson, John George. *A History of German Literature*. London: Blackwood, 1931.

Roth, G. K. *Fijian Way of Life*. London: Oxford University Press, 1953.

Sahlins, Marshall D. *Moala. Culture and Nature on a Fijian Island*. Ann Arbor: University of Michigan Press, 1962.

———, and Elman R. Service, eds. *Evolution and Culture*. Foreword, Leslie A. White. Ann Arbor: University of Michigan Press, 1960.

Sapir, Edward. "Culture, Genuine and Spurious," *American Journal of Sociology*, 29:401–429, 1924.

———. "Conceptual Categories in Primitive Languages," *Science*, 74:578, 1931.

Sauer, Carl Ortwin. *Agricultural Origins and Dispersals*. New York: American Geographical Society, 1952.

Sawyer, P. H. *The Age of the Vikings*. London: Arnold, 1962.

Saxo Grammaticus. *The First Nine Books of the Danish History of Saxo Grammaticus*. Trans. Oliver Elton. London: Norroena Society, 1905.

Sayles, E. B., and Ernst Antevs. "The Cochise Culture," *Medallion Papers*, 29, Globe, Arizona, 1941.

Schafer, Albert. "Review of *Culture and Community* by Conrad M. Arensberg and Solon T. Kimball," *Social Forces*, 44(3):434, 1966.

Schwidetzky, Ilse, and Hubert Walter. *Untersuchungen zur Anthropologischen Gliederung Westfalens*. Münster: Aschendorfsche Verlagsbuchhandlung, 1967.

Scientific American. "A Viking Settlement in America," *Scientific American*, 210(1):56, 1964.

Seeliger, Gerhard. "The Saxon Wars," *Cambridge Medieval History*. Cambridge, England: Cambridge University Press, 1936. 2:609–613.

Seligmann, C. G. *The Melanesians of British New Guinea*. Cambridge, England: Cambridge University Press, 1910.

Seltzer, Carl Coleman. "The Physical Anthropology of the Medieval Icelanders with Special Reference to the Question of Their Origin." Unpublished Ph.D. dissertation, Harvard University, 1933.

Shapiro, H. L. "The Distribution of Blood Groups in Polynesia," *American Journal of Physical Anthropology*, 26:409–416, 1940.

Shepardson, Mary. "Value Theory in the Prediction of Political Behavior: The Navajo Case," *American Anthropologist*, 64:742–750, 1962.

―――. "Navajo Ways in Government: A Study in Political Process," *American Anthropological Association Memoir* No. 96, 65(3), Pt. 2, 1963.

Shetelig, Haakon, and H. Falk. *Scandinavian Archaeology*. Trans. E. V. Gordon. Oxford: Clarendon Press, 1937.

Simmons, R. T. "A Report on Blood Group Genetic Surveys in Eastern Asia, Indonesia, Melanesia, Micronesia, Polynesia and Australia in the Study of Man," *Anthropos*, 51:500–512, 1956.

Simpson, George G. *The Meaning of Evolution: A Study of the History of Life and of its Significance for Man*. New Haven, Conn.: Yale University Press, 1949.

Skelton, R. A., Thomas E. Marston, and George D. Painter. *The Vinland Map and the Tartar Relation*. New Haven, Conn.: Yale University Press, 1965.

Skovmand, Roar. "Hunters and Food-gatherers," *Scandinavia Past and Present.* Ed. J. Bukdahl. Odense: Arnkrone, 1959a. 1:34–38.

————. "The Great Migrations," *Scandinavia Past and Present.* Ed. J. Bukdahl. Odense: Arnkrone, 1959b. 1:67–68.

————. "Hedeby and Birka," *Scandinavia Past and Present.* Ed. J. Bukdahl. Odense: Arnkrone, 1959c. 1:111–114.

Smith, Marian W. "Different Cultural Concepts of Past, Present and Future: A Study of Ego Extension," *Psychiatry,* 15:395–400, 1952.

Solenberger, Robert R. "Continuity of Local Political Institutions in the Marianas," *Human Organization,* 23:53–60, 1964.

Spate, O. H. K. "Islands and Men," *Man's Place in the Island Ecosystem.* Ed. F. R. Fosberg. Honolulu: Bishop Museum, 1963. Pp. 253–264.

Spencer, Herbert. *The Principles of Biology.* New York: Appleton-Century-Crofts, 1866–1867.

Spiegel, H. W. "The Altenteil: German Farmer's Old Age Security," *Rural Sociology,* 5:203–218, 1939.

Spjeldnaes, Nils, and K. E. Henningsmoen. "Littorina Littorea: An Indicator of Norse Settlement in North America?" *Science,* 141 (3577):275–276, 1963.

Spoehr, Alexander. "Cultural Differences in the Interpretation of Natural Resources," *Man's Role in Changing the Face of the Earth.* Ed. W. L. Thomas, Jr. Chicago: University of Chicago Press, 1956. Pp. 93–102.

————. "Marianas Prehistory," *Fieldiana: Anthropology Papers* No. 48, Chicago, 1957.

Sprockhoff, Ernst. "Zur Handelsgeschichte der germanischen Bronzezeit," *Vorgeschichtliche Forschungen* 7. Berlin: W. de Gruyter, 1930.

————. "Die nordische Megalithkultur," *Handbuch der Urgeschichte Deutschlands* 3. Berlin: W. de Gruyter, 1938.

Spuhler, J. N., ed. *The Evolution of Man's Capacity for Culture: Six Essays.* Detroit: Wayne State University, 1959.

————, and C. Kluckhohn. "Inbreeding Coefficients of the Ramah Navaho Population," *Human Biology,* 25:295–317, 1953.

Stang, Ragna. "The Viking Ships," *Scandinavia Past and Present.* Ed. J. Bukdahl. Odense: Arnkrone, 1959. 1:106–110.

Steffensen, Jón. "The Physical Anthropology of the Vikings," *Journal of the Royal Anthropological Institute of Great Britain and Ireland,* 83:86–97, 1953.

Stephen, Alexander M. "Hopi Journal," ed. E. C. Parsons, *Columbia University Contributions to Anthropology,* 23(1–2), 1936.

Sullivan, Louis R. "Anthropometry of the Siouan Tribes," *Proceedings of the National Academy of Sciences,* 6:131–134, 1920.

Summers, Catherine C. "Hawaiian Fishponds," *Bishop Museum Special Publication* 52, Honolulu, 1964.

Sumner, W. G. *Folkways: A Study of the Sociological Importance of Usages, Manners, Customs, Mores, and Morals.* Boston: Ginn, 1906.

Sveinsson, Einar Ólafur. "The Age of the Sturlungs," *Islandica* 36. Trans. J. S. Hannesson. Ithaca, N.Y.: Cornell University Press, 1953.

———, ed. *Brennu-Njálssaga.* Reykjavík: Íslenzka Fornritafélag, 1954.

———. "The Value of the Icelandic Sagas," Viking Society for Northern Research. *Saga Book.* London: University College, London, 1957–1959.

———. "Dating the Icelandic Sagas: An Essay in Method," Trans. G. Turville-Petre. *Viking Society for Northern Research.* Text series 3. London: University College, London, c. 1958.

Tacitus, Cornelius. "Germany and Its Tribes," *The Complete Works of Tacitus.* Trans. A. J. Church and W. J. Brodribb. Ed. Moses Hadas. New York: Modern Library, 1942. Pp. 709–732.

Tempels, Placide. *Bantu Philosophy.* Trans. A. Rubbens and Colin King. Foreword, Margaret Read. Paris: Présence Africaine, 1959.

Thomas, William L., Jr., ed. *Man's Role in Changing the Face of the Earth.* Chicago: University of Chicago Press, 1956.

Thompson, James Westfall. *Feudal Germany.* Chicago: University of Chicago Press, 1928.

Thompson, Laura. "Archaeology of the Marianas Islands," *Bishop Museum Bulletin* 100, Honolulu, 1932.

———. *Fijian Frontier.* Introduction, B. Malinowski. New York: International Council, Institute of Pacific Relations, 1940a.

———. "Southern Lau, Fiji: An Ethnography," *Bishop Museum Bulletin* 162, Honolulu, 1940b.

———. "The Native Culture of the Marianas Islands," *Bishop Museum Bulletin* 185, Honolulu, 1945.

———. *Guam and Its People.* Rev. ed. Princeton, N.J.: Princeton University Press, 1947a.

———. "The Problem of 'Totemism' in Southern Lau," *Oceania,* 17:211–225, 1947b.

———. "Relations of Men, Animals, and Plants in an Island Community (Fiji)," *American Anthropologist,* 51:253–267, 1949.

———. *Culture in Crisis. A Study of the Hopi Indians.* Foreword, John Collier. With a chapter from Benjamin Lee Whorf. New York: Harper & Row, 1950.

————. "Perception Patterns in Three Indian Tribes," *Psychiatry*, 14:255–263, 1951a.

————. *Personality and Government: Findings and Recommendations of the Indian Administration Research.* Mexico, D.F.: Instituto Indigenista Interamericano, 1951b.

————. "Applied Anthropology, Community Welfare, and Human Conservation," *Selected Papers, Fifth International Congress of Anthropological and Ethnological Sciences.* Ed. A. F. C. Wallace. Philadelphia: University of Pennsylvania Press, 1960a. Pp. 769–774.

————. "Core Values and Diplomacy: A Case Study of Iceland," *Human Organization*, 19:82–85, 1960b.

————. *Toward a Science of Mankind.* New York: McGraw-Hill, 1961.

————. "The Rural Community in Iceland: A Pilot Study Report," *VI Congrès International des Sciences Anthropologiques et Ethnologiques.* Paris: Musée de l'Homme, 1963. 2(1):305–310.

————. "Steps Toward a Unified Anthropology," *Current Anthropology*, 8(1–2):67–77, 1967a.

————. "Cultural Homeostasis: A Heuristic Concept in Understanding Culture Process." Paper presented at the annual meeting of the American Anthropological Association, Washington, D.C., 1967b.

————., and Alice Joseph. *The Hopi Way.* Ann Arbor, Michigan: University Microfilms, 1944.

————, and Alice Joseph. "White Pressures on Indian Personality and Culture," *American Journal of Sociology*, 53:17–22, 1947.

Thorarinsson, Sigurdur. *The Thousand Years Struggle Against Ice and Fire.* Reykjavík: Bókaútgáfa Menningarsjóds, 1956.

————. "The Oraefajökull Eruption of 1362," *Acta Naturalia Islandica* 2(2), Reykjavík: Naturugripasafn Islands Museum Rerun Naturalium Islandiae, 1958.

Thurnwald, Richard. *Economics in Primitive Communities.* London: Oxford University Press, 1932.

Titiev, Mischa. "Old Oraibi: A Study of the Hopi Indians of Third Mesa," *Papers of the Peabody Museum, Harvard University*, 22, Cambridge, Mass., 1944.

————. *The Science of Man.* New York: Holt, Rinehart and Winston, 1963.

Toynbee, Arnold J. *A Study of History.* Abridgement, D. C. Somervell. London: Oxford University Press, 1957.

Turville-Petre, E. O. Gabriel. *Origins of Icelandic Literature.* Oxford: Clarendon Press, 1953.

———. *Myth and Religion of the North: The Religion of Ancient Scandinavia.* London: Weidenfeld and Nicholson, 1964.

Tylor, Sir Edward Burnett. *Anthropology: An Introduction to the Study of Man and Civilization.* New York: Appleton-Century-Crofts, 1881.

Underhill, Ruth M. *Singing for Power: The Song Magic of the Papago Indians of Southern Arizona.* Berkeley: University of California Press, 1938.

———. "Papago Indian Religion," *Columbia University Contributions to Anthropology* 33, New York, 1946.

United States Public Health Service. Correspondence, 1967.

Veblen, Thorstein. *Imperial Germany and the Industrial Revolution.* New York: Macmillan, 1915.

Vogt, Evon Z. "On the Concepts of Structure and Process in Cultural Anthropology," *American Anthropologist,* 62:18–33, 1960.

Voth, Henry R. "The Oraibi Powamu Ceremony," *Field Museum of Natural History Publication 61, Anthropological Series 3(2),* Chicago, 1901.

———. "The Oraibi Marau Ceremony," *Field Museum of Natural History Publication 156, Anthropological Series 11(1),* Chicago, 1912.

Warner, W. Lloyd. *A Black Civilization.* New York: Harper & Row, 1937.

Washburn, Sherwood Larned, and Irven DeVore. "Social Behavior of Baboons and Early Man," *Social Life of Early Man.* Ed. S. L. Washburn. Chicago: Aldine, 1961.

Wax, Murray L., Rosalie H. Wax, and Robert V. Dumont, Jr. "Formal Education in an American Indian Community," *Supplement to Social Problems,* 11(4), 1964.

Wax, Rosalie H. "Les Notions de l' 'Ego' et de l' 'Id' dans la vieille Littérature Scandinave," *Revue de Psychologie des Peuples,* 12(3): 317–332, 1957.

Weber, Max. *General Economic History.* Trans. Frank H. Knight. Glencoe, Illinois: Free Press, 1950.

Wein, Hermann. "The Categories and a Logic of Structure," *Journal of Philosophy,* 49:629–633, 1952.

Weltfish, Gene. "The Ethnic Dimension of Human History: Pattern or Patterns of Culture?" *Selected Papers of the Fifth International Congress of Anthropological and Ethnological Sciences.* Ed. A. F. C. Wallace. Philadelphia: University of Pennsylvania Press, 1960. Pp. 207–218.

Whatmough, Joshua. *The Foundations of Roman Italy*. London: Methuen, 1937.

White, Leslie A. *The Evolution of Culture: The Development of Civilization to the Fall of Rome*. New York: McGraw-Hill, 1959.

White, Lynn, Jr. "The Historical Roots of Our Ecological Crisis," *Science*, 155(3767):1203–1207, 1967.

Whitehead, Alfred North. *Science and the Modern World*. New York: Macmillan, 1925.

Whorf, Benjamin Lee. "The Relation of Habitual Thought and Behavior to Language," *Language, Culture and Personality: Essays in Memory of Edward Sapir*. Menasha, Wis.: Sapir Memorial Publication Fund, 1941. Pp. 75–94.

————. *Language, Thought and Reality: Selected Writings*. Ed. John B. Carroll. Foreword, Stuart Chase. Cambridge, Mass.: M.I.T. Press, 1956.

Wolf, Eric Robert. *Sons of the Shaking Earth*. Chicago: University of Chicago Press, 1959.

————. *Anthropology*. Englewood Cliffs, N.J.: Prentice-Hall, 1964.

————. *Peasants*. Englewood Cliffs, N.J.: Prentice-Hall, 1966.

Wrasmann, Adolf. "Das Heuerlingswesen im Fürstentum Osnabrück," Verein für Geschichte und Landeskunde von Osnabrück. *Mittheilungen* 42(1):53–171, 1919.

Young, Jean I. "Glaed waes ic gliwum—Ungloomy Aspects of Anglo-Saxon Poetry," *The Early Cultures of North-West Europe*. H. M. Chadwick Memorial Studies. Eds. C. Fox and B. Dickins. Cambridge, England: Cambridge University Press, 1950. Pp. 275–287.

Young, Robert W., compiler. *The Navajo Yearbook 1951–1961*. Window Rock, Ariz.: Navajo Agency, 1961.

————, and W. Morgan. *The Navaho Language*. Phoenix: Phoenix Indian School, 1943.

Zimmerman, C. C., and M. E. Frampton. *Family and Society: A Study of the Sociology of Reconstruction*. Princeton, N.J.: Van Nostrand, 1935.

INDEX

A Note on the Type

The text of this book is set in CALEDONIA, a face designed by W.A. Dwiggins. It belongs to the family of printing types called "modern face" by printers—a term used to mark the change in style of type-letters that occurred about 1800. Caledonia borders on the general design of Scotch Modern, but is more freely drawn than that letter.

The book was composed, printed, and bound by Colonial Press, Clinton, Massachusetts. Typography by Al Burkhart.